Karel Kosík
and the *Dialectics of the Concrete*

Historical Materialism Book Series

The Historical Materialism Book Series is a major publishing initiative of the radical left. The capitalist crisis of the twenty-first century has been met by a resurgence of interest in critical Marxist theory. At the same time, the publishing institutions committed to Marxism have contracted markedly since the high point of the 1970s. The Historical Materialism Book Series is dedicated to addressing this situation by making available important works of Marxist theory. The aim of the series is to publish important theoretical contributions as the basis for vigorous intellectual debate and exchange on the left.

The peer-reviewed series publishes original monographs, translated texts, and reprints of classics across the bounds of academic disciplinary agendas and across the divisions of the left. The series is particularly concerned to encourage the internationalization of Marxist debate and aims to translate significant studies from beyond the English-speaking world.

For a full list of titles in the Historical Materialism Book Series available in paperback from Haymarket Books, visit: www.haymarketbooks.org/series_collections/1-historical-materialism.

Karel Kosík and the *Dialectics of the Concrete*

Edited by
Joseph Grim Feinberg
Ivan Landa
Jan Mervart

Haymarket Books
Chicago, IL

First published in 2021 by Brill Academic Publishers, The Netherlands
© 2021 Koninklijke Brill NV, Leiden, The Netherlands

Published in paperback in 2023 by
Haymarket Books
P.O. Box 180165
Chicago, IL 60618
773-583-7884
www.haymarketbooks.org

ISBN: 978-1-64259-820-9

Distributed to the trade in the US through Consortium Book Sales and Distribution (www.cbsd.com) and internationally through Ingram Publisher Services International (www.ingramcontent.com).

This book was published with the generous support of Lannan Foundation and Wallace Action Fund.

Special discounts are available for bulk purchases by organizations and institutions. Please call 773-583-7884 or email info@haymarketbooks.org for more information.

Cover art and design by David Mabb. Cover art is a detail of *Construct 32, Morris, Acorn / Rodchenko, Untitled Textile Design*, wallpaper mounted on linen (2006).

Printed in the United States.

10 9 8 7 6 5 4 3 2 1

Library of Congress Cataloging-in-Publication data is available.

*This book is dedicated to the memory of Gabriella Fusi and Anselm Min,
who contributed so much to the memory of Karel Kosík.*

∴

Contents

Acknowledgements XI
Notes on Authors XII

Introduction 1
   Joseph Grim Feinberg, Ivan Landa, Jan Mervart

PART 1
The Reform Years and the Origins of Dialectics of the Concrete

1   Karel Kosík as a Public Intellectual of the Reform Years   19
     Jan Mervart

2   Karel Kosík and His 'Radical Democrats': The Janus Face of *Dialectics of the Concrete*   39
     Tomáš Hermann

PART 2
Praxis and Labour

3   Praxis in Progress: On the Transformations of Kosík's Thought   57
     Francesco Tava

4   Labour and Time: Karel Kosík's Temporal Materialism   75
     Ivan Landa

5   Inception of Culture from the Ontology of Labour: The Original Contribution of Karel Kosík to a Marxian Theory of Culture   107
     Ian Angus

6   'The Philosophy of Labour' and Karel Kosík's Criticism of 'Care'   129
     Siyaves Azeri

7   Kosík, Lukács and the Thing in Itself   151
     Tom Rockmore

PART 3
Modernity, Nation, and Globalisation

8   The Ontological Dialectic and the Critique of Modernity: Based on the Interpretation of Kosík's Concrete Totality   165
    Xinruo Zhang and Xiaohan Huang

9   And the 'Thing Itself' Is Man: Radical Democracy and the Roots of Humanity   187
    Joseph Grim Feinberg

10 The Dialectic of Concrete Totality in the Age of Globalisation: Karel Kosík's *Dialectics of the Concrete* Fifty Years Later   205
    Anselm K. Min

PART 4
Intellectual Encounters

11 Kosík's Notion of 'Positivism'   229
    Tomáš Hříbek

12 Kosík's Concept of 'Concrete Totality': A Structuralist Critique   248
    Vít Bartoš

13 The World of the Pseudoconcrete, Ideology and the Theory of the Subject (Kosík and Althusser)   262
    Petr Kužel

14 Karel Kosík and Martin Heidegger: From Marxism to Traditionalism   281
    Jan Černý

PART 5
Influence and Reception

15 A Route of Critical Thought: Between Italian and Czech Intellectuals   307
    Gabriella Fusi

16   Karel Kosík in Mexico: Adolfo Sánchez Vázquez and *Dialectics of the Concrete*   316
       Diana Fuentes

17   Karel Kosík and US Marxist Humanism   325
       Peter Hudis

Postscript: Looking Backwards

18   Spirit of Resistance: Notes for an Intellectual Biography of Karel Kosík   345
       Michael Löwy

     References   355
     Index   375

Acknowledgements

We would like to thank Daniel Štěpánek for his help in preparing our list of references, author bios and index, all of which were crucial steps toward bringing this book to completion. We also owe thanks to Ashley Davies for his copy editing of our draft manuscript, to Simon Mussell for the final round of copy editing and to Miloslav Caňko for completing our index after typesetting.

Notes on Authors

Ian Angus
is Professor Emeritus at Simon Fraser University in British Columbia, Canada. He is the author of nine books, five edited or co-edited collections, and many essays in philosophy and the humanities. His 2009 book on the university appeared in Spanish translation as *Amar las preguntas. Acerca de la universidad y la educación* (Buenos Aires: Wolkowicz Editores, 2019). His most recent book is *Groundwork of Phenomenological Marxism: Crisis, Body, World* (Lexington Books, 2021). He has also published the book *The Undiscovered Country: Essays in Canadian Intellectual Culture* (Athabasca University Press, 2013). His website is at https://sfu.academia.edu/IanAngus.

Siyaves Azeri
is a professor of philosophy at the School of Advanced Studies, University of Tyumen in Tyumen, Siberia, Russian Federation. He is also an associate of the Thesis Twelve: Mardin Value-form Circle. Azeri has written on a large gamut of subjects in several international journals and books. His areas of interest include Hume's empiricism, Kant's transcendentalism, Marxian materialism, the problem of consciousness and the critique of epistemology. Recent publications of his have appeared in *Social Epistemology, Theory and Psychology, Critique, Socialism & Democracy*, and *Science & Society*.

Vít Bartoš
is Assistant Professor at the Technical University in Liberec, Faculty of Science, Humanities and Education, Department of Philosophy. He studies the philosophical problems of modern natural sciences and cognitive philosophy. His general philosophical approach is associated with Whiteheadian metaphysics and the philosophy of nature. He is also interested in Czech Marxist philosophy. His many articles include 'Egon Bondy aneb kouzlo pábitelské metafyziky', 'Co je význam?' and 'Biological and Artificial Machines'.

Jan Černý
is Assistant Professor at the Philosophical Faculty of the University of Hradec Králové. He has published the book *Jevení a spása. Subjektivita v materiální fenomenologii Michela Henryho* (Filosofia, 2019) and articles on phenomenology, political philosophy and modern Czech philosophy, including 'A Too-Future Eschatology? The Limits of the Phenomenology of Liturgy in Jean-Yves Lacoste' (*Open Theology* 5, no. 1, 2019).

NOTES ON AUTHORS   XIII

Joseph Grim Feinberg
is a researcher at the Institute of Philosophy of the Czech Academy of Sciences in Prague. His work focuses on political and aesthetic theory, Czech and Central European Marxism, nationalism and internationalism. He is author of *The Paradox of Authenticity: Folklore Performance in Post-Communist Slovakia* (University of Wisconsin Press, 2018) and editor of *Contradictions: A Journal for Critical Thought*.

Diana Fuentes
is Professor at the Universidad Autónoma Metropolitana (UAM) and the Universidad Nacional Autónoma de México (UNAM). She is the author of various articles on Marxism in Mexico. She is a founding member of the Asociación Gramsci México.

Gabriella Fusi
graduated in Theoretical Philosophy at Milan University under Professor Enzo Paci's direction, with a thesis on *Kosík and Richta: Philosophical Positions and their Political Implications*. She maintained contact with twentieth-century Czech and Yugoslav philosophers such as Karel Kosík, Jan Patočka and Gajo Petrović. She edited the book *Gajo Petrović: Socialism and Philosophy* (Feltrinelli, 1976). She co-edited with Francesco Tava *Karel Kosík. Un filosofo in tempi di farsa e di tragedia* [Karel Kosík: A Philosopher in Times of Farce and Tragedy] (Mimesis, 2013). She was among the authors of *Praxis – Društvena kritika i humanistički socijalizam* [Praxis – Social Criticism and Humanist Socialism] (Rosa Luxemburg Stiftung, 2012), with an essay entitled 'Talijanski intelektualci na Korčuli: između filozofije i politike' [Italian Intellectuals at Korčula: Between Philosophy and Politics]. She contributed to the publications *aut aut*, *L'ottavo giorno*, *Marx 101* and *Il Manifesto*. She passed away in 2020.

Tomáš Hermann
is Assistant Professor in the Department of the Philosophy and History of Science, Faculty of Science, Charles University in Prague, and is a researcher at the Institute for Contemporary History of the Czech Academy of Sciences. He is author or co-author of various articles and edited volumes on intellectual history and the history of science, esp. biology, in the Czech lands in the nineteenth and twentieth centuries, e.g. T. Hermann and A. Markoš (eds.), *Emanuel Rádl – vědec a filosof* (OIKOYMENH, 2004). He recently published (with M. Zelenka) an annotated edition of Roman Jakobson's book *Moudrost starých Čechů* (1943) including texts from the exile controversy and an extensive study (Pavel Mervart and ÚSD, 2015), and the chapter 'Disent a filosofie', in J. Suk et al., *Šest kapitol o disentu* (ÚSD, 2017).

Tomáš Hříbek
is a researcher at the Institute of Philosophy, Czech Academy of Sciences in Prague. He works on the philosophy of mind, the philosophy of science (biology), ethics (bioethics) and aesthetics. To date, he has published three monographs: on psychological externalism; on phenomenal consciousness; and on the ethics of assisted dying, respectively. His recent publications in English include chapters in the volumes *The Vienna Circle in Czechoslovakia* (Springer, 2019) and *Ernst Mach – Life, Work, Influence* (Springer, 2019).

Xiaohan Huang
is Professor at the Peking University School of Marxism. Her work focuses on Marxism and the philosophy of science. She has published several books and papers on systems theory and Western Marxism.

Peter Hudis
is Professor of Humanities and Philosophy at Oakton Community College. His current work in philosophy covers engagement in social and political theory as well as their sources in classical dialectic philosophy. He has published extensively on Marxist theory and is author of *Marx's Concept of the Alternative to Capitalism* (Brill, 2012) and *Frantz Fanon: Philosopher of the Barricades* (Pluto Press, 2015); he is also General Editor of *The Complete Works of Rosa Luxemburg*.

Petr Kužel
is a researcher at the Institute of Philosophy, Czech Academy of Sciences in Prague. He specialises in theories of the subject, Marxism, Egon Bondy and Louis Althusser. Kužel is author of *Filosofie Louise Althussera. O filosofii, která chtěla změnit svět* (Filosofia, 2014), and editor of *Myšlení a tvorba Egona Bondyho* (Filosofia, 2018). He is a member of the editorial collective of *Contradictions: A Journal for Critical Thought*.

Ivan Landa
is a researcher at the Institute of Philosophy, Czech Academy of Sciences, where he is head of the Department for the Study of Modern Czech Philosophy. His research focuses on Czechoslovak and East-Central European Marxism and dissident thought, as well as on the history of Hegelianism. Landa has published articles on Marx's philosophical anthropology, technology and politics, and Hegel's speculative theology. He is a member of the editorial collective of *Contradictions: A Journal for Critical Thought*.

Michael Löwy

is a sociologist and philosopher, whose main focus lies in analysis and interpretation of Marxist theories. His research aim is part of his lectures at the École des hautes études en sciences sociales in Paris. His monograph *The Theory of Revolution in the Young Marx* (Brill, 2003) has been translated into many languages.

Jan Mervart

is a researcher at the Institute of Philosophy, Czech Academy of Sciences in Prague. He is predominantly devoted to modern Czech and Slovak intellectual and cultural history. He has published two monographs on the role of the Writers' Union in the Czechoslovak reform process and on the normalisation of the cultural sphere in Czechoslovakia after 1968, and he has published several studies on Czechoslovak Marxism and Marxist intellectuals (e.g. 'Czechoslovak Marxist Humanism and the Revolution', *Studies in East European Thought* 69, no. 1). He is a member of the editorial collective of *Contradictions: A Journal for Critical Thought*.

Anselm K. Min

was Professor of Religion at Claremont Graduate University, Claremont, California, specialising in philosophy of religion and theology. In addition to over 80 articles on many areas of contemporary philosophy and systematic theology, he published four books, on Korean Catholicism, liberation theology, postmodernism, and the theology of Thomas Aquinas. He developed a systematic theology to address the challenges of a globalising world such as capitalism, imperialism, oppression, ecology and intercultural and interreligious relations. He passed away in 2020.

Tom Rockmore

is Distinguished Professor Emeritus at Duquesne University and Distinguished Humanities Chair Professor at Peking University. He has published studies and books on the history of philosophy, mainly on Kant, Fichte, Hegel, Marx, Lukács and Heidegger. In 2018, his monograph *Marx's Dream: From Capitalism to Communism* was published (University of Chicago Press).

Francesco Tava

is Senior Lecturer in Philosophy at the University of the West of England in Bristol. He specialises in moral and political philosophy, phenomenology and the history of philosophy. His publications include *Phenomenology and the Idea of Europe* (Routledge, 2018) and *Thinking after Europe: Jan Patočka and Politics* (co-editor; Rowman & Littlefield Publishers, 2016).

Xinruo Zhang received her PhD from Peking University and now works at the executive office of the Shanghai Stock Exchange. Formerly she was a researcher at the Research Center of Marxism in the Shanghai Administration Institute. Her work focuses on Marxism, especially Western Marxism. She has undertaken a National Social Science Foundation project called 'Research on the Contradiction of Modernity in China', completed in September 2018. She has also published several papers on Marxism, including an English review, published in *Science & Society*, of Sean Sayers' book *Marx and Alienation*.

Introduction

Joseph Grim Feinberg, Ivan Landa, Jan Mervart

Karel Kosík (1926–2003) was one of the most remarkable Marxist philosophers of his generation in Czechoslovakia. Together with the phenomenologist Jan Patočka, he is probably the best-known Czech philosopher in the modern age.

Kosík's reputation as a creative thinker and an insightful critic of both market-capitalist and Soviet-type societies is owed largely to his *magnum opus*, *Dialectics of the Concrete*. This book, first published in 1963, marked the culmination of a process of intellectual development that first took off in the mid-1950s, when Kosík, along with many of his generation, began to question the dogmas of Stalinist orthodoxy. Almost immediately after the book's appearance it became a philosophical 'blockbuster', quickly attracting the attention not only of philosophers, writers and artists, but also of the broader reading public. After its later translation into numerous languages, *Dialectics of the Concrete* would go on to enjoy international acclaim.

Nevertheless, to recall a phrase coined by a dark Swabian dialectician: 'what is familiar and well-known as such is not really known for the very reason that it is familiar and well-known'.[1] Likewise, the fact that Kosík has an enduring reputation does not necessarily mean that his ideas are 'really known' in the sense that they are still fruitfully interpreted or further developed, or even that his writings are still widely read. On the contrary, the opposite seems to be true, at least for the five decades or so that have passed since the moment when Kosík first gained widespread international recognition. Kosík's thought has been appreciated primarily for the historical role it once played. It is 'well known' as a historical document, but is overlooked and ignored as a living contribution to social thought.

Historians remember Kosík as an important figure in the Prague Spring of 1968, a courageous reformer who was silenced after the Warsaw Pact invasion put an end to his country's process of democratisation. But the ideas with which Kosík justified those reforms – the system of thought that helped make him a leading critic of the established system and a leading proponent of its transformation – are no longer widely studied. His work is looked upon as an intervention into a specific, local struggle, but it is no longer widely studied as a contribution to social and political philosophy.

---

1 Hegel 2018, p. 25.

1 *Dialectics of the Concrete*: Translation, Reception and Impact

Previously *Dialectics of the Concrete* was much discussed abroad. In various countries it was read by Marxists and phenomenologists, political scientists and Sovietologists, historians, literary critics, journalists and political activists. For the most part, international acclaim became possible only when the book began to appear in translation. The first was an Italian translation published in 1965.[2] This was no coincidence. The Italian philosopher Guido Davide Neri, a member of the 'Milan School' devoted to integrating Marxism with phenomenology, spent a year in Prague in the early 1960s, researching intersections between phenomenology and Marxism. There he met Kosík and became acquainted with the core ideas of *Dialectics of the Concrete*. After the book's publication, he initiated its Italian publication and helped with the translation. The book was enthusiastically received among Italian Marxists, especially those working on the frontiers of phenomenology and Marxism such as Enzo Paci and Pier Aldo Rovatti (both members of the Milan School). But it was Neri on whom the book made its deepest impact. In Neri's book *Praxis and Knowledge* (which was the outcome of Neri's research sabbatical in Prague, parts of it having been written during his time there), Neri included a chapter on Kosík's philosophy of praxis, in which he examined the epistemological implications of the ontology of labour.[3] Neri continued to follow Kosík's work in years to come, as can be seen for example in Neri's attempt to elaborate a philosophical analysis of 'actually existing socialism'.[4]

The Italian translation's importance reached far beyond the borders of Italy. Most significantly, it contributed to the dissemination of Kosík's ideas in the Hispanophone and Lusophone world during the 1960s, as the Spanish and Portuguese translations were both prepared from the Italian.[5] The Mexican philosopher Adolfo Sánchez Vázquez (who consulted the German translation made that same year) published his Spanish translation in 1967.[6] Sánchez Vázquez

---

[2] Kosík 1965a. As discussed below, however, an early, condensed presentation of the main argument appeared in French a few years earlier, in the Italian journal *aut aut*: Kosík 1961, pp. 203–13.
[3] Neri 1966.
[4] Neri 1980, in Neri 1980, pp. 130–55. For more on the Italian reception of Kosík, see Gabriella Fusi's contribution to this volume, pp. 307–15.
[5] The Italian text also served as the basis for a translation into Catalan: Kosík 1970.
[6] Kosík 1967b. In a Preface, Sánchez Vázquez explains that he took into consideration the German translation because of some terminological changes it incorporated. See Diana Fuentes in this volume, pp. 316–24. The Italian translation had been made from the first Czech edition, published in 1963, whereas the German translation was based on the third edition, from 1966.

had just finished his seminal *Philosophy of Praxis*, in which he described Kosík – along with the Polish philosophers Leszek Kołakowski and Adam Schaff – as a leading proponent of the 'philosophy of praxis'.[7] Sánchez Vázquez was – as was Neri – attracted by Kosík's attempt to develop epistemological implications out of an ontology of labour, as he argued that ontological commitments always imply certain epistemological commitments.[8] Kosík also influenced several philosophers and theologians of liberation, including Enrique Dussel. Kosík's reception in Lusophone countries dates primarily to 1969, when the Portuguese translation of *Dialectics of the Concrete* appeared in Brazil.[9] Kosík exerted some influence on Paolo Freire, who used some of Kosík's ideas in his theory of pedagogy.

A German translation of *Dialectics of the Concrete* was published in 1967 by Suhrkamp Verlag, and was later re-issued in several editions.[10] It stimulated debates among Sovietologists such as Nikolaus Lobkowicz, literary critics from the Konstanz school of reception theory (namely Hans Robert Jauss), and philosophers around the Frankfurt School, including Jürgen Habermas and Axel Honneth. Whereas Sovietologists like Lobkowicz praised the book as a revelation,[11] Habermas subjected it to critique. Most questionable in Habermas's view was Kosík's defence of *practical* materialism. In Kosík's robust concept of labour, labour takes on the role, in Habermas's words, of 'constituting the objectivity of possible objects of experience'.[12] Therefore other ways of constituting objectivity – either through recognition of persons or through linguistic

---

The third edition was slightly revised by Kosík, who left out a few passages, added several notes, and modified some concepts (e.g. substituting the term 'Materialism' for 'Marxism' in some places).

7   Sánchez Vázquez 1977, p. 30.
8   As Sánchez Vázquez notes: 'without praxis, or the creation of a socio-human reality, knowledge of reality is itself impossible'. Sánchez Vázquez 1977, p. 116. For more on Sánchez Vázquez's reception of Kosík's thought, see Diana Fuentes's contribution to this volume.
9   Kosík 1969a. Later on, this translation was published also in Portugal: Kosík 1977. Paulo Freire explicitly mentions Kosík in his essay 'Education, Liberation, and the Church' published in the journal *Religious Education*, no. 4, 1984, pp. 524–45.
10 Kosík 1967.
11 Lobkowicz 1964, pp. 248–51. Lobkowicz writes: 'This is truly an unusual book, comparable only to classic studies such as G. Lukács' *Geschichte und Klassenbewusstsein*. If, since World War II, there has been a Marxist-Leninist publication likely to persuade Western philosophers that Marxism-Leninism ought to be taken seriously, then this is the book. No propaganda. No trivialities. No sentence asserted because of the statement of a "Classic". Nothing of the shallow pseudo-clarity and of the scientism characteristic of so many Marxist-Leninist works; and very little of the muddled characteristic of Marxist-Leninist writings trying to stay close to, or rather to return to, Hegel'.
12 Habermas 1976, p. 27.

practice – are largely neglected. When Honneth later wrote about the book, however, he appreciated the fact that Kosík emphasised the role of recognition in his conception of praxis.[13] Among the literary critics who were active, beginning in the late 1960s at the newly founded University of Konstanz, Kosík's reflections on the work of art and on Marxist hermeneutics resonated and influenced the formation of 'reception theory'. Hans Robert Jauss, one of the leading proponents of *Rezeptionsästhetik* in Germany, stressed the importance of Kosík's understanding of the interpretative process as 'totalisation' or 'rejuvenation', in which the recipient plays a crucial role.[14]

The German translation served as the source for a French translation that appeared in 1970.[15] Kosík's reception in France had begun earlier, however, and was already deeply-rooted. Although the complete translation of *Dialectics of the Concrete* appeared relatively late, some of its main ideas concerning concrete totality circulated and exerted some influence in the Francophone world *via* a paper entitled 'Dialectique du concret', which Kosík presented at a philosophical colloquium in Royaumont in 1960 and published in the Italian journal *aut aut* two years later. Since Kosík was strongly influenced by György Lukács's French disciple Lucien Goldmann, who newly reinterpreted the concept of 'concrete totality' and used it to analyse world-view structures (*visions du monde*), it is no surprise that Kosík's ideas resonated with Goldmann (with whom Kosík met in person several times) and later on with some of Goldmann's students, including Michael Löwy and Marc Perelman. Jean-Paul Sartre was also attracted by Kosík's humanistic attitude and his brave attempt to break through the corset of official Marxism-Leninist doctrine.[16]

In East-Central Europe, leaving aside for a moment Czechoslovakia, Kosík's influence was rather modest. In spite of the fact that Kosík was read in Poland by Marxist philosophers belonging to the 'Warsaw School of the History of Ideas' (such as Bronisław Baczko and Leszek Kołakowski),[17] no Polish trans-

---

13 In his address upon the occasion of receiving the František Palacký medal from the Czech Academy of Sciences in May 2004, Honneth explicitly mentioned Karel Kosík and praised his contribution to social philosophy. See his interview with Marek Hrubec – Hrubec and Honeth 2004, p. 621.
14 Jauss 1970, pp. 7–37.
15 Kosík 1970. One year earlier, the German translation also provided the basis for a translation into Japanese: Kosík 1969b.
16 The second French edition, published in 1988 by Les Éditions de la Passion, included as an afterword Kosík's exchange of letters with Jean-Paul Sartre in 1975.
17 In the third volume of his monumental *Main Currents of Marxism*, Kołakowski mentions Kosík as an important Marxist revisionist in Czechoslovakia, as Kosík 'put forward a number of typically revisionist issues: a return to the idea of praxis as the most general category

lation was made. The same was true of most other countries in the region, with the exception of Hungary and the former Yugoslavia.[18] There, Kosík's humanist variant of Marxism found fertile soil among members of the 'Budapest School' (especially György Márkus and Agnes Heller)[19] and the 'Praxis School' (especially Gajo Petrović and Predrag Vranicki).[20]

The most important figure who introduced Kosík to Anglophone intellectual circles was the Italian-American philosopher Paul Piccone, publisher and editor of the journal *Telos*, which was founded during the rise of New Left in the late 1960s. From the start, Piccone devoted space in his journal to philosophical currents from East-Central Europe, and he published several extracts from *Dialectics of the Concrete* there in 1968 and 1969.[21] The book's complete translation, made directly from the Czech, appeared several years later, in 1976.[22] Piccone himself wrote an introduction to the translation, which in the end did not appear there but separately as an article in the journal *Critique*.[23] He notes in this article that the attractiveness of Kosík's philosophical project consists in his attempt to synthesise various philosophical currents – most importantly Marxism and phenomenology – without descending into mere eclecticism, in order to restate a Marxian materialist programme, highlighting the ontological importance of labour for our understanding of social reality. Through this emphasis, as Piccone believed, Kosík enriched the narrow framework of phenomenology.[24] Yet Kosík's influence did not restrict itself to phenomenolo-

---

in the interpretation of history; the relativity of ontological questions *vis-à-vis* anthropological ones, the abandonment of materialist metaphysics and the primacy of the "base" over the "superstructure"; philosophy and art as co-determinants of social life and not merely its products'. Kołakowski 1978, p. 469.

18 In Hungarian: Kosík 1967a. In Serbo-Croatian: Kosík 1967e. In Slovenian: Kosík 1967c. The only other partial translation into an Eastern or East-Central European language is by Pavel Prilutskiy, who in 2003 translated the book's first chapter into Russian. It remains unpublished but is available online as 'Диалектика конкретной тотальности' (http://www.cts.cuni.cz/soubory/reporty/CTS-03-12.pdf [accessed 21 August 2017]).

19 See Heller's comments on Kosík in her autobiography: Heller 1999.

20 See the chapter dealing with Marxism in Czechoslovakia in Vranicki's *History of Marxism*: Vranicki 1974, pp. 765–72.

21 The first chapter, 'Dialectic of the Concrete Totality', was translated in full. See Kosík 1968a, pp. 21–37; Kosík 1969e, pp. 35–54. In addition, the second chapter, 'History and Freedom', was translated in slightly abridged form and with the amended title 'Reason and History': Kosík 1969d, pp. 64–71. Although no translator or source is mentioned, one may speculate that these translations were made by Piccone himself from the Italian edition.

22 Kosík 1976.

23 Piccone 1977, pp. 43–52.

24 This interpretation of Kosík as a phenomenological Marxist is also illustrated by Bakan 1983, in McBride and Schrag 1983; Zimmermann 1984, pp. 209–33.

gical Marxism. James H. Satterwhite, who became familiar with Kosík while living in Prague in the early 1970s, would present Kosík within the context of Central and Southeastern European Marxist humanism,[25] as would Raya Dunayevskaya.[26]

While interest in Kosík in Western Europe and the Americas reached its high point in the 1960s and 70s, in China there has been growing interest in Kosík since the second half of the 1980s, as Chinese scholars have made efforts to enrich official Marxist-Leninist discourse, derived largely from Soviet DIAMAT and HISTMAT, with inspiration from less orthodox sources. In China, the process of interpreting and debating the significance of diverse traditions of Western and East-Central European Marxism is still in full swing.

In Czechoslovakia, *Dialectics of the Concrete* was widely reviewed soon after it appeared, by philosophers as well as historians, writers, and artists. Philosophically, the book was read by some as a landmark announcing a new phase of Marxist anthropology (in the sense of the 'philosophy of man'), by others as a study in ontology, and by others as an important contribution to the search for non-Stalinist Marxist theory and methodology. Of course, these readings did not necessarily exclude one another, and some authors combined multiple readings.

Jan Patočka, who interpreted *Dialectics of the Concrete* primarily as a work of ontology, saw in Kosík's book real philosophical insight. Patočka highly appraised Kosík's category of praxis as an expositional key to modern ontological, epistemological and existential questions. At the same time, Patočka criticised Kosík for not employing nuanced phenomenological categories that would enable him to depict the everyday praxis of the individual human being. The human being as a phenomenon must be, according to Patočka, not a secondary outcome of philosophical inquiry but rather a primary foundation of the philosophical approach. The phenomenology of life, he argued, is fundamental to anthropology, which precedes ontology. Thus ontology cannot be based on the analysis of abstract beings and things (even if they are dialectically conditioned); it must be based, rather, on the analysis of the existence of real human beings.[27] Nevertheless, Patočka also stated that Kosík's intellectual endeavours demonstrate the mutually intertwined continuity of classical

---

25   See Satterwhite 1992. Satterwhite also contributed to bringing Kosík's work to an international audience by editing *The Crisis of Modernity*, a collection of Kosík's essays from the late 1960s. See Kosík 1995.
26   Dunayevskaya 1989. For more information on Dunayevskaya's interpretation of Kosík, see Peter Hudis's contribution to this volume, pp. 325–42.
27   Patočka 2006a, pp. 325–6.

German philosophy, the Marxist tradition, and modern phenomenology and existentialism. According to him, with *Dialectics of the Concrete* Czech philosophy achieves what it had attempted in the first half of the nineteenth century: genuine participation in the thinking and making of the modern world.[28]

Ladislav Hejdánek, another non-Marxist philosopher, similarly welcomed Kosík's book as a rehabilitation of what he called a 'real philosophical approach'. On the one hand, he appreciated the humanistic character of Kosík's examination of man and his world.[29] On the other hand, he criticised Kosík for insufficiently developing his conceptions of ontology and praxis. According to Hejdánek, *Dialectics of the Concrete* limits itself to an ontological inquiry of Man's environment and ignores the complicated question of the meaning of nature.[30]

Kosík's colleague and fellow advocate of Marxist humanism Josef Zumr positively assessed several aspects of Kosík's work related to those addressed by Patočka and Hejdánek: its courage in addressing bourgeois philosophy (existentialism, phenomenology), as well as its confrontation with Marxist scientism and economic reductionism. Zumr was convinced that *Dialectics of the Concrete* signalled a new phase of philosophy based on an ontopoetic conception of man. Such an understanding of philosophy, he argued, was highly subversive in regard to both reified social relations and bureaucratic manipulation. At the same time it could provide a promising basis for further Marxist humanist inquiry.[31]

It was not only non-Marxists like Patočka and Hejdánek, however, who expressed reservations about Kosík's book. Kosík was also criticised by some of his Marxist humanist colleagues, including Robert Kalivoda, who criticised Kosík from the perspective of a synthesis of Marxism, psychoanalysis and Czechoslovak structuralism. Kosík's approach to dialectics, Kalivoda argued, is less concrete than it promises, and it fails in its analysis of concrete historical forms of emancipation. As Kalivoda put it, Kosík was elaborating merely a 'dialectics of the concrete', when he should have been developing 'concrete dialectics'. At the same time, much like Hejdánek, Kalivoda thought that Kosík's work helped reveal the position of the human being in the world, even if it

---

28   Patočka 2006a, p. 326.
29   Hejdánek 1963, pp. 118–20 (republished in Hejdánek 2010, pp. 31–4).
30   Hejdánek 2010a (a manuscript offered to Prague's *Filosofický časopis* in 1964 but unpublished until 2010).
31   Zumr 1963, p. 5. See also Bodnár 1963, p. 3.

failed to grasp the world in its wholeness, including the world beyond the human, as Engels had attempted to do in developing his 'dialectics of nature'.[32]

Within the context of 1960s Czechoslovakia, *Dialectics of the Concrete* was also perceived as providing sophisticated philosophical support for the reform communist current, as many within the Communist Party embarked on the path of de-Stalinisation and aimed at establishing what they saw as a more democratic form of socialism. Since the party itself during this period vacillated between support for and resistance to reform, the official ideologues of the Communist Party varied in their reactions to Kosík's work, as a result of which *Dialectics of the Concrete* sometimes enjoyed official approval and at other times became an object of censure.[33] After the suppression of the Prague Spring, however, the book's reputation was sealed as a symbol of so-called counter-revolution. In the 1970s and 1980s, Kosík was banned from all academic work, and if his work was mentioned at all it was only as an example of a 'dangerous revisionist deviation'. This situation changed somewhat after 1989. Kosík became publicly active again and gained some popularity as an essayist and commentator on current events. Nevertheless, in the atmosphere of triumphant capitalism his *magnum opus* remained almost forgotten, appearing to many as an ominous shadow of the dark communist past. Only in recent years, as Marxism has once again become recognised as a relevant part of the intellectual environment in the region, has *Dialectics of the Concrete* begun to attract significant attention among Czech scholars. Several of the contributions to this volume attest to this fact.

2   About This Volume

The idea of collecting papers on Kosík's *magnum opus* was motivated by a belief that *Dialectics of the Concrete* was not solely a historical document tied to a particular time and place. We are convinced that the book is worthy of careful rereading in entirely new contexts. Only then could it be truly said whether the book really stands the test of time. To be sure, our intention has not been to displace or completely diminish the importance of the historical context in which the book first appeared, since this context informs our understanding of the intellectual and political constellation in which Kosík's thought took

---

[32] For a detailed analysis of Kalivoda's and Kosík's approaches see Mervart 2017, pp. 111–26 (especially pp. 120–2).

[33] For more on the impact of Kosík's book on the Czechoslovak reform Communist scene, see Jan Mervart's contribution to this volume, pp. 19–38.

shape, and enables us to trace Kosík's impact on both Czechoslovak culture and on Marxist philosophy worldwide during the late 1960s and 1970s. Our general aim is to reintroduce Kosík's philosophy to English-speaking readers, providing them with something of a 'road map' or companion to help them more easily follow the argumentative thread of *Dialectics of the Concrete*, as well as the historical setting out of which the book emerged and the new settings that lent the book new meaning as it and its translations travelled the world.

The first step we took along this path was a conference entitled 'Karel Kosík and *Dialectics of the Concrete*', which was organised by the three editors of this volume in Prague, held on 4–6 June 2014. Our call for papers met with an enthusiastic response, enabling us to bring together a wide range of scholars who have been influenced by and have creatively reinterpreted Kosík's work. The conference participants included figures who were present during Kosík's first rise to prominence (such as Kosík's long-time colleague Josef Zumr, his student Johann Pal Arnason, and his admirers abroad Michael Löwy, Anselm Min, and Bertell Ollman), as well as others who have come to Kosík's work more recently, in entirely new contexts. We had a strong contingent of 14 participants from Czech academic institutions, but we also had seven participants working in China, eight in the United States and Canada, three in Italy, two in Latin America (Mexico and Brazil), two in Slovakia, as well as others working in France, Austria, Croatia, Macedonia, and Turkey. Their presentations, and the lively discussions they provoked, made it clear to us that Karel Kosík's thought can and should be a part of contemporary philosophical and social-theoretical debates.

The conference papers addressed Kosík's place in Czech and East-Central European intellectual history, as well as Kosík's influence abroad. A majority of papers focused on the significance of *Dialectics of the Concrete*, but others delved into other, less well-known aspects of Kosík's earlier and later work. Together, they offered the image of a diverse and original body of thought which, for all its engagement in its specific historical moment, is as relevant today as it was when it was written.

This range of themes is reflected in the papers included in this volume. Although some outstanding presenters were unable to turn their presentations into articles for the book, and although the practical necessities of publishing forced us to limit the number of papers we could include here, the following papers touch upon all the major threads of discussion that emerged during the conference.

The first section of this book, entitled 'The Reform Years and the Origins of *Dialectics of the Concrete*', is devoted to the social and intellectual background of Kosík's work. It situates the author of *Dialectics of the Concrete* in the historical moment of post-Stalinist Czechoslovakia and the growing push for reform within the Communist Party. Kosík is presented in *Jan Mervart's* paper as a Marxist-humanist thinker and public intellectual who played an important role in developing the notion of democratic socialism. The author examines in detail Kosík's political engagement after the Warsaw Pact invasion in August 1968, and draws attention to the antinomic character of Kosík's political strategy. *Tomáš Hermann* then turns his attention in his chapter to an earlier moment in Kosík's career, showing that the Marxist methodology employed by Kosík in *Dialectics of the Concrete* had already been used by Kosík in his earlier work on the Czech radical democrats who participated in the revolutionary events of 1848. Kosík's research on radical democratic thought, the results of which were published in his book *Czech Radical Democracy* (*Česká radikální demokracie*) in 1958, should not be understood only in negative terms as a departure from Stalinist-style Marxism-Leninism, but also as an original attempt to develop a new methodological approach, whose significance was later elaborated in *Dialectics of the Concrete*.

Dialectics of the Concrete has sometimes been perceived as a mere collection of 'closely related essays' rather than as a systematic inquiry with a systematic agenda for solving philosophical problems.[34] However, such reading obviously runs against Kosík's self-understanding, as he put it in a short introductory remark that was, surprisingly, not included in the English translation. In this note Kosík spells out his aim to elaborate a complex argument in which 'particular problems are linked to one another', 'shed light on one another', and in this way 'express the main idea'.[35] These 'particular problems' include a critique of fetishism and ideology, culture and politics, emancipation and revolution, praxis and labour, time and history, anthropogenesis and human nature, dialectics and rationality. The bond that holds them together relates to a more general question concerning the constitution and possible transformation of social reality. In dealing with each of these themes, Kosík argues that human beings are essentially onto-formative creatures who constitute and are able to change the very structure of social reality.

Kosík develops this idea primarily through his discussions of *praxis* and *labour*. These concepts also provide the common thread that runs through the papers included in the second section of our volume, which is devoted to Kosík's philosophy of praxis and ontology of labour. The papers in this section examine Kosík's conceptualisation of praxis as a way of moving beyond age-old dualisms of theory vs. practice, consciousness vs. being, and culture

---

34 Heller 1977, pp. 134–42, p. 134. Patočka 2006a, pp. 321–2.
35 Kosík 1966, p. 4.

vs. nature. The papers delve into various aspects of praxis, including its formative aspect, as manifested in labour; its normative aspect, as revealed in the mutual recognition of persons; its epistemic aspect, which is apparent in the openness of human knowing subjects toward social reality; and last but not least its existential aspect, which is related to the emotional frameworks of human minds. *Francesco Tava*, in his paper, argues that in *Dialectics of the Concrete* Kosík emphasised above all the formative aspect, thereby almost excluding other aspects. For him, labour is a model of human practice in general, which leads him to ground the philosophy of praxis on an ontology of labour. The contours of this ontology are outlined in papers by *Ivan Landa* and *Ian Angus*. Landa scrutinises Kosík's claim that labour constitutes human time in its three-dimensions: past, present and future. This claim, which was clearly intended to undermine Martin Heidegger's conception of original temporality, is further restated in a doctrine of temporal materialism, whose core consists in a descriptive analysis of the 'ecstasis' of the labouring process (which is itself composed of three aspects: product, producing, and intention) and in the derivation of temporal dimensions out of these aspects. Angus proceeds in another direction, focusing on culture and arguing that Kosík attempted to elaborate a 'phenomenology of the inception of culture from the ontology of labour'. Although labour is closely tied to economic structure, Angus points out that Kosík did not adopt a reductionist stance towards cultural production. In Angus's interpretation, this is because Kosík defined the sphere of culture in negative terms, as a realm of 'non-labour'. Precisely such a negative delineation allowed Kosík to theorise culture as a sphere which is on the one hand conditioned by economic structure, but on the other hand operates as an autarkic epistemic medium, disclosing social reality to human knowing subjects. However, Angus also criticises Kosík for subordinating both epistemic and existential aspects of praxis to the formative one, so that his conception of culture is ultimately contaminated with reductionism and economic determinism. Kosík's partial suspension of 'existentiality' has much to do with his ambivalent stance towards existentialism. As *Siyaves Azeri* argues, for Kosík existentialism implies a wrong-headed or 'fetishised' understanding of praxis. Here again, the main target is Heidegger with his conception of *Dasein* as 'care', which is criticised from the standpoint of the ontology of labour. For Kosík, care seems to be rather a distorted human form, manifesting itself in mere procuring: in manipulating and handling objects. But Kosík's principal objection to Heidegger consists in his claim that Heidegger elevated procuring to a trans-historical category, although in reality it is historical through and through, always bound to a specific mode of production: under capitalism procuring takes the form of abstract labour producing use values and measured in a purely quantitative way. Nevertheless, this was not Kosík's last word on existentialism. Later, after 1968, Kosík turned his attention to both epistemic and existential aspects of praxis. As Tava explains, Kosík focused on phenomena such as the comic, the tragic, and the ridiculous, borrowing a central insight from existentialism, according to which human beings are not neutral in their relatedness towards the world and to each other. He illustrated this insight with the phenomenon of self-sacrifice, which cannot be accounted for as a kind of constructive practice. Finally, *Tom Rockmore* asks how Kosík's ontology of labour enables knowledge of reality. Reminding us that Kosík writes within a tradition, going back to Kant, that sees reality as knowable only insofar as it is created by those who seek to know it, Rockmore shows that things-in-themselves can be grasped, according to Kosík, because they are themselves products of human praxis. And although this central idea had already been articulated by Kant and developed further by Hegel, Rockmore argues that Kosík contributed to epistemology by drawing out the implications of Marx's attempt to apply this idea to the economy, as expressed in the labour process.

The third section 'Modernity, Nation, Globalisation' opens with *Xinruo Zhang* and *Xiaohan Huang's* chapter, discussing Kosík's critique of modernity. It was modernity, they note, that transformed social consciousness and made it possible to arrive at 'concrete totality' as a philosophical expression of reality. Although 'modernity' is not thematised in *Dialectics of the Concrete*, it became central to Kosík's thought in the late 1960s, as he made use of this Heideggerian term (without thereby becoming a 'Heideggerian', the authors argue) in order to bring his critical approach to bear on a wide range of moral, cultural and political problems. The last of these comes to the fore in *Joseph Grim Feinberg's* chapter, which focuses on a specific aspect of Kosík's political thought. Grim Feinberg notes the recurring attention paid by Kosík to the concept of 'democracy', and he argues that in spite of the significant changes that Kosík's thought underwent over the course of his life, the figure of 'the people' appears rather consistently to play the role of a mediating term between two apparently contradictory notions of 'the human being'. While the human being appears sometimes as an absolute, abstract essence and sometimes as a socially constituted category, 'the people' is conceptualised both as constituted and as (potentially) self-constituting. The last two chapters in this section take Kosík's ideas beyond his own intellectual context, applying Kosík's conception of concrete totality to the problem of globalisation. *Anselm Min* makes it his task to bring the ideas of *Dialectics of the Concrete* into the present, taking into account not only broad social developments like intensified globalisation but also intellectual developments such as the widespread critique of Marxism that emerged in the years after 1968 and, especially, after 1989. Min argues that the notion of concrete totality enables us to grasp the central challenge of globalisation as the challenge of achieving 'global human solidarity'[36] while connecting solidarity to concrete practices, without allowing it to lapse into purely abstract ideology.

Up to now we have dealt with Kosík's thought primarily as a set of ideas developed by the author himself. However, Kosík developed many of his ideas indirectly, as he engaged with the views of other thinkers and criticised alternative conceptions. In elaborating his arguments negatively, Kosík was able to identify the thought-patterns and to articulate the insights that were fundamental to each thinker or intellectual current. He was then able to place these patterns in novel contexts and to employ them in developing completely new insights.

The aim of this volume's fourth section is to retrace Kosík's 'intellectual encounters' with important thinkers (Martin Heidegger, Herbert Marcuse and Louis Althusser) and intellectual currents (positivism, structuralism, phenomenology and critical theory). Kosík adopts core insights from existentialism and phenomenology, borrowing other ideas from structuralism, logical positivism and critical theory. Yet he was also critical of these approaches. In the case of positivism, he appreciated its sober anti-metaphysical approach, while he criticised its reductionist and naturalist mania to explain social phenomena solely on the basis of natural phenomena. In *Tomáš Hříbek's* view, Kosík's critique of positivism fails, since he did not distinguish between different strands of positivism and did not take into account, for example, Otto Neurath's attempt to merge positivism with methodological holism, which resulted in a 'holistic empiricism' freed of its naturalist inclinations to conceive the social realm in terms of physical features. Kosík's defence of holism is also central to a polemic he aimed at structuralism and systems theory. Kosík criticised both currents for overemphasising the role of autonomous structures and for replacing human subjects or collectivities with quasi super-subjects. Nevertheless, he was quite sympathetic to a functionalist approach to 'structures' and 'systems' that sees concrete parts as realisations of abstract statuses or functions. *Vít Bartoš* argues, however, that Kosík's appropriation and critique of both currents is parochial, due to his adherence to a *practical* materialism that favours human subjects and social reality over animal beings and natural reality. Kosík's conception of structural 'totality' thus appears, from this perspective, to be only partial. Hence, Kosík's text can be viewed as a striking example of Marxist ontology reaching a deadlock, since it blocks a dialogue with structuralism or general systems theory that theorise natural systems – and not only human beings or

---

36 This volume, p. 212.

social systems – as self-creating subjects. By the same token, Kosík's holism can be viewed as the antithesis of Louis Althusser's anti-humanist structuralism, since practical materialism implies the centrality of the human being. *Petr Kužel* undertakes a thorough comparison of Kosík's humanism and Althusser's anti-humanism, concentrating on their understanding of both ideology and the subject. Whereas for Althusser the subject is an ideological product and in this respect is trapped in a web of ideological beliefs (despite the fact that it can be involved in subversive actions), for Kosík the subject is theorised as revolutionary from the outset, with a capacity to destroy the 'world of the pseudoconcrete'. From here, Kužel concludes that Kosík's ontology of the subject offers an alternative to post-Marxist theories, whose main concern is to understand the subject emerging out of a revolutionary event. Kosík proceeds the other way around, conceiving revolution as it arises out of the subject. It should be further noted that while Kosík's practical materialism may have foreclosed dialogue with certain positivist and anti-humanist traditions, it also opened up a space for a fruitful intellectual dialogue between Marxism and phenomenology. After accomplishing its 'practical turn' in Husserl's late *Crisis of European Sciences and Transcendental Phenomenology*, and above all in Heidegger's *Being and Time*, phenomenology became more attractive for Marxism, as it was now concerned with everydayness and the life-world, both of which were amenable to Marxism's social analysis of practice. Still, Kosík moved beyond the phenomenological description of the structures of our practical coping with the world around us and turned towards a critical analysis of the economic structure hidden behind different ways of handling things in our environment. Within this context *Jan Černý* argues, as did Azeri in a similar way, that Kosík attempted to historicise Heidegger's notion of 'care' and to socialise Husserl's notion of 'life-world', analysing their common ground, namely economic structure. Later, in the 1990s, Kosík picked up the thread of Heidegger's late thought, exploring the essence of technology and reshaping it into a political program of 'metaphysical' democracy. Černý sees this as a retreat from Kosík's earlier revolutionary democratic position and as a shift towards modest traditionalism, renouncing revolutionary praxis altogether.

While we open this volume by situating Kosík's work within the context of Czechoslovak history, we conclude it in the sixth section with a look at the reception and influence of *Dialectics of the Concrete* abroad. Naturally, we were not able to cover all countries, language milieus and spheres of influence, but we believe that we have succeeded in collecting a number of important and characteristic cases. These tell of the reception of Kosík's work in Italy, Mexico, and the United States. In the first contribution to this section, *Gabriella Fusi* sheds light on the mutual influence between Czech and Italian Marxist intellectuals during the 1960s and 1970s. She points to contacts between Czech and Italian journals, describes common organisational activities, and focuses on the reception of Kosík's work by Enzo Paci and Guido Davide Neri. In the next paper, *Diana Fuentes* discusses the Mexican reception of *Dialectics of the Concrete*, which began with Kosík's attendance at the Thirteenth International Congress of Philosophy in Mexico City in 1963. Fuentes focuses especially on the work of Adolfo Sánchez Vázquez, who was instrumental in the publication of the first Spanish edition of *Dialectics of the Concrete*. In the third paper, *Peter Hudis* looks at the parallels between US Marxist humanism and Kosík's thought in *Dialectics of the Concrete*. Hudis introduces us to the commentary on Kosík's work by the leading North American Marxist humanist Raya Dunayevskaya. Hudis observes that Dunayevskaya developed her own version of Marxist humanism that was, much like Kosík's, based on the indispensability of philosophy. Marxist humanism, as it is presented in works of Kosík and Dunayevskaya, considers philosophy to be a challenging answer to the threat of the total dehumanisation of mankind.

We decided to conclude the volume with a postscript by *Michael Löwy*, who got to know Kosík personally while editing a French anthology of Kosík's essays.[37] In his contribution, based on lengthy conversations with Kosík and on the testimony of Kosík's contemporaries, Löwy pays homage to Kosík's lifelong opposition to all forms of political and ideological oppression.

37   Kosík 2003b.

PART 1

The Reform Years and the Origins of Dialectics of the Concrete

CHAPTER 1

Karel Kosík as a Public Intellectual of the Reform Years

Jan Mervart

1   The Czechoslovak Party Intelligentsia of the 1960s

Compared to other countries of the Eastern Bloc, the influence of the Twentieth party Congress of the Communist Party of the Soviet Union was rather controlled than spontaneous in Czechoslovakia. The only voices openly calling for immediate de-Stalinisation came from the circles of the party intelligentsia (including Kosík) and from students in larger cities such as Prague or Bratislava, as well as from some communist writers at the second congress of the Czechoslovak Writers' Union in April 1956. The party leadership and apparatchiks were very keen to suppress any efforts that would have striven for the assembly of an extraordinary party congress, or for further discussion of Khrushchev's speech. Soon after the Budapest events in the fall of 1956, Czechoslovakia was one of the most enthusiastic participants in an antirevisionist campaign, aimed at preventing any future 'counterrevolutionary tendencies'. Nevertheless, the more Czechoslovak cultural and intellectual life was fettered in the second half of the 1950s, the more relaxed was the atmosphere of the subsequent decade upon the delayed arrival of a process of political de-Stalinisation (in December 1962, the Twelfth Congress of the Communist Party of Czechoslovakia declared a fight against the 'cult of personality'), and when many previously politically delicate issues could be more or less articulated. The role of the Czech and Slovak communist intelligentsia (mostly scholars, writers, film makers or journalists) in shaping the heady atmosphere of 1960s Czechoslovakia is broadly examined in an extensive body of respective literature concerned with the Prague Spring of 1968 and its preconditions.[1] The following text is mostly concerned with Karel Kosík and the role he played as a public intellectual in the area of fomenting reform. To take this topic into consideration, it will be deliberately abstracted away from a detailed analysis of the reform communism of the 1960s. Nevertheless, there are several obser-

---

1   Golan 1971; 1973; Kusin 1971; Satterwhite 1992.

vations clarifying the specific features of the Czechoslovak party intelligentsia of that era that need to be remarked upon.

Intellectuals in former Czechoslovakia not only enjoyed the liberal atmosphere of the 'golden sixties', they massively contributed to form it; they were not merely a product of the political liberalisation (de-Stalinisation), they participated in producing it at the same time. Being publicly critical of the reality of so-called socialist society, discussing issues of censorship and official cultural policy, they helped to shift the quality of the Czechoslovak post-Stalinist regime to one of the most open state socialist regimes in the then Soviet Bloc.

The majority of the public intellectuals of the 1960s were former Stalinists, and were still party members in the 1960s; from this point of view, the term 'party intelligentsia' is more than suitable. They had mostly been born in the third decade of the twentieth century (Kosík personally in 1926) and started to be politically active during or immediately after the Second World War. In the second half of the 1950s, they underwent a complicated and usually painful personal de-Stalinisation process. At the same time, but no later than in the first half of the 1960s, they gained serious public authority as advocates of a delayed campaign against the 'cult of personality'. Kosík's generation, until recently a pillar of Stalinism, started a quest for a new legitimisation of communism's revolutionary attempts[2] through reform of the system. Simultaneously, the same generation contributed to the de-legitimisation of the Soviet form of Marxist-Leninist ideological dominance and opened up a space for specific reinterpretations of classical Marxist-Leninist dogmas in culture, philosophy, history or law. Despite the relaxed nature of the Czechoslovak post-Stalinist regime, this process was not of a linear character in the sense of continually increasing autonomy of the intellectual sphere. The reformist Party intelligentsia found itself in a constant struggle with party officials and up to the end of 1967, when Novotný was replaced by Dubček, its members could find themselves the target of an ideological campaign at any time.

Party intellectuals were still an immanent part of the system in the 1960s, and the era of dissent did not start until the beginning of the subsequent decade, when it was more than clear that reform communism was politically defeated for the time being. The subversion of Marxism-Leninism never crossed the boundaries of state socialism, and the party intelligentsia stayed and wanted to stay within it.[3] The vast majority of the critical ideas of the

---

2   For a specification of this generation see Liehm 1970. The book, which was originally called *Generation* in Czech, offers interviews with 14 intellectuals of that era. For a detailed analysis of the revisionist tendencies in the second half of the 1950s, see Kopeček forthcoming.
3   Such a separation from party policy as the *Open Letter to the Party* by Jacek Kuroń and Karol

1960s revolved around possible reforms of the existing socialist system, varying from official and mostly technocratic reformism (for example economic reform, scientific-technological revolution[4]) to its radical but still reformist form as in the case of Karel Kosík and other radical reformists.

For the majority of party intellectuals, the reform era of the 1960s represented a new form of the 'national road to socialism', which they had already enthusiastically supported after the Second World War. In their view, the Czechoslovak development was subordinated to its own specific historical and cultural preconditions, creating the possibilities for reform. A perspective of the Stalinist experience on the one hand and of the Czech cultural and democratic 'uniqueness' on the other was immanently present in their thought; as the Czech historian and Kosík's contemporary Karel Bartošek observed: 'no other country in the world has such an experience of developed bourgeois parliamentarianism as well as of Stalinist socialism'.[5] Similarly, party intellectuals sympathised with the idea that Czechoslovakia could be a suitable model for other socialist countries.

Similarly to other state socialist societies, Czech and Slovak intellectuals belonged to the most influential groups in socialist society.[6] If, however, in capitalist parliamentary democracies, public demands are (or are supposed to be) articulated through political parties and if art and the intelligentsia are subjected to a capitalist mode of production and substituted by the mass production of pop culture, in authoritarian societies such as state socialist Czechoslovakia in the 1960s, the intellectual and cultural sphere adopt, intentionally or unintentionally – regardless of whether a person was a Stalinist or a reformist – a highly political function. The irreplaceable role that public intellectuals played in authoritarian regimes is incomparable with that of Western societies. Because the intelligentsia tended to formulate public claims, their members were publicly recognised as respected authorities, and their influence

---

Modzelewski did not exist among the reformist party intelligentsia. In Czechoslovakia, similar radical voices emerged within the student movement, especial in the Revolutionary Youth Movement in 1968–69.

4 The post-Stalinist project of Scientific-technological revolution was a specific attempt to improve the quality of socialist society through applied science, effective management and the implementation of new technologies in production. In Czechoslovakia it was introduced with a proclamation of socialism in the early 1960s. It soon became the backbone of political reformism, and paragraphs on scientific and technological effectiveness appeared in the official reform programme (Action Programme) of the KSČ during the Prague Spring of 1968. See the most influential philosophical outcome of the project – Richta 1969.
5 Bartošek 2003a, p. 59 (the text was written in 1969).
6 Konrád and Szelényi 1979.

(symbolic capital) was much more significant than any of their Western counterparts. In an interview with the Czech cultural journalist Antonín Jaroslav Liehm, Kosík mentioned an illustrative conversation on that topic with Jürgen Habermas, who reportedly stated that compared to the censorship and ideological critique of philosophers in Czechoslovakia the situation in Western Germany was even worse, because intellectuals were ignored by the government as well as by the public, and therefore did not play a relevant role in the society.[7]

In this respect, the role of the intelligentsia in Czech society was even more specific, as the modern Czech national identity was based on it. In the nineteenth century, writers, university teachers, lawyers and other intellectuals belonged to the backbone of modern Czech society, and after Czechoslovakia was established in 1918 the state was referred to as the 'republic of professors' because its political elites, including the first two presidents (T.G. Masaryk and Edvard Beneš), were respected professors. From this perspective, the linkage between the nineteenth-century tradition, Stalinist 'engineering of human souls' and its replacement by reform communism is not surprising; the modes of understanding modernity and national progress had been changing since the nineteenth century, nevertheless reflections on the progressive development of the national community represented an inseparable part of reformist thought. At this point, it needs to be added that the 1960s can still be spoken of as an era of *graphosphère* as Régis Debray defines it,[8] in which intellectuals, 'men of letters', had not yet been replaced by TV stars.

2   Karel Kosík, Marxist Humanism and *Dialectics of the Concrete* in the Reform Years

The case of Karel Kosík was not an exceptional but a typical one. As a high-school student, the author of the *Dialectics of the Concrete* joined the anti-Nazi resistance group Předvoj,[9] he was editor in chief of its journal *Boj mladých* and

---

7   'We philosophers and sociologists are completely ignored [in Western Germany] both by the government and by the general public, and so we play no public or social role whatever' – Liehm 1970 (an interview with Karel Kosík in May 1968), p. 399.
8   Debray 2007.
9   This concerned a group of communist youth which was formed in the second half of 1943. Its main magazine was *Předvoj* (*Vanguard*), and up to 10,000 people were involved in its activity. A large number of them later belonged to the political or cultural elite of the state socialist regime, and it is evidently no coincidence that many made a significant contribution to the reform policy twenty years later. In addition to Karel Kosík we could name here the histor-

he spent the last days of the war in Terezín Prison while many of his comrades were executed.[10] Together with the economic crisis of the 1930s and the formation of the Popular Front, these were precisely the very historical moments which caused a large section of this generation to embrace communism already during the war. In such an understanding, communist engagement was not associated in the slightest extent with the implementation of bureaucratic directives and adherence to a strict party hierarchy. Despite the strictly pyramidal shape of the resistance's organisation, under the conditions of concealment the interpretation of party ideology was relatively unrestricted. Moreover, Stalinism was perceived as good and was primarily seen as the only opposition to Nazism (evil).

Předvoj was a group of communist youth, but due to the complicated circumstances of the war, the Czechoslovak communist leadership based in Moscow never recognised it as a part of the illegal Communist Party of Czechoslovakia (KSČ).[11] This explains the fact that Kosík and many others were able to join the party only after the liberation.[12] At the same time, the universities were reopened and Kosík started to study philosophy at Charles University in Prague. He collaborated with the newly established communist journal *Lidová kultura* [People's culture]. In 1947–49 Kosík studied in Leningrad and Moscow, and he returned to Czechoslovakia as a devoted builder of the new Stalinist civilisation, writing on Marxism-Leninism, the successes of the USSR, Stalin's works and so on.[13] With the establishment of the Czechoslovak Academy of Sciences, he started to work in the Cabinet for Philosophy. In 1954 he took part in a campaign against 'Masarykism' and so-called pseudo-humanism. Kosík did not hesitate to label T.G. Masaryk as an idealist and bourgeois thinker whose moralism and intellectual background did not provide an answer to the questions of the present day.[14] At first glance, nothing indicated any other fate for Kosík than a career of an official Marxist-Leninist philosopher following the party line.

---

ian Miloš Hájek or the philosopher Radovan Richta. See Wagnerová and Janovic 1968; also Lachout and Běláčková 2005.

10   Kosík was imprisoned on 11 November 1944 and released on 5 May 1945, when he almost died of typhus.
11   Mencl 2005, p. 37.
12   Membership of the KSČ is dated from 1 June 1945 – Archiv Akademie věd ČR (Archive of the Academy of Sciences of the Czech Republic). f. Filosofický ústav (Institute of Philosophy), kart. č. 3, inv.č. 22, sign. 042.
13   See for example: Kosík 1951a; 1951b.
14   Kosík 1954.

Nevertheless, at the same time Kosík was concerned with the Czech revolutionary tradition of the nineteenth century. As a member of the young communist generation, he critically followed up on Zdeněk Nejedlý's conception of Czech history. Nejedlý (born in 1878), a contemporary of T. G. Masaryk, was a professor of musicology. During the climactic period of Stalinism in 1948–53, he held the post of minister for Culture and Education. Simultaneously he was an intellectual guru of the Stalinist interpretation of Czech history and culture. Nejedlý called for an exploration of the popular traditions in Czech culture, which he understood in a positive revolutionary way and as specific historical preconditions for building the new communist society. In harmony with official history of philosophy, Kosík was preoccupied with the student revolutionary generation of 1848, which he interpreted as radical democratic. In contrast with the dominant interpretation of the Czech radical democrats, whose history was considered to be influenced by their Russian counterparts, Kosík placed his research within the context of the whole of Europe, including its western part.[15]

Together with the Twentieth party Congress in Moscow and its famous critique of Stalin's 'cult of personality', this was probably a decisive formative moment following the experience of the war in Kosík's intellectual development. At the end of 1956, together with Ivan Sviták, he initiated the first public anti-Stalinist debate in *Literární noviny* [Literary News] on the relationship between science and ideology. If ideology had recently been interpreted in a positive way in the official Stalinist discourse, as an inseparable part of political praxis, now Kosík understood it in a Marxian way as 'false consciousness' and demanded an end to the 'ideology dominion', which should be overcome by 'critical thought'.[16] This statement by Kosík prefigured the post-Stalinist era which began in Czechoslovakia in the second half of the 1950s.

The scientific paradigm changed and new themes appeared in the philosophical debate. Different thinkers began to engage with previously frowned upon topics such as a reassessment of the Marxist method, new approaches to epistemology or aesthetics, a reinterpretation of the 'people's democratic society' and its transformation towards socialism. New trends such as Marxist positivism or Marxist scientism, understood as 'clear', unideological post-Stalinist science appeared, nevertheless, the most influential as well as the most vigorous philosophical trend that emerged from the post-Stalinist situation was Marxist humanism.

---

15   This topic is elaborated in Tomáš Hermann's contribution in this book.
16   Kosík 2019a, p. 3.

This current was based on challenging the logic of 'external laws' in favour of an accent on human activity. The texts of Marxist humanists were preoccupied with questions such as the alienation of Man in modern society, modern art and its role in socialism, ideology and its critique, the Marxist relationship to Christianity or the future model of socialism. Similarly to Poland, the humanist approach of Czech scholars such as Robert Kalivoda, Karel Kosík, Milan Machovec or Ivan Sviták was formed within the framework of the history of philosophy. Crucial for the formation of Marxist humanism was the experience of working with original sources of Karl Marx and Friedrich Engels (*Economic and Philosophic Manuscripts of 1844*; the *Grundrisse*; *The Peasant War in Germany*), as well as of the broader Marxist tradition (Antonio Gramsci, György Lukács, Karl Korsch) or general philosophical tradition (Holbach, Hegel, Montaigne). The aforementioned critical relationship to Nejedlý's conception based on 'folkness' as the most significant feature of Czech culture and nationality during the course of history was also an important factor. An irreplaceable role was played by personal contacts and intellectual influences with representatives of the Polish school of the history of ideas, the Budapest school of Lukács's students and later (at the beginning of the 1960s) also the Yugoslav Praxis school and Western scholars such as Ernst Fischer, Erich Fromm or Roger Garaudy.

Karel Kosík finished his work on the Czech radical democrats in 1957. In this he defined the Marxist method in the sense of revealing the 'totality of relationships'.[17] A year later, at a conference about the Czech philosophical tradition, he warned against the economic determinism of the Stalinist era, as well as against excessive empiricism. In contrast with this, he pleaded for an application of philosophy (real Marxist method) to the history of philosophy, because 'the history of philosophy cannot in principle be of a higher standing than the philosophy of which it is a part'.[18]

Taking a similar perspective, Kosík started to elaborate upon the Marxist ontology of the social, which was, after several preparatory studies,[19] summarised in *Dialectics of the Concrete*. Soon after its publication in 1963[20] the book became a symbol of Czechoslovak Marxist humanism, because its main emphasis was on Man's free activity. Its unquestionable philosophical relevance will be deliberately left aside here, Kosík's contribution to Marxist philo-

---

17   Kosík 1958a.
18   Kosík 1958b, p. 9.
19   Kosík 1961 (Originally this was paper presented at a conference at Royaumont in September 1960); 1962.
20   Kosík 1963b.

sophy will be addressed rather within the context of Czechoslovak reform communism; as a specific critique of social institutions, which was understood in Czechoslovakia as a sophisticated subversion of the post-Stalinist regime.

His conception was based on an understanding of the human world as a 'concrete totality'.[21] Reality should be exposed as a complex of social relationships and as a dialectically conditioned unity of essence and phenomenon.[22] In contrast with a dialectical understanding of reality as a concrete totality, Kosík introduces the category of the pseudoconcrete, which was understood as the world of the everyday, its environment and routine atmosphere. The 'pseudoconcrete' part of reality is important for our further examination because it includes Man's fetishised praxis of procuring and manipulation, its ideology and fixed objects that are considered products of natural conditions. However, the world of the 'pseudoconcrete' is not a given substance, on the contrary, it has been created. It has to be demystified and recognised as a product of Man's activity, and destroyed in a process of overcoming through revolutionary praxis. The 'destruction of the pseudoconcrete' has to be accomplished in the following steps:

> (1) by the revolutionary-critical praxis of mankind which is identical with the humanisation of man, with social revolutions as its key stages; (2) by dialectical thinking which dissolves the fetishised world of appearance in order to penetrate to reality and to the 'thing itself'; (3) by the realisation of truth and the forming of human reality in an ontogenetic process; since the world of truth is also the own individual creation of every human individual as a social being. Every individual has to appropriate his own culture and lead his own life by *himself and non-vicariously*.[23]

Translated into the language of Kosík's contemporaries, social revolution was considered to have been as 'the key stage,' already accomplished after the Second World War. The second step of the 'destruction of the pseudoconcrete' lay in 'dissolving the fetishised world of appearance'. Regardless of whether Kosík meant this universally or not, it was understood as a subversion of the official Marxist-Leninist point of view. This could provide subsequent argu-

---

21 Although 'totality' was a category that experienced a revival in Eastern-European Marxism (compare especially with the works of Evald Ilyenkov), Kosík's conception was mostly inspired by Lukács 1979; especially by the first part *What is Orthodox Marxism?*, as well as by Marx's *Grundrisse*, which had recently been published. See Landa 2017, pp. 39–48.
22 'Totality signifies reality as a structured dialectical whole' – Kosík 1976, p. 18.
23 Kosík 1976, p. 8. Highlighted by Karel Kosík.

ments against the official party line, which was now demystified as the 'pseudo-concrete' sphere. The third step depended on the 'realisation of truth' and on 'the forming of human reality in an ontogenetic process', which presupposes man's activity as an authentic process. This could lead to the interpretation that in the revolutionary struggle, people do not necessarily need a Leninist conception of the party with its rules and imperative laws. If the party is needed as a professional political organisation, it has to be organised democratically. The individual resides here not as an obedient component of the socialist society but as a social and self-confident human being who is not a product of given historical conditions, but is able to create and re-create his environment.

In addition to this, Man 'has two different "means" that lead him to a cognition of human reality as a whole and to disclosing the truth of reality in its own reality: philosophy and art'.[24] The emphasis on the subversive role of philosophy (dialectical-critical thinking) and true art as well as on potential social changes, where the human individual plays a crucial role, was easy to understand in Kosík's era of flourishing intellectual and cultural activities. These aspects brought Kosík popularity with a broader Czechoslovak intellectual audience, but what made him enormously popular among the creative party intelligentsia were his arguments relating to contemporary art. Kosík observed art to be of a revolutionary quality: 'One of the main principles of modern art, poetry and drama, of painting and film-making, we feel, is the "forcing" of the everyday, the destruction of the pseudoconcrete'.[25] Art as creative activity played an important role in the destruction of the pseudoconcrete, because it made it possible to usher man 'into reality itself and its "truth"' and thus reveal the complexity of the world.[26] Kosík's statements were extremely influential. In the post-Stalinist era of constant controversies between party ideologues on the one hand and artists together with critical party intellectuals on the other, his arguments about art were understood as support for free expression. It was no coincidence that Kosík's book was nominated for a special award by the Czechoslovak Writers' Union. Despite the fact that the awarding was supported by such authors as Milan Kundera and Jan Skácel, who saw in *Dialectics of the Concrete* a philosophical work of extreme importance for the realm of art, the nomination was rejected by party officials.[27] Simultaneously, *Dialectics of the*

---

24   Kosík 1976, p. 73.
25   Kosík 1976, p. 49.
26   Kosík 1976, p. 79.
27   Literární archiv Památníku národního písemnictví (Literary Archive of The Museum of Czech Literature), f. Svaz československých spisovatelů (collection, Czechoslovak Writers Union), 21/C/16.

Concrete was enthusiastically reviewed in cultural-political journals such as *Literární noviny*, *Kultúrny Život*, *Host do domu*, *Kulturní tvorba* and *Plamen*.[28] The book was praised as an example of genuine Marxist philosophy, which was not only a programmatic declaration of what should or should not be examined, but represented a systematic inquiry targeting the most important questions of Man and society.

If Kosík was celebrated among the reformist party intelligentsia as a leading intellectual figure of his era, his work was also recognised by party ideologues and apparatchiks. Their attitudes towards Kosík's book oscillated between reserved critique and reserved celebration. Compared for example to another case of a successful Marxist humanist work, *Hussite Ideology* by Robert Kalivoda,[29] *Dialectics of the Concrete* did not receive any official award, though neither was it subjected to harsh critique. Nevertheless, in 1963–64 the party ideologues were disconcerted by the unanimously positive reception to Kosík's book in the cultural and intellectual sphere. The Central Committee (CC) secretary of the Communist Party of Czechoslovakia (KSČ) Vladimír Koucký regarded this phenomenon as a one-sided highlighting of the most problematic passages, 'for example the explanation of the category of praxis', of the book. Polemicising with such instances in the book, according to him it was feasible only 'with a deep understanding of materialist dialectics'.[30] When a year later the head of the Ideological division of the Central Committee of the KSČ Pavel Auersperg gave an account of the social impact of *Dialectics of the Concrete*, he stated: 'Despite its very abstract features and complicated form of expression, it has influenced an appreciable part of our cultural public, which has received it uncritically'.[31]

Without the attendance of Kosík, who considered it an ideological campaign against him (which, indeed, it partly was), the seminar was held in June 1965. It did not attract the broader attention of the party intelligentsia, nevertheless it is worth mentioning the most developed critique elaborated by Zdeněk Mlynář, a future important figure of the Prague Spring. He argued that Kosík's comprehension of politics as a part of Man's fetishised praxis in any given circumstances is no less than misleading. It limits politics to a tool of Man's

---

28 See for example Zumr 1963; Hejdánek 1963; Cvekl 1963; Červinka 1964; Blažek 1963.

29 Kalivoda 1961. In 1963, it was awarded by Klement Gottwald prize, which was regarded as the highest party acknowledgement in the field of science and culture.

30 Národní Archiv v Praze (NA – The National Archive in Prague), f. KSČ – ÚV 1945–1989 (collection, Communist Party of Czechoslovakia-Central Committee), 02/1 (Presidium of the Central Committee of the CPC 1966–71), sv. 58, a.j. 61, b. 12.

31 NA, f. KSČ – ÚV 1945–1989, 02/4 (Secretariat of the CC of the CPC), sv. 41, a.j. 78, b. 5.

manipulation (in Marx's words 'a dirty haggler') and closes off the path towards the realisation of Man through politics. If a kind of manipulation remains an immanent part of socialist politics, which favors the common interest over the individualistic interests of people, it does not necessarily mean that it must inevitably be isolated within the sphere of the pseudoconcrete and that true politics, in which Man is not merely an object but rather a subject in creating the conditions for realising the real and total Man, is not possible at all. It would not have been a failure if Kosík's elaboration of politics was incomplete, stated Mlynář, but it is a failure when Kosík's analysis posits itself as a final and enclosed solution. Such a trend must be politically criticised because it becomes, even if independently of author's will, a political issue.[32]

In the atmosphere of the post-Stalinist regime of the 1960s, this ideological type of critique served as an unintentional advertisement for Kosík's book: it made it simply more popular among reformist intellectual circles and in the sense of Habermas's remark it created a political issue out of it. Nevertheless, the type of sophisticated critique articulated by Mlynář questioned the important aspects of Kosík's conception. In reform communist circles, it challenged the very meaning of politics and its possibilities under socialist circumstances.

As Mlynář's attitude indicated, the positive reception to *Dialectics of the concrete* does not mean that there was no critique of it within Czechoslovak Marxist humanism whatsoever. For Ivan Sviták for example, it represented rather an 'abstract metaphysical' philosophy than an analysis of the real world. Kosík's style of argumentation would inevitably have failed in confrontation with contemporary positivism and scientism.[33] In a similar but more developed way, Robert Kalivoda considered *Dialectics of the Concrete* to be negatively influenced by Hegelian essentialism, which according to Kalivoda had culminated in a 'Lukácsian-phenomenological' trend which Kosík in his view represented. In deliberate opposition to Kosík, Kalivoda spoke about 'concrete dialectics' based on an analysis of concrete historical forms instead of on presumptions of a metaphysical quality. However, it seems that it was impossible to conduct a deeper discussion about Kosík's book due to tactical reasons. Such a debate would probably have been misused by the official party ideologues in order to discredit Marxist humanism as revisionism.

---

32 Mlynář 1965.
33 Sviták 1965 – NA, f. Ivan Sviták (personal colletion), kr. (box) 9.

3 Kosík and the Prague Spring of 1968

The enormous public influence of *Dialectics of the Concrete* was probably unintentional on the part of the author. Kosík had intended it as a contribution to a philosophical rather than to a public debate. As Jindřich Srovnal observed in an article, 'Kosík's book plays an obvious role in society, which is to a certain extent independent of its author'.[34] Nevertheless, this fact cannot overshadow an important aspect of Kosík's activities. Even if we agree with the hypothetical assertion that *Dialectics of the Concrete* was written apolitically as a contribution to systematic Marxist philosophy, it immediately gained an objective political dimension. Together with this, Kosík deliberately struggled to address a broader intellectual audience. He willingly engaged in public intellectual activities and debates. During the 1960s, he published several essays in cultural-political journals such as *Literární noviny* and *Plamen* (the first magazine was issued in a circulation of at least 150,000 copies every week). His texts predominantly focused on perspectives of culture, art and nation in the modern world. Using for example the literary works of Ernest Hemingway, Franz Kafka, or Jaroslav Hašek, he depicted reality as a 'dehumanised' and manipulated reality.[35] In many of his texts, he followed on from arguments (especially about art and its role) used already in *Dialectics of the Concrete*. And as was the case of his main work, the essayistic approach towards the manipulated praxis of modern world was understood as a critique of state socialist reality. Beginning in 1963, Kosík was also a member of the Central Committee of the Czechoslovak Writers' Union, an organisation of the party intelligentsia which had previously been Stalinist and in the 1960s became a centre for reform communism. At the famous fourth congress of the Czechoslovak Writers' Union in June 1967, which helped to destabilise Anonín Novotny's post-Stalinist regime, Kosík gave a speech where he – using the example of the Czech martyr Jan Hus who was burned to death in the fifteenth century – presented the topical dilemma of reason (political tactic) and conscience (truth).[36]

Despite the fact that Kosík insisted on a strict distinction between ideology and science and warned against exaggeration of the political successes of Czech and Slovak philosophers,[37] philosophy for him was not merely a matter

---

34 Srovnal 1965.
35 The anthology of these text edited by J. H. Satterwhite has the characteristic title *The Crisis of Modernity* – Kosík 1995.
36 See Kosík 1995e.
37 He stated for example: 'We have made very little contribution to the clarification of such basic problems as time, truth, existence or nature; in short, questions on which everything

isolated within a closed circle of professional philosophers but rather a public act. Or more precisely, he shared the conviction of his contemporaries about the necessity of public engagement through art and intellectual activity. In some respects, this was not dissimilar to the former Stalinist mission: at the moment when artists and scientists ceased to be henchmen of ideology, they started to be advocates of a 'truth' based on a critical reassessment of reality.

Kosík's work, intellectual authority and his emphasis on demystification and changing reality ranked among the sources that maintained an important current of the Prague Spring, namely the radical communist reformism that identified itself in a radical democratic sense and in opposition to official communist reformism, which was seen as more technocratic than democratic. When Kosík for example talked about shaping reality, it was understood as grasping and forming the nature of society, and it demanded radical changes in the name of democratic socialism. Radical reformists represented a loyal opposition to the reform communist party leadership of Alexander Dubček. They simultaneously supported and criticised the official reform communist program, attempting to create a political platform based on a coalition of intellectuals, workers and students that would be able to implement real structural changes leading to a democratic socialist society.

In the spring of 1968 Kosík published an essay entitled 'Our current crisis',[38] in which he presented a detailed analysis of the crisis of the system. Similarly to *Dialectics of the Concrete*, the author defined his analytical tools as critical thought, the goal of which was 'to reveal the basis from which our behavior and thinking are derived. It sets out to prove that, on that basis, all is not accurate and in order'.[39] Proposing ways out of the crisis, Kosík's main emphasis was placed, not surprisingly and in accordance with Marxist humanism as well as with his previous inquiries, on emancipated Man and on the permanent realisation of freedom: socialism 'has historical justification only to the extent that it is a revolutionary and liberating alternative'.[40]

Compared to *Dialectics of the Concrete*, in the Spring of 1968 Kosík was more concrete in his answers: the political crisis as well as the devalued sense of

---

depends, not just culture and politics but public life, interpersonal relationships, science, and so on'. Liehm 1970 (an interview with Karel Kosík in May 1968), p. 400.

38 As Karel Bartošek suitably observed, in modern Czech history such a type of critical analysis has periodically emerged every 15–20 years since the end of the nineteenth century (Bartošek 2003b, p. 73). Kosík deliberately referred to Masaryk's text of the same title – see Masaryk 1895. It was published as a serial over several issues of *Literární listy* in 1968. See Kosík 1995d.
39 Kosík 1995d, p. 32.
40 Kosík 1995d, p. 38.

politics should be overcome through a radical displacement of the police-bureaucratic dictatorship by a program of socialist democracy based on the federalisation of the Czechoslovak state, acceptance of a loyal socialist opposition to the KSČ, democracy of socialist citizens, legal dismissal of censorship and self-management of socialist producers. Such a radical reformist agenda was according to Kosík not merely of a national but rather of an existential character, because its fulfilment would enable an evolution of Man's potentiality.

Criticising the official reform policy, the essay referred to the conflict between pragmatism and technocracy on the one hand and conscience, human dignity, the meaning of truth and justice, honor and courage on the other. At the same time Kosík disagreed with the reform communist emphasis on expert knowledge as represented by economic reform and by the project of scientific-technological revolution. Both meant only a new form of mystification, which conceals the real problems of the modern world, and both endanger the revolutionary efforts through a new form of manipulation which is not in fact different from the former bureaucratic one.

Kosík was critical of the post-Stalinist regime of Antonín Novotný, which he considered a 'police-bureaucratic dictatorship', but he did not want to reduce the crisis of socialism to a correction of the previous state, as was demonstrated by the official reform communist rhetoric. In opposition to this, Kosík stated that there must be a distinction between the seeming and real meaning of socialism: 'these minimal little steps by which we reject political crime can neither hide nor postpone the urgency of the essential questions that we have as yet not touched upon, but without which socialism as a revolutionary alternative for the people of the twentieth century is inconceivable without posing anew the questions of who is man and what is truth, what is being and what is time, what is the nature of science and technology, and what is the meaning of revolution'.[41]

'Our Current Crisis' was not only analytical but, as is obvious, also a programmatic text. Together with articles by Robert Kalivoda or Antonín Jaroslav Liehm[42] it undoubtedly belonged among the most elaborated radical reformist propositions.

What the author considered in 'Our Current Crisis' was exemplified in the concrete radical reformist project of founding the new daily newspaper *Lidové noviny* [People's News]. Kosík was supposed to be the head of its editorial

---

41   Kosík 1995d, p. 39.
42   Kalivoda 1968a, b; Liehm 1968.

board. The newspaper was planned to be published by the Czechoslovak Writers' Union as a daily of Czechoslovak radical reformism and the cultural intelligentsia, with a special weekly cultural-political issue and with an English edition. The initiators of the project wanted to create a socialist variant of such dailies as *Le Monde* and *The Times*. In the programme of this never existing journal we can recognise Kosík's influence: *Lidové noviny* was supposed to inform 'truthfully', with humour but credibly, simultaneously it would have fought for democratic socialism and against any form of manipulation of Man. When Kosík in 'Our Current Crisis' stated that 'Socialist democracy is integral democracy or it is no democracy at all',[43] the newspaper's project copied this thesis and declared an overcoming of the political party's antagonism through the foundation of a broader socialist humanist coalition based on a mutual collaboration of communists, social democrats and Christians.[44]

When Kosík talked about the crisis of politics and its lost meaning, he was striving for a theoretical as well as for a practical change. His radical reformist endeavours culminated not only in essayistic writings; during the Prague Spring he also participated in several public meetings[45] and did not hesitate to become involved in actual political affairs. It was Kosík and a few other radical reformist intellectuals who became members of the Central Committee of the Communist Party of Czechoslovakia. They were elected at the extraordinary party congress held in the Vysočany ČKD factory immediately after the military invasion on 22 August. Due to the pressure of the Moscow party leadership, this congress was soon declared invalid, nevertheless a political compromise enabled some of the elected reformist members to be co-opted to the previously existing Central Committee.

At the session of the Central Committee in November 1968 he gave a radical reformist speech, where he warned of the self-isolation of the reform party leadership. He stated that while negotiations of the party leadership resembled the intrigues of a closed sect, there were thousands of demands from workers, cooperative farmers, intellectuals and students for a continuation of the reform policy. Instead of a Marxist analysis of the previous political development, a schematic interpretation of the 1968 events prevails which is not far from that

---

43   Kosík 1995d, p. 27.
44   This is derived from an extant conception of *Lidové noviny* which was approved by the Czechoslovak Writers' Union in May 1968 – see Literární archiv Památníku národního písemnictví, f. Svaz československých spisovatelů, 21/C/20. The project was apparently supported by some high ranking reform communists.
45   For example, the meeting Mladí se ptají [The Youth Asks], organised on 20 March with 20,000 people in attendance and aired by Czechoslovak Radio (Československý rozhlas).

of Moscow. According to Kosík, the meaning of the Prague Spring rested upon a metamorphosis of the working class from a passive object of manipulation into a 'real political subject' (an active political force) which 'wants to direct and manage the whole society in a new way'.[46] A mutual dialogue between the working class, cooperative farmers, intelligentsia and youth creates a new feature of politics, a 'revolutionary wisdom', which together with the 'wisdom of revolution' should become a 'guarantee against hysteria and demagogy, against the ambitions and the vanity of individuals, against cowardice, excessive caution, naivete, and illusions'.[47] If this is a new contribution of the working people to politics, the political leadership should regain their respect through the realisation of principled reformist politics. Whereas under the circumstances of the beginnings of the reintroduction of censorship, Kosík's November speech could still attract relatively broad public attention,[48] his subsequent and last speech on the same platform remained unpublished – public presentation of the pivotal session of the CC KPC was already strictly controlled in order to present a positive, conflict-free picture of Dubček's removal.[49]

On 17 April 1969, Kosík was one of the few speakers to raise an open voice of protest against the election of Gustáv Husák to the leadership of the Communist Party.[50] He asked a crucial question as to in whose interest it was to reestablish censorship and the old methods of political management: 'of these people who want to govern without the people, who do not want to respect people's living interests, who want to impose upon the people and nations of our country a nondemocratic solution to the contemporary crisis',[51] which would not eliminate the reasons for the crisis. Kosík declared that there were two alternatives of Czechoslovak development. Either a despotic system based not on revolutionary activities but on the party and a repressive apparatus together with the support of external forces would be reestablished, or the political strategies would be based on people's life interests. A constructive political programme

---

46   For the original of the speech see, LAPNP, f. Karel Kosík, kr. 4. It was published under a title 'The Only Chance – An Alliance with the People' (Kosík 1995l, p. 212).

47   Kosík 1995l, p. 214. The thesis about revolutionary wisdom and the wisdom of revolution had already been mentioned by Kosík in an interview with A.J. Liehm in May 1968 – see Liehm 1970, p. 412.

48   'Stůjte v poznané pravdě'. *Tribuna otevřenosti b* 1968, p. 5; Z diskuse na plenárním zasedání ÚV KSČS. *Rudé právo*, 16. 11. 1968, p. 3; 'Revoluční moudrost – moudrá revolučnost', *Nová mysl* (theoretical journal of the Czechoslovak Communist Party), 23, no. 1, 1969, pp. 16–19.

49   See the detailed elaboration in Doskočil 2006.

50   LAPNP, f. Karel Kosík, kr. 4. Poznámky k vystoupení na zasedání ÚV KSČ v dubnu 1969 (Notices to the speech at the CC session in April 1969).

51   Ibid., p. 3 (of the manuscript).

of further development must be based on a restoration of correct relationships between the party and the people and between socialist countries. Such a programme would have indispensably presupposed the equality and sovereignty of the people and of the whole country within the socialist bloc. The political leadership should defend and realise people's life interests and simultaneously it should periodically examine its mandate as given to it by the people. Political strategies and tactics must be subordinated to the people's interests and not vice versa. The political leadership must be vigorous and consistent, but always in a coalition with the people, under the people's control and in a relationship of mutual trust. Socialism means the liberation of Man, which brings more freedom in everyday life and not a new despotism. At the end of his speech, Kosík impressively stated that the realisation of such a programme represented the last chance for the current political leadership, otherwise it would be fully responsible for its own failure. From the long-term perspective, Kosík was right. Nevertheless, in 1969 it was his turn to go. At the subsequent session of the Central Committee in May, he was, together with some others, expelled from ranks of the Central Committee.

It was Gustáv Husák who started the process of so-called normalisation, which was accompanied by political purges in the party as well as throughout the whole society. At the beginning of Husák's departure from the reform communist policy, the circle of radical reformists belonged to the last actively rebellious 'islands' of party members. However, they were 'pacified' no later than by the spring of 1970, with the suppression of the Prague Spring and also Kosík's public intellectual activities. Similarly to thousands of others, in 1970 he was prohibited from holding any academic posts and, of course, he was expelled from the Communist party of Czechoslovakia. His works were banned and broadly criticised as a deviation from Marxist-Leninism. The author himself retired into a kind of internal exile, remaining in touch with the emerging socialist opposition but reserved in his activities.[52]

4 Conclusion

Kosík's texts show clearly that his advocacy for communist reformism as well as his real political engagement during the Prague Spring were not based on political pragmatism but on a revolutionary vision, the destruction of the pseudo-

---

52 This was especially apparent after a house search by the State security police in 1975 – cf. Kosík and Sartre 1975.

concrete. In accordance with Marxist humanism, this vision was based on authentic human activity, which was supposed to be able to overcome the contradictions of the existing type of modern state socialist society. Kosík did not introduce a programme of revolutionary change in a Leninist sense. Disillusioned by the results of the 1948 revolution, he saw the prospects for change rather in critical thinking and in the unrestricted political and cultural activity of the people than in sudden action of the working class with its vanguard represented by the party. Despite his sympathies for an alliance with workers and students, he never elaborated a deeper analysis of such a coalition, nor was he concerned with questions of practical political tactics for how to achieve it etc. Moreover, such matters as the state ownership of the means of production were not challenged in Kosík's conception. A critique of this type would have crossed the boundaries of communist reformism and even of its radical form, whose representative Kosík was. The type of an analysis that would have interpreted the economic basis of the existing system as 'state capitalist' for example was very rare in Czechoslovakia in that time. One of the few exceptions within this generation was represented by a text written by Kosík's personal friend Karel Bartošek[53] or an analysis by Egon Bondy, who unfortunately remained on the outskirts of the academic intellectual sphere.[54]

Dialectics of the Concrete as well as his essayistic writings gained enormous popularity, and Kosík became one of the most respected scholars of the reform communist era. His work and personal engagement were connected with the radical reformist critique of official reform communism. After the military invasion, as a philosopher and as a representative of that intellectual and political current, he was elected to the highest ranks of the party's executive body. If it has been already observed that Kosík was a typical example of the party intelligentsia of the 1960s, in addition to this there is a certain paradox residing in a tension between his philosophical work and public intellectual activities, the latter of which need to be specified.

For Kosík, true art and philosophy were not supposed to be explicitly involved in politics unless they wanted to a risk loss of their aesthetic or critical value. When Mlynář criticised Kosík for leaving the political sphere aside from further elaboration, it was, as a matter of fact, a legitimate critique. Kosík considers politics to be a part of the pseudoconcrete sphere and therefore a tool of a manipulation (*Dialectics of the Concrete*), and when he talks about what

---

53   Bartošek 2003a. A more radical attitude to this question can also be read in texts by Robert Kalivoda – see Kalivoda 1968a; 1968b.
54   Bondy 2016.

politics should be ('Our Current Crisis') he defines it in a negative sense as non-manipulation, and reduces it to an abstract, unrestricted political activity of party and non-party members, as well as to the activities of both nations (Czech and Slovak). Following Mlynář, Kosík's (non)conception of politics would not have been a failure as such. Nevertheless, it reveals its limits when Kosík attempts to go beyond intellectual debate and when he is confronted with real political praxis. At the time when Kosík decided to be co-opted onto the Central Committee of the Communist Party of Czechoslovakia in September 1968, he was probably aware that he was entering the pseudoconcrete sphere, with its own mechanisms, rules and decision-making principles. His speeches on this platform were undoubtedly exceptional and bold, nevertheless his reluctance to attempt to formulate effective political tactics within the sphere of manipulation embodies the limits of the whole radical reform communist project. The antinomic character of Kosík's radical reformism lay in a twofold approach to politics. He was aware that the actual occasion demands real political engagement and did not hesitate to become engaged. Simultaneously, this assumption was combined with his endeavor to stay 'clean', or more precisely not to become involved in the manipulative dimension of politics. This emphasis on a kind of 'political innocence' was crucial for him until the very end, when both he and his companions were expelled from the party. It was not only a matter of political tactics and compromises. It was also about a political opposition whose existence was absent at the crucial moments. At the time when Husák was elected, the radical reformists had no chance to resist other than to attempt to create a coalition with workers and students. Despite all their written proclamations in 1968, Kosík as well as others hesitated to embark upon such a step in 1969, because such spontaneous activity would ruin all hopes for a future dialogue with the party establishment. The reform communist part of their political identity limited them to remaining within the constraints given by the party; even after the party purges in 1970–71 most of them counted on an invitation for an early return to the party ranks. At the same time, the public intellectual as well as political activities of radical reformists mostly did not cross over from the sphere of the written word to the sphere of real (revolutionary) politics. Radical reformism was predominantly defined intellectually, using the written word and culture as a tool of politics, and practical political activity in the pragmatic sense, seen as the 'dirty part' ('sphere of manipulation'), was almost alien to it.

Although Kosík became the most famous Czechoslovak Marxist humanist already in the reform era, his work did not receive a worldwide reception until the English publication of *Dialectics of the Concrete* in 1976. At that time the author was already living outside of academia, while his book was barely available in Czechoslovak libraries. He tried to continue in his public intellectual activities after the fall of the state socialist regime, nevertheless his success was incomparable to that of the 1960s. First of all, the reform communist generation with its ideas of democratic socialism was not very popular within the optimistic atmosphere of the capitalist restoration of the 1990s, when the neoliberal doctrine was presented as the most progressive one. Kosík's conceptualisation of attributes of the post-1989 society such as 'supracapital' or 'lumpenbourgeoisie'[55] simply did not attract broader attention. Nevertheless, and most importantly, the media of public communication had changed. Whereas in the 1960s Czechoslovakia the printed word in the form of books, magazines, the daily press or leaflets still belonged among the main communication channels, subsequent decades have been characterised by different forms. As Regis Debray defines it, the era of the 'graphosphere' was replaced by the era of the 'videosphere'. This was already happening during the state socialism of the 1970s and especially of the 1980s,[56] and the capitalist restoration only accelerated and confirmed this process. Under the conditions of the new socio-economic order, Kosík could only experience what Jürgen Habermas had experienced earlier, or what Milan Kundera observed in exile, writing in his essay 'The Tragedy of Central Europe': 'If all the reviews in France or England disappeared, no one would notice it, not even their editors'.[57] In the 1990s, once it was possible for Kosík's old as well as new essays to be published, almost nobody noticed it; or at least his writings did not attract such attention as in the 1960s.

55 See Kosík 1997.
56 See for example Bren 2010.
57 Kundera 1984, p. 37.

CHAPTER 2

Karel Kosík and His 'Radical Democrats': The Janus Face of *Dialectics of the Concrete*

Tomáš Hermann

Karel Kosík's *Czech Radical Democracy*, subtitled *Contribution to the History of Ideological Disputes in Nineteenth-Century Czech Society* (*Česká radikální demokracie. Příspěvek k dějinám názorových sporů v české společnosti 19. Století*), was originally published in 1958.[1] Spanning over 480 pages, it is Kosík's most extensive work and probably his only monograph or synthetic work *sensu stricto*. Its subject is historical and regional: it focuses on nineteenth-century Czech social, political, and philosophical thought. In other words, it deals with intellectual history.[2] Three years later, Kosík finished his famous essay *Dialectics of the Concrete* (1963), which – unlike the above-mentioned work – has generally philosophical and systematic philosophical ambitions, and this holds regardless of whether we see Kosík's notion of praxis as an anthropological or ontological project (these being the two basic possible interpretations of this work). In this latter book, Kosík deals with the current perspectives of thought, thus turning his attention to the intellectual future.[3]

The two works, *Czech Radical Democracy* and *Dialectics of the Concrete*, differ both in their form and in their general subject. Most generally, one might be even tempted to believe that after dealing with a particular historical issue, Kosík turned his attention to a general systematic investigation. My claim, however, which I try to substantiate in the following, is that while the two works are clearly different, one cannot draw a clear line between the two projects. We should therefore take a closer look at *Czech Radical Democracy* and the context in which it was written. It constitutes the intellectual background in which the issues dealt with in *Dialectics of the Concrete* had emerged. And why should one speak within this context of its Janus face? Just as Janus looks in both directions of time and through the gates of Janus, one could go in both directions; Kosík's *Dialectics of the Concrete* points the way towards a reform of the Marxist philo-

---

1 This contribution was written as part of project supported by the Czech Science Foundation (GA ČR 16–07027S).
2 Kosík 1958a.
3 Kosík 1963b. In the following, we quote from the English translation, Kosík 1976.

sophy of the 1960s but also looks back at the deep personal and intellectual sources in which it originated. This way of viewing this work could reveal it in an unusual but new and interesting light.

This subject is too broad to capture adequately in one article. At the time we intend to focus on, i.e. the 1940s to 1960s, Kosík was one of the most prolific Czech philosophers, and his work is one of the most important contributions to Czech philosophy in the twentieth century. Moreover, the subject is not only philosophical: it is also embedded in the context of the social, political and especially ideological developments of the time. We therefore approach the subject by selecting some particular issues. In analysing them, we then try to capture the features characteristic of Kosík's development, subjects which could be further elaborated on or demonstrated either in his writings, in the experiences of his generation, or in the broader rich context of intellectual history of that period. To this end, we proceed in three steps. First, we outline some biographical and intellectual context and circumstances which inspired Kosík to write his book on Czech radical democracy. Then we use this perspective to describe this work and its structure, and finally we focus on *Dialectics of the Concrete* from the perspective of its link with *Czech Radical Democracy*.

The amount of attention we pay to the biographical and historical context and the impact of the Stalinist era in Kosík's development is not accidental or arbitrary. Even within the limited space of this contribution, it will hopefully be evident that one can understand the depth of intellectual transformation and development which Kosík and a large part of his generation had undergone only when fully taking this context into account.[4]

1 Stalinism and the History of Czech Philosophy

Kosík, who was born in 1926, belonged to a generation of young intellectuals born in the 1920s whose communist convictions were formed during the Second World War. He was part of a youth group of the Protestant congregation in the Smíchov district of Prague, where his older friends started introducing him to the classical works of socialist theory in 1943.[5] Their generational exper-

---

[4] Here I am referring to subjects addressed by the sociologist and Social Democrat in exile Karel Hrubý. In a number of articles, Hrubý disscussed Kosík's intellectual development from Stalinism to the Prague Spring, within the wider context of the experiences of his generation (see Hrubý 2018).

[5] Wagnerová (2006) offers a critical assessment of Hrubý (2018). She presents important information on Kosík's wartime intellectual development, which we draw upon in our contribution.

ience included disillusionment with interwar democracy and republicanism, Nazi occupation and its terror, the closing of Czech universities and the attendant loss of future prospects and values, accompanied with a search for practical solutions. They were keenly aware of the changing course of the war, symbolised by the defeat of the German armies at Stalingrad, and thought about ways in which they could make a concrete contribution to the war effort. They concluded that Marxism and the communist movement corresponded to their notions of resistance and the future transformation of the world better than Protestant Christianity. Kosík and his friends founded an illegal newspaper called *Předvoj* [Vanguard] and later a resistance group of the same name. They focused on political and organisational preparations for a social and national revolution, which was to take place at the end of the war with the aim of creating a new, better socialist society for everyone. Kosík, being the youngest member of the group, was in May 1944 asked to prepare another illegal journal, *Boj mladých* [Struggle of Youth], which aimed at mobilising broad strata of Czech youth. While observing strict secrecy in their operations, the Předvoj resistance group joined forces with other similarly-minded groupings, mostly formed by persons of similar age, and by the summer of 1944 grew into a large Czech resistance organisation. Contacts with the illegal central committee of the Communist Party of Czechoslovakia, which was at that time already severely decimated by repression and infiltrated by Gestapo agents, eventually became fatal, and in October 1944 led to the arrest of the leading representatives of Předvoj, including Kosík. In May 1945, his close friends were executed and only an accident saved him from being executed himself. Kosík felt a sense of moral obligation to his murdered friends, and this significantly influenced his views and his intellectual work throughout his life. One of his last philosophical essays, *Jinoch a smrt* [A Youth and Death], is just one of a number of Kosík's writings which deal with this experience.[6]

In the spring of 1945, Kosík returned from a Nazi prison as a convinced believer in communist ideology and revolution that would overcome the old world and lead humanity to a higher stage of life. He studied philosophy first at the Faculty of Philosophy of Charles University in Prague (1945–47), then in Leningrad and Moscow (1947–49), and started writings essays in support of the by then ruling communist ideology. Revolution and the Marxist theory of classes as interpreted by the Leninist and Stalinist theory of class struggle implemented by the dictatorship of the proletariat became the guiding principles of his philosophical, historical and political views. He ranked among the

---

6   Kosík 1995m.

mostly young people who adopted a basically Stalinist ideology, disguised by Marx's and Lenin's name, and learned its language, views and interpretation of the world. Guided by a vision of a new society and relying on experiences made of their Soviet model, they also embraced the idea of the transformation which a Communist Party must undergo to reach its goals and the methods necessary to achieve these objectives. They accepted the theorem of 'necessity and laws of class struggle' in Stalin's remorseless interpretation as a mandate to a dictatorship of the proletariat, which they wanted to serve to the best of their ability, and as a justification to suppress everything and everyone who would stand in the Party's way. This was accompanied by a series of political and ideological Stalinist campaigns against internal and external enemies, including enemies in science and philosophy. As Alexej Kusák, the historian of art, aptly put it, 'When we were growing up, it was not only the wartime nimbus and aureole of the victory of Nazism that for a large part of my generation and my nation made Stalin a respected and almost untouchable and revered personality. We also tried to see him as a thinker, even a thinker who defended certain cultural values within a theory which we, out of some strange idealism (whose content historians one day will have to investigate) adopted as our own'.[7]

Kosík, too, believed that all so-called 'people's democracies' must follow Stalin's leadership in their struggle for progress and peace, and that the law of intensified class struggle was absolutely binding for them.[8] He even defended Stalinist political trials in an article characteristically entitled 'Stalin Teaches us to Love our Homeland and Hate its Enemies'.[9] He challenged the humanistic and democratic legacy of the pre-war republic, as demonstrated by his participation in a campaign against the founder of Czechoslovak republic in 1918 T.G. Masaryk, the humanist philosopher and the first president of Czechoslovakia, and his 'Masarykism'. In the official journal *Filosofický časopis* [The Philosophical Journal], Kosík sharply criticised Masarykism as a counter-revolutionary ideology of the bourgeoisie, using the then common Stalinist language: 'Masarykism is nowadays the ideology of defeated and crushed classes which relied on exploitation. Its only public defenders are traitors to the country and imperialist agents abroad'.[10] On the other hand, Kosík did not espouse only the superficial contemporary propaganda. He found a real research topic which he, within his worldview, honestly investigated and to which he devoted most of

---

7   Kusák 1991, p. 5. This work was written in exile in early 1970s.
8   For instance, in his article 'Sovětsky svaz – bašta marxismu-leninismu' [The Soviet Union: A Bastion of Marxism-Leninism], Kosík 1951a.
9   Kosík 1951b.
10 Kosík 1954, p. 196.

his intellectual powers. This approach, however, gradually revealed the overly schematic views as deeply problematic.

In the Stalinist era, the official research goals of the history of Czech philosophy were determined by the approach taken by the historian, philosopher, and communist Minister of Education Zdeněk Nejedlý (1878–1962). In the spirit of militant Marxism, he formulated his approach in his 1946 lecture 'Slovo o české filosofii' [A Word About Czech Philosophy], which appeared in print in 1950.[11] It became the canonised doctrine. Nejedlý called for the creation of a new 'national Czech philosophy' grounded in Marxism-Leninism. One ought to note, however, that in Nejedlý's project, Marxism played mainly a proclamatory and political role. The emphasis was on the rejection of academic philosophy, which he saw as part of the legacy of the 'bourgeois' era. He contrasted academic philosophy with the – allegedly still suppressed – tradition of Czech thought as an expression of 'folk wisdom'.

Nejedlý played a chief role in the Sovietisation of Czechoslovak universities and the Academy of Sciences, which was established in 1952 based on a Soviet model. The Institute of Philosophy[12] was supposed to directly serve the interests of the ruling ideology and the cultural policy of the Communist Party of Czechoslovakia. One of its main tasks was to carry out a systematic investigation and evaluation of the history of Czech philosophy from the perspective of Nejedlý's claim and in accordance with Marxist-Leninist doctrine. Philosophy was supposed to be an expression of and part of the social movements and revolutionary traditions of 'the people', i.e. the predecessors of the current communist vanguard. In the older period the main focus was on the Hussite tradition, and in the newer era the nineteenth-century revolutionary tradition and the formation of the communist movement.

To achieve these goals, the newly established Institute of Philosophy employed a number of young communist researchers, among them Karel Kosík, who by then had the credentials of a radical communist who had studied at universities in the Soviet Union.[13] Kosík was assigned the task of studying the nineteenth century, because the revolutionary movements around 1848 were a subject he had intensively researched since his studies. Moreover, he had already published several articles on the ideas and social context of the work

---

11   Nejedlý 1950. Reprinted in Nejedlý 1953, pp. 258–79. On the contemporary discussion about Nejedlý's speech, see Křesťan 1999.
12   To be precise, the institution started out as the 'Cabinet for Philosophy of the Czechoslovak Academy of Sciences' and only later became a separate institute.
13   Kosík publicly espoused Nejedlý's concept of 'people's' philosophy at least until 1953; see Kosík 1953e.

of some Czech revolutionary democrats such as Emanuel Arnold (1800–69), Karel Sabina (1813–77) and Josef Václav Frič (1829–91).[14] Kosík thus seemed predestined for a long career at the Institute of Philosophy not only for ideological but also for professional, academic reasons. Shortly after joining the Institute, in 1953, he edited an extensive anthology called *Czech Radical Democrats: A Selection of Political Essays, 1848–1870* (*Čeští radikální demokraté. Výbor politických statí*), prefacing it with a long study called 'The Position and Importance of Radical Democrats in the History of Progressive Czech Politics and Ideology'.[15] These works were followed by numerous other editions and studies, in which Kosík researched his subject in an ever broader and deeper context, both Czech and European, and especially its relation to Russian post-Hegelian philosophy.[16] In 1958, this research culminated with the publication of the abovementioned monograph. Its final form, however, was influenced not only by Kosík's own intellectual development but also by the arrival of de-Stalinisation, which enabled a somewhat more critical approach to the original dogmatic scheme.

2 Czech Radical Democracy and the Poverty of Czech Philosophy

With respect to Kosík's *Czech Radical Democracy*, we ought to start by briefly mentioning several facts. The book is dedicated to the memory of Karel Hiršl and Vratislav Holát, i.e. two of Kosík's friends from the Předvoj resistance group who were executed during the war. This clearly shows that for Kosík, the subject of young radical democrats, their ideas, enthusiasm, 'progressive' views, but also their failure under certain historical conditions, is not just chosen at random. Rather, it is something that defines him. This personal and 'existential' aspect of the subject seems to be quite crucial if we are to understand the tenacity with which Kosík keeps returning to the subject and also his further development, in which he never quite abandoned the original claims, themes, and views. Instead, he kept trying to grasp the issue again and again with ever more clarity, and to give it a new interpretation.

Another factor that should be taken in consideration is that Kosík implicitly refers to and uses his numerous works on this subject from the entire preceding decade. In addition to providing the basic ideological framework, these works also contain a large amount of hitherto undescribed or unknown empirical

---

14 See Kosík 1948, Kosík 1952a and Kosík 1952b.
15 Kosík 1953b.
16 Kosík 1953a, Kosík 1953c, Kosík 1953d, Kosík 1955, Kosík 2019a.

material, biographical facts and interpretations of content. In his *Czech Radical Democracy* he treats all this as well-known facts, without explicitly dealing with it or repeating it. Instead, he takes his exposition to a comparative level which we would nowadays call history of ideas. Readers unfamiliar with his previous works therefore find *Czech Radical Democracy* very hard to understand. Otherwise, Kosík naturally proceeds in the spirit of revolutionary Marxist philosophy, which, however, due to the toppling of the 'cult of personality' and de-Stalinisation, had undergone certain changes. Despite a seeming conformity to official doctrine of the era, Kosík's work is thus rather multi-layered and challenging.

This relates to the third fact that should be taken into account. In this synthetic work, Kosík in fact attempts a completely new articulation of the 'Czech question', rephrasing it on a purely social level with the ambition of legitimising both the nineteenth-century revolutionary practice and the events which took place in Czech society after the communist takeover in February 1948. Kosík's ambitious goal is explicitly to present an alternative to the traditional 'national' approach to the subject, and implicitly to propose an alternative to Masaryk's democratic humanism and his formulation of a 'religious' meaning of Czech history. Already at the time of its publication, however, the book was viewed with a certain ambivalence, and contradictory feelings about it persist also because *Czech Radical Democracy* can be read as a product of then ideology, as history of political thought, as history of ideas or as a contribution to social history, all set within a broad Czech and European context.[17] One can see this work either as a typical example of 1950s ideology or as an original and elaborate synthesis, which sheds new light on the past and offers alternative approaches within the framework of the Marxist history of philosophy. Let us now try to outline some parts of the book's intentions, content and ways in which it inspired Kosík's intellectual development.

Kosík's main source of inspiration was contemporary Soviet historiography of philosophy, with which he was well acquainted. The new Soviet history of philosophy strongly emphasised the study of Russian Hegelianism and nineteenth-century revolutionary democratism, which were seen as domestic sources of the revolutionary communist movement. From this perspective, Czech 'radical democracy' represented a special case of radical and revolution-

---

17   In connection with the Czech philosophy of history, Kosík's notion of radical democracy was recently studied in detail by Andělová and Mareš 2015, who also include references to further reading on the subject. For the most important writings on the interpretation of Kosík's *Czech Radical Democracy*, see especially Kusák 1998, pp. 269–70., Šámal 2005, and Zumr 2011.

ary European movements which resulted in the 1848–49 revolutions. Because of the differences between the individual countries and their distinct social and economic conditions and development, Kosík decided not to adopt any established explanatory approach. Instead, he starts by proposing (in the first chapter) his own typology of European revolutionary democratism as a whole. He distinguishes two basic types, a 'peasant' democratism and 'plebeian/petit bourgeois' democratism (which in his view includes the Czech one) and describes their different manifestations over time and space eastwards and westwards of the Czech Lands.[18]

Kosík follows the transformations of radical democracy as a political and spiritual movement both in the European context and in the context of nineteenth-century Czech society, tracing its confrontations with other, both liberal and conservative, intellectual and political tendencies. In doing so, he interprets local historical conditions and attitudes of particular actors in the process through the lens of the typological structure he defined at the outset. This is why he tends to be critical not only of the liberal (or, in his words, bourgeois) historiography but also of the Soviet Marxist historiography wherever it overly emphasises the (Russian) national aspect and the autonomy of its development. In short, Kosík is highly critical of liberal/nationalist attitudes and their legacy, but also of simplistic economic and social determinism. Kosík's interpretation of the development of ideas, as described e.g. by Gramsci, Lukács, or Goldmann, was inspired by Marxist classics and genetic structuralism.

In the second and third chapter, Kosík applies his interpretative approach to an analysis of the formation of ideology of the Czech radical democrats and their opponents, and to the changes it had undergone during and after the 1848–49 revolutions.[19] It should be noted, however, that Kosík did intend a sort of revision of the Marxist methodology without abandoning it. His aim was to treat the developments in nineteenth-century Czech society fully within the framework of historical materialism. The partial criticism of Marxist schematism was supposed to lead to a more complex, more thorough and more convincing application of historical materialism. Kosík did not renounce any of the basic and a priori accepted ideological foundations of Marxism, which included first and foremost a materialist approach to history. Secondly, this historical materialism presupposed an almost teleological conception of 'pro-

---

18 Kosík 1958a, pp. 9–50, Chapter I, 'Problematika evropské revoluční demokracie 19. století' [On Nineteenth-Century European Revolutionary Democracy].

19 Kosík 1958a, pp. 52–240, Chapter II, 'Demokratická ideologie v Čechách' [Democratic Ideology in Bohemia], pp. 242–376, Chapter III, 'Politický program radikálních demokratů' [The Political Programme of the Radical Democrats].

gress' of intellectual development, which was seen as following certain strict rules. In particular, according to the omnipresent and 'objective' 'laws of progress', Kosík evaluates the ideological and philosophical positions of various thinkers while assuming that progress inevitably (in a Hegelian sense) leads to the highest and only true point of view, to wit, the one adopted by the evaluating philosopher and the ideology he advocates. And finally, Kosík defends the irreplaceable value of violent revolutionary practice and destruction of existing political units, which again amounts to a justification of current revolutionary communist polices.

These assumptions form a methodological departure which Kosík could not and did not want to leave behind. Despite various remarkable and novel interpretative observations, these tenets caused also some distortions which are the reason why the book is now an important historical document recording the development of Czech Marxist thought Just one example: Kosík completely leaves out Bernard Bolzano despite the fact that Bolzano's ideas about social reform had a profound impact on Czech society, including the radical democrats, who were moreover almost without exception his students. In short, Kosík is blind to anything he cannot explain within his typological construction of radical democrats.

For our purposes, the last chapter is of the greatest interest.[20] In it, Kosík deals with the Czech philosophical debates and discussions of 1846–50. This historically first debate about the need for a 'Czech philosophy' within the movement of the national revival focused on the reception of the new speculative philosophy of German idealism. Kosík explains the weaknesses of the otherwise ideologically highly preferred representatives of radical democracy, such as Arnold and Sabina – who did not even properly understand the dialectic principle – by claiming that this is a natural result of the priority of practice over theory in their work. He contrasts them with thinkers who had a more adequate grasp of current intellectual developments and who thus managed to bring Czech philosophy in touch with the most important philosophical movements of their times, such as the remarkably purely Hegelian thinkers Augustin Smetana (1814–51) and Karel Boleslav Štorch (1812–68).[21] At this point, Kosík

---

20   Kosík 1958a, pp. 378–473, Chapter IV, 'Radikální demokraté a bída české filosofie' [Radical Democrats and the Poverty of Czech Philosophy].

21   One should note that at the same time and under his supervision, Marie Bayerová was systematically editing and publishing the works of Augustin Smetana, so Kosík had plenty of material to draw on. His research took place on this broader platform, which gave rise to numerous remarkable works. The interpretations proposed by Bayerová and some others are, meanwhile, of much more lasting value than the ideologically driven interpretation proposed by Kosík, which all too clearly express the atmosphere of the times.

focuses on the so-called 'debate about the freedom of Czech philosophy'. He does not view this period from a historical and descriptive perspective, but rather as part of his own conceptual construction, summarising his evaluation as follows:

> The struggle for Czech philosophy, the debate about the 'national character' of philosophy, about the adoption or rejection of German philosophy, all this is just an idiosyncratic form of a battle between progressive and reactionary views, between dialectics and metaphysics, between theory and empiricism. This strange discussion meant so much that generally philosophical problems were debated even in backward Austria and in a land where the philosophical tradition had been violently severed.[22]

Kosík defends views once adopted by the Hegelians Smetana and Štorch against the advocates of the so-called 'philosophy of folk wisdom' (Sabina, otherwise a key radical democrat), or 'common sense' (Karel Havlíček's liberal democratism), but also against the inflexible metaphysics of Herbartism, as exemplified by František Čupr.[23] In this 1846–50 discussion about philosophy, Kosík finds the general foundations of Czech philosophy, which 'give us answers of immeasurably greater importance and reach than the temporal framework might suggest'. This debate, he claims, was the 'main battlefield and critical point in the origins of modern Czech philosophy' and that is why its evaluation should be seen as a 'contribution to the question of the philosophical tradition of Czech thought in the nineteenth century in general'.[24] This, from our point of view unremarkable and basically uninteresting statement, at the time conveyed a specific message, to wit that this should become a model for a new interpretation of the meaning of contemporary (Marxist) Czech philosophy as represented by Kosík and his colleagues, which was supposed to free itself from its dependency on political directives. In evaluating the debate and its participants, Kosík notably and critically violates the taboo of the value of 'folkishness' as the one of the few suitable sources of all positively viewed phenomena. Implicitly, he thus defends *the autonomy of philosophy*

---

22 Kosík 1958a, p. 382.
23 Herbartism was the philosophical, educational and aesthetic system created by followers of the German philosopher, psychologist and educationalist Johann Friedrich Herbart (1776–1841). In the Austrian-Hungarian Empire, Herbart's philosophical and aesthetic school represented a state-oriented philosophy that propounded a normative categorisation of reality.
24 Kosík 1958a, pp. 395, 398.

and free philosophical discussion. Nejedlý's crucial text 'A Word About Czech Philosophy', which played an irreplaceable role in inspiring Kosík's early philosophical endeavours and which he earlier explicitly espoused, analysed the same nineteenth-century argument but took the opposing side of the debate. Already here, Kosík is thus critical of Nejedlý's demands, opening a way to his own philosophical systematic position.[25] His views thus had a very actual background.

3 The History of Philosophy as Philosophy and *Dialectics of the Concrete*

Kosík's book about Czech radical democracy was not very successful. Czech historiansespecially viewed it with a decided degree of reserve. The problem was that according to Kosík's Marxist method, the history of philosophy is supposed to be primarily an expression of a systematic approach which contrasted to traditionally factually oriented Czech historiography. Nevertheless, one should also note that Kosík's *Czech Radical Democracy* had marked the beginning of attempts to revise communist policies (even before the subsequent campaign against so-called 'revisionism'). Paradoxically, Kosík argued his point by emphasising the role of the 'revolutionary' radical democrats as true predecessors of communists, and contrasted this with the re-constituted 'national' tradition as officially presented by Nejedlý. This revision went hand in hand with a return to the classics: not Lenin, however, but rather the chronologically more relevant Marx. At the time the book appeared, it was not yet clear how strong a foundation it would provide for the reform and reformism of the 1960s.[26]

It is known that Kosík was personally disappointed by the lukewarm reception and incomprehension with which his *Czech Radical Democracy* was received. Until the end of his life, he believed this book to be his main contribution to philosophy. Later, he was rather surprised, almost taken aback, by the nearly world-wide acclaim of his essayistic *Dialectics of the Concrete*.[27] This is

---

25   Kosík's apparent rejection of this concept, expressed in his analysis of a historical source, thus amounted to a formulation of an alternative to Nejedlý's position and thereby also to the demands of the cultural policy of the Communist Party. The history of debate about the freedom of Czech philosophy in the nineteenth century, including later assessments (both interwar and Kosík's), was recently re-analysed in Hermann 2012.
26   In addition to the sources already listed, see also Mandler 1995, p. 69.
27   According to a personal testimony of Dr Ingrid Strobachová, Kosík's student and friend.

not surprising if we take into account the systematic and intellectual connection between the two projects. In the introduction to his *Czech Radical Democracy*, Kosík places emphasis on 'method' as the main polemical instrument of the book and claims that 'Marxism is a method which spiritually reproduces reality as a *totality* of relations. It thus has nothing in common with the one-sided and subjective extraction of so-called 'topical' questions'.[28] The polemic is aimed against a one-sided Stalinist deformation of Marxism but is, at the same time, terminologically largely grounded in it. During his studies in the Soviet Union, Kosík had first-hand experience of the language used in contemporary proclamations and discussions of Lenin's and Stalin's interpretation of 'dialectics as a method of revolutionary activity' and the 'concrete nature of Marxist dialectic method', i.e. concepts which he himself had previously adopted and which penetrated even numerous Czech translations of Soviet philosophers.[29] Yet although he used them as a basis on which he originally expressed his approach to the study of radical democracy, in a later synthesis in 1958, he already uses them as a tool with which he fights the one-sidedness of the approach, an instrument he uses to articulate his criticism of the method. This transformation can clearly be seen in a lecture that is a sort of counterpoint to *Czech Radical Democracy*.

In the same year, in 1958, a conference was held on Philosophy in the History of the Czech Nation.[30] It represented a broad spectrum of various results achieved by the Czech Marxist philosophers but also manifested a certain relaxation of restrictions with respect to creative work and discussion which was brought about by de-Stalinisation. In many ways, this conference was a turning point. Kosík had the keynote address, which gave him the opportunity to summarise the methodological position adopted in his writing on radical

---

28   Kosík 1958a, p. 7.
29   See e.g. articles by M.A. Leonov 'Soudruh Stalin o dialektice jako metodě revoluční činnosti' [Comrade Stalin on the Dialectic as a Method of Revolutionary Activity], and 'Lenin a Stalin o konkretnosti marxistické dialektické metody' [Lenin and Stalin on the Concrete Nature of the Marxist Dialectic Method; Leonov 1950a, b], but also other contributions in the same anthology. It is nowadays very hard to see (and one rarely finds any mention of it in the existing secondary literature) just how important Stalin's booklet *On Dialectic and Historical Materialism* was to the post-war generation. It was a veritable pillar of discussions, of pro-communist argumentation, and later also a target of criticism. It was published in Czech already in 1945.
30   This conference took place in the well-known conference chateau of the Czechoslovak Academy of Sciences in Liblice, Central Bohemia, on 14–17 April 1958. It was the first of a number of ground-breaking conferences and meetings which characterised the 1960s reformist movement in culture and intellectual life.

democracy. It is most aptly summarised by the subtitle: 'The History of Philosophy as Philosophy'. The text of the lecture begins as follows:

> Experience gained through several years of work on the history of Czech philosophy can acquire its own philosophical significance only if formulated in a philosophical manner, which presupposes that it is stripped of any chance contingencies and empirical character, and can be summarised in a few *key concepts*. Only in this form can it become a subject of philosophical interest and thus also of discussion and criticism, specification, and further development.[31]

Further in the text, he introduces particular subjects. The fundamental notion of 'concrete totality', for example, is presented as a 'concrete historical totality' within which a philosopher is confronted with all the controversies and dialectic tensions both within the society and in the thinking of an individual. Other basic terms which form the structure of *Dialectics of the Concrete* – especially the issue of dialectics and praxis and the definition of philosophy as a conceptual reproduction of a particular reality, in this case a historical reality – were articulated here as part of the programme of the history of philosophy as philosophy. In the historical material, Kosík also discussed current problems such as a more thorough philosophical foundation of Marxism in confrontation with alternative philosophical views. This important (and published) lecture, which summarises the methodological framework of *Czech Radical Democracy*, thus forms a direct link between the historical and the systematic approach which Kosík later emphasised in order to coherently formulate his position.

Dialectics of the Concrete thus rests on the ideological foundations of an older work. What we witness is not a break but continuity, continuity both of the subject matter and a temporal one. In the original Czech edition, Kosík claims that the basic ideas of the *Dialectics of the Concrete* were expressed already in his 1960 lectures, i.e. soon after the publication of the *Czech Radical Democracy*.[32] The lectures in question investigated dialectics, concreteness, structure, and system. Another remark in *Dialectics of the Concrete* indicates that when thinking about the notion of 'concrete reality', Kosík drew especially on Lukács's *History and Class Consciousness* (1923), i.e. on a work of the pre-Stalinist era where Lukács explains the theory of totality as a basic methodolo-

---

31   Kosík 1958b, p. 9.
32   Kosík 1963b, p. 4.

gical principle of Marx's philosophy.[33] Kosík, however, also refers to a post-war discussion between Marxism and idealism about the issue of 'totality', which around 1948 clearly had a formative influence on him. In this connection, Kosík explicitly mentions his *Czech Radical Democracy* when drawing attention to a Czech historical modification of the narrow link between the notion of 'totality' and the issue of the 'revolutionary principle'.[34]

While writing *Dialectics of the Concrete*, a book which was completed already in 1962, Kosík until the early 1960s had been working on various studies which dealt with the subject of radical democrats.[35] The link between Kosík's long-term research of Czech radical democracy and the relatively short-term construction of the intellectual core of *Dialectics of the Concrete* – to which he moreover probably only afterwards added, under the influence of contemporary trends in Western Marxism and some Czech non-Marxist philosophers such as Jan Patočka, some phenomenological elements – is thus almost tangible.[36] From this perspective, *Dialectics of the Concrete* seems to function as if it were a fifth part of his investigation of Czech radical democracy, its revolutionary actions and intellectual ambition to lead 'the people'. From this viewpoint, the book is not just a systematic appendix to historical explanations but a personal expression of the inner meaning of a mutual link between dialectics, revolutionary ideas and philosophy, one he searched for in his historical investigations. Seen in this way, *Dialectics of the Concrete* is an accomplishment that makes the previous work, *Czech Radical Democracy*, complete.

The main philosophical approach ('destruction of the pseudo-concrete') is just the reverse of the 'revolutionary' method of transformation of reality. Kosík expresses it as follows:

> The destruction of the pseudo-concrete, the dialectical-critical method of thinking that dissolves fetishised artefacts both of the world of things and of that of ideas, *in order* to penetrate to their reality, is of course only another aspect of dialectics as a *revolutionary* method of *transform-*

---

33   Kosík 1976, p. 34, n. 13; Lukács 1971, especially chapter 'What is Orthodox Marxism?', which the author dates to 1919.
34   Kosík 1976, p. 34, n. 21.
35   E.g. Kosík 1963a.
36   Jan Patočka was a non-Marxist, but thanks to the intervention of his supporters was given a position at the Institute of Philosophy (though an administrative one) also in 1958. He became good friends with Kosík and in their joint reading of Heidegger began to influence him (testimony of Josef Zumr). This is probably the reason why Kosík decided to integrate in his current project some phenomenological notions which do not appear in his earlier work.

ing reality. To interpret the world critically, the interpretation itself must be grounded in revolutionary praxis. We shall see later on that reality can be transformed in a *revolutionary* way only because, and only insofar as, we ourselves form reality, and know that reality is formed by us. (Kosík's emphasis)[37]

If, therefore, the dominant topic of *Dialectics of the Concrete* is praxis, this connection clearly shows that it is an effort to defend and provide a foundation to a revolutionary practice. It is a subject which Kosík 'practically' identified with during the wartime era (in his anti-Nazi activities), during the post-war Stalinist period, and during the time when his intellectual views were maturing, a subject which now requires a deeper, total, philosophical articulation as opposed to the earlier, situational and one-sided treatments. Kosík lists three ways in which the pseudo-concrete can be destroyed:

> The pseudo-concrete is thus destroyed in the following ways: (1) by the revolutionary-critical praxis of mankind which is identical to the humanisation of man, with social revolutions as its key stages; (2) by dialectical thinking which dissolves the fetishized world of appearances in order to penetrate to reality and to the 'thing itself'; (3) by the realisation of truth and the forming of human reality in an ontogenetic process; since the world of truth is also the own individual creation of every human individual as a social being. Every individual has to appropriate his own culture and lead his own life *by himself and non-vicariously*.[38]

4 Conclusions

We could restate the gist of the above as follows: the first option is an expression of the communist ideology which Kosík earlier applied to historical issues but which remained an important part or perhaps even necessary precondition of the overall project of *Dialectics of the Concrete*. 'Social revolution' as the main factor in the formation of a human being is grounded in Kosík's own identification with Marxism-Leninism and its practical contribution to the transformation of Czech and international society.[39] The second point articulates the issue of the dialectics of the concrete on the level of conceptual reality. This com-

---

37 Kosík 1976, p. 7. Compare with Jan Mervart's text in this book.
38 Kosík 1976, p. 8.
39 For Kosík's conception of revolution in comparison with Robert Kalivoda see also Mervart 2017.

ponent of *Dialectics of the Concrete* inspired further developments in Marxist philosophy. And finally, the third way seems to signalise a dimension of *Dialectics of the Concrete* which at the time found even a non-Marxist audience, one that led to a broader dialogue with contemporary philosophy.

We tend to see Kosík's *Dialectics of the Concrete* through the lens of the second or third way. Already in 1963, this work entered the fast-changing Czech and European intellectual life, and inspired enthusiasm for creative Marxist philosophy as an instrument of analysis of social conditions and ultimately even the liberation of humankind. It is well known that soon thereafter, Kosík's views underwent a change. Once again he became one of the symbolic speakers of his generation. He called for a fundamental reform of socialism which would go hand in hand with a return to the previously suppressed humanistic tradition, independence of reason and freedom of conscience. From this perspective, *Dialectics of the Concrete* indeed stands at the beginning and charts the way to something new.

Dialectics of the Concrete is not usually seen as an advanced essayistic elaboration of the original radically leftist position and its starting assumptions, yet I believe that this is a possible and legitimate way of reading this work. In *Czech Radical Democracy*, Kosík identified its intellectual culmination in the work of Augustin Smetana, i.e. in an autonomous position of philosophy which reproduced spiritual reality in confrontation with the most advanced form of the philosophy of its time (in Smetana's case Hegel). Kosík attempted the same project and decided to find inspiration in Heidegger's fundamental ontology. In dealing with historical issues, he was confronted with the hermeneutic problem in the guise of Marxist conceptual structure and dialectics. Yet what he accomplished was not a revision of the starting ideological assumptions, but rather their particular and unique articulation and elaboration. This conclusion is supported by the fact that Kosík never rejected his early ideological assumptions. This helps us understand the continuity of his views as it manifested itself even in his reserve with respect to the dissent, in his contemplative essays about Czech culture, and even in his post-1989 writings. I believe that such an interpretation in no way detracts from the originality of *Dialectics of the Concrete*. Quite the opposite: by placing his position in its proper historical context, we can understand it better. And it also helps us understand that one of the lines of thought which resulted in the ideas of the Prague Spring, an unfulfilled dream of a union between democracy and socialism, leads all the way back to 1943, to a group of people in Prague-Smíchov and to the resistance unit Předvoj, whose legacy Kosík tried to articulate. At the same time, however, an honest assessment of this entire development, including its dark aspects in the Stalinist perversion of ideas, explains why it was in the end a futile dream beset by internal contradictions.

PART 2

Praxis and Labour

∴

CHAPTER 3

Praxis in Progress: On the Transformations of Kosík's Thought

Francesco Tava

One of the pivotal issues in the thought of Karel Kosík is that of *praxis*. Although various interpreters have recognised the centrality of this notion and identified its affinity with other theories of praxis drawn from the traditions of Marxism and Critical Theory,[1] an examination of the overall meaning of praxis in Kosík's output is still missing. This chapter aims to fill this gap by looking at three different stages of Kosík's reflection. First, I will clarify the meaning and function of the idea of praxis, as well as its relationship with the concepts of theory and labour, in *Dialectics of the Concrete* (1963). I will then address Kosík's subsequent works up to the failure of the Prague Spring (1964–69), in order to understand how his interpretation of praxis evolved throughout these crucial years of intellectual and political turmoil. I will conclude with an analysis of Kosík's late output (post-1989) that will reveal both the elements of continuity and the radical transformations that his reflection underwent.

1   Theory and Praxis in *Dialectics of the Concrete*

A widespread theme in *Dialectics of the Concrete* is the relationship and interplay between praxis and theory.[2] In this work, Kosík intends to counter the approach according to which philosophy must be eventually abolished by means of a transition from theory to praxis.[3] From his point of view, praxis is not to be understood as pure practical activity antithetical to theory, but rather as the authentic sphere of human being. Kosík's perspective radically alters the

---

1 On the idea of praxis in Kosík, see in particular Neri 1966a, pp. 197–207; Neri 1980, pp. 130–55; Schmidt 1977; Arnason 1991, pp. 77–8; Satterwhite 2009, pp. 142–7; Hauser 2012, p. 132 ff.
2 For a general analysis of Kosík's *Dialectics of the Concrete*, also with reference to the problem of praxis, see Landa 2012.
3 Such an approach stems from a peculiar interpretation of Marx's criticism of Feuerbach that had one of its strongest advocates in Engels, who theorised the substitution of philosophy by modern scientific and technical praxis. See Marx 2000a; Engels 1941. On this particular topic, see also Neri 1966b.

meaning of praxis within the Marxist debate: 'The problem of praxis in materialist *philosophy* is not based on distinguishing two areas of human activity [...]. Rather it is formed as a philosophical answer to a philosophical question: *Who is man, what is socio-human reality, and how is this reality formed?*'[4] According to this interpretation, praxis constitutes the authentic formative trait of humankind insofar as it allows human beings to enrich their own existence with the product of their actions. In this sense, objective production is only an instrumental component of praxis, whereas its true objective is nothing else than human constitution and flourishing. Kosík clearly instantiates the dynamic and creative aspect of praxis when he argues that 'praxis is the exposure of the mystery of man as an onto-formative being, as a being that *forms* the (socio-human) reality and *therefore* also grasps and interprets it'.[5] This emphasis is remarkable, as it identifies respectively the cause and the consequence of this process. It is, indeed, by framing the world that human beings learn how to interpret it and acquire knowledge of it. And it is by deploying these practical and theoretical attitudes that they can establish themselves as authentic human beings, i.e. as beings who are able to form their own reality as well as to formulate a *theory* of it. In other words, Kosík seems to suggest that the emergence of human praxis in the world precedes and founds all human efforts to know this world. Therefore, praxis cannot be conceived as a negation of theory, but rather as its prerequisite and fundamental basis.

A question arises from such a conception of praxis. Since humans can use their practical abilities to shape their social and political reality, one might wonder what prevents them from employing such abilities in order to establish their supremacy over the surrounding world. Kosík is aware of this possible outcome, and he underlines how praxis may also acquire a negative characterisation whenever it assumes the form of 'fetishised praxis', which essentially pertains to what Kosík calls the world of 'pseudoconcreteness', i.e. the world of 'procuring and manipulation'.[6] The Marxian critique of political economy has shown how this world is not the real one, but merely an appearance that correct praxis can help overcome:

> [T]he world that exposes itself to man in his fetishised praxis, in procuring and manipulation, is not a real world, though it does have a real world's 'firmness' and its 'effectiveness'; rather, it is a 'world of appearances' (Marx). The idea of a thing postures as the thing itself and forms

---

4 Kosík 1976, p. 136.
5 Kosík 1976, p. 137.
6 Kosík 1976, p. 2.

an ideological appearance, but it is not a natural property of things and of reality; rather, it is the projection of certain *petrified* historical conditions into the consciousness of the subject.[7]

This petrification typically occurs whenever the essential relationship between humanity and reality is explained in terms of organisation and supremacy of the former to the detriment of the latter. This mindset, which for Kosík is exemplified by technological rationality, denotes a transitive and exploitative relationship between human beings and their world, whereby external reality is nothing but the passive target of human determination. In contrast with this petrified idea of practical activity, Kosík outlines the possibility of an alternative praxis, which has the power to shatter this mindset. In this sense, Kosík's notion of 'revolutionary praxis' becomes particularly meaningful, as it reveals a way to counteract and overturn the world of pseudo-concreteness and the fetishised praxis that constitutes its fundamental core.[8]

In order to reject fetishised praxis and to achieve authentic human praxis, the whole mindset that allowed the emergence of the former must be radically rejected. According to that mindset, 'praxis was identified with technology in the broad sense of the word, and conceived and practised as manipulation, as a technique of conduct, as an art of handling people and things, in short, as the power to manipulate and as mastery over material both human and inert'.[9] In order to contrast with such an interpretation, praxis has to be understood not as mere superficial activity, but as something much broader, i.e. as a dimension of human existence that encompasses a vast range of phenomena and situations, which can be either active or passive, and which are often in conflict with each other. As it clearly emerges in *Dialectics of the Concrete*, praxis is not just the 'objectification of man and the mastering of nature', but also, in a deeper sense, 'the realisation of human freedom'.[10] This double characterisation reveals how praxis does not draw a straight line from humanity to the world, but rather entails a more complex dynamic, whereby humans can establish their position in the world and achieve the goals of their actions only as long as they are willing to open and expose themselves to reality's possible risks, even though this attitude entails jeopardising their own individual freedom. This dialectic between subject and object, and between life and the world, constitutes the

---

7   Kosík 1976, p. 5. Kosík's main reference point here is Marx's first volume of *Capital*.
8   On Kosík's idea of a 'revolutionary-critical praxis' and its link to dialectical reason, see Hauser 2012, pp. 132–45.
9   Kosík 1976, p. 134.
10 Kosík 1976, p. 139.

clearest definition of praxis. In order to grasp this dialectic, however, the classical dichotomy between activity and passivity has to be set aside, as both these ideas equally inform such a definition.

In order to demonstrate this point, Kosík particularly stresses that fact that beyond its formative element, which relates it to the notion of labour, praxis presents further and more complex traits that reveal a sort of ambiguity, which should not be seen as a flaw, but rather as its fundamental characterisation.[11] The argument that praxis is not just a human attempt to dominate the external world but also an effort to realise one's own freedom entails that praxis is not a mere labour technique, but first and foremost a 'struggle for recognition' in the sense that Hegel attributed to this term with regard to the master-slave dialectic.[12] If labour represents the fundamental sphere in which human beings discover temporality as the cycle that leads them from slavery to emancipation, it is only through praxis that this dialectical movement can actually be fulfilled. This fulfilment entails a transition from an *immediate* idea of the future – namely a future that is only understandable as a consequence of the present and that can only be achieved through the labour process – to a *mediated* idea of the future, which breaks the changeless dynamics of this cycle. Only from this rupture can an authentic struggle for recognition arise. Acknowledging this peculiar trait of praxis means realising that praxis encompasses two different moments:

> Thus apart from the moment of *labour*, praxis also includes an *existential* moment: it manifests itself both in man's objective activity by which he transforms nature and chisels human meanings into natural material, and in the *process of forming* the human subject in which existential moments such as anxiety, nausea, fear, joy, laughter, hope etc. stand out not as positive 'experiencing', but as a part of the struggle for recognition, i.e. of the process of realising human freedom.[13]

In other words, human beings can undertake a struggle for recognition and aim at embracing their own freedom only if they orient their action not exclusively towards determined and objective ends ('A mere objective relationship

---

[11] James Schmidt has particularly stressed the positive meaning of the 'ambiguity' that inheres in the notion of praxis. See Schmidt 1977, p. 75.

[12] Kosík 1976, pp. 138–9. For an analysis of the notion of 'dialectics' in Hegel and Kosík, see Landa 2012, p. 246 ff.

[13] Kosík 1976, p. 138.

to nature cannot generate freedom'),[14] but also to themselves – to the most hidden and intimate parts of their existence. In this sense, praxis shows a trait of 'passivity', i.e. a non-operational dimension in which its dynamic acquires a reflective bearing.

However, this emphasis on the existential dimension of praxis does not imply any sort of escape from reality, as it does not correspond to an attitude of introspection. In *Dialectics of the Concrete*, praxis never loses its character of revolutionary endeavour aimed at dispelling the world's pseudo-concreteness. Kosík clarifies this point by adding a third dimension of praxis, in addition to the formative and existential ones: 'Though it is a specific human reality that is formed in the happening of praxis, reality that is independent of man exists in it *in a certain way* as well'.[15] Kosík's biggest concern here is to prevent humans from becoming enclosed either in the mere product of their own praxis (understood as active, formative labour) or in themselves (in their being the unique bearers of a reflective, existential praxis that overlooks the surrounding material world). In order to avoid these risks, praxis must be able to target and alter both the external world – '[...] uncovering the universe and reality in their being' – and that part of reality that is exclusively human (feelings, emotions, values etc.) and that is normally associated with inner reflection rather than with concrete activity.[16] Acknowledging this multilevel character of praxis means ensuring that the human faculty to leave a mark on reality is not limited to people's material and contingent creations, but also involves human flourishing and personal enhancement.

2   From Praxis to Moral Action

The above showed how, according to Kosík's understanding, praxis is a multifaceted phenomenon. This interpretation in not limited to *Dialectics of the Concrete*, but further evolves in Kosík's later output. It is especially during the turbulent 1960s that the idea of praxis seems to undergo a decisive transformation. In 1964, only a year after the publication of *Dialectics of the Concrete*, Kosík gave a talk at a conference on the meaning of morality for Marxism, which was held at the Gramsci Institute in Rome. On this occasion, after describing the antinomy between humans and the system as one of the fundamental problems of Marxist ethics, Kosík arrives at the following question: 'Why are

---

14   Ibid.
15   Kosík 1976, p. 139.
16   Ibid.

people not happy in the modern world?'[17] In order to answer this question, Kosík points out how in the present age the economic structure, which had already been an object of his critique in *Dialectics of the Concrete*, becomes internalised. What follows from this is that human life is emptied of meaning insofar as all human values are levelled on this merely instrumental structure and therefore lose their centrality and authenticity: 'The transformation of all values into mere passing moments in the general and absolute race for more distant values has as its consequence the emptiness of life'.[18] In this situation, a dangerous inversion of means and ends takes place, insofar as values such as freedom and reason are reduced to mere instruments aimed at achieving better physical comfort and establishing a more efficient rational manipulation of people and things. This critique, which Kosík links to Marx's analysis of money,[19] recalls Hannah Arendt's analysis of work in *The Human Condition*, in which she highlights (also referring to Marx's viewpoint) the ineluctable tendency of *homo faber* to transform the world into material employed for its own building. 'Man, in so far as he is *homo faber*, instrumentalises, and his instrumentalisation implies a degradation of all things into means, their loss of intrinsic and independent value, so that eventually not only the objects of fabrication but also 'the earth in general and all forces of nature', which clearly came into being without the help of man and have an existence independent of the human world, lose their 'value because [they] do not present the reification which comes from work''.[20] This 'generalisation of the fabrication experience' causes the collapse of work into labour insofar as the difference between the two that Arendt had previously identified seems here to fade inexorably.[21] For this reason there arises the need for an idea of action that diverges from both labour and work.

Like Arendt, Kosík also strives for a solution to the condition of emptiness and levelling that the internalisation of the economic structure has generated

---

17   Kosík 1995h, p. 69.
18   Kosík 1995h, p. 70.
19   'Money thereby directly and simultaneously becomes the real community, since it is the general substance of survival for all, and at the same time the social product of all. But as we have seen, in money the community is at the same time a mere abstraction, a mere external, accidental thing for the individual, and at the same time merely a means for his satisfaction as an isolated individual. The community of antiquity presupposes a quite different relation to, and on the part of, the individual. The development of money in its third role therefore smashes this community', Marx 1973, p. 212.
20   Arendt 1998, p. 156. Arendt here is quoting from Marx 1933, p. 698.
21   Unlike labour, work produces things that are able to last, independently from the mere activity of the worker. See Arendt 1998, p. 136 ff.

both in capitalist and real socialist societies. Once again, this solution lies in the idea of praxis. According to Kosík, praxis has the power to invert this tendency towards levelling: '[...] historical praxis must transform the structure of the world' in order to define it as 'real community instead of levelling'.[22] This inversion can occur whether people recover their authentic judgement – not only the ability to distinguish between good and evil, but also the power to '[...] place good *in opposition* to evil, and evil *in opposition* to good'.[23] In this circumstance, praxis represents the dialectical transition from mere observation to moral action; from a condition of ethical paralysis, which characterises the internalisation of the economic structure, to a new openness: 'The contradictions of human reality are transformed into petrified antinomies if they are deprived of the unifying force that makes human praxis a totalisation and resuscitation'.[24] However, in order to achieve this goal, we must reject any monolithic definition of praxis. Praxis now takes on the shape and complexity of authentic moral action. In order to overcome the petrified antinomies that fix the position of human beings onto the general structure of the system, praxis cannot correspond to any of these fixed elements, but must rather contrast with them by preserving its inner complexity and establishing what Kosík calls a 'dialectical unity of contradictions'.[25]

Although Kosík does not fully develop the theme of praxis as moral action in his 1964 address, three years later he returns to the same subject on the occasion of another conference.[26] What does it mean that human praxis has to be understood as a 'dialectical unity of contradictions'? Understanding human praxis as a form of practical intentionality, i.e. in a sense that stresses exclusively its active and functional traits, for Kosík means overlooking all those passive aspects that essentially inform the very idea of praxis. These passive aspects reflect the errors, setbacks and contradictions that prevent us from achieving determined goals, but that nonetheless characterise human existence just as much as any positive and instrumental plan of action does. By considering these negative aspects as unrelated to praxis, human beings end up striving to regain control over them as though they were not essential components of human existence, but merely contingent factors that impinge on it from the outside. Understanding praxis as a mere activity does not permit humans to explain and withstand the unpredictability of existence, i.e. the circumstance whereby accidental out-

---

22   Kosík 1995h, p. 70.
23   Ibid. Emphasis mine.
24   Kosík 1995h, p. 75.
25   Ibid. Emphasis mine.
26   Kosík 1967. I will quote from the Italian translation of this text: see Kosík 2012a, 93–98.

comes can stem from intentional activities. According to Kosík, only by establishing an alternative and more inclusive idea of praxis will we finally understand '[...] how play and laughter can emerge from labor'.[27] Among the various interpreters of Kosík's philosophy the Italian phenomenologist Guido Davide Neri has particularly stressed the difference between human praxis and mere intentional activity. According to Neri's interpretation, the kind of praxis that Kosík has in mind has the power to envision conditions that are apparently opposite to it – such as stillness, imagination and dreaming – and to comprehend them not as if they were setbacks within an otherwise continuous process, but as necessary components of its own structure.[28] Only by acknowledging the complexity of his structure can we prevent

> [...] a reduction of the whole human reality to labour, with the consequence that all the ways of human existence appear as modifications of labour, or that all the domains of human reality that cannot be reduced to labour or understood on its basis must be considered as peripheral and secondary. It is therefore completely natural that, according to this idea, play – if compared to labour – appears only as pure play, namely as a secondary phenomenon, and that laughter, compared to the production of tools, is something utterly negligible.[29]

3 From Praxis to Play

We have seen how for Kosík human praxis has to undergo a fundamental transformation that reveals its less apparent traits: those of moral struggle, passive reflection, and contradiction. What emerges out of this transformation is a complex phenomenon that portrays well the relationship between human beings and their reality and that also seems to entail, among other things, a transition from praxis to play. If we compare Kosík's standpoint in *Dialectics of the Concrete* with his later output, we see how his attention gradually shifts from the active and creative aspect of praxis to a more complex dimension of it. Whilst initially the aim was to establish a revolutionary praxis with which humans could transform reality for the best, now the main focus moves to the intricate existential interplay that drives individuals towards one another and regulates their connection to the world that surrounds them – a connection in which humans transform the world as much as they are transformed by it. The

---

27 Kosík 2012a, p. 94.
28 See Neri 1980, pp. 145–6.
29 Kosík 2012a, pp. 95–6.

word 'play' often recurs in Kosík's writings to express this ambiguous aspect of praxis, which turns out to be both active and passive. To understand the use of this word, it is useful to look at its essential polysemy. Play denotes a recreational activity that has no other purpose than to provoke fun and amusement. However, play also means drama, and can describe a dramatic composition which is performed on a stage.[30] The etymology of this term shows that *drama* (δρᾶμα) derives from the Greek verb *draō* (δράω), which means to act, to perform, to do. A dramatic play is nothing but the combination of all the actions and passions that the various characters perform on the stage. Usually this combination is not linear but unfolds through a series of alternating patterns and sudden events in which the general situation develops along with the characters involved in it. It can be argued that this specific understanding of play provides the best possible description of the existential moment of praxis, which Kosík had already thematised in *Dialectics of the Concrete*. This for him is the moment when praxis diverges from mere labour and when the human subject starts that process of self-formation in which 'existential moments such as anxiety, nausea, fear, joy, laughter, hope, etc. stand out'.[31] All these elements, which characterise the human struggle for recognition, are summoned in the experience of play, which therefore corresponds to the true actualisation of existential praxis. However, it is in the 1966 essay 'The Individual and History' that Kosík provides the clearest exposition of his conception of play. According to Kosík, those who maintain that history is made by great individuals and those who believe that history is produced by supra-individual forces all agree on one thing: They all think that the making of history is a sort of privilege that is only granted to a few select actors, be they human or super-human. All others can only acquiesce to this superior order and are therefore relegated to a status of passivity, as if they were not actors but mere bystanders. In this situation, human nature is degraded '[...] to an anecdotal and secondary level: the human side appears in the form of insignificant details or in the sphere of private life'.[32] Consequently, phenomena that are typical of the human way of being and behaving, such as the ridiculous, the comic, the humorous, are marginalised and lose relevance when compared with the great endeavours of history makers. According to Kosík, this way of understanding history misses its concrete aspect. In order to challenge this interpretation and attain a better understanding of history, we have to identify 'certain dialectics in which the relationship between history and the individual is no longer expressed by

---

30 This polysemy is also contained in the Czech words *hra* (play), and *hrát* (to play).
31 Kosík 1976, p. 138.
32 Kosík 1995i, p. 125.

means of antinomies but rather as a movement in which the inner unity of the two members is constituted. *This new principle is the [principle of] play*.[33]

German philosophers such as Schelling and Marx have thematised the tight bond between history and play.[34] With this tradition in mind, Kosík proposes an interpretation of history through the lenses of play in order to fully acknowledge the inclusiveness of the historical process: '[H]istory is a play in which the masses and individuals, classes and nations, great personalities and average beings, all partake. It is a play as long as all people have a part in it and as long as all parts are included and no one is excluded. All genres are fully developed in historical tragedies, comedies, and grotesque plays'.[35] In this complex structure, all characters are equally involved in the making of history. In Kosík's words, everybody is involved in the same dialectics of acting and knowing. As already emerged in *Dialectics of the Concrete*, knowledge and action, theory and praxis are tightly intertwined in the same play, which is history. Only by directly engaging in the historical dialectics, by becoming actors and not mere bystanders, can human beings come to know themselves and their position in history and become capable of changing history from their own perspective. In other words, the only knowledge of reality we can possibly achieve is the knowledge that stems from our involvement in the historical process. Interpreting history as play also implies a substantial modification of the notion of historical temporality. From this perspective, there is no necessary consequentiality between past, present and future. The future is no longer seen as the progressive development of the present, which is in turn a progression from the past. Looking into the future through the lenses of an ongoing play, whose outcome (unlike in real plays) is unforeseeable, means understanding it as risk, uncertainty, and error. Only by openly embracing this risk element can we reject any reified conception of time whereby real history is replaced by history that is merely recorded.[36]

At the end of 'The Individual and History', Kosík explicitly reconnects the theme of play with that of praxis. Conceiving history and reality through the idea of play enables human beings to stop interpreting praxis as if it were a social substance, a historical factor that materialises regardless of the limited existence of individuals. By deconstructing historical determinism, Kosík sheds a spotlight on what praxis really is: 'the structure of the individual himself and

---

33   Kosík 1995i, p. 126. Emphasis mine; translation revised.
34   See Schelling 1978, p. 210; Marx 1955, p. 51.
35   Kosík 1995i, p. 127.
36   On the difference between real history and recorded history, see Kosík 1995i, p. 131.

of all individuals'.[37] What clearly emerges here through the mirror of play is a new idea of praxis, which surpasses its active and creative character and encompasses a much broader spectrum of reality, in which seemingly insignificant actions and passions, as well as historical enterprises, are all retained and valued.

4   On Humour and Laughter: Contrasting Normalisation

One of the aspects of human praxis that emerges most clearly in Kosík's analysis of play is that of ambiguity. The same action can acquire opposite connotations depending on which historical backdrop it takes place against, and the same theatrical play can turn from comedy to tragedy in the space of a few lines. The keen interest that Kosík showed, throughout his philosophical work, in the phenomena of humour and laughter might reflect attempts to further explore one of the facets of this ambiguity. In a 1963 essay, Kosík developed an original analysis of Kafka and Hašek, whose writings remained central also in Kosík's later output. Both Kafka's grotesque representation of reality and Hašek's joyful humour are in Kosík's mind two sides of the same coin, as they can both serve to contrast with what Kosík calls the 'big mechanism' of modern political power, meaning the various attempts by the ruling class to develop increasingly efficient mechanisms to exploit and dominate the rest of humanity.[38]

This line of thought further evolved in the following years and became particularly poignant in the aftermath of the Prague Spring.[39] In a 1969 article, Kosík decides once again to shed light on Hašek's literary hero, the good soldier Švejk, and on his idea of humour: 'When a person cannot identify with either of the warring sides because he sees limitations in both, he then becomes a target for attacks from all sides. With this approach he opens up a space that is free of any ideological baggage, and in this space a universal liberating humour is born'.[40] Kosík interprets Švejk's humour as a peculiar form of praxis that gives humans the strength to free themselves from any external control. The most powerful means of this liberating humour is laughter, which becomes the main issue of another paper that Kosík wrote in 1969 on the occasion of a

---

37   Kosík 1995i, p. 132.
38   Kosík 1995b, pp. 82–3.
39   On the role of Czech intellectuals in the years around the Prague Spring, see Kusin 1971; Falk 2003. For an analysis of Kosík's political commitment and philosophical thought, see Mervart 2012.
40   Kosík 1995g, p. 96.

meeting on the theme of 'laughter and liberation' in the editorial office of *Plamen*, a monthly journal of literature and culture that in those years became an important meeting place for reform-minded writers and free thinkers.[41] This is supposedly one of the last texts that Kosík wrote before he retreated into a long period of silence that lasted, with rare exceptions, until after 1989. The great importance that Kosík attached to the subject of laughter is attested to by the fact that he returned to it when, after the Velvet Revolution, he finally had a chance to conduct a series of lectures at Charles University, which he entitled 'Considerations on Laughter'.[42]

Towards the end of his 1969 article on laughter, Kosík argues that '[w]hoever listens carefully to speech will hear its laughter'.[43] This consideration emerges from the idea that speech and laughter are inextricably linked. 'Only a being gifted with language – in fact – is also able to laugh, and speech and laughter are not appendages to human existence, but are its constituent parts'.[44] Laughter is not a simple reaction to external stimuli, but rather indicates an authentic human practice that, due to its complexity, is comparable to speaking or thinking. Nonetheless, unlike speaking and thinking, laughter has the unique characteristic of temporarily dissolving all the bonds that keep human beings anchored to the present. Laughter frees humans from their anguish and enables them to access a new existential level on which all conventions are suspended. According to Kosík, anyone who bursts into laughter can reach a new level of receptivity – a multiplied readiness of mind that allows them to break out from everyday life. Moreover, the essence of humour lies in its timing: in the ability to conceive and deliver a message that immediately hits its comic target. In this respect, laughter is worlds apart from the lengthy and empty formulas of bureaucratic language to the point that one might interpret laughter as the perfect antithesis and antidote to any kind of political newspeak.

Another remarkable trait of laughter is its inner ambivalence. On the one hand, laughing at something allows us to distance ourselves from it and therefore to appreciate its true scale. On the other hand, laughter has the power to unite people. Kosík is particularly keen to stress this aspect. For him, laughter generates a deep bond among human beings, the essence of which is nevertheless difficult to identify. In this sense, his interpretation recalls that of Bergson,

---

41 See Kosík 1995n.
42 Parts of these lectures 'Úsměv a ústa' [The Smile and the Mouth], 'Výsměšnost' [Mocking] were later published in Kosík 1997, see Kosík 1997h and Kosík 1997l.
43 Kosík 1995c, p. 196. Translation revised.
44 Kosík 1995c, p. 184.

who maintained that '[h]owever spontaneous it seems, laughter always implies a kind of secret freemasonry, or even complicity, with other laughters, real or imaginary'.[45] After all, as Freud also pointed out, at least two people are required for something comical to happen, as laughter is essentially a social activity.[46] Kosík is interested in this ability of laughter to aggregate people: 'In this laughter is born a society of people who acknowledge each other, who do not laugh at each other but laugh together at their own ridiculousness, at their ability to make others laugh and to evoke a storm of laughter'.[47] A new and completely spontaneous idea of commonality seems to emerge from laughter, and this explains its unique political power. In thematising this political aspect of laughter, Kosík recalls Thomas Carlyle's description of the French Revolution, which began with the Parisian crowd bursting into thunderous laughter against the monarchy: 'it was one boundless inarticulate Haha; – transcendent World – Laughter; comparable to the Saturnalia of the Ancients'.[48] Similarly, in the spring of 1968, the people of Prague '[...] bid farewell to the old order with laughter'.[49] The protagonists of that turbulent season were those young people who took the floor in public debates and resorted to humour and jokes to spread the feeling of newfound freedom. On that occasion, laughter really became a powerful tool for political change. Nonetheless, the joyful humour of the young revolutionaries would soon be surmounted by the much darker laughter of the former regime that at that point was already swearing revenge:

> The ridiculous regime gives way, but does not give up, and history acts like a hidden encounter between the public laughter of people and the hidden grimace of those who are retreating, but who dream of revenge, of returning to a time when the laughter of the laughing crowds would go away.[50]

Although the tragic end of the Prague Spring prompted Kosík to conclude his analysis on this rather pessimistic note, the praxis of laughter requires further investigation to shed light on its inherent political essence and potential.

---

45 Bergson 2013, p. 9.
46 'Why is it, then, that I do not laugh at a joke of my own? And what part is played in this by the other person? [...] In the case of the comic, two persons are in general concerned: besides myself, the person in whom I find something comic. If inanimate things seem to me comic, that is on account of a kind of personification which is not of rare occurrence in our ideational life', Freud 1960, p. 176.
47 Kosík 1995c, p. 185.
48 Carlyle 1906, pp. 595–6.
49 Kosík 1995c, p. 186.
50 Kosík 1995c, p. 187.

By bursting into laughter, the people of Prague showed that they were not a crowd but a group of individuals. No matter how hard political regimes try to turn people into a uniform herd, over and over again, citizens will rise up and burst out laughing at them. This also shows how the existential praxis that we call laughter can help us achieve the same objective of the creative, revolutionary praxis that Kosík originally described in *Dialectics of the Concrete*, namely, the destruction of pseudo-concreteness and the liberation of humankind. By identifying the political dimension of laughter, Kosík found a way to meet this objective by following an alternative route.

5   Tragedy and Sacrifice: Towards a New Idea of Action

The aftermath of Prague Spring has shown how the human struggle for recognition, which for Kosík represents the main outcome of existential praxis, can sometimes collapse and leave room for a radically different reality. This happens whenever the comical facet of laughter, which is one of the brightest manifestations of such praxis, is replaced by its darker, grotesque side. This same phenomenon, however, persisted even after 1989 by taking on ever more diverse forms. In an article originally published in 1993, Kosík highlighted the emergence in the post-communist era of a new space of pseudo-concreteness, which resembles a modern version of Plato's cave.[51] The upward movement through which human beings struggled over the centuries to overcome the natural constraints of their existence and flourish seems to be replaced in the present time by a horizontal movement that merely repeats the same routine over and over again. Although such movement allows humans to move horizontally, i.e. to expand their material domination of the surrounding world, no real moral progress can have a place in such circumstances. As a result, human beings live is a sort an enormous cave, whose walls are no longer visible: 'The expanding cave increases in size by absorbing or occupying everything with which it comes into contact; its principle is that of expansive closure. [...] The inhabitants of the cave lack the measure and the dimension that would make reality a world in which human beings can freely and joyfully live'.[52]

Life in this modern cave is perfectly levelled. Individuals living in it are only allowed to follow predefined paths without unexpected events or sudden turns. As Kosík points out in another article from the same period, the character that best represents this peculiar human condition is that of Grete Samsa

---

51   See Kosík 1996.
52   Kosík 1996, p. 121.

from Kafka's *The Metamorphosis*.[53] According to Kosík, Grete always floats on the surface, preferring to act mechanically instead of developing her existential praxis, systematically ruling out of her existence any problematic element in order to preserve her everyday routine. It does not matter if this choice involves rejecting her own brother once he turns into a gigantic bug. As soon as Gregor's metamorphosis happens, Grete no longer considers him as human being. For Kosík, the sudden change in Grete's attitude is the real metamorphosis in this story: 'She directly intervenes in the action, and her behaviour is the real moment of reversal, that is, of the metamorphosis. The grotesque metamorphosis happens in the moment when Grete stops to consider her brother a person, when she renounces all doubt over whether he is a man or an animal, and his presence becomes unbearable to her'.[54] In Grete's view, this renunciation is necessary, as only by forgetting her monstrous brother will she be able to move forward. 'Grete Samsa, who is not shaken by any fact, not even by her brother's death, goes towards a kind of future that will be a copy of the past, and in her future life she will therefore replicate the sterility, the banality, the tradition of the past, and in this unproductive repetition she will invest all her youthful energy'.[55] In light of this, Grete for Kosík represents the 'anti-Antigone' of our times: Unlike Sophocles' Antigone, who bravely chose to flout social and political conventions by resorting to a deeper and more complex level of existence, Grete always opts for a superficial life.[56] Whilst the old Antigone refused to betray the memory of her brother even though in doing so she put her life in danger, today's Antigone is happy to reject Gregor's existence as long as this will allow her to go on with her ordinary life.

What Kosík sees in the figure of Grete is the loss of any sense of tragedy, i.e. of the ability to acknowledge any problematic and conflicting aspect in human life. In such circumstances, human praxis as we have described it so far seems to be radically negated as every action seems to conform to a purely utilitarian standard. In order to contrast this new form of pseudo-concreteness, human beings have to establish a new kind of praxis that is radical enough to break this crystallised structure. Acknowledging and fully embracing the tragic aspect of human existence is at the centre of Camus' essay on the myth of Sisyphus, which for various reasons recalls Kosík's analysis of the figure of Antigone. According to Camus, the tragic element of this story lies in the fact that Sisyphus is always perfectly aware of his condition: 'If this myth is tragic, that is because its hero is conscious. Where would his torture be, indeed, if at every

---

53   See Kosík 1993b.
54   Kosík 1993b, p. 16.
55   Kosík 1993b, p. 17.
56   On Antigone's ability to reach this plane of depths, see Patočka 2004b.

step the hope of succeeding sustained him? [...] Sisyphus, proletarian of the gods, powerless and rebellious, knows the full extent of his wretched condition: it is what he thinks of during his descent. The lucidity that was to constitute his torture at the same time crowns his victory. There is no fate that cannot be surmounted by scorn'.[57] According to Camus, even when human beings are faced with the most dehumanised activities, they can still preserve their authentic existential dimension as long they are able to detach themselves from such activities and to fully acknowledge their meaninglessness instead of accepting them uncritically. This tragic awareness allows humans to defend their individuality even in the harshest situations when there seems to be no path out of the cave. By recognising this aspect, humanity can really start a new praxis.

Kosík shares with Camus the objective of unearthing the tragic aspect of authentic human praxis, and he does so by identifying a 'new Antigone' – someone capable of contrasting with Grete's conduct, and of using her own praxis to break the levelling of the present. Only in this way will the human struggle for recognition finally be restored. To describe the kind of praxis that is able to achieve this goal, Kosík refers to the Czech writer Milena Jesenská. From his perspective, what characterises both Sophocles' *Antigone* and Jesenská is their ability to 'exit from the silent and fearful crowd' and to 'deviate from the queue' by directing their words and deeds against whatever they think represents evil in the world.[58] Milena Jesenská, through her work as a journalist during the Nazi occupation of Czechoslovakia[59] and her imprisonment in Ravensbrück, where she died in 1944, provides a great example of how to diverge from the established order and counteract its power.[60] This capacity for resistance is for Kosík the best representation of this renewed praxis. In another article from 1998, Kosík even argues that this resistant praxis is a prerequisite for individual freedom: 'The first prerequisite for freedom and condition for overcoming fatalism is being surprising – getting out of the flowing stream, deviating from the line, refusing to obey orders, staying out of the establishment, being an unclassifiable unity that rejects the fatality of the established order, because the only order lies in one's heart'.[61]

The tragic aspect of such praxis is represented by the conflict between those human beings who, alone, decide to undertake action, and the entire order of things that stands against them. No matter how hard they try to re-establish a

---

57 Camus 1955, pp. 185–6.
58 Kosík 1993b, p. 18.
59 See Jesenská 1983 and Hayes 2003.
60 On the figure of Jesenská, see Buber-Neumann 1989, Boella 2013.
61 Kosík 2004a, p. 32.

'dialectical unity of contractions',[62] in the end, as Jesenská's tragic death shows, the pseudo-concrete system will always prevail. Despite its unresolved and therefore tragic outcome, which recalls Sisyphus' journey, this praxis reflects what Kosík contended in *Dialectics of the Concrete*, i.e. that authentic praxis is a 'struggle for recognition' that aims towards the 'realisation of human freedom'. Despite the concrete setbacks that it has run up against, which eroded its most constructive, creative aspect, the existential element of praxis is still intact and resonates in Kosík's later works.

The extreme and most tragic representation of such praxis is sacrifice.[63] In an essay from the mid-1990s, entitled *A Youth and Death*, Kosík develops a broad analysis of the characteristics and consequences of human sacrifice, which ranges from the myth of Prometheus to the Christian tradition, to historical cases of people who decided to take their own lives. Among them, Jan Palach, the twenty-year-old Czech student who set himself on fire on 19 January 1969 in protest against the Soviet invasion, is the 'young man' who gives this essay its title. In recalling Palach's episode, Kosík rejects any celebratory tone. Palach's sacrifice is not motivated by abstract principles, such as freedom or peace, but by the strong desire to keep a distance from the dramatic outcome of the Prague Spring. Jan Palach wanted to be 'different from the others'[64] and to reject the usual order of things. Like Milena Jesenká, he also wanted to exit from the silent and fearful crowd. Both Milena and Jan carry on this negative and resistant praxis, which Antigone first introduced. The extreme alterity that such praxis enables is what can shatter the pseudo-concreteness of the present.

In order to protect this alterity, sacrifice must resist any utilitarian principle. It is no coincidence that the section of *A Youth and Death*, in which Kosík focuses on Palach, is entitled: 'The Uselessness of Sacrifice'. By sacrificing themselves, human beings do not act rationally in order to achieve predetermined ends. Their praxis is not decided on the basis of a means-ends scheme. In order to maintain its negative and contrastive trait, sacrifice must be – to use an expression coined by another Czech philosopher, Jan Patočka – 'sacrifice for nothing'. It must be a radical gesture that allows humans to '[draw] back from the realm of what can be managed and ordered' by taking back control over

---

62 See above: footnote 30.
63 On the nexus between tragedy and sacrifice, see Benjamin 1977, pp. 106–7: 'Tragic poetry is based on the idea of sacrifice. But in respect of its victim, the hero, the tragic sacrifice differs from any other kind, being at once a first and a final sacrifice. [...] The tragic death has a dual significance: it invalidates the ancient rights of the Olympians, and it offers up the hero to the unknown god as the first fruits of the new harvest of humanity'.
64 Kosík 1995m, p. 26.

their own death.[65] This outcome becomes possible, however, only as long as sacrifice is practically useless, i.e. only if it does not lead to any certain end.

In light of this characterisation, Palach's sacrifice acquires a new meaning. From Kosík's viewpoint, his value and power does not lie in any positive aspect but rather consists of its extreme negativity: 'His act is a rift, an interruption, a caesura that will always be unsettling and stimulating and will always foster productive discussions on the meaning of life'.[66] It is precisely in the midst of this negativity, where human praxis seems to fade, that a new opportunity for humans to recognise themselves in history unexpectedly arises. In the tragic rift of sacrifice, in its extreme emptiness, what is useless is not yet meaningless. Right there, a new existential dimension seems to flourish.

---

65   Patočka 1989, p. 332.
66   Kosík 1995m, p. 27.

CHAPTER 4

Labour and Time: Karel Kosík's Temporal Materialism

Ivan Landa

1 Introduction

Karel Kosík belongs to the group of Central European thinkers who from the mid-1950s onwards broke out of the rigid ideological straitjacket of the official Marxist-Leninist doctrine and attempted to bring into Marxism new impulses from existentialism, neopositivism, Hegelianism – and also from phenomenology.[1] With regard to phenomenology, in Czechoslovakia this was taken on board more systematically not only by Kosík, but also by Ivan Dubský, Jiří Pešek, Karel Michňák, Josef Cibulka, Jiří Černý and Milan Průcha.[2] However, among these authors Kosík deserves a special place: He is often accepted as an important representative of phenomenological Marxism in East Central Europe. Accordingly, his *Dialectics of the Concrete* is read as a fresh attempt at combining both philosophical currents by developing central motifs taken from the late Husserl and above all from the early Heidegger with the help of a Marxian conceptual toolkit, or conversely by picking up on Marxian or Marxists' key ideas and reinterpreting them in a conceptually novel way with the use of a phenomenological idiom.[3] For example, Husserl's notion of the 'life world', originally understood as an ahistorical, *a priori* structure of meaning, is seen to be reformulated by Kosík (drawing on Marx, György Lukács and Lucien Goldmann) as a 'concrete totality', namely as a socially and historically variable structure of meaning.[4] However, it is Heidegger's fundamental ontology

---

1   The research and work on this article was supported by the Czech Science Foundation (GA ČR) within the project GA16-26686S 'Karel Kosík and the Fate of Phenomenological Marxism in East Central Europe'. The chapter in its current form is a reworked and expanded version of an article originally published in Czech under the title 'Kosík, Heidegger a praktický materialismus' [Kosík, Heidegger, and Practical Materialism], in Landa and Mervart 2018, pp. 177–210. The permission for publication of this chapter has been granted by the Institute of Philosophy, Czech Academy of Sciences, as a copyright holder.
2   See Kosík 1963b; Pešek 1966; Michňák 1968; Michňák 1969; Průcha 1965.
3   Kosík 1976.
4   For the motif of the *Lebenswelt* in the context of Marx and Marxism see Šrubař 2007, pp. 277–316.

that is considered to be most relevant for Kosík, with its focus on *Dasein*, everydayness, care or procuring etc. Furthermore, fundamental ontology can even be associated with the theoretical agenda of the philosophy of praxis, pursued not only by Kosík, but by many other phenomenological Marxists.[5]

In the following text I am going to complicate this picture, revisiting the interpretation of Kosík as a phenomenological Marxist. I shall argue instead that in the early 1960s Kosík presented a philosophically powerful critique of phenomenology from a Marxist point of view.[6] As a matter of fact, Kosík engages in a dialogue with Heidegger's and Husserl's ideas frequently. Nonetheless, upon closer inspection one can see clearly that while presenting a philosophical position that is alien to him, Kosík is critical of it, preparing the ground for a defence of his own position, namely that of the philosophy of praxis. Thus a *prima facie* impression of appropriating motifs or concepts from Heidegger or Husserl is merely an optical illusion, resulting from the fact that Kosík quite often composes his argument *via negationis*: he starts out from a certain claim or conception and points to their blind spots, convincing the reader to look for alternatives. He also applies precisely this procedure to phenomenology. In this respect, Kosík's critique of phenomenology contains traits of his theory of human being as *praxis*, or as ontoformative being, which is argued for indirectly through a polemic with the Heideggerian conception of human being as *Dasein*. I believe that fundamental ontology is perhaps the most decisive philosophical position that contributed negatively to Kosík's formulation of his philosophy of praxis. Kosík's polemic with Heidegger is largely concerned with

---

5   To mention the most important representatives of the philosophy of praxis: Gajo Petrović, Evald Ilyenkov, Genrikh S. Batishchev, Guido Davide Neri, Jan Szewczyk, Adolfo Sánchez Vázquez or György Márkus.

6   Kosík's rather distanced attitude towards phenomenology did not escape the notice of Jan Patočka, who once remarked that 'Kosík, on principle, refuses to be a phenomenologist, as he seeks only a "rational kernel" in phenomenology'. Patočka concluded: 'From our point of view, we should regret that he is not enough a phenomenologist'. See Patočka 2006a, pp. 306–27, p. 326. – The intellectual aversion towards phenomenology among many East-Central European Marxists from the 1940s onwards was built up thanks to György Lukács, who in several writings from the post-war period rejected Husserl and Heidegger as irrationalists. Lukács 1949, pp. 37–62. See also Lukács 1980a. Surprisingly, this aversion was alleviated again by Lukács, whose *History and Class Consciousness* inspired many post-war Marxists to engage with phenomenology, existentialism or positivism, since Lukács here defended a methodological view of Marxism, saying that one can be an orthodox Marxist without subscribing to any propositional content or doctrine, but solely by accepting the dialectical method. I believe that this idea of methodological Marxism provoked a wave of revisionist critiques aimed at Marxism as a doctrine, and simultaneously opened up a space for a fruitful reception of other philosophical currents, e.g. phenomenology.

the core issue of fundamental ontology, that of time and temporality. I shall argue that Kosík defends a 'temporal materialism' which he bases on the 'labour theory of time', claiming that labour is constitutive for time to have a temporal structure, making it a distinctively human time. I believe that the 'labour theory of time' functions as a lever used against fundamental ontology and its 'temporal idealism', replacing it with the philosophy of praxis.[7]

I will proceed in the following steps. Firstly, I will cast some light on the intellectual background that shaped Kosík's thought concerning praxis and labour. I shall briefly sketch Marx's programme of practical materialism, outlined in the *Theses on Feuerbach* in 1844, in order to indicate not only the major differences, but also the common ground shared by phenomenology and Marxism. Secondly, I shall turn to Kosík's ontology of labour as one possible way of elaborating upon the programme of practical materialism. For Kosík, labour is a material and conscious activity, epitomising the teleological structure through which (1) artefacts, institutions or artworks come into existence qua social entities, and social reality is established; furthermore, (2) anthropological difference is instituted; and perhaps most importantly (3) time in its three-dimensional temporal structure is constituted. In the following step, I shall turn my attention to the 'labour theory of time', explaining why and in what sense practical materialism is always also a *temporal* materialism. Here I am drawing not only on Kosík's *Dialectics of the Concrete*, but also on Marx's *Grundrisse*, which seems to be a principal source for Kosík's reflections on labour and time. I shall then follow up with a reconstruction of Kosík's objections raised against the basics of Heidegger's fundamental ontology. He is mainly concerned with the question as to whether temporality is grounded by labour as both a material and conscious activity, or vice versa. As I suggested earlier, in criticising Heidegger and fundamental ontology, Kosík defends, *via negationis*, the philosophy of praxis and an ontology of labour. Finally, I discuss several arguments put forth by the Czech phenomenologist Jan Patočka, critiquing Kosík's temporal materialism. I assume that Patočka's critique, which had a strong influence on Kosík, motivated him to rethink radically the pro-

---

7 William Blattner describes Heidegger's position in *Being and Time* as 'temporal idealism' in his remarkable book (see Blattner 1999). The only work which is explicitly devoted to the 'labour theory of time' and ontology of labour within the context of Marx's work is Gould 1978, pp. 56–68. Gould was evidently familiar with Kosík's *Dialectics of the Concrete*, since she mentions it in the bibliography at the end of the book. However, she does not reconstruct the labour theory of time following on from Kosík, but in direct linkage to Marx's *Grundrisse*. The fact that there are a number of manifest parallels between Gould's and Kosík's line of argument can be attributed to the fact that Kosík also based his position upon Marx's manuscripts, and his materialist conception of temporality is an elaboration upon Marx's thought.

gramme of the philosophy of praxis in totally new terms, within a philosophy of technology, inspired by the thought of the late Heidegger. Kosík abruptly revises the paradigm of production and rejects the pathos of revolutionary praxis, turning his attention to everyday practices and coping with ordinary things. In this sense, Kosík became a phenomenological Marxist only in the late 1960s, when he started working on a grand, though unfinished project dealing with a 'critique of technological reason'.

2   Practical Materialism

The French philosopher Jean-Toussaint Desanti voiced serious doubts as to whether Marxism can be placed in a dialogue with phenomenology at all.[8] Analogous attempts are hindered by the very fact that each philosophical current rests upon incompatible principles, which belong to alien intellectual traditions. With regard to phenomenology: it is part of a tradition that stresses the primacy of consciousness. Its main concern lies in descriptions of logical acts that are involved within the constitution of various domains of meaning and objectivity. The 'entity' responsible for the execution of logical acts is proclaimed to be a transcendental 'I', which plays the role of the principle.[9] By contrast, Marxism epitomises a radical shift away from the transcendentalist tradition, even though this shift had already been initiated by German Idealism, which has some substantial affinities with phenomenology. Briefly speaking, German Idealism, still preoccupied with the issue of consciousness and self-consciousness, made an important step towards the objectification of reason or spirit, so that the transcendental 'I' stretched beyond the sphere of mere subjectivity to the domain of objectivity. Being inspired by such a shift, Marxism focused on human practice or the 'active side' of human being, understanding praxis as a principle that constitutes the sphere of 'objective spirit': social reality and socioeconomic formation.

When Desanti suggests that Marxism accomplished a 'migration of the spirit', we should understand such a shift as representing a break with the previous philosophical tradition. Henceforward, more attention is paid to the study of socioeconomic formations, i.e. to amalgams of economy, social structure, politics, culture and various shades of human practice.[10] At the same

---

8   Desanti 1963.
9   Desanti 1963, Introduction.
10 Ibid. As a matter of fact, a 'migration of the spirit' took place much earlier, in the work of Hegel, who thematised, under the heading of 'objective spirit', social relations, institutions

time, Marxism attempted to theorise the historicity of socioeconomic formations, focusing on the anatomy of social revolutions, so that revolutionary praxis became the most important shade of human practice. In both cases, social structure and historical change are conceived as being closely tied to labour as a material and conscious activity exercised by persons in space and time, instead of by a transcendental 'I' which performs merely ideal or logical acts.[11]

The programmatic text announcing the 'migration of the spirit' is the *Theses on Feuerbach*, produced by Marx in 1845. Brief in terms of volume yet rich in content, the *Theses* are almost a stenographic record of claims, backed up with only hints of an argument. Nevertheless, the text had an immense influence on later developments both in Marx's thought and within Marxist philosophy, which – in retrospect – can be seen as a more systematic elaboration and extensive commentary on those fragmentary theses.

The *Theses* attack different strands of materialism and idealism (especially German Idealism). Already the first thesis points out the 'chief defect' of materialism: 'The chief defect of all hitherto existing materialism – that of Feuerbach included – is that the thing, reality, sensuousness, is conceived only in the form of the *object or of contemplation*, but not as *sensuous human activity, practice*, not subjectively. Hence, in contradistinction to materialism, the *active* side was developed abstractly by idealism – which, of course, does not know real, sensuous activity as such'.[12] Accordingly, materialism of every stripe is defective, since it is based on a false ontology, which in turn implies an inaccurate epistemology and theory of practice, since both epistemology and the theory of practice follow on from ontology, thus replicating its vices.

---

or economy. Michael Gubser recently argued that Husserl's phenomenology also was from its outset practically oriented, offering a 'philosophy of praxis' *sui generis*. It made not only significant contributions to ethics or political and social philosophy, but also played an important role, as a theoretical framework, in discussions concerning reforms during the Prague Spring of 1968 or debates on human rights in the Charter 77 movement. See Gubser 2014, pp. 1–2. One should add that Marxism pays, in turn, considerable attention to various forms of consciousness and self-consciousness, under the rubrics of the phenomena of superstructure, ideology, class consciousness or vanguardism.

11 For that very reason Habermas rightly noted that for Marx 'the subject of world constitution is not transcendental consciousness in general but the concrete human species, which reproduces its life under natural conditions'. Habermas 1968, p. 27. Habermas explicitly claims that the turn from 'consciousness' to 'material activity' in Marxism was motivated precisely by an endeavour to overcome transcendental phenomenology through the philosophy of praxis, which accounts for 'constitution' in terms of *material* instead of *transcendental* activity.

12 Marx 1978b, p. 143.

As concerns ontology, materialism conceptualises things or reality as something objective in space and time, which exist independently of knowing subjects and their conscious states, as well as their bodily existence and material doings. In this respect, things and reality are simply given to knowing subjects, who access them epistemically, mainly through receptive knowledge in (outer) sensuous intuition. Emphasising objectivity and the givenness of things and reality on the one hand, and the epistemic passivity of knowing subjects on the other hand, materialism seems to ignore entirely the 'active side' of human beings and their – theoretical and practical – spontaneity. Things and reality are out there as ready-made objects, always at hand, which can be manipulated by acting subjects.

Pretty much the same objection applies to Feuerbach's materialism. Feuerbach accomplished an anthropological turn and paid attention to human beings as sensuous and bodily subjects who act materially in space and time. However, as Marx notes, Feuerbach did not succeed in providing an account of the bodily existence of human beings in terms of subjectivity or self-consciousness, which would have enabled him to grasp human practice as both material and conscious doing. As Marx puts it: 'Feuerbach wants sensuous objects, really distinct from the thought objects, but he does not conceive human activity itself as *objective* activity'.[13]

Quite paradoxically, it is German Idealism that is credited by Marx for theorising the 'active side' – although still in a mystified way. The 'active side' is theorised as an ideal activity that is performed by pure thought: either as synthesis, positing or dialectics. From this it follows that material things and reality are also conceived in terms of an ideal: their essence is made up of a conceptual infrastructure that is constituted due to the performance of logical acts by reason or spirit, which makes them epistemically accessible to finite knowing subjects. This conception of practice brings Marx to the conclusion that idealism 'does not know real, sensuous activity as such'.[14]

Now, the practical materialism proposed by Marx is able to surpass the aforementioned defects of both materialism and idealism. First of all, things or reality are not taken as objective in the sense of something given to knowing or acting subjects, but instead as subjective, namely as something produced and reproduced by human practice. In a similar vein, human practice is conceptualised as a material or objective doing, through which things and reality obtain a distinctively human form, which is by the same token a social form,

---

13   Ibid.
14   Ibid.

since human practice is not only a physical modification of things and reality, but rather consists in conferring social status upon them: X was produced as a hammer, but furthermore it is also a means of production, a commodity etc.[15] To sum up: practical materialism theorises practice as a material and inherently social constitution, rather than a mere manipulation of given or ready-made objects, which for Marx is a kind of practice 'in its dirty, wheeler-dealing manifestation'. Besides that, human practice represents a 'genuinely human attitude' to reality; in a most eminent way it takes the shape of 'revolutionary' or 'practical-critical' activity.[16]

The programme of practical materialism, portrayed in a nutshell, can be developed systematically in at least three different directions, depending on where the emphasis is to be placed: either on the sphere of objectivity or social reality (product), material constitution (production), or the self-conscious character of objectivity (producer). Accordingly, practical materialism can be worked out in a direction of social ontology, the ontology of labour, or the theory of subjectivity. Social ontology will focus on social or economic structure, studying its historical transformations and thematising things/reality as displaying human/social form (artefacts, institutions, commodity, technology, artworks etc.). The ontology of labour steps back, focusing not so much on products, but rather on both their material and social constitution, understood as labour and as performance of mutual acts of recognition. Finally, the theory of subjectivity looks at social reality and material-cum-social constitution through the lens of self-conscious characteristics, grasping them as 'self-conscious material reality' or self-conscious material activity, as Sebastian Rödl recently argued, partly following on from Marx: self-consciousness is spontaneous knowledge of oneself *as* oneself, which is not isolated at all from material, spatiotemporal reality.[17] However, attempts at a materialist theory of subjectiv-

---

15   This point was frequently elaborated by Marx in his later writings, especially in polemicising against the 'Robinsonades'. Marx basically argues that human practice is social, since it is made possible by previous practice, as acting subjects use tools, materials, know-how or propositional knowledge that is a product of 'past' practice; and by the same token the outcomes of their doings can be further used by other persons; last but not least, acting subjects are involved in practice as bearers of certain social statuses (as wage-labourers etc.). – To understand human practice in terms of material constitution implies that things/reality acquire their form only through human practice. As we shall see later on, Kosík construed material constitution broadly as praxis, which includes the material aspect of labour, the normative aspect of the mutual recognition of persons, and last but not least an affective aspect of existentiality.
16   Ibid.
17   Rödl 2011. pp. 11–12. Rödl reads Marx as saying that the chief defect of materialism is its empiricism, which makes it blind to 'self-conscious material reality'. Empiricism leads

ity are to be traced to the surrealists, mixing Marxism with Freudianism. As Záviš Kalandra noticed, the surrealist experiments were explorations of the 'subjective knowledge of the subject', stating that they had an ambition to provide, at the same time, objective 'knowledge of the human subject'.[18]

Within a broader scope, *Dialectics of the Concrete* can be read as an ambitious, though only partially realised attempt at developing practical materialism in all three directions. However, social ontology is sketched out only very roughly by Kosík, as he spends much of his energy elaborating his ontology of labour, while the theory of subjectivity remains on the periphery of his actual interest. The main task of practical materialism is explained with the following words: 'to discover productive activity behind products and artefacts' and 'to dig out the authentic subject of history from beneath the sediment of fixed conventions'.[19] I argue that Kosík's ontology of labour implies a 'labour theory of time', so that practical materialism is at the same time also temporal materialism. The human, or social form conferred on things and reality *via* labour is thus always a temporal form that is structured in three dimensions.

3   The Ontology of Labour

The term 'labour' refers to the 'active side' of human being, which manifests itself empirically in concrete and historically determined forms of labour. Hence, the ontology of labour can either begin with an analysis of empirical and historical forms in order to reach the ontological structure, or ignore those forms, focusing directly on the 'active side', analysing labour as such. In developing his ontology of labour, Kosík sets out on the second path. Accordingly, he does not start out from an 'ontic' sphere, moving on to the ontological structure, abstracting from all concrete forms of labour that are placed under scrutiny by empirical disciplines such as political economy, sociology, psychology or history. He rather approaches the 'ontological' sphere *directly*, assuming that the ontology of labour 'does not offer an analysis of work processes in their totality or in their historical development', as it is concerned just 'with a single ques-

---

to an understanding of material reality, including knowing subjects, solely as spatiotemporal objects given to knowing subjects in sensual intuition. In contrast Rödl, following on from Marx, proposes a 'true' materialism, whose aim is to explain 'in what way first-personal knowledge', which is spontaneous, 'can relate to the material reality'. Rödl 2011, p. 30.

18   See Kalandra 1994, pp. 18–19.
19   Kosík 1976, p. 8 [translation slightly modified – IL].

tion: What is labour?'[20] Hence: whenever Kosík refers to the 'ontic' sphere, i.e. using examples of concrete forms of labour, he takes them solely as models of ontologically significant practice – that of labour.

Kosík proposes the following answer to the question 'What is labour?': 'Labor is a *happening* which permeates the entire existence of human being and constitutes its specifics'. Furthermore, 'in labor something fundamental takes place with human being and its existence, just as with the world of human being'.[21] As I have suggested above, by 'labour' Kosík does not refer to any particular practice performed by human beings in space and time, but rather to the *practice as such*, which infuses – so to speak – the whole human life form. However, at the same time, labour also plays a role of *constitutive* practice, since it makes up the specifics of the human life form, differentiating humans from animals. In this respect, the concept of labour functions here both as a *genus* and as a *differentia specifica*.[22]

Let's turn to labour as a constitutive practice, which makes up social and anthropological difference. Kosík expounds such a constitution as a triple metamorphosis. Labour transforms the natural into a distinctively *social* realm. Furthermore, labour transforms animal nature into specifically *human* nature. And most importantly, labour transforms natural into *human* time, originating the temporal structure. All those metamorphoses contribute to the establishment of the human life form.[23] Accordingly, the biological infrastructure, including instinctive behaviour, natural needs and desires, is surpassed through labour in creating the realm of socially and historically mediated needs, practices and things.

Unfortunately, Kosík is too laconic in his exposition, and as a result he does not provide a detailed account of labour as a constitutive practice. He seems to be satisfied with revoking Hegel's master/slave dialectics, accepting it as an 'elementary model of dialectic itself', which makes explicit the basic ontological structures.[24] This model is allegedly construed by Hegel in such a way that the point of departure becomes an asymmetric relation, which holds between animal creatures confronted with natural needs or desires, such as hunger or sexual desire. The asymmetric relation activates dynamics, resulting in the

---

20   Kosík 1976, p. 118.
21   Kosík 1976, pp. 137–8 [slightly modified translation – IL].
22   Jan Patočka rightly pointed out that such a duality leads to a conceptual ambiguity, which I will explain in more detail below. Patočka 2006a, p. 323.
23   Kosík states: 'The three-dimensionality of human time as a constitutive dimension of man's being is anchored in labor as man's *objective doing*'. Kosík 1976, p. 122.
24   Kosík 1976, p. 121.

metamorphosis of the 'first nature' into the 'second nature', since the manner of how natural needs and desires are satisfied by animal creatures is altered. Usually, whenever an animal creature experiences a certain need, it *has to be* satisfied immediately, meaning that animal life is driven simply by 'biological imperatives'.[25] However, Hegel is primarily interested in an ontologically significant situation, in which the animal creature breaks free from the yoke of biological imperatives, cancels the immediacy of natural needs by holding them in check, and thus weakens the necessity of satisfying them right now. The main point seems to be precisely that this 'breakthrough' does not occur passively, as is the case whenever an animal is forced by external circumstances to put off the satisfaction of e.g. hunger, as nothing in its vicinity *can* serve as a food. Hegel assumes – at least according to Kosík's reading of him – that the situation becomes ontologically significant when the 'breakthrough' or holding desire in check happens actively, through a *consciously made resolution*, which in turn implies an *act of labour* that is both material and conscious. The act of labour is thus a mediating element, 'inserted' between natural needs and satisfaction, or consumption, by the animal creature.

Kosík follows on from Hegel's model, placing emphasis on labour as a mediating element, due to which animal desire (*Begierde*) is transformed into human desire (*Trieb*), contributing thus to the anthropogenesis and to the founding and shaping of the human life form.[26] However, these transformations depend on a shift within practice: from instinctive behaviour to an intentional activity. As Kosík notes: 'Having transcended the level of instinctive activity, and having turned into an exclusively human doing, labour transforms the given, the natural and the non-human, and adapts it to human needs even as it realizes human intentions in material of nature'.[27] Both labour and instinctive behaviour are material doings. Besides that, both, at least in the case of higher

---

25 Here I am adopting the term coined by John McDowell, which is used in his discussion of anthropological difference. See McDowell 1994, p. 117.

26 Kosík 1976, p. 131, n. 46.

27 Kosík 1976, p. 121. Kosík's philosophy of praxis was criticised by Robert Kalivoda, the Czech Marxist philosopher and aesthetician, from a naturalistic point of view. For Kalivoda, the philosophy of praxis takes praxis to be a *factum brutum*, and thus totally ignores the biological infrastructure of human existence with its basic needs and desires, which make up an 'anthropological constant'. See Kalivoda 2018, pp. 135–56, p. 150, n. 19. However, Kosík does not turn to biological infrastructure for the reason that praxis or labour constitute anthropological difference, setting up a 'second nature' without diminishing the 'first nature' at all. He assumes that in the case of humans, natural needs and desires are always filtered through the sieve of culture or civilisation. In this respect, there is no anthropological constant or purely biological infrastructure.

animals, are conscious doings. Nonetheless, only in the case of animal creatures who share the human life form is it possible to say that it is a conscious activity, which transforms the 'given, natural and non-human' according to intentions previously set up in their mind. Using Marx's example: a bee's or spider's doings resemble in various respects the doings performed by humans, since they are material activity, e.g. spinning a web, constructing a honeycomb cell etc.; they even look more skilful than the building of houses done by humans.[28] Still, the difference lies on the level consciousness, in the realisation of purposes and intentions, materialised in space and time with the help of materials, tools or machines.

In this way we finally arrive at the conception of labour as a *genus*, according to which labour epitomises *practice as such*. As a conscious activity it exemplifies a teleological, not solely a causal structure. This means that through labour not only physical properties of things and reality are modified, but also that intentions and purposes become materialised. Accordingly, material reality is formed on the basis of intentions and purposes, which in themselves reflect certain needs and desires. In this respect, intentions and needs are the structuring principles, guiding acts of labour. As Marx puts it, intentions 'determine the mode of [...] activity with the rigidity of law'.[29] From this it follows that normativity is in play already at the level of material activity, and does not enter only at the level of mutual recognition of persons. Importantly, further components of the teleological structure, namely material and tools, are also themselves exemplifications of the teleological structure. Only as such can they become a part of newly performed acts of labour. As they are products of *past* acts of labour, they are materialisations of intentions and therefore can reappear as use values in the labouring process. Those materialisations display a function, which was conferred on them and which also determines 'the mode of activity with the rigidity of law'. To put it crudely, teleological structure already implies the notion of normativity.[30]

---

28   'A spider conducts operations which resemble those of the weaver, and a bee would put many a human architect to shame by the construction of its honeycomb cells. But what distinguishes the worst architect from the best of bees is that the architect builds the cell in his mind before he constructs it in wax. At the end of every labour process, a result emerges which had already been conceived by the worker at the beginning, hence already existed ideally'. See Marx 1976, p. 284.

29   Marx states: 'Man not only effects a change of form in the materials of nature; he also realizes [verwirklicht] his own purpose in those materials. And this is a purpose he is conscious of, it determines the mode of his activity with the rigidity of a law, and he must subordinate his will to it. This subordination is no mere momentary act'. Ibid.

30   György Márkus, the Hungarian Marxist, makes precisely this point within his ontology of

The sketched account of labour as genus indicates that Kosík in fact conceptualises labour as objectification, since through labour the inner, ideal or mental becomes something outer, real or material. And as the act of labour is in itself a complex process, one can break down such an act into a series of partial objectifications, each contributing to the accomplishment of the final goal. For that reason, I assume that Kosík's ontology of labour embraces, in principle, the 'expressivist' theory of human practice. Charles Taylor introduced the term 'expressivism' in his monumental book on Hegel.[31] He uses the term to refer to the fact that our practices, artefacts or institutions are objectifications, which express the human self – not only the mental states of this or that person, but rather the self-identity of both a particular person and human communities.[32] So the basic idea behind the 'expressivist' theory is this: Certain *inner* powers or ideal structures, such as self-conception, can be realised only if they are employed. Unless we act, we cannot know what we think or feel, and more importantly, who we are. By the same token, through material properties we can express certain mental properties, thoughts or feelings, and furthermore: our self-conception. Hence, by those objectifications, which are expressions, we do not aim solely toward others, but also self-referentially toward ourselves. In short: we gain a full self-conception only through the permanent process of objectification. I think Kosík adopts pretty much the same position, although for him the paradigm of objectification is labour taken as a genus of human practice. Accordingly, he takes things and social reality as the expressions of both mental and physical states of particular persons, and more importantly as the expressions of the human life form as such. Analogically, labour is not

---

labour, which resembles in many respects that of Kosík. Accordingly, Márkus claims that 'while objects of nature are, so to speak, "neutral" to the mode of their use, products of human labour as objectifications are not; in the real context of social life they have a normal, a *"proper"* use [...]. A glass is intended for drinking and, roughly speaking, something *is* a glass when it is normally and systematically used in this function. And humanly produced objects become social use-values precisely through the fact that there are definite *rules* [...], which circumscribe both the end and the manner of their use'. See Márkus 1986, p. 52.

31   Taylor 1975. See also the book by Ernst M. Lange, who similarly argues that Marx holds an 'expressivist' theory of human practice. Lange 1980.

32   Taylor 1975, p. 13, n. 1, see also p. 15 and p. 16, where Taylor notes: 'It is this fuller model of subjective expression which underlies what I have called here the expressivist theory. If we think of our life as realising an essence or form, this means not just the embodying of this form in reality, it also means defining in a determinate way what this form is. And this shows in another way the important difference between the expressivist model and the Aristotelian tradition: for the former, the idea which a man realizes is not wholly determinate beforehand; it is only made fully determinate in being fulfilled'.

only a modification of physical properties of things (or of mental properties of persons), but it is moreover an objectification, through which human intentions and the human life form become manifest as well as constituted.

However, there is still an ambiguity in Kosík's ontology of labour, which is closely linked to the conception of labour as both *genus* and *differentia specifica*.[33] It manifests itself especially in the equivocal use of the terms 'labour' and 'praxis'. Kosík frequently defines praxis in a same manner as labour: praxis is defined as a 'sphere of human being', and it is further specified as an element that 'permeates the whole of man and determines him in his totality' and so on.[34] Apparently, labour as genus is identical to praxis, grasped as pure 'ontoformativity'. This results in equating the ontology of labour with the philosophy of praxis. However, at the same time, labour is taken to be something that constitutes human specifics. Hence, it is not a genus, but rather a species of praxis, one among many, alongside mutual recognition of persons or existentiality. The ontology of labour is then only a part of the philosophy of praxis, just as the theories of recognition and of affectivity.

Kosík does not bring much light into this opacity. Unsurprisingly, he presents his philosophy of praxis by referring again to a further elaboration of Hegelian master/slave dialectics. In Hegel's model, roughly speaking, social statuses or social facts depend on the exercise of mutual recognition among persons.[35] This mutual recognition is not exercised solely individually, but collectively, as Kosík emphasises. Furthermore, the acts of recognition do not take place in some social vacuum, and so they are already situated within a 'social space', which is in itself a product of past praxis. Any attempt to emancipate oneself from the social space, e.g. in social revolution, appears foolish, since a revolutionary collapse of the social space is simultaneously the constitution of a new one. Another moment of praxis, namely existentiality, relates to an important feature of human practice, namely its affective and emotive facet: human practice is always imbued either with fear, or anxiety, joy, laughter, hope etc.[36] As Kosík remarks: 'Praxis is not an *external* determination of man: neither a machine nor a dog have or know praxis. Neither a machine nor a dog know

---

[33] As I mentioned earlier, Jan Patočka had already pointed out the conceptual ambiguity in Kosík's ontology of labour. Patočka 2006a, p. 323.

[34] Kosík 1976, pp. 136–7.

[35] Kosík provides the following example of the act of recognition that institutes social status and normative structure: 'Gods exist only for those who recognise them'. Furthermore, he notes that 'beyond the borders of a country these turn to mere wood, just as a king becomes a common man'. Kings or gods are only a 'social relationship and product', or simply: social constructs made by humans. Kosík 1976, p. 168.

[36] Kosík 1976, p. 139.

the fear of death, the anxiety of nothingness, or the joy of beauty'.[37] Hence, although animal creatures are affective and emotive, Kosík reminds us, referring to Hegel, that they are *not* engaged in a struggle for recognition, which consists in a conflict between animality and humanity, between biological and social, between first and second nature. By the way, if there is any trace of the positive influence of Heidegger on Kosík in *Dialectics of the Concrete* at all, then it can be tracked down to the philosophy of praxis, implying – with its stress on the moment of existentiality – a theory of subjectivity, which was not elaborated in further detail by Kosík.

4 Temporal Materialism

Kosík's temporal materialism can be boiled down to the following claim: Labour constitutes a temporal structure which is a constitutive 'dimension of [human] being'.[38] In *Dialectics of the Concrete* it is possible to encounter two readings of such a claim. While a weaker, 'expressivist' reading suggests that labour is only a manifestation of a temporal structure, in a stronger reading labour itself constitutes this temporal structure. In my view both readings are compatible for Kosík, since he states: 'The three-dimensionality of time as a form of [human's] own being manifests itself in human being and constitutes itself in the process of objectification, i.e. in labour'.[39] As objectification, labour forms a temporal structure, which is by the same token manifested in or through labour, as well as through a variety of human practices such as play or linguistic practice, in this way becoming transparent to humans. Thus both readings make up a doctrine of temporal materialism. However, in presenting this doctrine I will focus solely on 'constitution', instead of on 'manifestation', since the former seems to be much more contentious and less evident than the latter.

However, I shall first begin with the terminology. I follow on from John McTaggart's discussion concerning the use of temporal predicates that reveal the important characteristics of temporal structure. Whereas McTaggart defends temporal nihilism, according to which time is not real, I will employ those characteristics in order to explain Kosík's temporal materialism. I believe that, despite his nihilist conclusion, McTaggart introduced useful terminology and

---

37 Kosík 1976, p. 137.
38 Kosík 1976, p. 121.
39 Kosík 1976, p. 138 [modified translation – IL].

important distinctions that are instrumental in understanding the tenets of the 'labour theory of time'.[40]

McTaggart introduced the concepts of the *moment* and *event*, defining the *moment* as 'a position in time', and the *event* as 'the content of a position in time'.[41] We usually describe moments either as 'earlier-simultaneous-later', or as 'past-present-future'. According to McTaggart's nomenclature, the first description orders moments in an 'A-series', while the second description orders them in a 'B-series'. With regard to an A-series, events do not occupy permanent positions in time, so it is aptly used for describing change. An event E *successively* occupies one position after another, first being a future, then a present and finally a past one. Furthermore, the order within an A-series is asymmetrical, centred at the present moment ('now'), so that E is a future or past event relative to this 'now'.[42] By contrast, in a B-series events occupy permanent positions in time, even though the series is always 'lengthening' as further events happen. Moreover, a B-series exemplifies a decentralised order, which is still asymmetrical, since no moment enjoys primacy over others. So, if one event E_1 happens to occur earlier than another event E_2, E_1 is then forever to be described as 'earlier' than E_2. An important feature of a B-series, due to the permanency of moments, pertains to the fact that we basically distinguish them by using conventionally established determinations ('hours', 'days', 'months', 'years' etc.), whereas within an A-series moments do not take on any conventional determinations.[43]

Kosík's chief claim, according to which temporal structure is constituted through labour, can be reformulated now in at least two ways in the light of the above distinctions: Firstly, that labour constitutes A-time in its three dimensions: past, present and future; and secondly, that labour constitutes B-time in its three dimensions: earlier, now and later.[44] To be sure, none of the formu-

---

40 Carol Gould used the heading of the 'labour theory of time' in her interpretation of Marx's *Grundrisse*. Gould 1980, especially the chapter 'Ontology of Labour: Objectification, Technology, and the Dialectics of Time', pp. 56–68. See also Brockhaus 1984, pp. 91–5, p. 92.
41 McTaggart 1908, pp. 457–74.
42 McTaggart 1908, p. 458. Here I basically follow Koch's interpretation of McTaggart, stating that an A-series is 'nunc-centric', while a B-series is decentralised. For Koch, an A-series has its centre 'now' and 'here', when or where embodied subjectivity, capable of epistemic self-relation, appears. See Koch 2006, p. 134.
43 Interestingly, McTaggart introduced a third way of how to order the moments, which he referred to as a 'C-series'. This resembles both a static and symmetrical arrangement of items, so that it is not a temporal order at all.
44 I am adopting this distinction between A- and B-time from Hugh Mellor. See Mellor 1998, pp. 8–11.

lations denies that many events, if not most of them, take place within time without being bound to the act of labour. For example, the development of the solar system or the origin of life on Earth took place long ago, without the existence in the universe of humankind, for whom the 'active side' is characteristic. However, the sense of Kosík's temporal materialism is merely that there is an ontologically significant connection between the human life form, labour and temporal structure, which requires clarification. Thus, whenever Kosík speaks of 'time', what he is referring to is always 'human time', which is related to the human life form.[45]

The question is: Does labour constitute A-time or B-time, or perhaps both? Is labour intimately related to a temporal succession of moments, or rather to a relationship between moments? In *Dialectics of the Concrete* Kosík focuses almost exclusively on the first formulation, relating to *subjective* A-time. Far less attention is paid by him to the second formulation, relating to *objective* B-time. A-time is subjective, since it is centred on the knowing and acting subject, while B-time is objective, as it is decentralised and composed of moments fixed by dates (regardless of the fact that these are conventional products of human linguistic practice). In my presentation, I shall rather concentrate on the first mentioned formulation, asking whether it is possible to meaningfully claim that subjective A-time is constituted through labour in all of its three dimensions.

Kosík's analysis of labour as genus culminated in the finding that labour embodies a teleological structure, which exhibits both subjective and objective aspects. It is a material activity, in which intentions and purposes, which reflect human needs, are consciously materialised. The material upon which the act of labour is performed undergoes changes of its qualities, with the contribution of tools. The material and tools, however, in themselves are nothing 'given', but are also the product of labour. As a result, it applies that objects which are a part of the labour process as products become inner elements of the teleological structure. The aforementioned aspects of labour, in Kosík's view, are the material origins of temporal structure (A-time).

---

45 Carol Gould makes a similar point in her interpretation of Marx's *Grundrisse*. See Gould 1980, p. 57. Here she substantiates the thesis that 'for Marx, in the *Grundrisse* at least, labor creates time or introduces time into world', further claiming that 'labor is the origin of time – both of human time-consciousness and of the objective measure of time'. Accordingly, labour is at the genesis of both A-time and B-time. Besides that, labour is the condition that enables us to form time-consciousness, or a temporal understanding of both natural and social phenomena. Gould 1980, pp. 56–7. As I have suggested above, Kosík holds a more moderate position, arguing exclusively in favour of the hypothesis that labour is the origin of A-time and its temporal dimensions, without elaborating a 'labour theory of B-time'.

Let us recall that A-time is subjective, since at its centre is an acting subject. And it is precisely this centre that is closely linked with the act of labour. Marx called this 'living labour'. He assumed that in living labour the form undergoes a change, without any change of content occurring. This purely *formal* change affects not only objects, which take on new qualities, but also intentions or plans, which are materialised. For example, in labour a piece of wood is transformed into a table, by which the intention to *make a table* is materialised in this piece of wood. The course of this transformation can be broken down into steps or sequences. It is necessary to perform these in order to reach the goal. For example, if we are building a house, this involves a whole range of activities and functions, which are ordered in a certain manner: from the laying of the foundations, insulation and plumbing etc. to the walling of the ground floor, construction of the perimeter walls, reinforcement of the beams or construction of the roof. It is significant that 'living labour' is not performed aimlessly, but that it contains a finality. The act of labour has a direction, as it is oriented towards a certain goal, in which labour is 'living' only up to the moment when the goal is achieved. This means that in 'living labour' we have a succession, which has its centre in the act of labour or in the acting subject, and whose moments are ordered in a mutually asymmetrical relationship.

Let us elaborate upon this finding with regard to Marx's reflection on the 'temporality of things' as presented in the economic manuscripts *Grundrisse*. Kosík does not mention this reflection explicitly, but there cannot be the slightest doubt that he took inspiration from and developed upon it. Marx's economic manuscripts *Grundrisse*, written within the period of 1857–59, contain this dense passage, which Kosík most probably drew upon: 'The transformation of the material by living labour, by the realisation of living labour in the material – a transformation which, as purpose, determines labour and is its purposeful activation (a transformation which does not only posit the form as external to the inanimate object, as a mere vanishing image of its material consistency) – thus preserves the material in a definite form, and subjugates the transformation of the material to the purpose of labour. Labour is the living, form-giving fire; it is the transitoriness of things, their temporality, as their formation by living time'.[46]

---

[46] Marx 1973, pp. 360–1. In his analysis Marx relates to the 'simple production process'. This means that he does not engage with the complex production process in which the accumulation of capital takes place. His reflections herein are developed within the following context: he attempts to map the very complex correlation between 'living labour time', 'objectified labour time', 'living labour capacity' and 'production costs'. Marx takes the view that 'living labour time reproduces nothing more than that part of objectified labour time

A number of important points are hinted at here, in particular the idea that living labour, performed here and now, is realised in material. When 'realisation' is referred to, this means that this concerns a transformation, a change of form. Transformation is not a destruction or abolition of the preceding form, or the imposition of an absolutely new form which would be 'external to the inanimate object'. Even if the preceding form is abolished, it is at the same time preserved – in Hegelian terms: it is 'aufgehoben'. Another idea is concealed in the range of metaphors, for example, 'living, form-giving fire', 'transitoriness of things', or 'temporality of things'. How are we to interpret the claim that labour constitutes the 'temporality of things'?

Marx conceptualises labour as objectification. Living labour is thus objectification taking place 'here' and 'now', whose moment is material and tools, namely the products of labour. Marx's position is now approximately the following: If these aforementioned objects are moments of living labour, their content or 'substance' is thereby retained. This 'substance', as he notes, is 'viewed economically [...] objectified labour time'.[47] In the case that objects do not become a moment of living labour, they are left 'as a mere thing, at the prey of processes of chemical decay etc'.[48] This means that it is possible to identify an item (material, tools) and objectified labour time. This then exists in a dual manner: either in a 'unilateral objectified form' as a 'mere thing', when it is left 'at the prey of decay', or as a 'means and end – of living labour', when it has material being.[49]

As a mere thing labour is 'vanished', it is objectified labour time, which constitutes only the 'external form of its natural substance'. Marx's example is a form of cylinder which is external to iron, or a form of table external to wood or plastic, etc. An analogy of living labour would thus be a living tree, in which the content is retained in the form of a tree, i.e. in such a form which is 'natural' to wood. To the same degree it applies that in the form of a table, wood

---

(of capital) which appears as an equivalent for the power of disposition over living labour capacity, and which, therefore, as an equivalent, must replace the labour time objectified in this labouring capacity, i.e. replace the production costs of the living labour capacities, in other words, must keep the workers alive as workers', since production costs are not merely costs for the production of an object, but also for the reproduction of labour power. Living labour capacity is a certain skill which is applied or implemented in the labour process (e.g. craft skill applied in the production of a table). However, this capacity must reproduce the goal of 'producing'. Marx accordingly states that labour capacity is objectified labour time expended on its 'production'. Marx 1973, p. 359.

47 Marx 1973, p. 360.
48 Ibid.
49 Ibid.

has an 'unnatural' form, because it has not grown into such a form, which is alien to it. However, as material being an object becomes a part of living labour, which – figuratively speaking – breathes life into the form and content (table and wood): 'Objectified labour ceases to exist in a dead state as an external, indifferent form on the substance, because it is itself again posited as a moment of living labour; as a relation of living labour to itself in an objective material, as the *objectivity* of living labour (as means and end [*Objekt*])'.[50] Living labour, as has been stated a number of times, alters the material in accordance with the purpose of labour: 'The transformation of the material by living labour [...] thus preserves the material in a definite form, and subjugates the transformation of the material to the purpose of labour'.[51] And it is precisely this change or transformation that Marx interprets as its 'temporalisation'. The fact that the object ceases to be a mere thing left at the prey of chemical decay and becomes a material being of living labour, in its result means that it is temporalised. For this reason it is said of labour that it is the 'temporalisation of things'.

Marx illustrates his conclusion with the aid of the following illuminating example:

> When cotton becomes yarn, yarn becomes fabric, fabric becomes printed etc. or dyed etc. fabric, and this becomes, say, a garment, then (1) the substance of cotton has preserved itself in all these forms. (The chemical process, regulated by labour, has everywhere consisted of an exchange of (natural) equivalents etc.); (2) in each of these subsequent processes, the material has obtained a more useful form, a form making it more appropriate to consumption; until it has obtained at the end the form in which it can directly become an object of consumption, when, therefore, the consumption of the material and the suspension of its form satisfies a human need, and its transformation is the same as its use. The substance of cotton preserves itself in all of these processes; it becomes extinct in one form of use value in order to *make way for a higher one, until the object is in being as an object of direct consumption.*[52]

For Marx, labour is a process culminating in consumption. It is therefore possible to understand labour as a progressive 'increasing' of use-value, which we can illustrate as the series: cotton → yarn → fabric → printed/dyed etc. fabric → garment. The individual phases always demonstrate the transformation that

---

50   Ibid.
51   Marx 1973, pp. 360–1.
52   Marx 1973, p. 361.

has taken place. The new form raises the use-value, and at the same time narrows down the number of possibilities of further transformations, entirely in accordance with the narrowly profiled set of needs that are satisfied in consumption. As Marx notes, change of form is an ever greater adaptation of the object to a certain need, which culminates in its satisfaction. This means that it is directed towards the product or better: to the act of consumption, by which the *dimension of future*, which is constituted in labour, manifestly comes to the forefront.

We may further divide acts of labour into phases, just as the material and tools used can be sorted according to their particular functions, which at a certain moment become constituents of living labour. Material enters into it as objectified labour time: first it is cotton, second yarn, third fabric etc. So this material as well as tools form a *dimension of the past*, as products of dead labour, despite the fact that it was once living labour. A series of phases of the labour process are located in a mutual relationship which is asymmetrical, since yarn cannot precede cotton, fabric yarn etc. In this the act of labour or living labour is always at the centre of the process (present) directed towards a certain goal (future), utilising material and tools (past). As such it is the originator and at the same time a synthesis of the past, present and future.

I think Kosík follows on precisely from the outlined reflection on the 'temporality of things', when he asserts that temporality of A-time is constituted in labour. Through the act of labour, 'living labour time' (present) is constituted, synthesising objectified labour time (past) with intentions or purposes (future). However, Kosík takes the assumption concerning the 'temporality of things' to extremes. According to him, we can comprehend the temporalisation of things in living labour also in the sense that temporality (= living labour time) is spatialised in a form of use-value. Kosík thus extends the analysis of A-time by an analysis of space, although in truth he does so only in passing: 'As objective doing, labour is a special mode of identity of time (temporality) and space (extension), as two fundamental dimensions of human being, of a specific form of man's movement in the world'.[53] This means that temporality, or more precisely, a synthesis of three dimensions, containing a form of succession and change, is constituted in labour. Whereas living labour is a time succession, the labour product 'appears as the condensation or *abolition* of the time succession, as inertness and duration'.[54] The product of labour is therefore an 'incarnation' of the labour process and of temporal succession, in which the

---

53   Kosík 1976, p. 122.
54   Ibid.

product is the spatialisation of temporality. However, we could similarly consider the temporalisation of space whenever an object becomes a component of the act of labour. As such labour 'appears as a cycle of activity and duration, of movement and objectivity', or a transition of time into space and space into time.[55]

5 Against Heidegger

Let us now take a look at Kosík's critique of Heidegger from the standpoint of temporal materialism. First of all, we must emphasise that Kosík considered Heidegger to be a thinker who deserves the credit for the reorientation of the attention of phenomenology from themes such as 'intentionality', 'reduction' or the 'transcendental Ego' to the 'active side'. At the same time, however, Kosík reproaches him for failing to reach the position of the philosophy of praxis. His tone in *Dialectics of the Concrete* is therefore predominantly polemical, in which his main objections are directed towards Heidegger's allegedly inadequate conception of human practice and of temporality.

It is certainly not without interest that Kosík took part in a dialogue with Heidegger in connection with the question as to what is economy. There are various paths that could be taken in seeking a response to this question, and Kosík surprisingly inclines towards the phenomenological method. He justifies his decision in the following words: 'Important for the authenticity of our further reasoning is not how people answer the question about economics but rather what economics *is* to them, prior to any questioning and any contemplation. One always has a certain understanding of reality that precedes explication. Itself an elementary layer of consciousness, this pre-theoretical understanding is the basis for the *possibility* of the culture and the cultivation through which one ascends from a preliminary understanding to a conceptual cognition of reality. The belief that reality in its phenomenal appearance is peripheral [...] leads to a fundamental error [...]'.[56]

The search for an answer to the question concerning the nature of economy must therefore begin with a detailed analysis of the pre-theoretical understanding of the actors who are part of the economic reality, who experience and understand it in one way or another. To be sure, political economy always builds upon this pre-theoretical understanding, whether it corrects it or develops fur-

---

55 Ibid.
56 Kosík 1976, p. 36.

ther upon it. In addition, Kosík is of the opinion that the economic structure cannot be reached directly, but rather has to be arrived at *via* a number of mediating steps, in which it is necessary to start from the phenomenal appearance. We should therefore reformulate the initial question differently. Instead of asking what economy is, we should ask: How is economic reality given to us, how does it appear to human beings?[57]

Kosík's answer is as follows: 'The primary and elementary mode in which economics exists for man is care'.[58] Although Kosík here adopts the central concept of Heidegger's fundamental ontology, his intention is to demonstrate that care is in fact only a 'reified' praxis, since it is neither a *constitution* of social reality nor its *revolutionary* transformation.[59] It is important to stress that Heidegger chose *care* as the starting point of his analyses, in order to arrive at more fundamental, ontological structures, expounding our pre-theoretical understanding of being via a description of practices such as the use of tools or the manipulation of objects. And he reveals the most general framework of such an understanding, which according to him is original temporality. William Blattner thus appositely refers to Heidegger's approach here as 'the phenomenology of everyday life', since Heidegger's aim is not to present a philosophy of praxis but to reveal the temporal structure of human existence.[60]

However, according to Kosík, the phenomenology of everyday life, oriented towards diverse manifestations of 'care', merely reveals that care is only a 'reified' mode of praxis. Accordingly, if human being is primarily care, social reality appears to humans as something given, in which they exist in a mode of procuring, as Heidegger terms the practice linked with care. Kosík criticises such a conception of the 'active side' and also proposes to replace fundamental ontology with an ontology of labour (or philosophy of praxis). He states: 'Procuring as the universal reified image of human praxis is not *the process of producing and forming* an objective-practical human world, but is rather the manipulation of ready-made implements as of the total of civilisation's resources and requirements'.[61] Elsewhere he adds: 'Procuring is praxis in its *phenomenally alienated form* which does not point to the *genesis* of the human world [...], but rather expresses the praxis of everyday manipulation, with man employed in

---

57   Kosík 1976, p. 37. To be sure, Kosík uses phenomenological method to arrive at the conclusion that social reality or economic structure as its essence is nothing 'given'.
58   Ibid.
59   Kosík 1976, p. 112.
60   Blattner 2006, p. 9. See also the commentary on *Being and Time* by Dreyfus, in which he characterises Heidegger's position as the 'hermeneutics of everydayness'. See Dreyfus 1990.
61   Kosík 1976, p. 41.

a system of *ready-made* "things", i.e., implements'.[62] And finally he notes: 'The shift from "labour" to "procuring" reflects in a mystified fashion the process of intensified fetishisation of human relations, a fetishisation through which the human world reveals itself to the everyday consciousness [...] as a *ready-made* world of devices, implements and relations, a stage for the individual's social movement, for his initiative, employment, ubiquity, sweat, in one word – as procuring'.[63]

If, together with Heidegger, we theorise the 'active side' as procuring, we thereby obscure the fact that social reality and the economic structure are products of practices of concrete people and social groupings. In addition to this, the conception of the 'active side' as procuring, i.e. as the manipulation of objects that are at our disposal, conceals the fact that in modern societies, it is human beings who are manipulated by objects and by a whole system of apparatuses (interestingly, this is the point stressed by Heidegger in his late reflections on the essence of technology). This has an important consequence. Whereas Heidegger sees the facticity of human existence in our 'thrownness', Kosík demonstrates that such facticity comprises a further layer, namely that human beings become a component of a system of apparatuses and functions, so that the 'active side' is reduced to mere manipulation. Heidegger is thus exposed to a similar objection, raised by Marx against traditional materialism in *Theses on Feuerbach*, namely that traditional materialism knows *praxis* only 'in its dirty, wheeler-dealing manifestation'.

However, Heidegger's analysis of care supposedly has a further weakness, connected to an interpretation of the temporality of human existence, which is an obstacle to a better understanding of both being and time. Such a harsh criticism grows out of Kosík's conviction that temporality is closely linked with material and conscious activity, i.e. with labour conceptualised as objectification. As Kosík states: 'Without objectification there is no temporality'.[64] Hence Kosík assumes that Heidegger, in his analysis of care, ignores the objective or material aspect of labour, and as a result also neglects to thematise ontocreativity and its linkage with temporality.

In the opening passages of *Being and Time*, Heidegger outlines a plan of fundamental ontology, the declared aim of which is to understand being from time.[65] In the course of his reflections, Heidegger reveals the basic ontological

---

62   Kosík 1976, p. 39.
63   Ibid.
64   Kosík 1976, p. 122.
65   Heidegger 1996, p. 16. Heidegger notes that 'being is to be conceived in terms of time', and he further explains: 'The meaning of the being of that being we call Da-sein proves to be

structure of human existence, or *Dasein*, for whom it is symptomatic that 'it belongs to its most proper being to have an understanding of this being and to sustain a certain interpretation of it'.[66] This ontological structure is conceptualised as temporality. However, Heidegger does not conceive temporality as a medium in which human existence would be simply 'located'. It is rather so that temporality permeates throughout human existence, or more precisely speaking human existence itself is temporal in its essence. One of the main tasks of fundamental ontology therefore consists in an 'elaboration of the *temporality of being*'.[67]

Although this issue is closely linked with the common or 'vulgar' conception of time, it nevertheless cannot be simply reduced to it. We may describe the common, or 'vulgar' conception of time as A-time, which is characterised by change, or by the succession of moments: future, present and past. Or it can be also depicted as B-time, i.e. an invariable order of moments that can be dated.[68] However, for Heidegger temporality means something else, as he claims that both A-time and B-time 'originate from temporality'.[69] If he speaks of temporality, what he means here is the *inner* structure of every moment of time, which is described by him as a synthesis of three ecstasies: futurity, present and having-been.[70] Heidegger therefore seems to approach to original temporality analogously to A-time, although importantly he abstracts from the features of A-time, namely from succession and change, and keeps its three dimensions as simultaneous ecstasies, each of which is for him 'equally original': they are always there at once in a single moment.[71]

The original temporality is manifested in human self-understanding, which is defined partially by what the human being has been hitherto, and partially by what he or she intends to become. Accordingly, human beings are directed into the future, by which they transcend their existence 'here' and 'now'. *Via* their actual or imagined possibilities, humans gain a certain self-understanding, so

---

temporality. [...] Time must be brought to light and genuinely grasped as the horizon of every understanding and interpretation of being. For this to become clear we need an *original explication of time as the horizon of the understanding of being in terms of temporality as the being of Da-sein which understands being*'. Heidegger 1996, p. 15.

66   Heidegger 1996, p. 13.
67   Heidegger 1996, p. 17.
68   On this way of interpreting 'vulgar' time as B-time, as well as on 'datability' see Heidegger 1996, pp. 382–3.
69   Heidegger 1996, p. 16.
70   Heidegger 1996, p. 302.
71   Heidegger 1996, pp. 302–3. For more on this point see Koch 2006, p. 412; and Blattner 1999, p. 125.

that they choose one or another option, while the implicitly ultimate possibility, which is strictly speaking a necessity, is death.[72] However, at the same time this self-understanding is defined by what human beings have been, what they have become, which options they have chosen or neglected etc. Heidegger refers to this aspect as 'thrownness'. Importantly, Heidegger adds that the 'having-been arises from the future'.[73] The realised possibilities acquire their significance only thanks to what a human being can still become in future. In this respect, death as the ultimate possibility concludes not only the future horizon and the present situation, but also the past or the 'having-been'. Last but not least, human beings somehow 'find themselves' in a present situation, making the present the past in actualising their plans, while encountering within their surroundings concrete things, living creatures and other people. Heidegger thus assumes that in every 'now' we have the following tripartite structure: anticipation, making present and thrownness. Without this the 'now' would shrink to a point moving on a time-line, i.e. a repeating – reappearing and simultaneously always disappearing – moment.

Kosík's main objection to the aforementioned conception of original temporality consists in a claim according to which particular ecstasies do not have an equal standing in the tripartite structure of original temporality. Heidegger evidently gives priority to only one ecstasy, namely the future, as human beings' self-understanding is primarily constituted from the standpoint of their *future* possibilities. In a summary of his position, Heidegger says the following: 'Temporality is essentially ecstatic. Temporality temporalizes itself primordially out of the future'.[74] Kosík criticises this primacy given to the future in Heidegger:

> In care, the individual is always already in the future and turns the present into a means or a tool for the realisation of projects. Care as the individual's practical involvement favours the future in a certain way, and turns it into the basic time dimension, in whose light he grasps and 'realises' the present.[75]

---

72 See §65 bearing the title 'Temporality as the Ontological Meaning of Care' – Heidegger 1996, pp. 397–404.
73 Heidegger 1996, p. 299.
74 Heidegger 1996, p. 304. Heidegger elsewhere notes: 'In enumerating the ecstasies, we have always mentioned the future first. That should indicate that the future has priority in the ecstatic unity of primordial and authentic temporality, although temporality does not first originate through a cumulative sequence of the ecstasies, but always temporalizes itself in their equiprimordiality'. Heidegger 1996, p. 302.
75 Kosík 1976, p. 42.

If we give priority to future possibilities and to anticipation, we are prioritising something that is not yet objective at the expense of objectivity: both the past ('dead labour') and the present ('living labour'). Accordingly, Kosík notes: 'Since care is anticipation, it invalidates the present and fastens onto the future which has *not yet* happened'.[76] By contrast with this, temporal materialism places emphasis on the circumstance that all three ecstasies are constituted simultaneously in the act of labour. In other words, temporal materialism prioritises the present, since it is in the present, namely in the act of labour, that a synthesis of the ecstasies of time takes place, as well as the synthesis of time and space. This emphasis on the act of labour gains prominence in Kosík's discussion of Heidegger's conception of death. Heidegger understands care primarily as 'being-toward-death'.[77] Kosík assumes that being-toward-death devalues the existence of the 'here' and 'now' – not only the act of labour, tools and material, but also the whole sphere of objectivity, which makes up culture and civilisation. In opposition to this Kosík proposes another view, claiming that human being 'discovers his mortality and finitude *only* on the basis of civilisation, i.e. on the basis of his objectification'.[78] Thus, confronted with the 'having-been' or the past in a shape of 'dead' labour, or spatialised labour time, encountering things that are not the moment of any act of labour, that are 'at the prey of processes of chemical decay', things devoid of any use-value, such as a broken gramophone, worn out shoes etc., we learn what it means that we will die one day. Therefore, it is not through care, but rather through 'dead' and 'living' labour that the 'authentic character of human time' is opened up.[79]

6 Ontology Up-Side Down?

In the second half of the 1960s, Jan Patočka, a Czech phenomenologist of the older generation, sketched out a remarkable critique of Kosík's ontology of labour from a phenomenological point of view. Although he defends Heidegger against Kosík, Patočka nonetheless simultaneously appreciates with overt sympathy Kosík's attempt to undermine the pillars upon which fundamental ontology rests. At the centre of Patočka's attention is above all Kosík's polemic with Heidegger's conception of temporality, as well as Kosík's own temporal

---

76 Ibid.
77 Heidegger 1996, p. 303.
78 Kosík 1976, p. 137.
79 Kosík 1976, p. 42.

materialism. It is not without interest that Patočka maintained a distanced position from *Dialectics of the Concrete* shortly after its publication in 1963. On 15 March 1964 he wrote to his friend, the art historian Václav Richter that Kosík is a 'sensation', despite the fact that nobody knows precisely 'what he is actually saying and what he is aiming at'.[80] Two years later, Patočka again in a letter to Richter notes: 'I will not write (specially) about Kosík'.[81] Regardless of this declaration, Patočka proceeded to engage in detail with *Dialectics of the Concrete* in several texts, although it is true that none of these texts focuses 'specially' on Kosík. As soon as in 1965, in one of his shorter reviews he dealt critically with Kosík's central thesis, according to which time, or more specifically temporal structure, is constituted in labour.[82] However, Patočka did not present a thoroughgoing critique until 1969, in an article (originally a lecture) on contemporary Czech philosophy. Here he proposed an interpretation according to which Czech philosophy, in one of its most productive branches, has attempted since the mid of 19th century to elaborate a 'philosophy of the active side'. And *Dialectics of the Concrete* is considered to represent a recent outcome of such an attempt.[83] Despite the fact that Patočka regards this tradition as innovative, he nonetheless formulates a number of objections, by means of which he attempts to point to its limits. Last but not least, it is necessary to mention Patočka's article published in *Festschrift* for Martin Heidegger in 1970, in which Patočka scrutinises Lukács's critique of Heidegger from the beginning of the 1950s.[84] Let us summarise the core of Patočka's critique of Kosík on the basis of these three texts, focusing especially on the issue of temporal materialism.

Patočka acknowledges that it is absolutely apposite to understand the 'philosophy of praxis' either as a supplement or as an alternative to the 'fundamental ontology of existence', since Heidegger's ontology has its shortcomings, especially as regards the absence of the social dimension of human existence. According to Patočka, terms such as the 'call of conscience' or 'being-toward-death' are conceptually ill-equipped to capture the social dimension. As a result, fundamental ontology should turn to Marxism or other currents and adopt more appropriate conceptuality, e.g. the concepts of *alienation*,

---

80   Patočka 2001, pp. 127–8.
81   Patočka 2001, p. 145.
82   Patočka 2004a, pp. 204–10, see p. 209.
83   Patočka 2006a, pp. 306–27, see especially pp. 321–7.
84   See Patočka 1970, pp. 394–411. Czech translation in Patočka 2006b, pp. 214–29. Patočka stresses here that Lukács's critique of Heidegger and Husserl should be blamed for the delay in the reception of phenomenology among Marxist philosophers in the early 1950s.

fetishism, or *objectification*. As Heidegger didn't elaborate any philosophy of praxis, Patočka considers it important to enhance fundamental ontology with analyses of labour.[85] At the same time he has some misgivings concerning a resolute rejection of the project of fundamental ontology and unreserved acceptance of the ontology of labour. This would be a fatal philosophical mistake, since it would result in a position in which a rich variety of phenomena and deeper ontological structures, including the temporal, were reduced to just a single explanatory principle, namely to labour, or ontocreativity.[86]

According to Patočka, this reduction is unjustified, which becomes clear if we take the opposite perspective and adhere to Heidegger's fundamental ontology of existence (enhanced by the ontology of labour). From this perspective, Kosík's position is unsustainable for the reason that it is not consistent. It puts the cart before the horse when it attempts to derive temporality from labour, when in reality the situation is that labour as both material and conscious activity presupposes an original temporality. This is taken into account precisely by fundamental ontology, which enables us to understand the relationship between labour and temporality, or more precisely to understand the temporality of human existence, far better than temporal materialism. Since ontology cannot begin 'as if shot out of pistol', we need something to rest our ontology upon, and support is provided only by the phenomenological perspective, which starts with a concrete human existence that relates to itself and pre-theoretically understands its own existence. The aforementioned perspective guarantees that ontology is really a 'dialectic of the concrete', rather than a dialectic of the abstract and impersonal.

Patočka's chief objection therefore refers to the inadequacy of the methodology. Accordingly, the ontology of labour is not anchored in concrete social reality, as it proceeds from ontological structures to phenomena.[87] However, there is then a danger that in this way the 'impersonal' and would-be 'objective' machinery of dialectics would be applied as *deus ex machina*, whenever we try to explain any mediation or metamorphosis, such as the constitution of social reality, anthropological difference, temporal structure or the human life form. Furthermore, Patočka is convinced that such anonymous dialectics makes it in principle difficult for human beings to form any self-understanding or self-

---

[85] Patočka 2006a, p. 325.
[86] Ibid. According to Patočka, the ontology of labour has the ambition to 'explain the origin of essential structures of humanity, in particular of time, in the sense of original temporality', from labour. Patočka 2006a, p. 323.
[87] A similar objection was raised by Zimmermann 1984, pp. 209–33; and Ballard 1990, pp. 121–41.

conception, since 'objective' dialectics resembles processes in nature that are devoid of any self-understanding. Hence, Kosík in his ontology of labour merely revives Engels's dialectic of nature.[88]

Consequently, we are urged to occupy the opposite position. In Patočka's view it is necessary to start from phenomena: from concrete human existence (*Da-sein*), which exemplifies a certain life form, or more precisely from the self-understanding which human existence has of itself. Patočka thus recommends starting from mere 'anthropological fact', i.e. from 'life as it is lived', as it is experienced from a first personal perspective. If we accept anthropological fact as the starting point of ontology, we can – surprisingly – expand upon the implications of practical materialism as it was conceived by Marx in the *Theses on Feuerbach*. This starts out from a material object, which differs from other objects in that is conscious of itself, but in a different manner than it is conscious of the other objects.[89] – As such, Heidegger's approach, beginning from analyses of care and culminating in a revelation of the basic structure of original temporality, may appear far more convincing – and in fact more materialist in the intentions of the *Theses on Feuerbach*.

A further objection relates to the claim according to which temporality is constituted in labour. Kosík, as we have seen, substitutes a concrete analysis of this constitution in part with a description of Hegel's master/slave dialectic, and in part ensues from Marx and his reflections on the temporality of things. It is precisely Kosík's dependency on Hegel's model that Patočka picks up on. He asserts that in this model the central point is the proclaimed connection between labour and holding desire in check. In this, to hold desire in check covers the following: that labour is inserted as a mediating element between need and its satisfaction; and that animality is thereby transformed into humanity, 'first nature' into 'second nature', or that temporality is constituted together with this process. However, Patočka objects that here again there is an anonymous dialectic of nature at work, which leads to a situation in which 'non-human practice turns into a human one'.[90]

Upon closer examination, Hegel's model, or more precisely Kosík's adaptation of this model, in itself contains an unarticulated or displaced assumption that in reality there is a more fundamental principle than labour, namely

---

88 Kosík was reproached for his 'objectivism' also by the Czech Marxist philosopher Milan Průcha, who rightly noted: 'Kosík remained basically untouched by Husserl, Heidegger, and the entire existential ontology in the fundamental issues, so that he can even be accused of scientism'. Průcha 1966, pp. 24–5.
89 See Rödl 2011, p. 30. See also Patočka 2006a, p. 322.
90 Patočka 2006a, p. 323.

'release from the bondage to instinct, the temporality of human life, its finitude'.[91] As a result Patočka rejects the notion that the 'three-dimensionality of human life' would be constituted either from 'desire held in check', or from labour.[92] Here, the ontologically original is not emancipation from 'biological imperatives', but rather temporality. Only due to original temporality is it possible for humans being to transcend their existence 'here' and 'now', that of immediate satisfaction of basic needs and desire, and anticipate other possibilities.

Patočka therefore argues as follows: Practical materialism understands labour as a transformation of animal needs and desires, while deferring animal desire implies emancipation from 'biological imperatives'. Hence, labour presupposes not only a 'first nature': basic needs and desires, but at the same also a postponement of their satisfaction until later. However, it is already 'first nature', not the 'second', that is in itself a concrete phenomenon which displays a temporal structure. Accordingly, temporality is rather a condition under which labour is possible as a material and conscious activity, *via* which something ('first nature') can be transformed into something else ('second nature'). Labour therefore does not constitute temporality. Moreover, the precise opposite is the case: temporality constitutes labour as ontocreativity. Therefore, labour 'already implies quite a specific understanding of the dimensionality of time, namely a conception, concentrating *on the present moment*, focusing on *the present moment*, which is ever new'.[93] Patočka concludes his critique as follows: 'Kosík's immensely bold attempt to explain 'out of labour' the very structure of time, its three-dimensionality, is evidently an attempt at something which is impossible, namely to reduce the irreducible'.[94]

7   Conclusion

Let us first consider his methodological objection. This states that Kosík does not start out from an anthropological fact, and as a result also overlooks the fact that praxis is, above all, the sphere of meanings and their constitution, rather than of objectivity. However, once we realise that Kosík's ontology of labour follows, in principle, a programme of practical materialism, as sketched out by

---

91   Patočka 2004a, p. 209.
92   Ibid.
93   Ibid.
94   Ibid.

Marx in the *Theses on Feuerbach*, it immediately becomes clear that Patočka's objection is not particularly justified. Accordingly, Kosík intends to demonstrate that it is necessary to understand the sphere of objectivity in terms of subjectivity, hence as a sphere which is saturated with meanings, since material objects in space and time manifest a human life form that is imprinted on them by humans via acts of labour. In this, labour as a material-cum-conscious activity is a mediation, serving to ensure that meanings are imprinted upon these objects. Also, in his analysis of social reality and its structure, Kosík proceeds phenomenologically, even if he subsequently rejects the phenomenology of care as merely a reified appearance of praxis. Asking the question as to what is economy implies that the ontology of labour should be followed up with the phenomenology of labour, as is the case e.g. in the work of Simone Weil, taking into account the first personal perspective of the actors who are closest to the reality, and who experience it in or through their activity. Alternatively phrased, social reality cannot be simply examined objectively from a third personal perspective, developing ontology abstractly. However, it is similarly possible to undermine Patočka's further objection, according to which an anonymous dialectic of nature is at work in Kosík as a notorious *deus ex machina*. Kosík's analysis of anthropogenesis etc. focuses precisely on the act of labour, i.e. on 'living labour' as coined by Marx. Accordingly, the act of labour, which is a material and conscious activity, is centred on the subject. It is therefore possible to understand it not only as an objective dialectical process, but again *subjectively*, from a first-person perspective, namely as a dialectic which is neither conceivable nor real without self-conscious material beings that can also form collective self-understanding.

Nonetheless, Patočka's critique was of immense significance for Kosík's further intellectual development, and motivated his 'Heideggerian turn'. Although Kosík never abandoned Marxism with its stress on human emancipation, from the end of the 1960s the pathos of ontocreativity and of revolutionary praxis little by little disappears from his work, especially after the failure of the Prague Spring of 1968. Instead of these, everyday practices and concrete phenomena such as comicality, tragedy, sacrifice, affectivity and emotions come to the forefront of Kosík's analytical focus.[95] Hence, to use the terminology of the *Dialectics of the Concrete*, the affective or existential aspect of praxis now comes to the fore. For Kosík, it is in everyday practices and most elementary experiences, and more precisely in contact with ordinary things that lack a use or exchange value, i.e. things that cannot be manipulated to serve as a material and tools

---

95 See Francesco Tava's contribution to this volume, pp. 57–74.

in an act of labour, that he seems to seek an emancipatory potential which could enable a transformation of the predominant ontology, and thus radically change our approach towards both nature and social reality. The departure from the paradigm of labour goes hand in hand with turn to the late Heidegger's reflections on the essence of technology. Kosík became a phenomenological, and more specifically Heideggerian Marxist, only after the *Dialectics of the Concrete*.

CHAPTER 5

Inception of Culture from the Ontology of Labour: The Original Contribution of Karel Kosík to a Marxian Theory of Culture

Ian Angus

Three significantly different interpretations of the Marxist philosophical heritage can be distinguished by what they regard as the foundational level of analysis: class struggle, the 'anarchy of the market', to use Lenin's phrase, and that which focuses on the labour process.[1] Each of these imply political projects that differ fundamentally and entail significantly different evaluations of 'Marxist' political regimes of the twentieth century. If class struggle is the fundamental level of analysis, a classless society is the political project, such that it remains undetermined as to what the relationship of the classless society is to the organisation of labour. If the anarchy of the market is the problem, then the solution is state regulation of the economy. Some combination of these two defines the dominant tendency of twentieth-century Marxism that has attained political power – even though it might rightly be commented that the classless society has been more ideology than reality. The priority placed on the labour process implies that the organisation of labour is the criterion for political success. This interpretation of Marxism has been the least politically successful, even while it launches a fundamental critique of the hierarchical organisation of labour in both capitalist and Communist societies. The interpretation of Marxism through the priority of labour depends on a view of human being as fundamentally a praxis that manifests itself in labour. An ontology of labour thus undergirds an interpretation of Marxism as the emancipation of labour. Karel Kosík's *Dialectics of the Concrete* is an important text within this stream of interpretation.

---

1 This paper was funded by the Social Sciences and Humanities Research Council of Canada, #435-2012-0209. A revised and expanded version has been included in *Groundwork of Phenomenological Marxism: Crisis, Body, World* (Lexington Books, 2021).

1   Introduction: Human Being as Praxis

It is not too much to say that twentieth-century philosophy is in its essence praxis philosophy, that is to say that its starting point is human being in its practical activities, such that science and reflection become secondary and derived formations. The focus on language, often called the 'linguistic turn', only becomes a genuine turn from the previous priority of representational language in science and philosophy when language is understood as language-in-use, as a form of doing in the human world, and only secondarily as a description or analysis of that world. But it is equally the case that, when the derived status of science and reflection in an ontological sense becomes derogation in an ethical sense or relegation to epiphenomenal status, then praxis is understood as a reduction of human being to its given world. To avoid a merely polemical reversal of the relationship between praxis and reflection, it must be shown how forms of representation emerge from praxis. What is needed is not a reductionism but a phenomenology of the inception of culture from the ontology of labour. Karel Kosík termed this essential issue of the relationship of praxis to human being 'openness'.

> Abolishing philosophy in dialectical social theory transforms the *significance* of the seminal nineteenth-century discovery into its very opposite: praxis ceases to be the sphere of humanising man, the process of forming a socio-human reality as well as man's *openness* toward being and toward the truth of objects: it turns into a closedness: socialness is a cave in which man is walled in. Images, ideas and concepts that man takes for spiritual reproductions of nature, of material processes and of objects existing independently of his consciousness, are in 'reality' a social projection, an expression of man's social position in the *form* of science or of objectivity. In other words, they are *false* images. Man is *walled in* within his socialness. Praxis, which in Marx's philosophy had made possible both objectivation and objective cognition, and man's openness toward being, turns into social subjectivity and closedness: man is a prisoner of his socialness.[2]

Kosík aims to restore Marx's conception of praxis as openness, which requires a restoration of Marx's relation to philosophy, since philosophy is the practice of openness and is, as such, a practice of the being of human being. Here we may well see a profound though unacknowledged debt to Heidegger in Kosík's idea

---

2   Kosík 1976, p. 106.

of philosophy. Openness grounds negativity, and thus Kosík's conception of the dialectic, in its reach toward totality that is the very definition of praxis. The existential openness of human being parallels the task of philosophy whose openness opposes any closing in by a social system.[3]

In aiming at a recovery and revitalisation of Marx's thought on praxis as the essence of human being, Kosík criticises the reduction of Marxism to a theory of the influence of the 'economic factor' on human life. 'The factor theory avers that one privileged factor – economics – determines all other factors: the state, law, art, politics, morals'.[4] Such an economic determinism not only occludes the active, world-making ontology of human being, but also justifies rule through technical manipulation of this supposed determinism by a bureaucratic elite. Kosík's critique not only exposes this error but also explains its production as a consequence of the historical dynamic of praxis itself. Capitalist society produces the economic sphere as an abstracted and self-contained sphere that correlatively produces a specific sort of economic knowledge applicable to that society. This abstracted sphere of activity can then be interpreted to determine one-sidedly other aspects of human life. Thus, the 'factor theory' of orthodox Marxism is itself a product of capitalist society, such that a historically isolated aspect of human praxis can be hypothesised to determine the whole. Communist society, in operationalising economic determinism, thus culminated the truncated praxis of capitalist society.

The key concept in Kosík's appropriation of Heidegger and simultaneous recovery of Marx's theory of praxis is 'totality', which accounts for the genesis of social reality through which 'the social whole (the socio-economic formation) is formed and constituted by the economic structure. The economic structure forms the unity and continuity of all spheres of social life'.[5] An important question arises concerning if, and how, the whole of human praxis can be

---

3   The definition of the human being and philosophy in terms of openness conceals an ambiguity in Kosík's reliance on Hegel to illuminate Marx's conception of totality. It seems that unlike a Hegelian totality of determinations, totality in Kosík remains more like an indeterminate phenomenological horizon. This may be a deeper influence of Heidegger, or Husserl, than that indicated within the text. This issue is, as far as I can see, addressed nowhere in *Dialectics of the Concrete*. I have previously pointed out the stakes for a Heideggerian Marxism in obscuring this difference (Angus 2009; Angus 2005). Paul Piccone has noted that Kosík's totality is a horizon and that it therefore corresponded to the open totality of the Prague Spring though it is not clear whether this is a criticism or an appreciation (Piccone 1977, p. 51). Other of Piccone's works suggest that he is more inclined toward a Lukácsian-Hegelian closed conception of totality (Piccone 1971). I have argued that the distinction between these two conceptions of totality is philosophically fundamental in order to endorse the phenomenological concept of horizon (Angus 2000, pp. 66–70, pp. 93–6).
4   Kosík 1976, p. 64.
5   Ibid, italics removed.

determined as a 'socio-economic-formation' and why this can be explained by 'economic structure', but it is clear that only insofar as it can explain the 'unity and continuity' of the entirety of historical human being can it be considered a recovery of Marx's thought. What is the nature of Kosík's determination of philosophy as praxis, as labour, and as economic structure, such that it can be framed as 'a philosophical answer to a philosophical question: *Who is man, what is socio-human reality, and how is reality formed?*'[6]

Kosík's ontology of being human defines human being as praxis, goes on to define praxis as labour, and show that labour is organised in a determinate historical form as economic structure. It is important to understand the nature of this theoretical determination, which moves from the most universal toward the most specific, from praxis through labour to economic structure. Evidently, there are philosophies that are not praxis philosophies; there are praxis philosophies that do not focus on labour; and there are labour philosophies, or more correctly ideologies, that focus on the economic factor rather than economic structure. Kosík begins with the most abstract characterisation of his approach to philosophy – praxis versus contemplative – and then at the next step characterises praxis as labour, and then labour as organised through economic structure. At each point the initial abstract characterisation is given greater concreteness due to its increasingly specific theoretical determination. In this way, economic structure is not distinguished from other kinds of structure; labour is not distinguished from other forms of human activity; and praxis is not distinguished from other forms of human being. There are not, as it were, a series of distinct concepts at the same level of abstraction – for example, labour, play, prayer, etc. – from which one is chosen – which would of course raise the question concerning by what criteria one of several possibilities is deemed more fundamental. There is a logic of increasing specification from universal to concrete, in which each greater determination produces greater content while at the same time requiring that competing concepts, which do occur at a given level of abstraction, be founded upon the next specific level. For example, one does not choose labour over play, but shows that labour is a specification of praxis, so that play would also be a form of praxis that is founded upon labour. This logic of determination from abstract to concrete excludes other possibilities through each concretion, so that the specific form of Kosík's ontology emerges not only from the increasing concretion but also from its justification for the rejection of other possibilities.

---

6 Kosík 1976, p. 136, emphasis in original.

Thus to say that the being of human being is praxis is to say that it is *not*, at least in the first place, or fundamentally, contemplative, theoretical, or artistic; though for this to be more than a polemical assertion, what is not-praxis – the contemplative, theoretical, and artistic – must be shown, in the second or third place, to be a product and mutation of praxis. To say that the essence of praxis is labour is to say that it is *not*, at least in the first place, or fundamentally, politics, art or technics; though, for this to be more than a polemical assertion, what is not-labour – politics, art and technics – must be shown to be, in the second or third place, a product and mutation of labour. To say that the essence of labour is economic structure is to say that the historical conditions of labour are such as to organise a distinction between labour and not-labour. It is this not-labour founded upon labour that is the origin of culture.

Insofar as human being has been determined philosophically as praxis, further determined praxis as labour, and further still as economic structure, which institutes its specifically Marxist dimension, it demands a non-reductionistic theory of the inception of culture from labour. The inception of culture from the ontology of labour is the point at which the openness of human being is captured and continued by philosophy as the realisation of human being. Kosík's Heideggerian concept of labour as a happening (*Geschehen*) in which human being expresses itself is followed through in his theory of culture, or not-labour, where he understands human reality as disclosed through philosophy and art (rather than culture as explained by the economic factor). This logic of this specifying determination means that the alternative initially rejected – labour not culture – must be recovered in a non-reductive and non-polemical form. In this sense, accounting for the inception of culture is a crucial test for the adequacy of an ontology of labour.

I will show that Kosík's notion of culture as not-labour, defined only by a privative, is an original contribution to a Marxian theory of culture. The following sections will address two fundamental issues in the inception of culture from the ontology of labour. (1) Kosík's critique of Marcuse's synthesis of Marx and Heidegger on the origin of culture through either an 'essential excess' in labour (Marcuse) or the negation of social necessity by 'not-labour' (Kosík). (2) I follow Mildred Bakan's critique of Kosík's failure to account for the role of language in labour and culture to show its roots in Kosík's resorting to Engels' developmental account of language from labour (rather than consistently maintaining an ontological analysis). In conclusion, I suggest that, by incorporating these two critiques, Kosík's non-reductive account of culture could sufficiently account for the autonomy of culture, especially the key themes of individuation, death and laughter. The foundation of a theory of culture in the ontology of labour shows how the determination of praxis as labour does not diminish its universality but provides a basis for the autonomy of culture – in which human being as openness finds expression in philosophy and art.

2   Ontology of Labour as the Foundation for Culture

Labour is understood by Kosík as the ontological character of human being. Labour in this sense is not accessible through a sociological description of forms of labour, nor work processes and activity as such, or different kinds of work. 'Labour is a *happening* (*Geschehen*) which permeates man's *entire* being and constitutes his specificity'.[7] In this context Kosík refers to 'On the Philosophical Foundation of the Concept of Labour in Economics', a 1933 essay by Herbert Marcuse, which was the first attempt to synthesise Marx's concept of labour with Heidegger's ontology. There, Marcuse defined labour as an occurrence or 'happening' (*Geschehen*) following Heidegger's definition of historicity as 'the constitution of being of the "happening" of Da-sein as such'.[8] It is in this dialogue between Kosík and Marcuse that characteristics of the ontology of labour which are pertinent to the inception of culture can be brought out.

Marcuse's early essay on the philosophical foundations of labour and Kosík's account in *Dialectics of the Concrete* share a common polemical object in the orthodox Marxist reduction of labour to an aspect or factor, then argued to be the significant factor in human life that determines the rest, and which can therefore only be assumed to be a primordial need or biological given. In contrast, when labour is understood ontologically as a happening, or event, that permeates the entirety of historical human being, it shows, according to Marcuse, 'an essential excess of human Dasein beyond every possible situation' or that 'human being is always *more* than its Dasein at any given time'.[9] Labour is the fundamental motility of human being that places it into history and a situation that it can always surpass through its 'primordial negativity'.[10] Marcuse specifies the ontology of labour in three characteristics: duration, permanence, and burdensomeness. Duration in Marcuse's usage refers to the fact that labour surpasses any specific act or process of labour in being an orientation to human life as a whole. Permanence refers to the products objectified in the labour process such that the historical form of a human world is constructed. Labour as a

---

7   Kosík 1976, p. 119; cf. Kosík 1967d, p. 197.
8   Marcuse 2005, p. 127; Heidegger 1996, p. 17; Heidegger 1986, pp. 19–20.
9   Marcuse 2005, p. 136.
10 Marcuse 2005, p. 139.

burden does not refer to the degree of its difficulty or irksomeness, but to the 'law of the thing' under which labour works; labour must respect the nature of its materials and the practical necessities of its exertion to successfully produce its object.[11] Marcuse's notion of 'essential excess' is usually called 'surplus productivity' in Marxist terminology and would constitute the first characteristic of reading Marx's 'transhistorical characteristics of labour' as ontology.

Kosík generally endorses Marcuse's specification of the ontology of labour, no doubt because of their common appropriation of Heidegger to recover Marx's conception of labour as a happening that permeates the whole of human being. He builds upon the temporal elements of Marcuse's analysis to analyse the three-dimensionality of time in human being: First, the temporal process of labour is transcended (*Aufhebung*) in the product which endures through time such that products collectively constitute the human built world. Second, in the process of labour, the results of past labour are transformed by future intentions.[12] Human time is thus rooted in objective praxis whereby human being transforms the given historically-determined situation through first adapting itself to that situation.

Nevertheless, Kosík is critical of Marcuse on one fundamental point. Kosík asserts that Marcuse does not distinguish between labour and praxis, that 'labor is characterised as the essence of praxis and praxis is defined essentially as labour'. Indeed, Marcuse refers to 'this happening itself: labour as the specific *praxis* of human Dasein in the world'[13] so Kosík's characterisation is apt enough, but how does Marcuse come to this identity and how does Kosík's view distinguish between the two?

Kosík's claim that praxis and labour must be distinguished from one another might be interpreted along the lines of the distinction between *technē* from *praxis*, or labour from politics, as many commentators – such as Hans-Georg Gadamer, Hannah Arendt and Jürgen Habermas – have done.[14] We would have

---

11   Marcuse 2005, pp. 129–30.
12   Kosík 1976, p. 122; Kosík 1967d, p. 203.
13   Marcuse 2005, p. 127.
14   Kosík's distinction between labour and praxis is not based on the notion that they are intrinsically different sorts of activities, an essential and ontological distinction that is rooted in Aristotle's distinction of *technē* from *praxis*, or making from doing, that is perhaps clearest in the opening passage (1094a) of *Nicomachean Ethics*: 'Every art or applied science (*technē*) and every systematic investigation, and similarly every action and choice, seem to aim at some good; the good, therefore, has been well defined as that at which all things aim. But it is clear that there is a difference in the ends at which they aim: in some cases the activity is the end [i.e. *praxis*], in others the end is some product beyond the activity. In cases where the end lies beyond the action the product is naturally

two, or perhaps many forms of human activity, and the issue would be how to ground their unity in an ontology of human being. Thus it could be claimed that the problem is that Marcuse saw all human action through the prism of labour and was thereby tied to Marxist productivism. However, Kosík and Marcuse agree that labour is a happening that permeates the whole of human being and, even more, labour is understood as the ground from which human being discloses Being itself. Moreover, as we have seen, Kosík himself determines praxis by labour and labour by economic structure. Therefore, this sort of division of human being by placing labour in opposition to other forms of activity is not a viable interpretation of Kosík's critique of Marcuse. What is meant by Kosík comes to light in his account of the genesis of culture from labour.

Marcuse's first statement of the identity of praxis and labour (quoted above) occurs immediately prior to his consideration of the possibility that play might be equally primordial with labour in defining human praxis. He argues that, while play may or may not have an object as does labour, the relation to the object is substantially different. Play does not orient itself to the content and law of the object as does labour, but insofar as is possible negates the sway of the object in favour of humanly created rules of the game – which can in principle be violated but which the players voluntarily recognise. Play in this sense negates the objectivity of the object and thus creates a freedom that is impossible in labour. For this reason, play is an intermittent activity in human life that involves a turning away from the activities that routinely dominate human life. Therefore, 'the way that life happens in play is not a happening that is completed in and through itself: it is essentially dependent and points inherently to another doing'.[15] The characteristics of labour that Marcuse then elaborates – duration, permanence and burdensomeness – are derived precisely from that which is not operative during play. These characteristics explain the *historical* dimension of human being as rooted in the *motility* of labour as negation of a given state, so that '[l]abor presupposes a well-determined *relation to time* that thoroughly penetrates Dasein and guides its praxis'.[16] While Marcuse dis-

---

superior to the activity' (Aristotle 1962, p. 1). This distinction has influenced Western philosophy significantly up to Hannah Arendt (see Lobkowicz 1967, pp. 9–15; Arendt 1958, pp. 12–17, pp. 136–44, pp. 175–81). Hans-Georg Gadamer used it to suggest that ancient practical philosophy undertook a prior posing of the dilemma involved in the translation of scientific knowledge into technical innovation (Gadamer 1977). This distinction has been used by Jürgen Habermas under the influence of Hannah Arendt and Hans-Georg Gadamer (Habermas 1973, p. 286, n. 4).

15   Marcuse 2005, p. 128.
16   Marcuse 2005, p. 141.

tinguishes between labour and play, he does not place play on the same ontological level as labour.

The distinction between labour and praxis must be sought then, not as a distinction within praxis into labour versus other sorts of activity, but as a distinction that arises from within labour as praxis itself. There are two aspects of labour, according to Kosík, which were not properly grasped by Marcuse and which constitute the meaning of his remark that Marcuse failed to distinguish between praxis and labour. The first, which can be called hominisation, refers to the formation of human being from a prior animal. The second refers to the notion of 'metamorphosis in general' which is based on the happening of labour understood through hominisation, and grounds the notion of culture as not-labour – which is the specific contribution of Kosík to a phenomenological-Marxist theory of culture.

This dense formulation needs to be spelled out in more detail. Kosík is arguing that the specificity of the specific-universal account of labour can be understood from the viewpoint of the process of hominisation. This process is at once a specific process, but one that, in creating the human, comes to pervade the whole of human being. This transformation is not only a specific transformation, but is the model for transformation outright, since it is the origin of dialectics as such. 'The dialectical mediation of this happening does not *balance* opposites, nor are its opposites constituted in an *antinomy*. Rather, in the process of *transformation* a unity of opposites is *formed*'.[17] Hominisation is a specific happening that originates dialectics as the universal process of the happening of labour that grounds historicity and therefore of the later specific historical forms of labour. There is no explicit reference here, but it is clearly a philosophical formulation of Engels' theory that labour initiated the transition between animal and human.[18] This is also the problematic that dominates György Lukács's work *The Ontology of Social Being*, which struggles repeatedly and without success to explain the process of the 'leap', as he calls it, between animality and humanity on the presupposition that this is the main issue of an ontology of labour.[19] However, an ontology of human being is not oriented

---

17 Kosík 1976, p. 121, emphases in original.
18 Engels 1940, pp. 279–96.
19 Lukács 1980b, p. 15, p. 20, p. 21, p. 31, p. 35, p. 43, p. 50, p. 65, p. 67, p. 79, p. 135, p. 136. The argument by Ernest Joós that Lukács's ontology of labour cannot account for the origin of personal identity is instructive at this point given the structuring assumption in Lukács's ontology that the key problem is the Engelsian one of the historico-anthropological origin of human labour from animal activity. One need not agree with Joós's last word that the person is essentially a Christian concept in order to accept his main argument (Joós 1983, pp. 106–14).

toward the genesis of humans from pre-human animals, but to the essential features of human being once human being is established as such. Kosík is certainly correct to note his fundamental difference from Marcuse on this point. The recourse to Heidegger for an ontology of labour that could be synthesised with Marx to ground both a conception of human being and historical inquiry into forms of production of necessity rejects the problem of hominisation in order to address the ontology of human being directly as it is for humans, or in Marx's words, 'labour in a form in which it is an exclusively human characteristic'.[20] There is an essential difference between *genesis* understood in historical-anthropological terms from its meaning as an onto-genetic layering of human experience in ontology.

This difference has a further consequence in a difference between how Marcuse and Kosík address the relation between freedom and necessity that is the foundation for their accounts of culture. All human doing is not labour in the ontological sense according to Marcuse. Only activity that is self-actualisation, happening, is human labour.[21] Human activity that simply fits into the given organised structure of the world is not labour in the ontological sense. By interpreting human praxis as labour and thereby labour as the being of human being, Marcuse is required to make a distinction between human activity that attains self-actualisation and that which does not. He makes a fundamental distinction between 'doing in the service of 'material' production and reproduction, that is, providing, procuring, and maintaining Dasein's basic necessities' and 'the labour that goes beyond these necessities and that is and remains tied to making Dasein happen'.[22] Simple material reproduction is not labour, only labour that goes beyond the necessity of production for reproduction makes human being happen. He argues that such self-actualising labour can 'happen freely' because it 'has attained a certain distance from the most necessary and immediate things'.[23] In this way, Marcuse associates authentic labour, in Heideggerian terminology, as the highest form of human self-actualisation, with Marx's description of the realm of freedom and, correlatively, associates merely ontic labour, as material reproduction immersed in immediate things, with Marx's realm of necessity.

---

20 Marx 1977a, pp. 283–4. Marx elsewhere certainly uses labour to *demarcate* the difference between animal and human, to stress their ontological difference, but feels no necessity to explain a *transition* between the two, which has its origin in Friedrich Engels's *Dialectics of Nature* and is the foundation for the necessity to explain the 'leap'.
21 Marcuse 2005, p. 143.
22 Ibid.
23 Marcuse 2005, p. 148.

One might be forgiven for thinking that Marcuse's distinction between labour as ontic and as ontological adequately fulfils Kosík's demand that labour be understood as 'a specific happening or as a specific reality that constitutes and permeates man's entire being'.[24] However, a second look would observe that the relation is rather the reverse in Marcuse: in orthodox Heideggerian fashion, Marcuse begins with the ontological account as the ground for a historical, ontic one, whereas Kosík's philosophy of labour begins from the specific labour that grounds hominisation, which then comes to pervade the whole of human being. This 'before' is not meant in a temporal sense, but in a logical and ontological one: for Kosík, ontology is grounded on a specific historical-anthropological genesis, whereas for Marcuse ontology is the foundation for determining historical forms. Thus, Kosík characterises his discussion of the 'ontology of man' as a 'digression', indicating that for him the universal, ontological question is on the way to understanding a historical-anthropological genesis that founds history and ontology.[25]

Following out this notion of the specific happening of hominisation into the genesis of culture, Kosík asks '[w]here is the limit of labour, or the measure of its distinctiveness?', that leads directly to a discussion of freedom and necessity in which art is the activity most characterised by freedom.[26] Art is labour as free creation, whereas the 'specificity of labour [is] [...] determined by *extraneous* purpose'.[27] This 'extraneous purpose' is identical to the 'law of the thing' which Marcuse sees as an ontological characteristic of labour that distinguishes it from play.[28] Kosík agrees that labour is determined by necessity so that 'one and the same activity can be both labour and not-labour, depending on whether or not it is performed as a natural necessity', in order to conclude that the distinction between freedom and necessity doesn't fully capture the distinction between labour and not-labour.[29] In using the term 'not-labour' as distinct from labour, Kosík clearly does not want to distinguish what is not labour by any substantive characteristic differing from that of labour, but to say that it is *exclusively* distinguished from labour *only* by the negative characteristic that it is not labour. What is labour is thus determined by the social organisation of necessity and what is not-labour is that which is free creation entirely defined by the criterion that social organisation does not define it as

---

24 Kosík 1976, p. 123.
25 Ibid.
26 Kosík 1976, p. 124.
27 Ibid.
28 Marcuse 2005, p. 130.
29 Kosík 1976, p. 124; Kosík 1967d, p. 206.

necessary. He goes on to give an account of the realm of freedom as a historical distinction growing out of the realm of necessity, and thus as a historically transient distinction, so that the conceptual juxtaposition of labour and freedom remains captive of this historical moment. Kosík sums up his argument with the statement that 'such human doing which is determined only by internal purposiveness and does not depend on natural necessity or social obligation is not labour but free creation, *irrespective* of the realm within which it is realised. The real realm of freedom thus begins beyond the *boundaries* of labour, although precisely labour forms its indispensable historical basis'.[30]

Whereas Marcuse *defines* labour ontologically as creative happening, and thus subsumes much actually-existing labour under ontic necessity that is not 'really' labour, Kosík defines the purpose of a philosophy of labour to be realised in free artistic production, or not-labour, which labour within the realm of necessity makes possible. This is the meaning of Kosík's remark that 'a philosophy of labour [...] is consequently a philosophy of not-labour'.[31] While these positions are very close at some points, they are divided fundamentally insofar as Marcuse sees the essence of labour as fulfilled in the realm of freedom, whereas Kosík sees the realm of freedom as not-labour. This difference embodies two utterly opposed perspectives toward the 'law of the thing' under which they agree labour works: for Kosík, freedom is only beyond this law of the thing, whereas for Marcuse it is not the law of the thing that freedom escapes but necessity as it is socio-historically defined. To sum up in a slogan: Marcuse sees the realisation of human being in free labour still working under the law of the thing, whereas Kosík sees freedom as beyond labour – which is indeed properly understood through this law. This is why ontology is the foundation for Marcuse, but only a digression for Kosík. When Kosík accuses Marcuse of failing to distinguish between labour and praxis, he is aiming at this fact: that Marcuse sees fulfilment *within* labour, whereas Kosík sees freedom *outside* it. The realm of freedom, art and culture is thus for Marcuse a realm in which labour comes into its own, whereas for Kosík it is a realm beyond labour that is made possible by labour. Kosík asks: 'Does this mean that political activity, science and art *are not* labour? A sweeping negative answer would be just as incorrect as the assertion that science, politics and art indeed are labour'.[32] The footnote to Marcuse indicates that he sees in him such an assertion. While Kosík regards his own answer as not so sweeping, it is most certainly in the negative. Not-labour is grounded in labour and itself grounds culture.

---

30   Kosík 1976, p. 125.
31   Ibid.
32   Kosík 1976, p. 124.

Kosík distinguishes praxis from labour because, while labour is the prerequisite of creative freedom, creative freedom – though it is still praxis – is not labour. For Kosík, the inception of culture is at that point in labour that exceeds natural necessity as defined by the prevailing economic structure. Thus, it has no ontological dimension such as Marcuse's 'excess' and Marx's 'surplus productivity'. Culture is consequently defined solely as not-labour, which is a privative characterisation devoid of any positive content. What are the advantages of such a definition?

Any positive definition of culture, such as Marcuse's, requires both a justification of that definition against competing alternatives and, insofar as it is a Marxist definition, requires a grounding of that capacity or possibility in human labour. Such a justification and grounding would itself be a cultural argument, construction and invention, so that it would need to play the double role of accounting for culture *per se*, including the competing definitions (even if incorrect), and substantiating itself as correct. This would lead to a hermeneutic circle very much like that which Heidegger describes in *Being and Time*,[33] though applied not to Being outright but to culture: in order to justify a conception of culture one would have to use cultural resources made possible by that conception of culture itself. This would mean that any theory of culture would be always-already immersed in a cultural way of life that it could describe and extend but could not theorise from the ground up, and would encounter difficult problems in its relation to other cultural formations. It may be that these problems could be adequately addressed in Heideggerian form: by suggesting that the circle is not vicious, as it appears, but that cultural inquiry consists in widening and deepening the circle of cultural interpretation and not in escaping it. One could not in this manner give an account of the ontological *genesis* or *inception* of culture such as Kosík requires. In this sense, Marcuse is consistent in identifying culture as free creation with labour and denying that the prevailing economic structure is labour at all, with the result that he cannot really bridge culture and labour even though his notion of 'excess' grounds its possibility.

This is the first advantage of Kosík's privative definition of culture: it avoids a hermeneutic circularity by grounding culture solely in the negation of labour in its historically-determined form, such that the justification of culture is not self-referential but refers to labour as both ontological and historically specific. It follows from this definition that the realm of culture does not fulfil the potential of a prior ontology but, by negating its historical form, opens itself up to

---

33   Heidegger 1996, pp. 5–7.

possibilities not realised in that form. Moreover, the form of activity in culture is not tied either to the form of activity in the ontology of labour or its negation (in play, for example). The form of activity is left entirely undetermined, which is to say, left to free invention through the activity itself. Kosík's conception of culture is characterised by openness through its privative determination from labour. The realm of culture can be described and justified as a whole since it is determined by labour, but this realm determines its own content and form precisely because as not-labour it is not tied in its content to the historically-realised possibilities of labour, thereby opening up to that which is unrealised. Its form does not take the form of labour, nor must deny the form of labour, but is free to determine its own appropriate form in the light of its content of unrealised possibilities.[34] Marcuse, on the other hand, is caught in exactly this oscillation: while he denies that culture takes the form of play in his early Heideggerian theory, his later theory of culture goes on to identify it with play.[35] The privative definition does not say that culture *is not* labour, it says that culture *is* not-labour. It is not a negation of the verb but of the noun, such that the form and content of culture are not determined by that which they negate but affirmed by what makes them possible.

However, despite the real advantages of describing the inception of culture as not-labour, Kosík fails to capture the ontological characteristic of labour as surplus productivity or excess that grounds its capacity to produce not-labour. Only because labour does not exhaust all its productivity in sustaining the immediate worker can the inception of culture as not-labour be possible. For this reason, Kosík's ontology of labour, insofar as he intended to develop one, is lacking by comparison with Marcuse's.

3   Culture as Language

Kosík's theory of the inception of culture from labour is presented in three parts: First, an argument against determinism by the economic factor, with a correlative defence of 'economic structure' as a non-reductionist conception of the totality of human life understood as praxis. Second, an argument against viewing art as merely the expression of social reality, with a correlative account of its formative role in human reality. Reality is not known prior to culture but disclosed in it. '[A] work of art expresses an entire world only insofar as it *forms*

---

34   Kosík 1976, p. 124.
35   Compare Marcuse 2005, pp. 136–7 with Marcuse 1962, pp. 165 ff.

it. It forms a world insofar as it discloses the truth of reality. Insofar as reality speaks out through the work of art. In a work of art, reality addresses man'.[36] Third, these two theses on the inception of culture are deployed to clarify the famous segment from the final pages of the introduction to Marx's *Grundrisse*, where he refers to fact that the Greek arts 'in a certain respect [...] count as a norm and as an unattainable model'.[37] Since this passage has long been a problematic one for Marxist theory because it appears to run counter both to the historical character of his thought and to the base-superstructure Marxist theory of culture, Kosík's explanation of this passage can be taken as the nutshell of a non-reductionist theory of culture that forms human reality in a manner that is not shut in by its social production but *opens out* to become a 'timeless' acquisition. Timelessness is not, however, outside human history but is rather the interaction between the work and its audience through history. '[T]he work is a work and lives as a work because it *calls for* interpretations and because it has an *influence* of many meanings.'[38] The influence of a work contains an *event* that links audience and work in this history of interpretation. The event of a work is a happening that discloses human reality sufficiently that it can be explored in many ways from different social locations and in different social contexts. A cultural work is seen by Kosík as a disclosive happening that is a creative forming of human reality, whose meaning is explored historically through a process of totalisation. The location of cultural theory within Marxism has here become central: the role of culture in disclosing the totality of human reality in philosophy and art means that even 'economic structure' and 'the economic factor' must be understood as cultural productions. Further, it even suggests that Marxism in its true meaning is itself a cultural theory of human reality.

Mildred Bakan has argued that Kosík's theory of labour lacks an account of the role of language.[39] To put the critical point in positive terms closer to Kosík's formulation, the *not* of not-labour consists in a freeing of language from the form it takes within the ontology of labour such that culture constitutes an opening of human being.

Language that accomplishes reference to what is absent can itself be taken back to the unique mutuality of intersubjective human address. That *opening* to Being that Kosík and Heidegger both speak of is also 'the mutual *opening* of person to person in terms of the potentiality for speech. And the context of per-

---

36   Kosík 1976, p. 74.
37   Marx 1973, p. 111.
38   Kosík 1976, p. 80.
39   Bakan 1978, pp. 244–53.

son to person mutuality – the precise context of dialogue – is also the context of oppression as a violation of recognition. [...] The demand for recognition that Hegel grounds in the telos of the absolute idea is itself implicit in speech as the mutuality of personal address [...]'.[40]

The dialectic of recognition as a failure of mutuality motivating a dialectic of its eventual achievement presumes that the failure can be seen precisely as a failure, such that the motivation for continuation can be immanent. The seeing of a failure as a failure of mutuality is grounded in the mutuality of address in language. There is, in this sense, a contradiction in the position of the slave with respect to the master in that the slave must be sufficiently non-human to be the instrument of another's will in order to fit the definition of a slave, but also must be sufficiently human to understand the commands that the master utters. This contradiction, which is essential to the dialectic of recognition as a process of immanent negation, can only be seen to be a contradiction through the mutual address implicit in language.

For Bakan, there is a categorical difference between work and speech that must be accounted for within the ontology of labour.[41] Whereas work is oriented toward transforming a given state of things into an imagined future organised around a product, speech is oriented to the mutuality of understanding. 'Insofar as we are open to each other dialogically, we let each other be. [...] To be open to *things*, however, in terms of *work*, is to be open to their *possible transformation*'.[42] These are not different activities but different components of the same activity of labour. For clarity we may adopt definitions here: language is intersubjective communication, whereas work is the object-producing transformation of nature. These are two abstract aspects of labour insofar as human

---

40   Bakan 1983, p. 87.
41   Bakan's compressed argument in the review agrees with Paul Ricoeur's analysis on all points: while every word can always be referred back to action – and this is the legitimacy of a Marxist theory of culture for Ricoeur – it simultaneously is a break from immediate praxis initiating 'a first reflective withdrawal, which, thanks to the interval, the gap hollowed into the plenum of the gesture in the act of being performed, allows for the projective design of the total gesture' (Ricoeur 1965, p. 201). We should note the theoretical trajectory of Ricoeur's argument, which is identical to that of Bakan: on the basis of an understanding of work as the transformation of nature into human products, the necessity of language to the operation of work is noted, and then the emancipation of language from its immediate immersion in work is analysed, such that language in an extended and mediate sense grounds culture. (I consider it likely that Ricoeur's analysis influenced Bakan in making her argument, even though she does not refer to him, since she was well aware of his work when the review was written. I studied with Mildred Bakan as a graduate student at York University when she wrote the review.)
42   Bakan 1983, p. 88. See Heidegger 1996, p. 250.

labour is *social* labour and thus incorporates both work and language in every actual instance. Language speaks of the absent with equal facility as of the present. It informs the imagination and therefore grounds temporality. Thus, the imagination of the future product that is constructed in work is impossible without language.

Bakan's critique of Kosík is that he does not grasp the importance of language to work.[43] But is the paradigm of work as object-oriented transformation, which indeed requires the addition of language, sufficient to cover what Kosík means by 'labour'? Since Kosík understands 'labour as a happening and a *doing* in which *something* happens with man'[44] referring to the *social being* of humans,[45] it implicitly assumes a reference to language and communication as the ground of social life even though Bakan's critique is correct to say that there is no actual theory of language either in Kosík's ontology of labour or in his account of the origin of culture. He comes closest to addressing this issue when he poses the question of the specificity of human being: he repeats the orthodox Marxist gesture of addressing human specificity by contrasting it with non-human animal specificity. Referring to Hegel and Diderot, and eschewing any reference to Engels's classic text that influenced all subsequent Marxism on this point, Kosík diverts the question of the specificity of human being in labour to the historico-anthropological one of the 'transformation of animal appetite into human desire, the humanising of appetite on the basis and in the process of labour'.[46] Kosík thus follows Engels in supposing that the specificity of human labour and being is properly described by explaining its origin from animal being. One key aspect of this theory is its derogation of language in favour of its derivation from a technical, or object-forming, concept of labour.

Engels's theory of the transition from ape to man runs this way: certain apes encountered a way of life that required their hands to be used differently from their feet; this led to an erect posture and eventually to the ability to fashion tools with the hands; (whereas animals can *use* objects encountered in the environment as tools, only humans *construct* them, according to Engels); the hand, and then the whole body, was transformed by the process of labour; the development of labour brought greater social organisation in coordinated activity, leading to the development of language and the bodily transformations that it required, especially in the larynx and brain.[47] One should

---

43 Bakan 1977, p. 249; Bakan 1983, p. 87.
44 Kosík 1976, p. 120.
45 Kosík 1976, p. 112, p. 177.
46 Kosík 1976, p. 121; Kosík 1967d, p. 200.
47 Engels 1940, pp. 279–85.

note three major aspects of this theory: (1) it is a theory of hominisation that attempts to derive the specificity of human labour from the historico-genetic process of coming-to-be human; (2)] that language is derived from a prior labour process which was initially animal and later human – that is to say, it assumes a state of non-linguistic production from which language originates – as Engels says, 'first comes labour, after it, and then side by side with it, articulate speech';[48] and (3) labour functions in this theory as both the *explicandum* and as the *explicans*; specifically-human labour organised through language is explained through its causal origin in not-yet-human labour without language in the transition-period of hominisation. In this sense, Engels conflates labour, which is for Marx *social* labour, into object-production in work lacking social communication, in order to *explain the historical origin* of social labour from work.

This is the sense in which, as Bakan says, Kosík ignores language. Kosík *assumes* labour to be social and thus linguistic but does not account for this assumption in his ontology. In this sense, like Engels, he subsumes labour under the paradigm of work as object-production, whereas, for Bakan and others such as Ricoeur,[49] labour includes both work and language – both object-production and social communication. This is because they are concerned not with the genesis of human labour but with its essential characteristics, as was Marx in *Capital*:

> We are not dealing here with those first instinctive forms of labour which remain on the animal level. [...] We presuppose labour in a form in which it is an exclusively human characteristic [...]. But what distinguishes the worst architect from the best of bees is that the architect builds the cell in his mind before he constructs it in wax.[50]

This imagination in the mind is, according to Ricoeur and Bakan, grounded in the reflective capacity of language in a manner not addressed by Kosík. It is the mutuality of language that grounds the social aspect of human labour, not its transformative capacity in work as the Engelsian heritage claims. It is not language as opposed to work that is at issue here, but language immediately *within* labour as the coordination of its social component and, founded upon this, language as *emancipated* from its immediate embeddedness in labour to form the basis of culture. Language within labour is the basis for the emancipation of

---

48   Engels 1940, p. 284.
49   Ricoeur 1965.
50   Marx 1977a, pp. 283–4.

language in what Kosík calls 'not-labour', which grounds the independence of culture. This absence of language in labour is why Kosík's account in *Dialectics of the Concrete* cannot adequately ground a theory of culture.

Language operative in labour becomes freed from immediate immersion in labour due to the surplus productivity of the labour that grounds not-labour. Language thus acquires the freedom of language characteristic of cultural creation. Language is in this sense the significant mediation between labour and culture. For Kosík's half-hearted ontology of labour to capture the inception of culture adequately, it would need to shed its commitment to an Engelsian historico-anthropological theory of hominisation in favour of a fully ontological account of labour as surplus productivity and the social, that is to say, always-already linguistic.

It is in this sense that we speak of the 'inception' of culture. There is no a-cultural human being, but since the being of human being inheres in praxis as elaborated in the ontology of labour, the origin of culture from labour is an essential theme in the being of human being. 'Origin' in this sense does not mean historical origin, nor even a pre-historical temporal period from which hominisation might originate such as in the model proposed by Engels. It is 'origin' in a genetic and ontological sense that is at issue here. Culture is generated from labour ontologically in the sense that it is made possible within labour, grounded in labour, but diverges from labour in its essential characteristic. The capacity of labour to originate a split within itself such that it gives rise to culture, a split that is co-extensive with labour historically but describes the ontological dependency of culture, is the fundamental theme of the inception of culture. By 'inception' we mean to point to the split within labour that originates culture as non-labour. This split is grounded in labour as negation of a given state for an imagined future one, such that surplus productivity negates simple reproduction. This negation *within* labour grounds the *privative negation* of labour as not-labour.

4 Individuation, Death and Laughter

Kosík's account of culture as not-labour is a non-reductive, unique account of the inception of culture from the ontology of labour. However, as we have seen, he slips from maintaining this ontological account in two places, where he relies instead on Engels's orthodox Marxist account of hominisation. In the first place, Kosík substitutes the coming-to-be of labour as historico-anthropological genesis for an ontological account that would also admit of determination into ontic, historical forms. Marcuse's Heideggerian theory is more adequate in this respect insofar as the fundamental character of labour as producing an excess shows how non-labour is ontologically generated – unlike Kosík's appeal to hominisation. In the second place, Kosík resorts to Engels' theory in order to explain the historico-anthropological genesis of human from animal desire which necessarily subordinates language to labour – labour understood in the first place as without language or pure object-formation in work. It is this that accounts for the absence of a theory of language in Kosík's account of culture.

Any theory of the inception of culture from labour must account for the role of language in culture. One possibility is that language is superimposed upon labour in the same moment that culture is instituted from labour, in which case language would be a specifically cultural aspect of human being. But this would have the consequence that labour itself would be understood as non- or pre-linguistic on the model sketched by Engels. Insofar as the ontology of labour is concerned with specifically human labour, the social character of human labour requires that language be understood as inherent in labour processes. An explanation will also be required as to how language operative in labour can become freed from immediate immersion in labour to acquire the freedom of language characteristic of cultural creation. Language is in this sense the significant mediation between labour and culture.

In conclusion, I want to indicate how an ontological account of labour as both object-formation and language can describe the onto-genesis of culture in a manner that opens its content to individuation, death, and laughter. With these themes, the inception of culture from labour as a privative negation is sufficiently grounded phenomenologically.

Labour consists of an object-orientation in work and a language component in which the language component is subordinated to, and held in check by, the object-orientation of work. The surplus productivity of labour (excess) is the ground for the non-exhaustion of human time in labour. The language component of labour is thereby emancipated from its tie to product-orientation and comes into its own. Rhetoric, understood as form of expression oriented to persuading individuals to adopt a form of life, becomes a major cement for social groups. Speaking is always a speaking-about, and thus oriented to an object – which is the work, but the speaking-to, or other-orientation, comes to the fore with the loss of the domination of object-production. Loosening of the tie of language to object-formation occurs through excess, grounding individuation and thus personal identity, and thereby the ability of culture to describe the historical differentiation of labour in imaginative forms.

This is the onto-genetic inception of culture as fundamentally language and speaking-to-another within not-labour.

Within the realm of creative freedom, play – which can be defined as the invention of rules that bind voluntary social activity – and the invention of genres of play, comes into its own as the expression of human being. This ontological account of the origin of personal identity in culture is thus compatible with, and requires completion by, a cultural theory of the diversity of relations between individual and social identity in different historical and cultural forms. Personal identity is articulated in the dialectic between the self and the other through increasing differentiation. The origin of personal identity is in the distinction between the self and the other that grounds this dialectic. A self-other dialectic is introduced by play, whose differentiation takes many different cultural forms, and which allows the development of a conception of the individual as distinct from all other humans.[51] Awareness of the significance of individual human death arises with individuation and reverberates through culture.

Laughter is the realisation of the possibility of play brought forth by the activity of labour. By laughter I mean neither simply jokes nor wit but a state of human experience that manifests human being. Laughter is an ability to rise above the being of the world through a negation of the power of its necessity. Labour overcomes reality through transforming it, laughter overcomes reality by short-circuiting it. It is quick, not painstaking. Laughter removes in a flash the burdensome law of the thing and replaces it with the law of magical realisation. Labour is the experience of gravity in the weight of the world as against our desires. Laughter is the reversal of gravity. It replaces weight with lightness and fulfils desire immediately, a-temporally. For this reason it is difficult to locate within history. Laughter is the ahistorical irruption of pleasure in the immediate satisfaction of desire. Thus it is the thorough privative negation of labour and, as such, is at the root of culture.

With a specification of the ontological root of individuation, death, and laughter culture is located as the privative negation of labour. Privative negation of specific labour organisation opens up spaces for play such that the dialectic between these cultural spaces and those organised by labour grounds a history of individuation. Historical forms of individuation allow for and demand privative thematisation of death as the end of the personal identity of an individual. Laughter is a privative negation of the whole sphere of labour insofar as it dismisses the law of the thing in one swoop. Laughter is the most

---

51 The absence of personal identity, or individuation, has been pointed out by previous critics, but even the most thorough account by Mildred Bakan, who locates it with respect to the concept of teleological totality in light of our split from nature (Bakan 1983, pp. 91–2, Bakan 1978, p. 253), is not internal to Kosík's account, whereas it is merely noted in the review of *Dialectics of the Concrete* by N. Lobkowicz (Lobkowicz 1964, pp. 248–51).

thorough realisation of the power of culture as not-labour in that it negates labour not in specific forms but universally and forever. It is that a-temporal, unconditional freedom created, cultivated, and protected within culture whose universal privation of labour allows human being to emerge from its given world and to glimpse the worlding of worlds itself.

Creative freedom outside labour in culture returns toward the realm of necessity to articulate the possibility of creative freedom within the labour process. Marxism can be understood in this sense as the realisation of the project of culture within the sphere of labour, the turning of necessity into freedom, and the completion of the odyssey of spirit. Human historical action in 'revolution', or world-transforming activity, aims at the re-appropriation of the ontology of human being through the creative freedom that it makes possible. The ethical principle of this revolution is that every individual within a society take responsibility for the performance of necessary labour and have access to all the forms of culture made possible by necessary labour.

Kosík's philosophy of labour has been shown to be an account of labour performed under necessity, which creates a world of not-labour within which freedom and artistic creation can be experienced. The goal of labour is not-labour, such that the specific act that inaugurates human being as dialectical metamorphosis contains the goal of abolishing itself as a defining characteristic of human being. It is for this reason that Kosík defends the autonomy of philosophy from any social formation. He is critical of Marcuse's attempts to interpret Marxism as the surpassing of philosophy by social theory.[52] Philosophy is characterised by an openness toward all being and in this sense is one of the paramount aspects of non-labour.

> Man is not walled in by the subjectivity of his race, socialness, or subjective projects, in which we would merely define himself in different ways. Rather, through his being, i.e. through praxis, he has the ability to transcend his subjectivity and to get to know things as they are. The being of man reproduces not only socio-human reality; it spiritually reproduces reality in its totality.[53]

Openness to totality is the essence of the being of being human for Kosík which manifests itself in praxis as labour and, through labour's construction of not-labour, grounds both the openness of culture and its freedom from the 'law of the thing' (Marcuse) that rules labour. It is in this sense that Marx's project of the liberation of labour is the culmination of philosophy.

---

52 Kosík 1976, pp. 102–4, p. 128, n. 10, 11.
53 Kosík 1976, p. 152.

CHAPTER 6

'The Philosophy of Labour' and Karel Kosík's Criticism of 'Care'

Siyaves Azeri

1   Introduction

Karel Kosík's elaboration on the interpretations of Marx's *Capital* emphasises the inherent unity between the philosophical and the economic: an authentic interpretation of Marx's *Capital* should deal with all the themes and concepts that have been proposed in the text. Accordingly, economic aspects of *Capital* cannot be properly grasped without grasping its philosophical aspects and vice versa.[1] Kosík's own method of criticising existentialism is a peculiar application of such a holistic outlook: for instance, he refers to categories such as labour, abstract labour and concrete labour in order to formulate a criticism of the notion of 'care'.

Kosík also applies the aforementioned method to the interpretation of *Capital* while criticising those views that separate the philosophical-logical 'form' and the economic 'content' of *Capital*. According to these views, logic is a set of universal rules that is applicable to different contents, and *Capital* is a book of applied logic. Kosík mocks such approaches, stating that by the same token one can also interpret *Capital* as a work of 'applied grammar' since the economic 'content' of the book has also been expressed in linguistic forms and sentences.[2]

Marx criticises Hegel for being a 'crude empiricist'. Empiricism concedes that essence and appearance are different; however, it ontologises and absolutises this difference, and relates essence and appearance mechanically and causally. Rather than ideally and conceptually reconstructing the peculiar logic of specific phenomena, empiricism applies a ready-made, 'abstract' and 'universal' logic to the so-called 'world of appearances'. Thus with regard to Hegel's theory of state, Marx writes, 'Hegel's true interest is not the philosophy of right but logic. The philosophical task is not the embodiment of thought in determinate political realities, but the evaporation of these realities in abstract

---

1 Kosík 1976, p. 96.
2 Kosík 1976, p. 97.

thought. The philosophical moment is not the logic of fact but the fact of logic. Logic is not used to prove the nature of the state, but the state is used to prove the logic'.[3]

Kosík formulates this conceptual shortcoming, which is also shared by the inheritors of Enlightenment dualism, and attempts to criticise it with reference to Marx's materialist method. Phenomenon is different from yet internally related to essence: it covers it (veils it) and yet reveals it. 'Grasping the phenomenon negotiates *access* to the essence. Without the phenomenon, without this activity of manifesting and revealing, the essence itself would be beyond reach'.[4] Grasping the essence requires a progression from the abstract to the concrete. According to Kosík, the fundamental question of materialist epistemology is the relation between concrete and abstract totalities; that is, how concrete totality is to avoid sinking into abstract totality. De-contextualising and absolutising the fact (severing the facts from the context and attributing a static character to them) amounts to a degeneration of the concrete into abstract totality.[5]

The method of abstract principles distorts the whole picture of reality and is equally insensitive to details. It registers these details but fails to grasp their significance. Such a method can be seen, for instance, within traditional 'Marxist' movements where one tendency creates a hierarchy of social problems but conceives of 'class struggle' or the 'inner contradiction of the capitalist society' as an abstract absolute; the resolution of these other problems (which are considered secondary) is postponed to the aftermath of the abstractly conceived revolution; another tendency categorises these issues in a hierarchy, but this time horizontally: hence, totality or the real is reduced to the sum-total of all these issues, whereas the method of ascending from the abstract to the concrete identifies the common generic root behind all these phenomena, thus identifying their historical significance in relation to the essential contradiction of the capitalist society. Thus Kosík states, 'Totality is not a ready-made whole, later filled with a content and with properties and relations of its parts; rather, totality *concretizes* itself *in the process of forming its whole as well as its content*'.[6]

Kosík assumes a critical stance towards both scientism and daily life and the popular view, because both approaches are blind to their own historicity

---

3 Marx 1977b, p. 18.
4 Kosík 1976, p. 3.
5 Kosík 1976, p. 28.
6 Kosík 1976, p. 29.

and presuppositions; both views, therefore, ontologise, absolutise, and thus fetishise their own stances. Yet Kosík's criticism of daily life and scientism is qualitatively different from Heidegger's: Scientistic blindness to historicity is a consequence of a specific type of historical human activity and thus has a genesis; it is not a natural 'defect' or a sign of 'inauthenticity', but an inevitable mark or a necessary form of knowing activity under the capitalist relations of production.

2 Roots of Fetishism

In his criticism of existentialism and the notions of 'care' and 'procure', Kosík uses the aforementioned method to show how Heidegger's existentialism is rooted in and shares the fetishistic view of the world specific to capitalism. In order to disclose this kinship, Kosík refers to the category of abstract labour as a historical-specific form of wealth (value)-producing labour in capitalist society.[7]

Kosík takes on the question as to 'why the essence is not immediately perceptible?' and – in what way is the 'essence concealed?'[8] He responds, 'Man undertakes a detour and exerts an effort in exposing truth only because he somehow assumes that there is a truth to be exposed and because he has a certain cognizance of the "thing itself"'.[9] The reason for the detour is that 'the concealed basis of things has to be *exposed in a certain activity*'.[10]

Reality is the reality of the activity. This is an inevitable consequence of the Marxian materialist stance that rejects the rationalist-empiricist conceptualisation of the basis of knowing as observing-learning and replaces it with activity-changing-manipulating.

Dialectics is a critical-revolutionary method of grasping and transforming the world of the things: 'reality can be transformed in a *revolutionary* way only because, and only insofar as, we ourselves form reality, and know that reality is formed by us'.[11] The 'real world' that is concealed by the world of the pseudoconcrete is not a real world in contrast to an unreal world; nor it is a transcendental world in opposition to a world of subjective illusions; rather, it

---

7   Kosík 1976, p. 38.
8   Kosík 1976, p. 3.
9   Kosík 1976, p. 4.
10 Ibid.
11 Kosík 1976, p. 6.

is a world of human praxis.[12] Both the world of the pseudoconcrete and the world of essences are real; they are one and not one at the same time, as they are both products of human activity. A Marxist analysis of reality is bound to show the historical-specificity of this structuring of the world; it should reveal the historical limits of this world; the historical necessity of its existence and thus the historical possibility of changing this structure with reference to the internal dynamics and intrinsic contradictions within the very structure of this reality. 'Dialectics is after the "thing itself". But the "thing itself" is no ordinary thing; actually it is not a thing at all. The "thing itself" that philosophy deals with is man and his place in the universe or, in different words: it is the totality of the world uncovered in history by man, and man existing in the totality of the world'.[13]

There is no fixed 'essence' beyond the phenomenon: The Kantian conceptualisation of the world of the 'things-in-themselves', for instance, is an uncritical reproduction of the fetishised picture of the phenomenal world; hence it is ossified, trans-historical, and incomprehensible: 'The world of reality is not a secularized image of paradise, of a ready-made and timeless state, but is a process in which mankind and the individual *realize* their truth, i.e. humanize man. It is a world in which truth *happens*'.[14] Practical critique or the destruction of the world of the pseudoconcrete is not a process of unveiling the ready-made, given reality: The world of the pseudoconcrete is exactly the world of independent existence of the products of human activity; the fetishised world of things, where human activity is reduced to utilitarian practice and its reason to instrumental rationality. 'Destroying the pseudoconcrete is the process of forming a concrete reality and of seeing reality in its concreteness'.[15]

A genuine conceptual reconstruction of reality should reveal reality in its totality. 'Totality does not signify *all facts*. Totality signifies reality as a structured dialectical whole, within which and from which any *particular fact* (or any group or set of facts) can be rationally comprehended'.[16] Conceiving the totality does not mean beginning from fixed premises; such a fixed method would be an uncritical reproduction of the method of applying prefabricated logic to phenomena. Rather, it means beginning from abstract and relative premises in order to grasp the reality, natural and social, its wholeness, with all its contradictions. 'The very concept of fact is determined by the overall

---

12 Ibid.
13 Kosík 1976, pp. 152–3.
14 Kosík 1976, p. 7.
15 Kosík 1976, p. 8.
16 Kosík 1976, pp. 18–19.

conception of social reality'.[17] The main question is 'what is social reality?'; the question concerning fact is a moment of this more fundamental question.

For instance, with regard to history, Kosík asks whether history is that which is reflected in human minds that were present at the time of, say, a particular set of events, or whether history is that which really occurred. How is a historian to deal with this? Should she just present history as the reconstruction of the 'reflection' of events in the human mind or should she reconstruct history as it *should* have happened? In the case of the former, the distinction between the essential and the peripheral disappears, which according to Kosík amounts to an abandonment of science.[18] What about 'nature'? Are the so-called laws of nature really within nature or are they reflections or some ideal reconstructions of the human mind? Although science is an idealisation, an ideal reconstruction, it is the reconstruction of some essential aspect of reality and thus it is objective. The ideality-objectivity of scientific reconstruction of 'laws of nature' and objective natural processes is very similar to the ideality-objectivity of value that is incorporated in commodities. Value is an ideal reconstruction, a concept and yet it is the expression of the real, objective movement of commodities under the capitalist relations of production. That it is ideal does not deprive it of its reality and objectivity; that it is objective and real does not mean that it is independent of human activity. Value is the expression of the economic movement of objects within the context of a peculiar type of productive activity, that is, under capitalism. A proper, dialectical scientific exposition of what value is and how it determines the movement of commodities reveals the genesis of this category, its forms of appearance, its historical specificity and limits. Such is the case with natural scientific laws: after all, these are laws of the activity of humans within nature; they are objective and real but in an ideal manner; they are the expression of the mode of the human activity of manipulating the environment and the 'reflection' of the ways humans historically relate themselves to their surroundings. Hence, Kosík continues, 'Mystification and people's false consciousness of events, of the present and the past, is a *part* of history. A historian who would consider false consciousness to be secondary and a haphazard phenomenon and would deny a place in history to it as something false and untrue would in fact be destroying history'.[19]

Kosík's criticism of the approaches that advocate 'abolishing philosophy' is a criticism of the undialectical stances that ignore the aforementioned complexity.

---

17   Kosík 1976, p. 25.
18   Kosík 1976, p. 26.
19   Kosík 1976, p. 27.

It is not true that philosophy is merely an alienated expression of alienated conditions and that this description exhausts its character and mission. Only particular historical instances of philosophy might amount to false consciousness in the absolute sense, but from the perspective of philosophy in the real sense of the word, these would not amount to philosophy.[20]

According to Kosík, the assumption that philosophy is an inverted reflection of the inverted world is based on an idealistic conceptualisation of history not as a history of human activity, not as a history of class struggle, but as history itself; of the history of ideas that have been covertly attributed with a reality of their own.[21] Furthermore, such a formulation suffers from an inner contradiction as it assumes that history exists up to a point but then comes to halt at a certain point. 'A dynamic *terminology* conceals a *static* content; reason is historical and dialectical *only up to a certain phase* in history, up to a turning point, whereafter it changes into trans-historical and non-dialectical reason'.[22]

One of the arguments concerning the abolition of philosophy is based on the idea that the transition from Hegel to Marx is not a transition from one philosophical stance to another, but a transition from philosophy to a theory or criticism of society. This position covertly assumes that there is a continuum in the 'evolution' of philosophy or an independent logic of the emergence of ideas from within ideas. However, 'from the standpoint of materialist dialectics, neither the history of philosophy as a whole nor its individual stages can be interpreted as a 'transition from one philosophical position to another one', because such an interpretation presupposes an immanent evolution of ideas, which materialism denies'.[23]

Kosík, in this regard, criticises Marcuse's view which contrasts Marx and Hegel and claims that the philosophical categories and concepts of the former are social and 'economic', while the economic and social categories of the latter are 'philosophical'. This formulation openly contradicts the Marxian materialist position that seeks to reveal the social and economic content of all ideas in different epochs, since it is not an abstract spirit that philosophises but always a particular, historically determinate concrete human person.[24] What is revealed through Kosík's criticism is the trans-historical core of such formu-

---

20   Kosík 1976, p. 102.
21   Ibid.
22   Kosík 1976, p. 103.
23   Kosík 1976, p. 105.
24   Ibid.

lations, which consider 'labour' only as a trans-historical category. Capitalism's fundamental contradiction, according to these views, is the one between the sociality of labour and individuality of appropriation of the products of labour. Marx, accordingly, refers to this social essence in order to criticise the individual mode of appropriation in capitalist society. Therefore, there is no room in a post-capitalist society for categories and concepts of capitalist society, as a post-capitalist society is the realisation of this social essence of labour. Kosík states,

> The theory of 'abolishing philosophy', however, grasps the 'socio-economic content' of concepts subjectively [...] The statement that all philosophical concepts of Marx's theory are socio-economic categories expresses the double metamorphosis Marxism has undergone in transition from philosophy to social theory. First, the historical reality of discovering the character of economics is obscured. Second, man is imprisoned in his subjectivity: for if all concepts are in essence socio-economic categories, and express only the social being of man, then they turn into forms of man's self-expression, and every form of objectivation is only a variety of reification.[25]

Kosík's depiction of capitalism based on *Capital* is decisive for understanding his position regarding existentialism. He presents capitalism as a system where value appears as a mystified and mystifying subject and where humans are but masks and personifications of this abstract subject. The abstract and contradictory structure of capitalism is manifest in its basic unit, the simple commodity, which assumes a double-character as the unity of use-value and exchange-value (value); this dual character itself is the result of the double-character of labour as the unity of useful (concrete) labour and abstract labour. Marx's *Capital* is the description and analysis of capitalist society which is formed through the movement of this subject (value or commodity).

3 Abstract Labour and the Philosophy of Labour

Capitalist society is a society mediated by abstract labour, which is the source of the valorisation of capital. Marx, as early as the *Paris Manuscripts* identifies the dual character of labour under capitalist relations of production: 'The

---

25 Kosík 1976, p. 106.

worker is the subjective manifestation of the fact that capital is man wholly lost to himself, just as capital is the objective manifestation of the fact that labour is man lost to himself. But the *worker* has the misfortune to be a *living* capital, and therefore an *indigent* capital, one which loses its interest, and hence its livelihood, every moment it is not working'.[26] This double-character is characterised here in one of its particular forms of manifestation, namely alienation:

> The worker produces capital, capital produces him-hence he produces himself, and man as *worker*, as a *commodity*, is the product of this entire cycle. To the man who is nothing more than a *worker-and* to him as a worker-his human qualities only exist insofar as they exist for capital *alien* to him [...]. The worker exists as a worker only when he exists *for himself* as capital; and he exists as capital only when some *capital* exists *for him*. The existence of capital is *his* existence, his *life*; as it determines the tenor of his life in a manner indifferent to him.[27]

In *Capital* Marx states that like the commodity, the unit of capitalist society, which has a dual character that is crystalised in the inner contradiction between use-value and value, 'labour, too, has a dual character: in so far as it finds its expression in value, it no longer possesses the same characteristics as when it is the creator of use-values'.[28]

Labour – as useful labour – is a condition of human existence independent of the form of each society; it mediates the relation between human society and nature.[29] Note that it is only useful labour that assumes such a character. 'As values, the coat and the linen have the same substance, they are the objective expressions of homogeneous labour'.[30] 'Homogenous labour' signifies 'abstract labour'. Simple average labour that is simply expressed in the value of a commodity is the labour-power possessed by every human being in its organism. This simple average labour may vary from epoch to epoch or from society to society, but in a particular society it is given.

In the case of use-value, the labour contained in a commodity counts qualitatively only; with reference to value, however, it counts quantitatively: From the standpoint of the former, it concerns the 'how' and 'what' of labour, from the standpoint of the latter, it concerns the 'how much' of the temporal dura-

---

26 Marx 1974, p. 75.
27 Ibid.
28 Marx 1982, p. 132.
29 Marx 1982, p. 133.
30 Marx 1982, p. 134.

tion of the labour. Labour's dual character means that on the one hand, it is an expenditure of human labour-power; it is abstract human labour that constitutes the value of commodities. On the other hand, it is the expenditure of a particular human labour-power that produces use-value.[31]

Marx's theory of value does not imply that value is a market category only (that is a category of the mode of distribution only): Marx's statement that in capitalism 'direct labour time [is the] decisive factor in the production of wealth', suggests that his category of value should be examined as a form of wealth whose specificity is related to its temporal determination. 'An adequate reinterpretation of value must demonstrate the significance of the temporal determination of value for Marx's critique and for the question of the historical dynamic of capitalism'.[32] Abstract labour can be understood in terms of the 'ideal'. Abstract labour is not the sum total or a generalisation of various aspects of concrete labour; rather, it is the expression of something real: abstract labour is the expression of the ideal being of value as something real, objective, yet non-physical and non-material. Value, abstract labour etc. as social forms have an objective, mind-independent yet relational existence: they exist as ideals, in the realm of the ideal. They are modes of existence of the capitalist social relations (of production). 'Abstract labour is not a substance that one can touch, see, smell or eat ... Commodities acquire a purely social reality in so far as they are expressions of one identical social substance. Viz. human labour [...] it follows as a matter of course that value can only manifest itself in the social relation of commodity to commodity'.[33] Abstract labour is labour subsumed to abstract time, where abstract time signifies empty time as homogenous time.[34]

The one-dimensional treatment of labour as 'labour in general' is common to classical political economy, to classical German philosophy and also to traditional Marxism (the latter reduces Marx's criticism of capitalist society to a criticism from within labour). Kosík draws attention to this 'double character of labour', its relation to the 'double character of the commodity', and the consequent 'movement of the automatic subject (value)'.[35] The subject of the movement of capitalist society is commodity or value. According to Kosík, describing the structure of capitalist society means: 1) determining the laws of the movement of this subject; 2) analysing its individual shapes (forms of

---

31 Marx 1982, p. 137.
32 Postone 2003, p. 123.
33 Bonefeld 2010, p. 266.
34 Bonefeld 2010, p. 267.
35 Kosík 1976, p. 109.

appearance); and 3) presenting a holistic picture of this movement.[36] If this be the case, human subjects or agents as social relations in capitalist society are determined by capital as a social relation and by its self-movement: 'The capitalist is a social relation decked out with a will and a consciousness, mediated by things, and manifested in *their* movement'.[37]

Comparing Marx's *Capital* to Hegel's *Phenomenology*, Kosík draws attention to one common element in both: for both, the subject of cognition is not a mere observer that has a god-like view of the world but is an active agent that can cognise the world only through her own activity and herself as the product of this activity. Yet the world of the active agent that is cognised afterwards is not the world that existed prior to activity, neither is the consciousness identical to what it was – if it was at all – before the activity. Hence, Kosík points toward an epistemology of act-change in contradistinction to the empiricist dictum 'observe-learn'. Kosík calls this the cultural motif of '*Odyssey*'.[38]

Marx, unlike Hegel, does not start with consciousness, not with the spirit, but with a concrete unit, a commodity which is not only an object of the senses, but also a product, a creation of a historically-specific form of social labour.

> Marx starts out with the historical form of the social *product*, describes the laws of its movement, but his entire analysis *culminates* in finding that *these* laws express in a certain way the social relations and the production *activity* of *producers*. To depict the capitalist mode of production in its totality and concreteness means to describe it not only as a lawlike process in itself, i.e. as a process carried out without, and independently of, human consciousness, but also as a process whose laws deal with the way people are *conscious* of both the process itself and of their position in it.[39]

The world of economics is the world of the social relations that lie beneath this surface; economics is the world of those social relations that produce economic entities and categories, which appear as if they have a momentum of their own. Marx's critique is not a critique of masks (the forms of appearance of social relations of production) but of the essence that necessarily assumes these forms. 'Economics is the objective world of people and of their social

---

36 Kosík 1976, p. 110.
37 Kosík 1976, p. 116.
38 Kosík 1976, p. 111.
39 Kosík 1976, pp. 111–12.

products; it is not the objectual world of social movement of things'.[40] Therefore, the core of Marx's critique of political economy is the critique of this transient form of economy and of fetishism. 'As long as this historical form of economics exists, i.e. as long as the social form of labour creates exchange-value, there also exists a real prosaic mystification. When mystified, particular relations into which individuals enter in the course of producing social life appear inverted, as social relations of things'.[41]

Drawing on the generality and historical determination of labour in capitalist society, Kosík criticises 'scientific' and sociological approaches to work; he criticises such approaches for their fetishised conception of labour and for presenting labour or work in its 'concrete' terms as some transhistorical activity of producing and manipulating the world. Kosík states that the task of a philosophy of labour 'is not to *generalize* partial findings of various sciences, let alone to present an apology for a particular historical form of labour'.[42] There are two aspects to be noted; first, the philosophy of labour, as a conceptual investigation of reconstructing the process of labour, should aim at forming a concept of labour, which will signify the logical-generic root of forms of labour. Second, labour is not a transhistorical form of activity; it is historically determined; in particular, labour under capitalism is a historically-specific form of labour. Thus follows Kosík's treatment of labour in two distinct categories: labour as a philosophical category and labour as an economic category. As a philosophical category, labour is the activity of objectification of human tools and meanings and the humanisation of the environment and nature.[43] Economically, however, labour is the activity that produces specific forms of wealth; it is a historical-specific activity: under capitalist mode of production, it is two-fold abstract-concrete labour that amounts to the production of value and commodities as the bearer of value. Labour in general or labour as a philosophical category is the historical basis of labour as an economic category; yet the two are not identical.[44] Therefore, freedom is not actualised via labour but beyond its boundaries: 'The real realm of freedom thus begins beyond the *boundaries* of labour, although precisely labour forms its indispensible historical basis'.[45] Free *time*, in contrast with leisure that is the product of work, is possible only if

40   Kosík 1976, p. 115.
41   Ibid.
42   Kosík 1976, p. 117.
43   Kosík 1976, p. 122.
44   Kosík 1976, p. 127.
45   Kosík 1976, p. 125.

reified labour is abolished, i.e. when historical-specific double-sided capitalist labour is abolished.

With work, the human being gains three-dimensionality: past, present, and future. Whereas the animal always lives in the present, the human lives in the past, the present, and the future. With labour the human gains control of time; by contrast, the animal is solely controlled by time. Labour is a mediation that amounts to the human's delayed response to stimuli. In a sense, labour is the source of abstraction and therefore of meaning: 'The being that can resist immediate satiation of its craving and can "actively" harness it forms a present as a function of future, while making use of the past. *In its doing it uncovers the three-dimensionality of time as a dimension of its own being*'.[46] Time, then, is the time of labour.

> The three-dimensionality of time and the temporality of man are based on objectification. *Without objectification there is no temporality*. As objective doing, labour is a special mode of identity of time (temporality) and space (extension), as two fundamental dimensions of human being, of a specific form of man's movement in the world.[47]

Under the capitalist relations of production, time assumes an abstract, universal character; it becomes the abstract time of abstract labour. Therefore, the general aspect of labour is internally and dialectically tied to its historical-specific form: with abstract labour concrete labour is abolished, yet to reappear as a moment of abstract labour. The abolition of concrete labour is realised in the emergence of abstract labour; yet the product of abstract labour, that is value, is bound to appear only in the concrete, useful product of labour, namely, in use-value. Thus the realisation of abstract time is necessarily tied to the time of labour.

With labour the human being appears as an objective subject. The product of labour as an artefact independent of individual consciousness is the prerequisite of human history and the continuity of her existence. The tool of labour, therefore, is the most important mediation between the human being and reality. Realistic views of human reality, from Anaxagoras to Aristotle and Hegel, therefore, emphasise the centrality of the tool for the human being in contrast to intentionality, which is dear to romanticist philosophy:

---

46   Kosík 1976, p. 121.
47   Kosík 1976, p. 122.

There is widespread opinion that man is the only being aware of its morality: only he faces a future opening up ahead, with death at its end. The existentialist interpretation of this opinion idealistically distorts it. From the finitude of man's existence it infers that objectification is a form of *flight* from authenticity, namely from being-toward-death. But man knows his morality only because he organizes time, on the basis of labour as objective doing and as the process of forming socio-human reality. Without this objective doing in which man organizes time into a future, a present and a past, man could not *know* his totality.[48]

Approaches that separate the realms of freedom and necessity take a historically transient form of division of labour as a trans-historical condition: they eternalise and ontologise the existing relations of production. Furthermore, they identify *free* time with leisure time. Labour under the capitalist relations of production is a compulsion imposed by the abstract social goal of production of surplus-value and the self-valorisation drive of capital. The uncritical interpretation of the labour process therefore sees in the labour process only external compulsion, without conceiving its true source. Hence there follows a superficial division between labour and freedom etc. Moreover, this blindness to the historicity of the labour process and the particular forms it acquires amount to abhorring the abstract element as the source of inauthenticity and evils in the world. Such an approach is merely the other side of the coin of absolutising and eternalising the existing relations of production. 'A philosophy of labour, i.e. an objective human doing *through which*, in the happening of the necessity, real prerequisites of freedom are *formed*, is consequently also a philosophy of non-labour'.[49]

Labour that produces value is not 'labour in general', although the latter is the basis of the former. Labour in the philosophical sense is the source of human social reality. If this be the case, it is inevitable that capitalist society is the product of a historically-specific form of labour, which is labour that has a two-fold character: useful or concrete labour and abstract labour. Abolition of capitalist labour, therefore, is not the abolition of labour in the philosophical sense of the term, but is the abolition of labour as a necessity imposed on people by the self-valorisation drive of capital.

There is no freedom-in-general as there is no production-in-general; freedom both as a concept and as a condition of human existence is historically

---

48   Kosík 1976, p. 123.
49   Kosík 1976, p. 125.

determinate. If the prerequisites of freedom are formed in the realm of necessity through labour, then every historical form of labour will amount to a specific form of freedom. In capitalist society, therefore, freedom is bound to capitalist labour, the specificity of which is its dual character. Capitalist labour is the unity of concrete and abstract labour. Abstract labour is labour that is subordinate to abstract time, that is, time as a universal independent variable. Through labour the human being dominates time, but under capitalist relations of production, the very product of human activity dominates the producers; 'Time is everything, man is nothing: he is at the most time's carcass'.[50] Under the capitalist relations of production, freedom too attains an abstract form; it becomes a function of the specific form of capitalist wealth – value. Production of value requires a free labourer; free in a dual sense: free from the means of production and free as the owner of her specific commodity, that is, labour-power. However, since value is bound to express itself in commodity form, in the form of money or use-value, there is a concrete aspect to this abstract freedom. Although limited, the worker that exchanges her labour-power with capital, as the owner of the money she is paid for her labour, is free to use the money as she wishes. 'Freedom is not a state, but rather an historical activity that forms corresponding modes of human coexistence, i.e. social space'.[51]

The view that considers objectification a 'flight from authenticity' is blind to this dual nature of labour and the dual character that freedom acquires under the capitalist relations of production. It unconsciously realises that the (abstract) time of objectification through capitalist labour subsumes humans, but it identifies the capitalist form of objectification with 'objectification-as-such'. In doing so, it eternalises and ontologises capitalist labour. Where Hegel sees only the positive side of labour,[52] this approach sees its negative side only; this being the case, it replicates the Hegelian one-sided view of labour symmetrically.

4 Criticism of 'Care'

Abstract labour is general value-producing human labour, the expenditure of which is measured by abstract time. This aspect, according to Kosík, becomes manifest in the fetishisation of human relations and also in wage-labour. The shift in German classical philosophy from 'labour' to 'procuring' (Hegel to

---

50 Marx 1992, p. 41.
51 Kosík 1976, p. 147.
52 Marx 1974, p. 131.

Heidegger) is the manifestation of the dominance of abstract labour in capitalist society and a degraded reaction against this abstractness. German classical philosophy knows only 'labour' as the transhistorical, immediate activity of manipulating nature. The absence of such a transhistorical concrete labour and determination and subjugation of 'labour' by abstract labour finds its unconscious 'ideological' manifestation in the shift from labour to procuring. 'Procuring' is a mystified, fetishised interpretation of and a nominal replacement for concrete labour. It is a romantic rage against abstract labour, but from within the very context that is determined by abstract labour.

Procuring is the phenomenal aspect of abstract labour. Labour has been divided up and depersonalised to the extent that in all spheres – material, administrative, and intellectual – it appears as mere procuring and manipulation. To observe that the place occupied in German classical philosophy by the category of labour has been taken over in the twentieth century by mere procuring, and to view this metamorphosis as a process of decadence represented by the shift from Hegel's objective idealism to Heidegger's subjective idealism, is to highlight a certain phenomenal aspect of this historical process.[53]

Heidegger sees labour as transhistorical; thus concrete labour's determination by and subordination to abstract labour in capitalist society seems to represent the dissolution of labour and its replacement by some abstract entity. Therefore, he offers a return to the 'essence' of labour; an essence that does not exist; he abhors phenomenally conceivable labour as the manifestation of abstract labour and suggests a return to the allegedly authentic 'labour' in the form of procuring. Heidegger does not see that concrete labour's determination by and subordination to abstract labour is the inevitable consequence of the self-movement of capital. Concrete labour under capitalism cannot emerge except as a moment of abstract labour. It is the necessary form of appearance of abstract labour (as the generic root and the essence of labour). Heidegger dreams of a direct return to an essence where no such essence persists. Thus Kosík states, 'Procuring is praxis in its *phenomenally alienated form* which does not point to the *genesis* of the human world but rather expresses the praxis of everyday manipulation, with man employed in a system of *ready-made* "things", i.e. implements'.[54]

Heidegger's conceptualisations of anxiety and care confirm the aforementioned interpretation. Anxiety and fear, though different, are kindred phenomena and mostly conflated. Fear is to fear something in-the-world, whereas

---

53   Kosík 1976, p. 38.
54   Kosík 1976, p. 39.

Dasein's running away from itself is not running away from something in the world but from something like itself, namely Dasein. '*The turning-away of falling is grounded rather in anxiety, which in turn is what first makes fear possible*'.[55] Being-in-the-world is a basic state of Dasein. Therefore, '*That in the face of which one has anxiety is Being-in-the-world as such*'.[56] The characterisation of anxiety as being anxious about the threat of something that is 'nowhere' (and therefore everywhere) signifies the abstractness of the threat: 'What oppresses us is not this or that, nor is the summation of everything present-at-hand; it is rather the *possibility* of the ready-to-hand in general; that is to say, it is the world itself'.[57]

Anxiety is anxious about being in the world. In a sense, as it is anxiousness in the face of the abstract, it negatively brings about the apparent possibility of Dasein coming about itself (that is, Dasein not running in the face of itself). The self-sameness that is existentially 'experienced' due to anxiety is the reflection of the fear of the abstract omnipresent element, the abstract aspect that appropriates every simple entity in the world; the abstractness that turns every particular concreteness into a moment of itself. Thus Heidegger concludes, 'in anxiety one feels "*uncanny*"'.[58] 'Uncanniness' also means not-being-at-home (since the 'home' is occupied by the things, the 'others' that are moments of the abstract). Heidegger is quite straightforward on this:

> This character of Being-in was then brought to view more concretely through the everyday publicness of the 'they', which brings tranquilized self-assurance – 'Being-at-home', with all its obviousness – into the average everydayness of Dasein. On the other hand, as Dasein falls, anxiety brings it back from its absorption in the 'world'. Everyday familiarity collapses. Dasein has been individualized, but individualized as *Being*-in-the-world. Being-in enters into the existential 'mode' of the '*not-at-home*'. Nothing else is meant by our talk about 'uncanniness'.[59]

To fall means to be dragged toward daily entities; this state of being attracted by the public, by the ordinary, manifests itself in the form of feeling 'at home' in everyday life (not to feel threatened by either the abstract or the outsider). The feeling of the uncanny, which is the expression of Dasein's authenticity via anxiety, functions like a call in the face of absorption into and thus confirma-

---

55   Heidegger 1962a, p. 230.
56   Ibid.
57   Heidegger 1962a, p. 231.
58   Heidegger 1962a, p. 233.
59   Ibid.

tion of the everyday world. 'This uncanniness pursues Dasein constantly, and is a threat to its everyday lostness in the 'they', though not explicitly'.[60] It is worth noting how the threat of the abstract ('nothing and nowhere') and that of the 'they' go hand in hand in triggering the anxiety and the consequent uncanniness. Falling and the feeling of uncanniness resemble the anti-Semitic idea that considers the degradation of a community of equals (*Volksgenossen*) into society as the source of evil and fear.[61] For the anti-Semite, society is rootless and declares rootlessness as its purpose: it demands abstract equality before the law and defines accumulation of wealth in form of value (abstract labour) as its final end. The other, the 'they', which is the source of the feeling of uncanniness, is a parasite to be exterminated so that the community can regain its lost purity.

Because of its thrownness into the world, humanity's confrontation with Being, according to Heidegger, takes the form of a confrontation with things. In this way, being of the ready-to-hand entities becomes the dominant form of understanding being; being, accordingly, acquires the meaning of reality. In this way, even the being of Dasein moves into this horizon and 'Being in general' acquires the meaning of 'Reality'. Such a diversion will eventually derail the general problematic of the meaning of Being.[62] By entering the world of everyday, familiar objects and reality, Dasein's conception of itself is degraded; even its existence is degraded; it loses its ontological significance and falls down to the level of everydayness and commonality.

The question of reality and the external world can only be resolved on the basis of identifying the appropriate kind of access to the real. Traditionally, grasping the real has been identified with the knowledge that is acquired based on beholding (looking, observation). To the extent that the Real is understood as something in itself and independent of consciousness, the question of the meaning of the real becomes linked with the questions as to whether the real is independent of consciousness or whether consciousness somehow is prior to the Real. Furthermore, the question about the nature of our primary access to the real should also be answered in order for us to be able to decide if knowing can assume this function at all.[63] In a sense, Heidegger proposes that the 'pragmatic' or the 'utilitarian' approach to reality is responsible for the inverted understanding of both the question of being and the mode that is considered primary for grasping the real. Such an approach has some truth in it in that

---

60   Heidegger 1962a, p. 234.
61   Bonefeld 1997, pp. 63–4.
62   Heidegger 1962a, p. 245.
63   Heidegger 1962a, p. 246.

human modes of knowing, manipulating, and appropriating the world cannot be thought of in isolation from human consciousness, which is historically determined. The problem, however, is that Heidegger de-historicises and ontologises the utilitarian approach; in this, he replicates the very illusion that is produced by the utilitarian-pragmatic mindset appropriate to the capitalist mode of production. Consequently, the characteristic of humanity's practical (and productive) behaviour under the capitalist mode of production – the dual character of labour – is ontologised, fetishised and consequently ignored. For instance, he assumes that identifying knowing with beholding (observing) is a transhistorical characteristic of all 'metaphysics' and thus it signifies an ontological error common to all theories of knowledge throughout history. It is in this sense that his 'criticism' of idealisms and realisms falls within the very tradition at which this criticism is aimed. Thus Heidegger is only critical of 'instrumental reason' in contrast with reason as such; however, instrumental reason is merely the other side of the coin of reason. There is no reason-as-such. As Bonefeld puts it,

> The moral obligation to lead the exodus to a better world and the immorality of instrumental reason are historically and theoretically two halves of the same walnut: Revolution and its containment in the name of revolution itself. 'The thought of happiness without power is unbearable because it would then be true happiness' (Horkheimer and Adorno, p. 172). Instrumental reason is the mode of existence of the expanded reproduction of the *status quo*. It allows merely technological revolutions and serves the continuous project of bourgeois revolution by fashioning human existence as a resourceful tool for profitable calculation.[64]

Existentialism, i.e. philosophical anthropology, is a mere reaction to a historically transient form of conceptualisation of humanity that reduces the human to a calculable physical entity. Yet as a form of idealism it commits the fallacy of separating human existence from nature; it reduces nature to a projection of subjective imagery. In doing so, it replicates the reductionist positivist conceptualisation of the human since this latter formulation too separates the human and nature, or the historical and the natural.

> Only when man is included in the design of reality and when reality is grasped as the totality of nature and history will the conditions for solv-

---

[64] Bonefeld 1997, p. 66.

ing the philosophical problem of man have been created. While a reality without man would be incomplete, man without the world would equally be a mere fragment. Philosophical anthropology cannot recognize the character of man for it has locked him into the subjectivity of his consciousness, race and socialness, and has radically separated him from the universe. Learning about the universe and about laws of natural events *always* also amounts to direct or indirect learning about man and his specificity.[65]

The anthropological reaction to reductionism is a reaction to the quantitative concept of the human. Quantitative conceptualisations of the human and her consciousness are the reflection of an approach that reduces all nature to quantifiable things, which are externally related. Such an approach is a form of appearance of the logic of capital as self-valorising value, which is rooted in abstract labour, that is, value-producing labour or labour subsumed to abstract time. However, philosophical anthropology defines itself as a complement to a philosophical conceptualisation that excludes the human – the subject of conceptualisation – from its conceptions. This reaction, in turn, is a reflection of a rage against the abstract from within the framework of the concrete.

Capitalist society is the world of implements; of interconnected functions: machines are plural; they are abstract tools determined by the logic of abstract labour and commodity production. The pre-capitalist world, the world of the plane,[66] however, is the world of immediacy and particular concreteness. Capitalist social relations are different from other overt forms of relations among individuals in non-capitalist societies (e.g. kinship or individual domination); in contrast with the concrete particularity of such overt relations capitalist social relations assume a general, abstract form. The problems of the twentieth century, of capitalist society, cannot be conceived from within the framework of pre-capitalistic concreteness. 'Procuring as abstract human labour in its phenomenal form creates an equally abstract world of utility in which everything is transformed into a utilitarian instrument. In this world things have no independent meaning and no objective being; they acquire meaning only insofar as they are manipulable'.[67] In the modern world particularity is replaced by absolute universality. Procuring is the reified image of human praxis; procuring is not a process of producing and forming an objective-practical human world

---

65 Kosík 1976, p. 152.
66 Kosík 1976, p. 40.
67 Ibid.

but is the process of manipulation of the world of ready-made things (manipulation of fetishes).[68]

The time of 'care', according to Kosík, is the future; it is the time of projection; of fear, expectation, hope etc. In this, it is the denial of the present.[69] The present in this mode of time appears as a projection of the future; the now becomes subordinate to the not-yet. This can be interpreted as an aspect of the abstractness of time; a practical form of appearance of abstract time as the independent, universal variable. This projection is possible because time in this abstract mode is divisible into equal segments which are identical to each other and universally quantifiable. Time as an abstract universal is all the same; the present would be the future, as they are both identical. Since the future is not here yet and since through this abstract universal projection of the future the present is neglected, life appears to the philosopher of care as nothingness.

The everyday of capitalist society is different from that of pre-capitalist societies.[70] Kosík pursues the differences caused by the emergence of the abstract, universal concept of time: 'The everyday is above all the *organising* of people's individual lives into every day: the replicability of their life functions is fixed in the replicability of every day, in the time schedule for every day'.[71] The replicability of the everyday is the manifestation of the repeatability of abstract time (the minute, the hour, the day) as a universal independent variable. Each segment of abstract time is identical to others, as it is devoid of any kind of concrete content. For the naïve consciousness, the everyday appears as the natural world of familiarity, whereas history or war appears as a transcendental reality that disrupts the familiar world and throws it into catastrophe. The cleavage of life into the everyday and history appears as the historicity of the History and the ahistoricity of the everyday. 'History changes, the everyday remains'.[72]

5   Conclusion

The method of the philosophy of care takes the everyday as an inauthentic historicity, which is to be rejected and transcended; however, in this it mystifies the everyday and reality: 'If the everyday is the *phenomenal* "layer" of reality, then the *reified* everyday is overcome not in a leap from the everyday to authenti-

---

68   Kosík 1976, p. 41.
69   Kosík 1976, pp. 41–2.
70   Kosík 1976, p. 42.
71   Kosík 1976, p. 43.
72   Kosík 1976, p. 44.

city but in practically abolishing both the fetishism of the everyday and that of History, that is, in practically destroying reified reality both in its phenomenal appearance and in its real essence'.[73] This standpoint of the philosophy of care is reminiscent of Bruno Bauer's stance with regard to the 'emancipation' of the Jew. Bauer 'demands [...] that the Jew should renounce Judaism, and that mankind in general should renounce religion, in order to achieve civic emancipation'.[74] Instead of questioning the relation between political emancipation and human emancipation in general, Bauer restricts his criticism to a particular form of the state – the so-called 'Christian state' – rather than the state in general. Thus, by reducing the state to the concrete form it assumes under a certain circumstance, that is, by considering the state devoid of its determinations, he ontologises and fetishises this 'concrete' Christian state, thereby mistaking the phenomenon for the essence. Bauer, disregarding the 'secular' basis of theological questions, merges history with superstition. The core of the matter is that religion, alongside other superstitions, is not a source but a showcase of the miserable human condition, and it is reproduced within the existing social relations. In other words, neither religious superstition nor other forms of 'ideologies' are realities in and of themselves; regardless of their historical roots, they are phenomena of the existing society and expressions of the general inequality and unfreedom under the existing mode of production. Fetishising and ontologising religion, Bauer, alongside others, only deals with such phenomena in theological terms. Bauer demands that the Jew denounce Judaism; through such a demand he leaves the root of the problem untouched. Interpreted from the perspective of a mature Marx's critique of political economy in *Capital*, the secular basis of religion turns out to be the self-valorising value, that is, capital as a social relation. Bauer conflates the domination of the abstract – capital – with its concrete forms of incarnation – religion and the religious state.

In a similar vein, the philosophy of care advocates an escape from the 'everyday' to the so-called authentic. However, the 'authentic' is itself a perverse image of the 'inauthentic' everyday, just as god is the alienated image of humanity purported onto heavens. The escape to 'authenticity' is a rejection of the apparent state of alienation, while holding fast to the essential material relations that yield such an alienated state. As Fritsche puts it, 'the decision to cancel society does not prevent the authentic Daseine [English plural of Dasein] from taking over modern technology and capitalism as an economic system'.[75]

---

73   Kosík 1976, p. 45.
74   Marx 1975b, p. 149.
75   Fritsche 1999, p. 289, n. 64.

Disregarding the determination of social reality by value amounts to an affirmation (albeit unintended) of the very basis of the so-called 'inauthentic everyday'. With such a dismissal of the essence of the problem, the critique of the everyday turns into a mere criticism of the shadows of capital – a reproduction of the commodity-fetishes – the pseudo-concrete – that seem to have a life of their own and the relations among which appear as social relations.

Misrecognition of the abstract, i.e. value, which dominates contemporary society as the concrete in the form of the 'everyday', amounts to the philosophy of care's pseudo-critical stance that may effect a break with bourgeois society, but does not break with capitalism. This stance, at the political level, yields reactionism and the sanctification of violence in the name of cleansing the 'home' of degrading elements. As the everyday represents the determination of the ready-to-hand, the break with the everyday also appears as promoting indeterminacy. Instead of setting indeterminacy as a goal in face of the determination of social life by capital, the philosophy of care sanctifies it, in form of the denial of the present and a 'critique' of the inauthentic everyday, as an ontological and authentic position – a criticism which Postone calls a 'reified response to a reified understanding of historical necessity'.[76] The philosophy of care fails to see that indeterminacy is appropriable only once the constraints exerted by capital are overcome and thus advocates 'a "tiger's leap" out of history'[77] onto authenticity.

The reified everyday and the fetishised reality (historicity) are two moments or modes of existence of the same social reality of the capitalist relations of production: the former is an appearance of the concrete, the latter a manifestation of its abstract aspect. The philosophy of care criticises the former from within the framework of the latter, but it assumes the latter as the authentically concrete, in contrast with the abstract inauthenticity of the former.

---

76 Postone 2006, p. 95.
77 Ibid.

CHAPTER 7

Kosík, Lukács and the Thing in Itself

Tom Rockmore

Since Marx's position turns on a historical approach, it is useful to note that Kosík's most significant work, *Dialectics of the Concrete* (1963), clearly belongs to its historical moment. It appeared in 1963 in the days when Marxist humanism was flourishing, when the problem of rethinking the relation of Marxism and Marx's later writings to previously unknown earlier writings like the *Paris Manuscripts* and the *Grundrisse* was central to discovering a new side of Marx, when Marxism-Leninism was in power in the Soviet Union and throughout Eastern Europe, and before the intellectual counterattack began in Althusser's defence of orthodox Marxism. Yet within the context of Marxist studies since that time when Kosík was writing, his book seems astonishingly up to date. And in another sense, though his study is obviously inspired by Marx, it is not an exercise in Marxist philosophy, or rather it is more than a contribution to Marxism, since it also counts as an original contribution to philosophy.

Kosík's important book, perhaps like all original philosophical texts, develops in different directions from a conceptual centre. In order to focus the discussion, I will be concerned here with merely a single aspect of Kosík's position in this work: his contribution from a critical Marxist perspective, certainly critical with respect to orthodox Marxism, to the problem of knowledge. This is an important theme in different ways in German idealism, in Marx, and in post-Marxian Marxism.

The origin of Marx's position lies in his early critique of Hegel's *Philosophy of Right* and in related texts. Engels, who invented classical Marxism, was self-taught in philosophy. He was aware of the limits of his understanding of this domain.[1] Later Marxists who, like Lenin often rely on Engels to understand Marx, often do not know enough about philosophy to grasp the limits of what Engels says about Hegel and German idealism, whom he dismisses in favor of materialism. The significance of this point lies in the fact that in different ways, Hegel remains a central reference throughout Marx's later writings. Hence Marx's theories can usefully be understood against the background of

---

1 He was, as he said in a letter to Ruge, self-taught and not knowledgeable in this domain. See Engels's letter to Ruge, dated 26 July 1842, in Marx and Engels 1975, p. 545.

his diagnosis of and solution for what he obviously regards as the unresolved difficulties of Hegel and German idealism in general.

The theme of a specifically Marxian approach to cognition with the aim of solving the problem of German idealism is popular in the debate, particularly during the Soviet period, early on in Lukács, then later in Ilyenkov, Kosík, Kołakowski and others, to mention only a few names. This has the advantage of understanding Marx's position not as sui generis, not as unrelated to its context, but rather, as he may have understood it, as an effort not merely to ignore but rather to carry forward the debate.

In order to limit the scope of the paper, I will concentrate my remarks on comparing and contrasting efforts to solve the supposedly unsolved problem of the thing in itself, which in different ways runs throughout German idealism and is supposedly solved in Marx's position. In response, I will be pointing to a sense in which Marxian materialism does not break with, but rather extends German idealism in further developing cognitive constructivism.

1   On the Thing in Itself

The fact that in a sense we live in different worlds is brought home by the difficulty of interpretation. Philosophical interpretation, like all forms of interpretation, indicates that interpreters often 'see' starkly different texts. All forms of Marxism, starting with Engels, are at least in some distant sense interpretations of Marx. The history of Marxism shows us that, though they agree on his importance, interpreters of Marx understand his position from often radically different points of view, hence identify different, often incompatible views they attribute to the author of *Capital*. Though Marx is often depicted as breaking sharply with German idealism, there are strong elements of continuity as well, for instance as concerns the thing in itself, a concept which is central for both German idealism as well as Marx and certain forms of Marxism.

For present purposes I will limit the discussion to the views of Engels, Lukács and Kosík. All three understand the cognitive problem as turning on the thing in itself, which they understand very differently. This concept is understood in many ways in a long debate. Suffice it to say here that Kant popularised this term in reinterpreting Plato's canonical distinction in his notorious theory of forms (or ideas) between forms, which refer to reality, and appearances, which refer to objects in the surrounding world. We do not know if Plato accepted any version of the theory of forms, which has been attributed to him in the debate over more than two millennia. According to Plato, objects, also called appearances, are effects which 'participate' in forms, which are their causes. An ontological relation of cause to effect leads from forms to appearances. But no path leads from appearances to forms, which are known through intellectual intuition by philosophers only.

This theme recurs in the critical philosophy. Kant, who denies intellectual intuition, thinks that all knowledge begins in experience. He refers to reality, which does not appear and, hence, cannot be known, as the thing in itself, or noumenon, in a short as an object of thought, but not as given in experience. The term 'thing in itself' is understood in many ways, including epistemologically as a cognitive limit and ontologically as mind-independent reality.

2   Engels and Lukács on Cognition

Engels is the inventor of classical Marxism, which lies at the root of all later forms of Marxism. Lukács and Korsch, Lukács more than Korsch, invented Hegelian Marxism in the early 1920s. Lukács especially emphasises a Hegelian dialectical approach in refuting the mechanistic approach of the Second International, in placing Marx's relation to Hegel in the centre of the effort to grasp Marx, in depicting this relation not as simple but rather as complex, and in arguing in detail that Marx solves the cognitive problem at the heart of German idealism.

As concerns philosophy, it is appropriate to note the difference between Engels and certain philosophically sophisticated later Marxists such as Lukács, Korsch, Marcuse, Habermas, Kołakowski and Kosík. In his study of Feuerbach and elsewhere, Engels depicts Marx as following Feuerbach to leave idealism for materialism, philosophy for science, mythology for truth. Lukács, who is politically in agreement with Engels but philosophically deeply opposed, was a product of German neo-Kantianism and increasingly familiar with Hegel. His grasp of German idealism was acquired before he turned to Marxism, and later deepened in a long series of writings, often on Hegel. He depicts Marx as overcoming the problem of classical German philosophy through a theory closely related to post-Fichtean Hegelianism. Kosík, who like Ilyenkov and others was active during the Soviet time. Like other Marxists of this period such as Petrovic or Paci, he turned toward post-Husserlian phenomenology, especially Heidegger, in appropriating and rethinking selected concepts.

Engels takes what today would be called a positivist approach to philosophy, perhaps more precisely scientific empiricism close to the Vienna Circle approach. He infamously discards the Kantian thing in itself, which is overcome in his opinion by practice and industry, in favour of scientific cognition of mind-independent reality. According to Engels, Marx solves (or resolves) the problem of the relation of thinking and being, the central problem of philosophy, through discovering the scientific laws of society. In other words, Marx solves the fundamental problem of philosophy in turning to science. From Engels's positivistic perspective, science and only science is the source of truth. And Marx's position is a form of science, hence also a source of truth.

Lukács, who in effect denies Marx leaves philosophy, points to Engels' basic misunderstanding of the thing in itself as practice and industry, in suggesting the relationship of Marx to Hegel is central to the Marxian solution of the problem of knowledge. For Lukács, idealism fails to 'know' the thing in itself, which is 'known' through Marx and Marxism, more through Marx than Marxism, above all through Hegelian Marxism. Lukács suggests a deep continuity between Marxian materialism and Hegelian idealism, hence between materialism and idealism, or between Marx and German idealism.

In turning away from Marxism, Lukács rereads Marx not outside of but rather within the German idealist tradition. In replacing the Hegelian absolute through the proletariat through what Lukács calls the identical subject/object, Marx discovers the real historical subject, hence solves (or resolves) the problem of the thing in itself. This is certainly one way to read Marx's reference to Vico's view that we can know what we make, since, as Lukács notes, 'the object of cognition can be known by us for the reason that, and to the degree in which, it has been created by ourselves'.[2]

This claim suggests four points. To begin with, Lukács stresses the very early Marx and not, say, economic crisis, the party as the vanguard of the proletariat, the transition from idealism to materialism, the abolition of private property, the dictatorship of the proletariat and so on in the transition from capitalism to communism. Second, as noted, he reads the proletariat as an identical subject-object, hence from the closely Hegelian perspective of so-called identity theory. He further turns to class-consciousness, hence to the famous Hegelian master/slave analysis, in stressing Marx's link to German idealism. Lukács finally looks beyond Hegel toward Fichte in pointing to a conception of the subject as active and never passive. This point can be supported by Marx's concern with Fichte's view in formulating his conception of the subject in the third of the *Paris Manuscripts*.

The opposition between Engels and Lukács in reading Marx is clear and important. Engels points to a break between materialism and idealism, between Marx and German idealism, to solve the problem of the thing in itself. Lukács, on the contrary, points to a deep continuity between Marx and Hegel

---

2 Lukács 1971, p. 112. See also Vico 1948, p. 85 and p. 105 (§§ 331 and 376).

in order to resolve the same enigma. For Engels, Marx leaves Hegel behind in turning from idealism to materialism. For Lukács, on the contrary, Marx does not leave Hegel (or idealism) behind but rather builds on Hegel in solving the problem of German idealism in a further, better form of philosophy.

3   Kosík on the Pseudo-concrete

There is political discontinuity between Engels, Lukács and Kosík, philosophical discontinuity between Engels and Kosík, and limited philosophical continuity between Kosík and Lukács. Once he became a Marxist, Lukács consistently sought to be politically orthodox in adapting to the changing views of Western political Marxism. For instance, in *History and Class Consciousness* (1923) he refuted classical Marxism, which was the basis of Soviet Marxism. Yet he publically abandoned this view in the next year in aligning himself on Lenin's views in his little study of the unity of Lenin's thought.[3]

Kosík, who was not politically orthodox, is close to Lukács as concerns the Marxian constructivist view of cognition. Cognitive constructivism is introduced into modern philosophy by Hobbes, Vico, and independently by Kant. In his Copernican revolution Kant, who famously points to the fruitless effort to adapt thought to the object, suggests that as an experiment we adapt the object to our thought. This is the main insight situated at the heart of modern constructivist epistemology. Kant's constructivist turn leads to the difference between finding, uncovering or discovering what we know either through direct intuition or representation, or on the contrary making, producing or constructing it as a condition of knowledge.

In the *New Science*, Vico develops an anti-Cartesian concept of cognition according to which we know and can only know what we construct. In calling attention to the distinction between nature and history, he argues that only God, who made nature can know it, but human beings, make and also know history. Marx notes this point approvingly in *Capital*.

Kosík, who refers to Vico three times, never directly mentions the latter's cognitive thesis. Yet he reformulates this point in drawing attention to a distinction between the abstract, the pseudo-concrete and the concrete. Kosík's distinction is important in identifying the difference between the constructivist approach running through German idealism and what it rejects.

---

3   See Lukács 2009.

Without mentioning German idealism, Kosík also formulates a constructivist approach in distinguishing between the idea and the concept of a thing as two categories of human praxis. He has in mind the difference between phenomenon and essence. According to Kosík, the idea of the thing stands in as a false or ideological appearance for the thing in itself.[4] The problem consists in knowing the thing in itself by destroying what he calls the pseudo-concrete to grasp the essence. Kosík offers two suggestions from his dialectical perspective towards knowing the thing in itself: to consider that dialectical thought is grounded in revolutionary praxis; and to consider that the real world is not fixed but grounded in the activity of finite human beings in the social world.[5]

These two suggestions respond to very different conceptions. The first view, or the view that the real world is grounded in revolutionary praxis, is a political thesis, which aims toward the supersession of private property and the transformation of capitalism into communism. This initial view is based on the second, logically preceding view, which points toward constructivism. For there is a basic difference between nature, which is independent of human beings, and the social world, which is constructed by human beings in their interactions between themselves and between themselves and nature. Constructivism, which takes many forms, leads to the ontological view that we construct ourselves and our human world in and through what we do, as well as to the cognitive view that we can and do know the world and ourselves since we construct them in and through what we do.

Kosík goes on to discuss concepts of concrete totality, forms of praxis, and so on. If we ignore these other concepts for the moment, we can note that for Kosík constructivist epistemology is distinguished from, but related to, Marx's concern to ascend from the abstract to the concrete. Kosík points out that Marx, who begins *Capital* in discussing commodities, is able, through this concept, to construct a model of modern industrial society. The model is concrete since the different concepts 'fit together' in a single totality.

This point bears on the meaning of 'materialism', which is unclear in Marxism, but less so in Marx. Kosík plausibly suggests this term basically refers to what is concrete as opposed to what is abstract.[6] That further suggests that we give up the classical view of materialism as reducing everything to atoms and the void, the form of materialism Marx studies in his dissertation, or the current view of materialism as related to physicalism. The difficulty lies in grasping

---

4 Kosík 1976, p. 5.
5 Kosík 1976, p. 7.
6 Kosík 1976, p. 28.

the 'concrete'. According to Engels, whose grasp of Hegel is suspect, imprecise, not well informed, the latter begins from thought to go to reality, whereas we should start with reality to go to thought. Engels seems to believe that we can directly grasp the mind-independent real, above all through natural science, but that Hegel, who is presumably ignorant of science, overlooks the need to begin with the empirical world.

Engels's claim, which is regarded as authoritative and often cited in Marxist writings, is not only false, but even unrelated to Hegel's texts. Engels simply reverses Hegel's procedure in the *Phenomenology* where the latter begins with experience, which precedes any theory about it. For Hegel 'concrete' means 'conceptually-mediated'. Marx, who formulates a similar approach in the *Grundrisse*, is clearly concerned with the classical philosophical theme of how thought grasps objects. Engels suggests that the way Marx does this, in his (i.e. Engels's) opinion the way we should all follow, is to turn away from philosophy toward science.

Marx takes a different approach in following Hegel's lead, even though he seems unaware of how close his view is to Hegel's. Marx seems to believe that, though we cannot directly grasp the world, we can build up a concrete conceptual theory by starting from simple relations between categories and experience. For instance a commodity is both a concept as well as an object, which is made by someone within the process of production in meeting specific reproductive needs. In retrospect, Marx appears to construct his model of modern industrial capitalism on the basis of his view of commodities. Kosík applies this approach to what he calls 'false totality'. The proper way to build up a totality, or structured representation of social reality, is opposed by Kosík to various forms of false totality, which appear concrete, but are in fact abstract.[7]

4 Kosík on Marx and Economics

This approach is especially useful with respect to economics, in which Kosík claims the concrete is replaced by the abstract. The result is an only apparently 'ready-made' world, in which reified human practice is concealed rather than revealed. Unfortunately Kosík appears to obscure this important insight in relying on Heidegger. Kosík points out that the latter regresses to subjective idealism, and that his conception of authenticity leads to 'aristocratic romantic

---

7 Kosík 1976, p. 31.

stoicism'.[8] This seems to me to capture a valid insight. Yet he obscures this insight by attaching it to the Heideggerean distinction between presence to hand and ready to hand. Thus the surprising term 'procuring' seems to refer to the ready to hand, and the ready made, whereas praxis relates to the genesis, production and reproduction of the world of human praxis.[9] Yet the canonical Marxian conception of the subject as the ensemble of social relations seems incompatible with this Heideggerean view.[10]

Kosík's account of *homo oeconomicus* is not a claim about the conception of human beings utilised by economists, but rather about the reality of the situation of the individual in capitalism. This account is particularly interesting. Rather than taking an abstract conception of the subject as the economic model, Kosík suggests that the economic process of modern capitalism reduces human being merely to its use-value in creating economic value. According to Kosík, economics presupposes a system, which only began to exist with the rise of capitalism. The system and economic man, or finite human being, which in capitalism is reduced to a cog in the economic machine, in short a mere abstraction in the system, are inseparable. In consequence, what is transitory, or only a mere stage in social development, mistakenly appears to be permanent, even a category of reality itself. Another way of putting this insight is that reality loses the aspect of concrete human reality, or what is experienced, in favor of an abstract approach. Kosík, on the contrary, thinks that we can only grasp society from the perspective of dialectical reason if it is based on an underlying economic structure.

Kosík further applies his economic analysis to *Capital*, whose logical structure, he claims, must in some way 'match' the structure of reality. What this means is intuitively clear but in practice less than clear, in fact obscure. Since, like Marx, he does not appeal to the infamous reflection theory, dear to Engels, Lenin and many orthodox Marxists, this raises the central cognitive question: what would it mean to say that the logical structure matches the structure of reality? This is the Marxian version of the question of the relation of thought and being, a theme for which neither Kosík nor anyone else appears to have an answer.

In place of a clear response, he turns to the role of human praxis in respect to the rule of dead labour over living labour in describing, on the basis of an analysis of the commodity, Marx's starting point. Kosík calls this process the odyssey of commodities in structuring modern industrial capitalism through

---

8   Kosík 1976, p. 49.
9   Kosík 1976, p. 41.
10   Kosík 1976, p. 47.

economic laws, shapes (Gestalten) and a structured whole.[11] Hence, as Marx points out in the Introduction to the *Grundrisse*, in one of the rare analyses of method in all his writings, the analysis of the commodity turns out to be the answer of where to begin in building up a so-called logical structure to match reality.

Kosík goes on to make two remarks in comparing and contrasting Hegel's *Phenomenology* and Marx's *Capital*. To begin with, he contrasts Hegel's path of natural consciousness pressing forward to self-knowledge with Marx's odyssey of concrete historical praxis. Though they differ in their objectives, it appears that Kosík, who accepts the view that Marx and Hegel are basically different, overlooks the deep similarity in their views with respect to knowledge. One way to put the point is to say that both belong to the Kantian tradition for which, as the Copernican revolution suggests, we know only what we in some way construct. Marx is not Hegel and his theory differs in basic ways from Hegel's. Yet they share their own versions of the Kantian insight that we construct the social world and ourselves, which we know in finally only knowing ourselves so to speak. On this level, Marx is clearly restating the same constructivist message as Hegel, not for knowledge in general but rather for knowledge of modern industrial capitalism.

Kosík, who overestimates the distance between Marx and Hegel, further misrepresents Marx's achievement. He is correct that economic analysis uncovers social being, or the objectivity of social activity, hence human praxis. In other words, economic analysis, which does not concern the movement of things, but rather of people, is, hence, not about what is permanent but rather about what is transient. He is correct as well that Marx's intent is not to formulate a theory of human consciousness but rather to formulate a scientific reconstruction of the anatomy of modern industrial society. Yet he is incorrect to suggest that the result is in any sense, any sense at all, more than a theory. 'Marx's *Capital* is not a theory but a theoretical *critique* of a *critical* theory of capital'.[12] For at the end of the day, Marx is offering a theoretical reconstruction of human praxis, hence a description of human reality, which, however, remains a theory.

This difficulty is not confined to Kosík. Theory is a kind of practice, hence can always be refuted by practice. This is true for Marx's theories as well, which depend on, hence must respond to what we find in practice. The point that Marx goes beyond theory is a frequent claim in Marxism. It is reiterated independently by Ilyenkov, who asserts, but neither demonstrates nor even seeks

---

11   Kosík 1976, p. 110.
12   Kosík 1976, p. 111.

to demonstrate, that through Marx's position there is immediate access to reality, in this case to economic reality, which is situated beyond or rather prior to concepts.

One could argue, following Lukács, that only Marxism allows us to pierce the veil of ideological illusion to grasp social truth. Ilyenkov makes a different argument. His view, which seems unclear, apparently relies on a claim for direct intuition of what is, a view current in the debate as early as Plato, or on reflection. According to Plato, philosophers are capable of directly intuiting or in other words 'seeing' reality. A similar view is restated in the notorious reflection theory. If we apply this theory to economics, it leads to the view that the economic categories of *Capital* 'reflect' mind-independent economic reality objectively and independently of their theoretical interpretation. Yet no argument has ever been devised to show that we in fact directly intuit or otherwise grasp reality as it is. It has also never been shown how to 'reflect' the mind-independent world on the level of mind. And, finally, following Hegel, Marx denies immediate empirical claims in relying on a grasp of experience through categories or concepts, such as labour, the commodity, use-value, exchange value, and so on.

This point, which can be generalised, bears on the claim to go behind the pseudo-concrete in order to grasp the essence. Such a journey starts with the appearance in traveling deeper toward what we take to be the essence. We do not and cannot directly intuit reality. Rather we formulate a theory intended to grasp the essence in starting from the appearance. Theories are reconstructions of what at some level is given in experience as the appearance of what later, on the basis of the theory, we at least for the moment accept as correct, hence as an acceptable view of its essence. Yet since we do not and cannot know that we have in fact reached the essence, we must always be ready to accept that a distinction between what we take to be the essence, or the *Erscheinung*, is in fact merely *Schein*. For any theory, even Marx's, can always be refuted by practice.

5   Kosík on Praxis and Constructivism

Kosík's approach to praxis is original and very interesting. He suggests that the materialist form of the relation of theory and praxis cannot be understood on the Aristotelian model of contemplation and activity, nor through the so-called primacy of praxis over theory, which, in his opinion, simply devalues theory. An example might be Italian Fascism, which promotes action at all costs and an approach to know that wholly devalues theory in basing knowledge on faith rather than reason. Apparently distantly following Heidegger, Kosík suggests 'praxis is the whole of man', and that human being forms reality.[13] He draws the cognitive inference in pointing out that it is because human beings produce social reality that they can reproduce, hence know it.[14] This is his way of putting Marx's discovery that everything in history is the doing of human being.[15] In other words, history is the unfolding of human possibilities.[16] This point is a sophisticated restatement of Marx's famous claim that man is the root for man. Kosík, however, closes with the denial that this is an anthropological perspective, which, according to Kosík, would separate human being from the world.

Kosík ends the book in responding to the question: how does a dialectical approach know the thing in itself? His answer is that this is possible if and only if the investigation is carried out from the perspective of finite human being, who constructs and knows only what it in some way constructs. This is his answer to the question: what is Marx's theory of knowledge? Now a theory of knowledge always presupposes a conception of truth. Kosík, who began the book with the statement that dialectic is concerned with the thing in itself, which does not show itself immediately, apparently presupposes a variation on the Heideggerean conception of truth.

Yet this 'static' view of truth seems incompatible with a dialectical approach. Heidegger's view that every revealing is also a concealing is not demonstrated nor even argued. In Heidegger's account, this must be taken on faith, whereas Marx clearly argues there are good reasons, rooted in self-interest based on class distinctions why for the most part we are unaware of social reality.

According to Marx, a socially-distorted form of the social context leads in turn to mistaken accounts. This claim can be understood in at least two main ways. One way is the view that the economic system itself tends to conceal the real situation. This view rests on the idea that the system itself in its role as an actor tends to hide itself. Yet it is implausible that economic phenomena are anything other than as Kosík says the result of human activity. According to Kosík, a dialectical approach centres on finite human being and its place in the universe from the perspective of human being.[17] The other, more plausible view is that human beings, who consciously or unconsciously act to further their own self-interests, are responsible for the mistaken understanding of the social context. This view, for instance, was arguably again at work in the great

---

13   Kosík 1976, p. 137.
14   Kosík 1976, p. 139.
15   Kosík 1976, p. 143.
16   Kosík 1976, p. 145.
17   Kosík 1976, pp. 152–3.

recession of 2008. It is, then, interesting that for so many observers, the true causes were unknown whereas it seems likely that the self-interest of individuals well placed in the financial community was the main cause of the crisis.

6   Conclusion: Kosík, Lukács and the Thing in Itself

I come now to my conclusion. Kosík and Lukács both claim in different ways against Kant that Marx enables us to know the thing in itself, which we can understand as the result of the activity of finite men and women. This activity is objectified in a series of social structures that human beings construct and hence can, for that reason, know. The difference lies in the grasp of German idealism, hence in the evaluation of their respective accounts of Marxian theory. Lukács relies on detailed knowledge of the German idealist tradition in his treatment of Marx. Kosík, who is working mainly within Marx's writings in isolation from their surroundings, and who, like many Marxists of his generation, further relies on Heidegger, perhaps overestimates the originality of the Marxian approach. According to Kosík, Marx and Marx alone allows us to grasp the thing in itself through dialectical thought, hence to solve (or resolve) the great basic question of German idealism. Yet in Fichte, Hegel and Marx each in their own way provide a form of the constructivist insight that we know we do not know the mind-independent world or nature. But we can and do know what we construct and then reconstruct as the social world from the perspective of the activity of finite human beings. It follows that Marx's specific contribution does not merely consist in the turn from a representational to a constructivist approach to cognition. It rather lies, as Kosík further seems to suggest in his insightful remarks on economics, in the application of a constructive approach to specifically economic phenomena, which are situated at the centre of modern capitalism.

PART 3

Modernity, Nation, and Globalisation

CHAPTER 8

The Ontological Dialectic and the Critique of Modernity: Based on the Interpretation of Kosík's Concrete Totality

Xinruo Zhang and Xiaohan Huang

1   Introduction

There is a common judgement in both Chinese academia and the Western world about Karel Kosík being a Heideggerian.[1] We deeply doubt this judgement due to its failure to illustrate that Kosík's philosophy – particularly his dialectic – is inherited from the Hegelian-Marxian tradition, and due to its misunderstanding of Kosík's use of Heideggerian terms in his writings. However, we do not assert that Kosík is not related to Heidegger in any way; on the contrary, the exposure of the concrete crises of modern time, influenced by Heidegger, helps Kosík deepen his dialectical thoughts. What should be discerned here is Kosík's basic philosophical position – the way he appropriates reality and the use of language as he might intend to borrow several Heideggerian phrases or expressions to describe the crisis of the modern world.

Therefore, in order to interpret *Dialectics of the Concrete*, we should also read *The Crisis of Modernity*, collected essays written by Karel Kosík around 1968, and edited by a US scholar named James H. Satterwhite, which has received little attention in comparison with the former. *Dialectics of the Concrete* is mainly a theoretical discussion of the existence of human being and society as well as the relations between human beings and the world. To grapple with such matters, Kosík emphasises 'totality' by starting from the various angles of daily life, political and economic issues, culture, arts, history and so on, which comprise the main content of *The Crisis of Modernity*. On the other hand, in order

---

1   Quite a few Chinese scholars consider Karel Kosík to be a Heideggerian or a Heideggerian Marxist. See *Jutidebianzhengfa yu xiandaijingpipan: kexike zhexuesixiang yanjiu* [《具体的辩证法与现代性批判：科西克哲学思想研究》; *Dialectics of the Concrete and the Critique of Modernity: A Study of Karel Kosík's Philosophy*], written by Li Baowen (李宝文) from Heilongjiang University (Li 2011). For a Western interpretation, see 'Karel Kosík's Heideggerian Marxism' by Michael E. Zimmerman from University of Colorado, Boulder (Zimmerman 1984).

to illustrate the social and historical causes and cultural origins of the modern crisis itself, Kosík's dialectical view offers us a unique perspective and a proper method to grasp the essence of modernity.

2   From 'Concrete Totality' to the 'Ontological Dialectic'

'Concrete totality' is considered one of the key concepts of Kosík's philosophy. Before we approach this, we should first discern several other concepts. The first question is 'what is reality?' For Kosík, reality is a 'concrete totality, i.e. a structural, evolving, self-forming whole',[2] which is a dynamic, forming existence. He refuses to take reality as 'the sum of all facts'.[3] Therefore, 'reality' means 'essence' for Kosík. Next, what is 'fact'? 'A fact is coded reality'.[4] Facts are the phenomenal forms of reality, which presents itself directly but variously in front of us. Therefore, 'fact' for Kosík means 'phenomenon'. He states that 'all cognition is a dialectical oscillation between facts and context (totality)', which means dialectics should deal with the relations between 'reality' and 'fact', or more precisely, dialectics should give us an ongoing essential cognition of the world. Since human cognition can never cover all facts, all properties of all things, and all relations and processes, it is wrong to conceive reality as merely the sum of all facts, because new aspects or additional facts can always emerge with the expanding of our experiences. It is anti-dialectical to simply stop where empiricism stops. Reality is a structural dialectical whole within which and from which any particular fact (or a set of facts) can be rationally comprehended. Thus facts themselves are not like atoms; a series of facts is not an addition of atoms. All facts exist in a structure of meaning that is mutually related to the totality. 'The reality of facts is opposed to their facticity not so much as a reality of different order and independent of facts, but rather as an internal relation, as the dynamics and the contradictory character of totality of facts'.[5] Kosík also states that 'the logical relationship expresses the fact that a generalisation is the internal connection of facts and that a fact itself mirrors a certain complex. The ontological essence of every fact reflects the whole reality, and the objective significance of a fact depends on how richly and how essentially it both encompasses and mirrors reality'.[6] We should notice

---

2   Kosík 1976, p. 18.
3   Ibid.
4   Kosík 1976, p. 26.
5   Kosík 1976, p. 27.
6   Kosík 1976, p. 25.

here that Kosík uses the phrase 'ontological essence', and he also mentions 'the essence' various times within this context, which gives us a clue to reviewing the difference between him and Heidegger.

Many scholars consider Kosík to be a 'Heideggerian Marxist' and insist that he has combined Heideggerian philosophy with Marxian philosophy, just like Marcuse or other philosophers. We should be very careful in making such a judgement. As in the case of Kosík, it is not so proper to define him as a 'Heideggerian Marxist' because there are crucial differences between Kosík and Heidegger. The aim of Heideggerian philosophy is to deconstruct metaphysics and its 'essence'. As for the question *'was ist Sein?'*, Heidegger asserts that traditional philosophy always focuses on *'Sein'* i.e. *'being'*, but barely discusses the predicate *'ist'*. This is to say that Heidegger wants to discuss *'how to be'*, and his ontology is not about being itself, but rather the existing status, i.e. the process of becoming. In Chinese, we have named Heideggerian philosophy 'CunZaiLun' (存在论), which is different from 'BenTiLun' (本体论), but in English the two are referred to using the same word – 'ontology'. Kosík's ontology is not identical to Heidegger's. He does not deny 'essence', but rather gives essence two dimensions: both being and becoming. In the first part of *Dialectics of the Concrete*, Kosík repeats several times that the 'thing itself' – the essence, the structure of a thing – does not show itself directly and immediately, but it exists and needs to be known by us. He says that 'the essence, unlike phenomena, does not manifest itself to us directly, and the concealed basis of things has to be exposed in a specific activity. This is precisely why science and philosophy exist'.[7] Therefore, Kosík does not mean to discard 'essence' and he basically inherits from Lukács the 'totality dialectic' in order to rebuild the concept of 'totality', because this is the only way to know the world better.

In fact, the concept of 'totality' or concepts related to 'totality' emerged as early as from the Ancient Greeks. Parmenides raises the concept of 'one', although it is somewhat different from the more recent concept of 'totality'. Parmenides' 'one' is a chaotic and simple concept that does not contain any concrete elements, and is not a consequence of dialectical thinking. Kosík argues that in classical German philosophy, 'totality' has been elaborated as a central concept for polemically distinguishing dialectics from the standpoint of empiricism. Empiricism always dwells on haphazard phenomena and cannot arrive at a comprehension of the development of reality, i.e. the essence. So when we come to grasp the essential aspects of reality, we should develop a dialectical

---

7   Kosík 1976, p. 4.

concept of totality in order to save the concept from being grasped one-sidedly and directed to a completely different way of social praxis.

In *History and Class Consciousness*, Lukács places 'totality' in an important position, taking it as the only way of interpreting Marx's dialectical method. He says,

> This dialectical conception of totality seems to have put a great distance between itself and reality, it appears to construct reality very 'unscientifically'. But it is the *only* method capable of understanding and reproducing reality. Concrete totality is, therefore, the category that governs reality. The rightness of this view only emerges with complete clarity when we direct our attention to the real, material substratum of out method, viz. capitalist society with its internal antagonism between the forces and the relations of production.[8]

In spite of using the phrase 'concrete totality', Lukács makes it clear that totality has methodological priority over parts or particularity. There is no doubt that the emphasis on 'totality' is a dialectical step, but Lukács has an exaggerated view of it. He overestimates the function of totality and puts it in an awkward position which opposes any part. The totality and the parts are not in an evolving structure. Because he does not have a view of internal relations, he cannot understand that the parts are as important as the totality. Dialectical truth does not fit together neatly like the pieces of a puzzle, but allows for the kind of multiple one-sidedness that is the necessary result of studying a subject within the different perspectives associated with its different aspects.[9] Every part or every concrete fact is in the meaning structure of the whole. The whole is not the sum of every part, but rather in a dynamic progression which contains them together as mutually functioning. This is why Kosík goes further than Lukács.

The methodological principle for dialectically investigating objective reality is the standpoint of concrete totality.[10] Social reality can only be known within concreteness as well as totality. 'Totality' is reality, and it is only right in the sense of 'concrete totality', which differs from Lukács. However, since Lukács presents his totality as having primacy over the moments of the totality, the parts of the whole, to give primacy to the moments of the totality over the whole is to hypostatise the totality and to give it a life and independence from

---

8   Lukács 1971, p. 10.
9   Ollman 2012, p. 219.
10 Kosík 1976, p. 22.

the concrete reality of which it is meant to be the basis. Kosík at one moment criticises Lukács,

> Hypostatising the whole or favoring it over its parts (over facts) is one path that leads to a false totality instead of to a concrete one. If the whole process represented a reality which could be indeed genuine and higher than facts, then reality could exist independently of facts, independently in particular of facts that would contradict it. The formulation that hypostatizes the whole over the facts and treats it autonomously provides a theoretical substantiation for subjectivism which in turn ignores facts and violates them in the name of 'higher reality'.[11]

This is exactly Lukács's deficiency, which Kosík calls 'false totalisation'. On the contrary, 'concrete totality' has nothing to do with holistic or other one-sided concepts of wholeness. Dialectics cannot grasp totality as a ready-made or formalised whole determining the parts, because the genesis and development of totality are components of its very determination.[12] Therefore, totality concretises itself in the process of forming its whole as well as its content. This undoubtedly sounds a little Heideggerian. However, we should know that Hegel talks about forming and becoming as well as Marx. Hegel defines dialectics as the movement of concepts and ideas. Marx constructs the whole of human society with praxis, which he himself calls 'sensuous activity'.

As far as we know, Kosík has represented a real dialectical principle of 'totality', i.e. 'concrete totality', which is a unity of the whole and the parts, phenomenon and essence, subject and object, and so on. To put it more elaborately, we summarise three aspects of 'concrete totality':

1. Concrete totality is a structural, evolving, self-forming whole, not the mechanical sum of facts or parts, not the accumulation of all aspects, matters and relations.
2. Totality cannot exist independently as some kind of entity. Totality is not a ready-made whole, but rather an organic system of internal relations. It constructs and forms itself within the mutual interactions of parts and the whole structure as well.
3. Totality is built within human society by human praxis. It is not a formulation of facts. We should not interpret it from an objective perspective, but rather from a subjective angle.

---

11   Kosík 1976, p. 27.
12   Kosík 1976, pp. 28–9.

Overall, 'concrete totality' is a 'dialectical totality'. It means not only that the parts internally interact and interconnect both among themselves and with the whole, but also that the whole cannot be petrified in an abstraction superior to the facts or parts, because dialectical thinking essentially conceives of reality as a whole that is not merely a sum of relations, facts and processes, but also the structure, the very process of forming them as well. 'Concrete totality' is the unity of ontology, epistemology and methodology. This leads us to the 'ontological dialectic'.

The ontological dialectic contains two mutually existing dimensions: 'what is reality' and 'how it becomes what it looks like and what it really is'. Here, as we discussed before, although influenced by Heidegger, Kosík is not strictly speaking a Heideggerian. Where Heidegger was principally concerned more with the 'is' of 'what is being' than with the nature of 'being', Hegel remains concerned with both the 'is' and the nature of 'being', making his analysis of the nature of 'being' a characterisation of how the 'is' unfolds itself through becoming. Like Hegel, Kosík's 'concrete totality' must equally be concerned with the 'is' and the 'being' of the question of being. This is fundamentally different from the standpoint view of Heideggerian phenomenology. Again, Kosík is like Hegel in that he takes the concrete as the fundamental reality of the whole: the concrete Idea (*Idee*) that is the whole in Hegel is the negation of the negation of the subjectivity of the Concept (*Begriff*) and its objectivity. We will discuss the difference between these two thinkers later in the next part.

The dialectic itself evolves. Hegelian dialectic is considered to offer a fresh light in idealism, although it comes up with a mystical system and logical extreme. Marx inherits the dynamic element from the Hegelian system and puts forward a materialistic dialectic. Lukács summarises,

> By taking the inner contradictions of metaphysics to extremes, by breaking up their immobile façade, by uncovering the concealed dynamic of the contradictions of the real world, Hegel not only points the way to dialectical thought, he also shows that it is not the private monopoly of privileged geniuses but a faculty inherent in all human thought which had been ossified by the habit of metaphysics. The logical continuation of this road could only be the discovery of materialist dialectics, for this alone can reflect the dialectical movement of reality itself in such a manner as to do away with the Kantian prohibition altogether. But materialist dialectics and historical materialism necessarily go hand in hand.[13]

---

13   Lukács 1975, p. 395.

When it comes to Kosík's 'ontological dialectics', the dialectic he deals with is the essential way of human living and the relationship between the human and the living world. Kosík's thoughts on 'totality' are quite incisive and profound. It is a great development of Marx's dialectical thoughts, while Kosík inherits another element from Marx – criticism of the living world. His main interest is in trying to rebuild the relations between the whole and the parts as his theoretical basis, which serves his greater philosophical theme that is to explain the relations between individuals and society. For Kosík, the core of the 'concrete dialectic' is to interpret how modern humans live in the modern world and the meaning of their lives.

3   Individuals and the Living World: From Marx to Kosík

For Marx, human being has three main meanings that every individual shares: (1) A human being is a conscious being. Consciousness is a particular human capacity not shared by non-human animals. Marx claims that an individual is a conscious, dynamic and natural being. Human activities entail initiative. Unlike animals' negative or mechanical response to nature, human beings have rationality and judgement. Human consciousness thus differs from animal consciousness by reason of the fact that it includes an awareness of the self as being a member of a species, as sharing a common nature with others, as being one kind of being among other kinds of beings. (2) A human being is a social being. Although human beings are natural beings, the essence of human being is not what is natural or physical, but rather what is social. In his *Theses on Feuerbach*, Marx makes a famous and crucial claim, namely that 'the human essence is no abstraction inherent in each single individual. In its reality it is the ensemble of the social relations'. He then says that because Feuerbach does not recognise this, 'Essence, therefore, can be comprehended only as "genus", as an internal, dumb generality which naturally unites the many individuals'.[14] We should be careful about the notion 'genus' here. Although Marx uses the term (sometimes translated as 'species'), especially in his earlier writings, he never stops where Feuerbach stops. For Marx, an individual always has a background of a social class. (3) A human being is a practical being. Again, in the *Theses on Feuerbach*, Marx states: 'The chief defect of all hitherto existing materialism (that of Feuerbach included) is that the thing, reality, sensuousness, is conceived only in the form of the object or of contemplation, but not as

---

14   Marx 2000a, p. 172.

sensuous human activity, practice, not subjectively'.[15] Here, practice does not merely refer to moral activity in the sense of traditional German philosophy, but rather means undertaking real productive activities, i.e. labour. By producing the means of subsistence, people are indirectly producing their actual material life. Therefore, labour is the main and necessary bridge that links people to nature, as well as to society.

Nevertheless, labour has a historical content through different periods of history and thus has different meanings. When labour becomes the means of surviving or a tool for living that can be sold as a commodity in a certain stage of history, it is separated and alienated from people themselves. Marx elucidated the relationship between the individual and labour through the concept of alienated labour. In an alienated society, such as capitalist society, workers become commodities as they rely on selling their labour power for a living. The more commodities they create, the cheaper it becomes to reproduce their labour power, because people cannot appropriate what they create but can only use their negligible salary to buy what should be theirs in the first place. Therefore, through the process of labour, this labour solidifies itself into an object, makes itself a thing, the objectification of labour. Here we should notice that Marx's dialectic plays an important role in explaining this relationship. For Marx, a product is never merely a thing, but is also a form of relations. First of all, it represents the relationship between subject and object. Once a product has been created, it carries the power of objectification. People actualise themselves by making products. Secondly, it represents the relationship between use value and exchange value. As soon as a product becomes a commodity, it has both use value and exchange value, although the former is expunged in the market and the latter remains behind in an abstract form, raising another relationship, i.e. the relationship between seller and buyer. Labour power as a commodity itself refers to the relationship between labourers and capitalists.

What should be highlighted here is the secret of the 'commodity', which Marx calls the secret of the whole capitalist society. Lukács pointed out in *History and Class Consciousness* that Marx reveals the real relationship between human beings via the phenomenon of reification. He states that 'The essence of commodity-structure has often been pointed out. Its basis is that a relation between people takes on the character of a thing and thus acquires a "phantom objectivity", an autonomy that seems so strictly rational and all-embracing as to conceal every trace of its fundamental nature: the relation between

---

15   Marx 2000a, p. 171.

people'.¹⁶ Marx describes the basic phenomenon of reification as follows: 'A commodity is therefore a mysterious thing, simply because in it the social character of men's labor appears to them as an objective character stamped upon the product of that labor; because the relation of the producers to the sum total of their own labor is presented to them as a social relation, existing not between themselves, but between the products of their labor'.¹⁷ As long as the real social relations hidden in the form of 'commodity' have been found out, there is nothing mysterious about it. Then, the relations connecting the labour of one individual with that of the rest appear not as direct social relations between individuals at work, but as material relations between persons and social relations between things. It is only a stage in the history of human development that the relationship between self and labour becomes alienated. Marx does not use the theory of alienation to understand the individual in capitalism but to understand capitalism from the standpoint of the individual. This is achieved by focusing not only on the individual but on those elements of his nature which are then thoroughly mystified by the operations of the capitalist market, and this mystification too is an integral part of what is meant by 'alienation'.¹⁸

Lukács in *History and Class Consciousness* also wishes to emphasise the importance of socialised individuals and stresses the priority of class beyond individuals,

> The individual can never become the measure of all things. For when the individual confronts objective reality he is faced by a complex of ready-made and unalterable objects which allow him only the subjective responses of recognition or rejection. Only the class can relate to the whole of reality in a practical revolutionary way. (The 'species' cannot do this as it is no more than an individual that has been mythologized and stylized in a spirit of contemplation.) And the class, too, can only manage it when it can see through the reified objectivity of the given world to the process that is also its own fate. For the individual, reification and hence determinism (determinism being the idea that things are necessarily connected) are irremovable. Every attempt to achieve 'freedom' from such premises must fail, for 'inner freedom' presupposes that the world cannot be changed. Hence, too, the cleavage of the ego into 'is' and 'ought', into the intelligible and the empirical ego, is unable to serve as the foundation

---

16   Lukács 1971, p. 83.
17   Marx 2000, p. 473.
18   Ollman 2012, p. 252.

for a dialectical process of becoming, even for the individual subject. The problem of the external world and with it the structure of the external world (of things) is referred to the category of the empirical ego. Psychologically and physiologically the latter is subject to the same deterministic laws as apply to the external world in the narrow sense. The intelligible ego becomes a transcendental idea (regardless of whether it is viewed as a metaphysical existent or an ideal to the realized).[19]

Kosík goes further than Lukács when he reserves the most essential meaning of the 'Individual' by putting forward the notion 'autonomy' as he asserts,

> The historicity of the individual is not only his ability to evoke the past, but also his ability to integrate in his individual life what is generally human. Man, just like his praxis, is always imbued with the presence of others (his contemporaries, his predecessors, his successors) and he takes over the present and transforms it either by acquiring autonomy or not acquiring it. Autonomy means: first, to stand, not to kneel (the natural posture of the human individual is to hold up his head, not to be on his knees); second, to show one's own face and not to hide behind a borrowed mask; third, to portray courage, not cowardice; and fourth, to remain aloof from oneself and from the world in which he lives and distinguished the particular the general, the accidental and the real, the barbaric and the human, the authentic and the nonauthentic. [...] Autonomy does not mean to do what others do or to do something different than others, but neither does it mean to do something regardless of others. Autonomy is an independence of or isolation from others. It means establishing contacts with others in which freedom can exist or can be realized. Autonomy is historicity, the center of the activity in which the instantaneous and the 'matatemporal', the past and future, unite; it is the totalisation in which universally human qualities are reproduced and revived in the particular (the individual). The individual can change the world only in cooperation and conjunction with others. But even in reified reality and change of reality and in the interest of a really revolutionary change of reality every individual as an individual has occasion to express his humanness and preserve his autonomy.[20]

---

19   Lukács 1971, pp. 193–4.
20   Kosík 1995i, pp. 133–4.

Obviously, Kosík adopts Marx's view on the relationship between individuals and the living world, especially taking Marx's notion 'labour' (or 'practice' in a broader sense) as an inner element of subjects. For Kosík, labour is the direct practical way of human being. It makes an individual who he/she is. Labour is an action as well as a historical process. Human beings are able to define themselves and recognise their essential meaning of living through labour and only through labour. However, Kosík also emphasises the importance of living or everyday life, which did not become a crucial aspect in the content of both Marx and Lukács. For Kosík, every individual's mental activity or psychological status should also be considered necessary and sufficient conditions of obtaining freedom. Otherwise, practice becomes merely instrumental procurement. This perspective is surely influenced by Heidegger but no doubt becomes a crucial vantage point for Kosík to open up his view on the relationship between individuals and the living world.

Kosík develops his discussion by noting the 'pseudoconcrete world'. He states that 'the collection of phenomena that crowd the everyday environment and the routine atmosphere of human life, and which penetrate the consciousness of acting individuals with a regularity, immediacy and self-evidence that lend them a semblance of autonomy and naturalness, constitutes the world of the pseudoconcrete'.[21] That is to say, the pseudoconcrete world is a world in which everyone lives for himself/herself as an alienated individual. Kosík deeply exposes 'the world of the pseudoconcrete' and lists four types of 'pseudoconcrete'. These are: 'the world of external phenomena'; 'the world of procuring and manipulation'; 'the world of routine ideas'; and 'the world of fixed objects'.

The world of external phenomena is the general world of the modern era. Kosík argues that 'the world of the pseudoconcrete is the chiaroscuro of truth and deceit. It thrives in ambiguity. The phenomenon conceals the essence even as it reveals it. The essence manifests itself in the phenomenon, but only to a certain extent, partially, just in certain sides and aspects'.[22] That is to say, reality is the unity of phenomena and essence. Although the phenomena represent the essence, they are not identical in the first place. If we simply equate phenomena with essence, the phenomena are then all we obtain. Moreover, if we separate essence from phenomena and give it an independent existence as the only reliable entity, the essence itself becomes unreal and unknowable. Therefore, 'to capture the phenomenon of a certain thing is to investigate and

---

21 Kosík 1976, p. 2.
22 Ibid.

describe how the thing itself manifests itself in that phenomenon but also how it hides in it'. Because external phenomena have their own orders, structures and laws and the relations between us and external phenomena are direct and immediate as such, it is hard for us to discern the phenomena from the essence, but easy to misplace the phenomena instead of the essence. The rapid development of technology and science also consolidate the world of phenomena as they are created by omnipotent science and reason.

The world of procuring and manipulation is built by man's fetishised praxis. It appears as a utilitarian world, in which manipulation becomes universal, activity is distorted, and subjects are submerged. The most important character of the world of manipulation is that 'labour' turns into 'procuring'. As Kosík says, 'procuring as abstract human labor in its phenomenal form creates an equally abstract world of utility in which everything is transformed into a utilitarian instrument',[23] thus people in this procuring world become implements, pure objects, and lose their own essences. Therefore, modern civilisation turns the practical world into a static world, a reified world, where human praxis has been transformed into manipulation of both things and people. Modernity is a process by which a rational subject ensures his/her subjectivity and meaning, while subjectivity also perishes and becomes its opposite. On the one hand, procuring tears human labour apart into thousands of mechanical operations, so the human world is not creatively reformed but becomes an unchangeable world; on the other hand, procuring creates an alienated world where everything becomes implements and tools. What Kosík points out here is that we cannot just reject this procuring world by means of some romantic evasion, because the world is actually formed within human history and it is the consequence of modernity itself. It cannot be evaded or ignored, but only conquered and changed by ourselves. So the first step has to be to realise that the manipulation of human being is closely related to the process of objective understanding. Objective understanding is ultimately the inevitable way in which every individual comes to know the world, but the problem is that 'an individual might be submerged in objectivity, in the world of manipulation and procuring, so completely that his subject disappears in it and objectivity itself stands out as the real, though mystified, subject'.[24]

The procuring world creates a sense of the 'everyday' and routine ideas. Kosík, like Heidegger, attempts to use the word 'everyday' to represent the most usual, universal, and indispensable living style. The sense of the 'everyday' has

---

23   Kosík 1976, p. 40.
24   Kosík 1976, p. 47.

been engendered through reified praxis, and is the ideological form of human praxis. No matter who lives in the 'everyday', the most prominent character of this lifestyle is repeatable, replicable and replaceable. People have undertaken boring operations every day without thinking why or how. Their subjectivities are unconsciously stripped from the mechanical environment. This is the result of modernity. Individuals become components of a known world and take the 'everyday' for granted as their own world because they are so familiar with it that it is unusual to break a regular rhythm. Therefore, as Kosík says, in the modern era, the 'everyday' has no history because history changes and the 'everyday' remains. Kosík states that 'While the everyday appears as confidence, familiarity, proximity, as "home", history appears as the derailment, the disruption of the everyday, as the exceptional and the strange. This cleavage simultaneously splits reality into the historicity of History and the ahistoricity of the everyday'.[25] In modern times, ahistoricity has fully penetrated every aspect of our lives, including our mind.

The world of fixed objects is not the objects of the natural world, but rather the objects of human praxis. However, these objects always exist there, giving people impressions that they are natural and unchangeable. It is not easy for people to figure out that they are actually the consequences of their own praxis and the creatures they make by their own actions. Kosík points out that all of the 'economic system', 'merchants', and 'capital' built by people can be called 'fixed objects'. In the world of 'fixed objects', everyone is transformed into 'homo oeconomicus', abstracting from his/her subjectivity and becoming an element of the whole lawlike system. Kosík states that 'the purely intellectual process of science transforms man into an abstract unit integrated in a scientifically analyzable and mathematically describable system. This reflects the real metamorphosis of man performed by capitalism. Only under capitalism did economics develop as a science'.[26] That is to say, only under modernity did man become 'homo oeconomicus', who totally loses his/her authenticity and essence as a real human being. Kosík reminds us here that 'economic man' is a reasonable abstraction under modern circumstances. It can only be understood within the whole economic system. This is also the standpoint from which Marx chooses to criticise Adam Smith and the whole of classical political economy, because Marx has a sense of historicity and he knows that 'economic man' is not something eternal but historically existing. Therefore, any theory

---

25   Kosík 1976, p. 44.
26   Kosík 1976, p. 50.

based on 'economic man' and the whole economic system is fake, ahistorical, and therefore a misunderstanding.

As a matter of fact, Kosík is not the only scholar who sees the importance of individuals as well as integrality. Mészáros also argues,

> [A]ccording to the Marxian conception, the 'social and political structure' had to be transformed in its integrality, and such transformation had to be accomplished by the social individuals referred to in our last quotation from *The German Ideology*. As Marx also made it very clear in another work written in the same period of revolutionary upheavals, the historic task had to be accomplished by the social individuals by restructuring 'from top to bottom the conditions of their industrial and political existence, and consequently their whole manner of being'.[27]

Therefore, it is clear that for both Marx and Kosík, there is never a Robinson Crusoe living in isolation outside of social contexts. An individual must be within relations, i.e. undertaking labour to connect with nature and society; living socially with other people. However, Kosík stresses the concrete meaning of how an individual lives as the individual by keeping his/her essential connection with others as a social being. The reason why Kosík could surpass his predecessors is mainly because the social content of his era changed in the twentieth century. History brought great sorrow in the form of wars, dictatorships, and all kinds of living problems brought about by developing technologies. Human beings have become the victims of modernity simultaneously as they are its beneficiaries. Kosík experienced more concrete changes and problems through the second half of the twentieth century, which gave him a sharper perspective in criticising modernity to fill with his ontological dialectic.

4 The Critique of Modernity

We have now come to the last part, which can be considered as the answer to the question 'why has the relationship between individuals and the living world been constantly alienated and distorted?' That is to say, as we have discussed how Kosík deals with the relationship between individuals and the living world by reinforcing the aspect of daily life, we can draw up a draft of how he criticises modernity.

---

27 Mészáros 2011, p. 19.

What is modernity? Since the Enlightenment and the Industrial Revolution, a modern style of social life has emerged that is closely related to the capitalist spirit. What we call the 'capitalist spirit' here refers to a reason-oriented, technologically dominant way of living and thinking. Modernity has penetrated every aspect of our modern lives, including economics, politics, culture, and ideas. It not only affects the pattern of our practicing world, according to Kosík, but also deeply formalises our routine thinking. Both the physical world and mental world under modern conditions are mediated and pushed ahead by modernity – a so-called universal way of living, reasonable, abstract, but depersonalised, which has been regarded as the only efficient pattern for nearly everyone. Hegel faced the issue of modernity. In *Phenomenology of Mind*, he states the following:

> The manner of study in ancient times is distinct from that of the modern world, in that the former consisted in the cultivation and perfecting of the natural mind. Testing life carefully at all points, philosophising about everything it came across, the former created an experience permeated through and through by universals. In modern times, however, individual finds the abstract form ready made.[28]

This means that modern philosophy is dependent on a universe of existing abstractions rather than beginning from concrete phenomena that presented themselves directly to us. This also formularises the basic living status of modern times, which is also dependent on abstractions. Modernity requires and mutually interacts with the individualistic ideology. Mészáros points out,

> For the dominant individualistic ideologies have their institutional counterpart – including the practical teleology of the market and the 'hidden hand' of its 'parallelogrammatic' interactional instrumentality – which effectively operate in accordance with the well established structures of material inertia. At the same time, the conditions for the successful functioning of a collective 'true consciousness' – which, in order to be able to successfully engage in a lasting global control of its tasks, would require as its material ground a non-inertial institutional framework – are as yet nowhere in sight today, even in an embryonic form.[29]

---

28   Hegel 1973, p. 94.
29   Mészáros 1998, p. 432.

Hence, the individualistic ideology is the main base of modernity, embedded in the modern production process and social lives.

In *The Crisis of Modernity*, Kosík discusses several detailed issues. First of all, reason and conscience exist only as two mutually independent variables, indifferently or antagonistically disposed to one another during modern times. The division of reason and conscience seems as natural to us as facts and value, scientific technology and ideology. Kosík tells us that these divisions are consequences of history because when we trace our history back, we are able to find the opposite situation: a fifteenth-century Czech intellectual defends the unity of reason and conscience, thereby also defending a specific concept of both reason and conscience. 'Unity is so important to the character of reason and to the nature of conscience that when this unity is lost, reason loses its substance and conscience its reality'.[30] Kosík's words remind us of the critique of 'instrumental reason', which is a certain variant of Reason. There is no doubt that 'instrumental reason' is reason split from conscience, because it has been instilled and put into use only according to the laws of the world of manipulation, i.e. utility and reified praxis. In *Dialectics of the Concrete*, Kosík claims 'unreason becomes the reason of modern capitalist society'.[31] We should discern rationalist reason and dialectical reason. Rationalist reason is the foundation and substantiation of the modern world, which has inevitably caused irrationality, while dialectical reason seeks to shape reality reasonably.

Secondly, Kosík points out that the mystified political system is the origin of the political crisis. Modern politics proceeds with absolute demands and seeks to subordinate all. Kosík asserts: 'Politics has become, for modern humanity, fate: each person, in some measure, clarifies by way of political issues the meaning of his or her own existence'.[32] There are several political issues discussed in the context: (1) The contradiction between rulers and people who are governed although they do not want to be, i.e. the issue of the political system (whether political power is focused on people or not). (2) Class is highly related to the political structure of a society, the property relations of a society, and the direction in which a society chooses to go. So Kosík studies the class issue in particular, which is a central problem in political modernity. He focuses on concrete Czech problems including bureaucracy and dictatorship. The workers were locked up in the factory and became tools and implements. They lost their freedom of publishing, speech, and knowing, as well as their political rights. The division of intellectuals and workers was accomplished,

---

30   Kosík 1995e, p. 14.
31   Kosík 1976, p. 56.
32   Kosík 1995d, p. 17.

and they were unable to act together.³³ They were unaware of being people within a social totality, which deepened the crisis. (3) The fate of socialism is related to scientism, which has already had a considerable impact on capitalism. Kosík criticised the phrase 'science and technology revolution' because it concealed the real revolution that people needed.

Thirdly, Kosík argues that under a certain political system we should be very cautious about the culture we share, particularly one which has been taken advantage of by politicians or reformers. Culture can resolve precious little and influence few people, when it has lost its essence deep within the general public. Kosík states that 'far more noticeable is the impotence of culture, owing to the fact it has never succeeded in humanising power, enlightening rulers, or getting to the heart of everyday practical human relations, so that man might live "poetically" on earth'.³⁴ In modern society, culture has been inevitably affected by materialised, mechanised, and technologised civilisation, which is based on exchanges, merchandise, and techniques, in a way formulised by numbers. Culture should be formed within the general public, especially the working class, and it comes out of their essential everyday lives, reproducing the power of labour, and being the objectification of human power. However, essentially speaking, 'culture is based on works, lives in works, and survives in them'.³⁵ In modern times, culture is closely bound up with products and human delusions instead of desires, in deconstructed and manipulated everyday life. As a result, Kosík finds that this degeneration of culture has caused many vicious consequences, including the loss of morality, indifferent and detached human relationships, a distorted interpretation of history and reality, ideological language, as well as political crises.

Overall, we can conclude from the discussions above that Kosík has been focusing on the crisis of modernity by starting from the basic manner of how human beings actually live in modern times. What benefits Kosík's capacity for criticising modern society is his ontological dialectic, his particularity of being aware of the dialectical relationship between human beings and the living world. Modern politics, especially the political events that took place in Czechoslovakia around 1968, along with 'the crisis of political system', 'the crisis of political personality', 'the crisis of class', 'the crisis of nation', 'the crisis of socialism', and 'the crisis of mortality and culture', etc. have also affected him deeply. He goes straight to the heart to point out that neither Stalinism nor capitalist democracy is able to provide an alternative to nihilism, an alienated

---

33   Kosík 1995d, pp. 25–6.
34   Kosík 1995j, p. 101.
35   Kosík 1995a, p. 103.

and dangerous way of leading a modern life. He says, 'Nihilism ruins people, breaks their backbone, corrupts their ethics, and devalues thought. Most of all, however, it degrades, empties, and makes futile all criticism as sheer negation and all critics as having only three instruments at their disposal: an axe, incense, and ashes'.[36] He also points out that the core of the universal procuring system in modern times is 'technical rationality', which is itself inclined to be objective and omnipotent. The logic of 'technological reason' is what this system obeys at all times.

Hence, the deep-rooted cause of the alienation between human beings and the living world is the alienation of human practice. People living in the twentieth century shared two common phenomena. On the one hand, individuals becoming human beings under a procuring system, from the perspective of daily life; on the other, from the perspective of social life, the economy becomes superior to human beings. Therefore, human beings become subjects enslaved to the objective technology-based world. Truth is subservient to utility and accuracy, while dialectics has been degraded to a pure mechanised method or just an assembly of unchanging rules. Modernity, in Kosík's view, has been driven by so many alienated powers, such as the desire to rule, to possess, to become well-known or to become something compelling yet pseudo, something deprived of real desire for truth and justice. In spite of paying all kinds of attention and considerations to what is not really worth caring about, people have inevitably sunk into a pseudo-world where they are not able to discern for themselves what kind of life pattern is real or good. The actual make-up of social phenomena is not immediately apparent and the direct forms of appearance of social being are not subjective fantasies of the brain, but moments of real forms of existence, the conditions of existence of capitalist society. It seems obvious to the people who live in capitalist society, indeed it strikes them as 'natural', to stick with these forms and not to strive to comprehend the more hidden interconnection (intermediary terms, mediations) through which these phenomena interconnect in reality, and through whose identification they can be understood only in their correct context.[37]

Now we move back to the theme we have taken up throughout the whole essay: Kosík's ontological dialectic based upon his understanding of 'concrete totality', which has surely been discussed in *The Crisis of Modernity*, wherein Kosík discusses the living status (crises) of human beings under modern circumstances and the relationship between individuals and the outside world

---

36   Ibid.
37   See Lukács 2000, pp. 79–80.

(time and space) many times. He states that 'an individual remains an individual, but if he gets into the proximity of history, he becomes either the great individual making history or the helpless person being crushed by history'.[38] The power of pushing history forward is not something superstitious or 'superindividual forces' like Hegel's 'world spirit', but rather the resultant forces of people, especially workers, in which case history is no longer one-dimensional or merely an object, but rather is something shaped with various dimensions. These diverse dimensions come out of human praxis and all the possibilities produced by individuals themselves. Kosík criticises the fact that Marx's notion of 'praxis was interpreted more or less as a social substance outside the individual and not as a structure of the individual himself and of all individuals. The analysis of the reified modern industrial societies, relationship to the individual led to practical consequences opposed to those that were intended'.[39] Therefore, neither depersonalisation in modern society nor the disintegration of the individual solves the impact of modernity. In Kosík's view, the individual lives in society as a part of the whole but this should not entail a denial of his/her individuality, and human sociability need not conflict with his/her personality as well.

5 What Can China Learn from Kosík?

In *The Crisis of Modernity*, Kosík discusses several detailed issues in Czech history and raises the 'Czech question'. However, as a matter of fact, those issues that arose with modernity are also taking place in China. With the recent installation of a new Chinese government, a series of daunting but most urgent issues remain to be dealt with, for instance, food safety problems, government corruption, severe environmental issues, the socialist path within globalisation, and so on. All these problems have an impact on Chinese people as well as the government, which urgently calls for solutions, both theoretically and practically.

With the reformation that Deng Xiaoping started in the 1980s, China has become entrapped in a super-complicated pitfall that on the one hand involves global economics, which requires a 'free' market, and on the other is governed by a central socialist government, which is supposed to resist it. In the intervening years, some interest groups reaped staggering profits out of the reform,

---

38 Kosík 1995i, p. 123.
39 Kosík 1995i, p. 132.

for instance, the bureaucratic class, state-owned enterprises, and capitalists. In recent decades, house prices have soared incredibly, inflation has been sharply aggravated, and people's welfare has not improved as much as it should have. Therefore, plenty of intellectuals have begun to appeal for 'social justice' and have turned against the 'one-party dictatorship' as well as its official ideology – Marxism – especially Chinese liberals, who insist that the government is excessively interfering in public affairs and expropriating people's rights and interests. It is a great pity that they tend to turn to the Western model of democracy and impute these social problems to Marxian thought. However, the apparent triumph of Western capitalist models is not, in any clear sense, the victory of a predictively powerful theory; indeed, the even more recent events of the worldwide recession and instability in the Middle East have generated little serious thinking.[40] Capitalism is not a good choice when facing those social problems. This does not mean that Marx was wrong or socialism has come to an end. On the contrary, it requires proper dialectical thought to help clear our vision, so that we can jump out of the complicated pseudoconcrete to tear the disguised phenomena apart.

Of course, the circumstances in China and the developed Western countries are distinct. For historical reasons, China does not have a complete civil society that is separated from the government, i.e. we have not undergone a successful political emancipation which clearly separates normal public life from political life. Moreover, China has a long history of centralised feudal autocracy, which leads Chinese people to adapt to group life and rely more on governments. Because China does not have as fully developed a civil society as the United States and other Western capitalist countries do, people may not be able to realise actual relationships between the self, others, and the state. In other words, China remains at a beginning stage when individuals and the state interact directly, and only after further development can it reach a higher level. But on the other hand, globalisation simultaneously affects China, focusing increasingly on the problems of integration into the world economy, which causes a necessary development of civil society. However, so-called globalisation is based on the rapacious and extractive needs of global capital, which is fundamentally in conflict with socialist structure.

China is on its way to modernity, as a result of which we have encountered complexity within social development. In spite of our particular cultural and social causes of problems, we share something in common with Western modernity, for instance, the procuring system brought about by modern civilisation,

---

40 Margolis 1992, p. 329.

psychologically caring for daily life, mental compressive stresses, deteriorated relationships between human beings and the environment, distorted illusions of reality, and so on. However, Kosík has pointed out the real key point of getting rid of alienation, i.e. the 'concrete totality' – a practical process that reconstructs reality and the relationship between human beings and the living world. His ontological dialectic has demonstrated a great vitality in analysing the distorted phenomena ahead of us, hand in hand with a revolutionary practical appeal to rebuild both humanised nature and social relations. It will require the government's endeavour, but moreover every Chinese citizen's participation and effort. Because everyone, as an individual, has the autonomy to integrate in his or her individual life what is generally human. Everyone should regard himself/herself as a revolutionary subject to bring in everyone to the evolution of society. Meanwhile, the individual can change the world only in cooperation and conjunction with others. That is to say, we can only succeed in a unity in which everyone is concrete and alive. Individualism, nihilism and capitalism are not viable options.

6 Conclusion

In this essay, we have discussed several opinions based upon interpretations of Kosík's work. First of all, we claim that Kosík is a Hegelian-Marxian scholar rather than a 'Heideggerian Marxist', although we do not deny that he has been influenced by Heidegger's critique of modernity, which on the other hand becomes his crucial perspective in his analysis of modern society. Secondly, we have stressed Kosík's concept of 'concrete totality' in *Dialectic of the Concrete*, analysing its philosophical meaning within the context, and compared it with several other interpretations of 'totality', especially that of Lukács. Thirdly, the link between 'concrete totality' and the 'ontological dialectic', which evolves from the Hegelian tradition, has been illustrated. We indicated the essential meaning of the 'ontological dialectic' by drawing an outline of 'the relationship between individuals and the living world'. Fourthly, we have compared Kosík's view of the 'individual' with both Marx's and Lukács's view. It is the certain historical conditions and abundant social changes that bring about differences. All three thinkers pay great attention to the historical and social structure of capitalist society, but Kosík focuses more on individuals' daily lives and their alienated living status in modern times. He utilises Marx's analysis of capitalism, absorbing and developing his dialectical thinking in order to reveal new social crises that Marx did not encounter in his age. Fifthly, we have also discussed several main issues that Kosík discusses in *The Crisis of Modernity* to articulate how his ontological dialectic works with real social problems. Finally, we have tried to use Kosík's theory to offer a few comments on contemporary China. Overall, we have proved that with the ontological dialectic and the critique of modernity, it is possible to excavate the distorted social relations from within diverse spheres in modern times, or at least that Kosík shows how we might approach reality dialectically.

CHAPTER 9

And the 'Thing Itself' Is Man: Radical Democracy and the Roots of Humanity

Joseph Grim Feinberg

Karel Kosík was a humanist. He was also a humanist who problematised the meaning of the human.

The central tensions of humanism run through Kosík's work. Kosík held up the human being as a transcendent ideal in contrast with an alienating reality, even while he pointed toward the historical contingency of this transcendent ideal.

Kosík never fully resolved this tension, but he pointed to one possibility for resolution. In his notion of 'democracy', especially 'radical democracy', a term emerges that mediates between the absolute, abstract human ideal and the relative, concretely alienated person. This term, 'the people', points to an alternative conception of humanity, grounded in social form and emancipatory struggle. If the people's activity is 'radical', it reaches for humanity's roots.

1 To Grasp Things by the Root

'Dialectics', writes Karel Kosík in the first sentence of *Dialectics of the Concrete*, 'is after the "thing itself"'.[1] To be dialectical is to be dissatisfied with mere appearances, to seek out the essence of things, to unveil the real structure that determines the form of appearances.

A few years earlier, in a 1958 article called 'Classes and the Real Structure of Society', Kosík described Marxism in only slightly different terms, as a 'genetic-historical method', a method for approaching things by looking for their origins.[2] In that same year he published *Czech Radical Democracy* (*Česká radikální demokracie*), which among other things traces the genesis of Marxism to the radical democratic movements of the nineteenth century.[3] Dialectics, in other

---

1 Kosík 1976, p. 1.
2 Kosík 2017, p. 192.
3 Kosík writes, 'Marx became a communist after having been a radical democrat. This fact is extraordinarily significant for understanding not only revolutionary democracy, but also

words, through the study of historical developments, breaks through the superficial appearances of the present, identifying the structures that lie beneath. Marxism, in other words, reaches for 'things themselves' by unearthing their temporal and ontological roots. Kosík, after all, was a radical, and this was just how Marx defined radicalism: 'To be radical is to grasp things by the root'.[4]

A question remains, however: what is to be done once the root has been grasped?

On this point Kosík's position is ambivalent. Does the solution to the problems we face lie in a return to the essential, or is the essential itself the root of our problems? Should we 'become metaphysical', as Kosík puts it in his 1993 essay 'Democracy and the Myth of the Cave',[5] or is this metaphysical moment only transitory, leading toward a moment in which apparently eternal essences might be transformed? Should we go 'back' to the roots, or should we grasp them in order to tear them up?

And in either case: what are the roots?

2   But for Man the Root Is Man

'The "thing itself" that philosophy deals with', writes Kosík in the final paragraph of *Dialectics of the Concrete*, 'is man'.[6] He was perhaps alluding to the statement by Marx quoted above. 'To be radical is to grasp things by the root', wrote Marx, and then he continued: 'But for man the root is man himself'.[7] Radical, dialectical thought seeks to understand human affairs by identifying what lies beneath them and what they grow out of. But what lies beneath human affairs is itself a human affair. The human being is absolute, dependent on nothing other than itself. Kosík, like Marx – and unlike, for example, anti-essentialists of the postmodern age – would insist on the reality of essences that give shape to superficial existence. But the essences he identified were themselves a part of human existence, socially formed.

---

communism. [...] [T]he often debated question of the relationship between communism and democracy can best be clarified by tracing the development of the founder of Marxism.' Kosík 1958, p. 22.
4   Marx 1978a, p. 60.
5   Kosík 1996, p. 123.
6   Kosík 1976, p. 152. Or, in a fairer but perhaps less poetic translation, the 'thing itself' is 'the human being'. The Czech word *člověk*, although grammatically masculine, is semantically gender-neutral and etymologically unrelated to 'man' (*muž*).
7   Marx 1978a, p. 60.

The human being and its creations can only be explained by reference to the human being. But still: what exactly is the human being? Kosík poses this question explicitly, but once again his answer is ambivalent.

The human being, writes Kosík in *Dialectics of the Concrete*, 'is no ordinary thing; actually, it is not a thing at all'.[8] In 'Democracy and the Myth of the Cave', however, he would observe that 'Man is always exposed to the danger of degenerating into "something", being transformed into a mere "what"'.[9] Although the philosophical approach in Kosík's late essays differs from the approach in *Dialectics of the Concrete*,[10] on this point he was quite consistent: the human being appears as an object that is actually a subject; but it is also a subject that is always on the verge of becoming an object. The human being is an object of inquiry that also sets the terms of inquiry and makes inquiry possible; it is a product of objectifying socio-historical processes, but is also a creative actor in those processes. Yet at the same time the human being continually risks losing the subjectivity that would seem to be its due. The human being is distinguished by its capacity to create itself and its conditions, but it does not always exercise this capacity. Or, more precisely, it is not always in active, subjective control of its creative activity. *In principle* it is absolute and self-determining, but *in practice* it is relative, relational, determined by all manner of things outside itself. *A priori* the human being appears to be an absolute, metaphysical principle, yet *a posteriori* it reveals itself to be a dialectical principle, whose absolute self-determination exists only in a potential that has never yet been realised.

'[T]he human being is praxis', writes Kosík, again in 'Democracy and the Myth of the Cave'.[11] The human is a being whose essence is the ability to create essences; or, as Kosík puts it in this essay, the human being's essence is its ability 'to found the world'. But there is no guarantee that this potential will be realised. Perhaps this is why, in his discussion of the human being, Kosík returns repeatedly to the question of *democracy*. The question of democracy is the question of whether humanity – that is, the collective of human beings and the human understood as a collective being – can actively determine its own potential creativity.

Here, yet again, Kosík is ambivalent. Kosík points toward the possibility of a radical, post-humanistic conception in which the human being appears fully rooted in society, criticising society and uprooting society only by virtue of

---

8   Kosík 1976, p. 152.
9   Kosík 1996, p. 122.
10   Cf. Jan Černý's contribution to this volume, pp. 281–303.
11   Kosík 1996, p. 122.

its position *within* the social totality. But he hesitates. Although in *Dialectics of the Concrete* he opposes metaphysics with dialectics,[12] he appears unwilling to definitively abandon a metaphysical conception of the human being as an absolute standard, an unchanging measure of the ever-changing social world. And by the time of 'Democracy and the Myth of the Cave' (published thirty years after *Dialectics of the Concrete*), Kosík's affection for metaphysics has become explicit.

These tensions in the thought of Kosík, a humanist critic of uncritical humanism, reveal tensions that run through humanism more generally. And nowhere is this tension more apparent than in Kosík's discussion of the human being's potential to determine its own social existence – that is, in Kosík's discussion of democracy.

3   Man the Answer

In 'Democracy and the Myth of the Cave', Kosík poses democracy as a question. With humanity beset by generalised manipulation and a technology-induced loss of meaning and truth, Heidegger had remarked that philosophy becomes impotent and 'only a god can save us'. But no such god exists, Kosík observes, because the roots of humanity's problems lie in humanity itself, and humanity must find its own way out of the morass into which it has wandered. Then, he asks: 'If there is no divine salvation', can we expect to be saved by 'democracy'?[13]

Kosík does not rush to answer affirmatively. 'Contemporary democracy' hardly seems up to the task, because it has become complicit in the ruling system of mass manipulation. The citizenry has become pacified by an apparent abundance of consumer goods; the incessant expansion of the market, which is the 'hidden ruler'[14] of contemporary society, gives the impression of openness and choice, while it quells popular demands for anything else. As for the system of elections, of selecting rulers who absolve us of the 'burden of decision'[15] – is it simply an illusion of freedom within the 'cave' of mass-manipulated falsehood?[16]

The late Kosík's despair, however, is not complete. He holds out hope for a *different* kind of democracy, a democracy governed by a different kind of *demos*,

---

12   Kosík 1976, p. 17.
13   Kosík 1996, p. 121.
14   Kosík 1996, p. 120.
15   Kosík 1996, p. 117.
16   Kosík 1996, p. 122.

by a 'people' that is 'adequate to the idea of democracy'.[17] How should this 'people' be defined? Kosík responds with a linguistic banality that is as apparent in English as it is in Czech: 'The people are people, and people is the plural of person'. Or, translated differently, 'the people is the human being in plural'.[18] The question of democracy is therefore a search for the human being, a search for a people that is adequately human, human enough to be a free subject that founds and re-founds the world. Humanity appears as the answer to the question of democracy, a kind of *deus ex machina* that could save us in place of a god. 'Contemporary' democracy operates on the level of mere appearances, shadows on the wall of an enormous cave; but it could arrive at its essential truth by becoming *human*.

That was Kosík in 1993, when he had become pessimistic about humanity's chances of saving itself from technological civilisation. But even in the late 1960s, when he was more optimistic about humanity's prospects, he expressed himself in similar terms. In 'Our Current Crisis', for example, written in early 1968, Kosík discusses a crisis facing 'the nation' (*národ*); here he does not write directly of 'the people' (*lid*),[19] but the problem is analogous to the one posed in 1993, and the solution is fundamentally the same. The Czech nation, caught in an undemocratic political system, manipulated by bureaucratic administration, is unable to act as a subject in control of its own affairs. The way out of the crisis lies in the nation's ability to realise its humanity: 'we are a nation', Kosík writes, 'only insofar as we distinguish ourselves from a colony of ants or an indifferent mob'.[20] The nation is only adequate to the idea of nationhood if it can make itself a free subject that is also a collection of individuated free subjects. If Czech intellectuals have long debated the 'meaning' of Czech national history, Kosík observes that the key underlying question is '*primarily* about the *human being*'.[21] The issue is partly geographical, as Kosík follows oth-

---

17 This is how Johann Arnason puts it in his slightly loose translation of this passage. The passage in Czech reads more literally as 'how must the people be defined in order to be the people of democracy?' Kosík 1996, p. 122; Kosík 1993a, p. 184.

18 These are my more literal renderings of the Czech original: 'Lid jsou lidi, lid je člověk v plurálu'. Kosík 1993a, p. 184. Arnason's translation reads: '[...] the people constitutes a plurality of human beings [...]'. Kosík 1996, p. 122.

19 The existing English translation (Kosík 1995) erroneously renders the word *národ*, which unambiguously means 'nation', as 'people'. An editorial note offers one possible explanation: the translation was made from an earlier translation into Serbo-Croation, in which the word *narod* can mean either 'nation' or 'people'. For whatever reason, the translation includes a number of imprecisions, which I correct here in quoting from that volume.

20 Kosík 1995d, p. 29.

21 Kosík 1995d, p. 31. Here, and in later quotations, I have restored Kosík's italics, which the existing English translation left out.

ers – most notably Tomáš Garrigue Masaryk – in calling on the Czech nation to overcome its tendencies toward isolationism and contribute to humanity as a whole. But here Kosík's emphasis is on something existential: Answering the so-called 'Czech question' means seeking, in specific Czech conditions, 'the truth of human existence', beyond the separate and superficial issues of 'mere policy, nationhood, simple patriotism, mere nation-building'.[22] The question of the nation, like the question of the people, is answered by the human.

4 Man the Question

In the same 1968 essay, however, Kosík also calls into question the unchanging essence of the human being and casts doubt on its ability to provide an answer to questions posed by the people and the nation. Kosík notes Machiavelli's belief that the human being was inherently 'more inclined to evil than good', which led Machiavelli to a rather inhumane conception of politics.[23] But, as Kosík observes, Gramsci would later counter that 'there is no abstract "human nature", fixed and immutable' and that 'human nature is the totality of historically determined social relations'.[24] This would seem to offer a devastating critique of the approach Kosík has just elaborated, which posits the human being as the measure of politics. If the human being continually changes, can there be any meaning to the assertions that the people or the nation must 'humanise' themselves? By what measure can their 'humanity' be judged?

Nevertheless, although Gramsci's rejection of human essence is clearly more historically materialist than Machiavelli's belief in the human's essential inclination toward evil, Kosík does not immediately accept it. To accept it uncritically, he claims, would mean to accept the view that human essence is determined entirely by power, since power is what continually transforms those social relations which, according to Gramsci, produce human essence.[25] And if human essence is determined entirely by power, 'power becomes all powerful, since it can alter anything, including the very "nature" of man'.[26] This conclusion

---

22 Kosík 1995d, p. 31.
23 Kosík 1995d, pp. 32–3.
24 Gramsci 1971, p. 133. Cited in Kosík 1995d, p. 33.
25 In Kosík's rendering, Gramsci appears very much like a forerunner to Foucault as a theorist of how power relations generate systems of thought, including the notion of humanity. But I am not aware of any evidence that Kosík was familiar with Foucault's work at this time. (Foucault, by contrast, probably was influenced by Gramsci, at least indirectly, through Althusser.)
26 Kosík 1995d, p. 34.

would be 'unacceptable', but according to Kosík it is also unnecessary. Human essence could be understood precisely as the human capacity for transforming social conditions – and thus for transforming human essence. This capacity enables the human being to '*transcend* the set of circumstances in which it lives and to which it cannot be reduced',[27] thus making it possible for people living in one set of social relations to understand people from another set of relations.[28] According to Kosík, only a complex view of human essence, which neither accepts human essence as unchanging nor views it as *entirely* determined by changing circumstances, enables us to understand the dialectical irony of revolutions, which can both 'liberate' the human being (from its erstwhile essence) and in doing so can subject the human being to manipulation (imposing a new human essence).[29] Because 'power is not all-powerful',[30] the human being is able to maintain a semi-independent perspective on its manipulation and its ability to assert an alternative subjectivity – an independent essence – in the face of power.

In the course of this qualified and problematised assertion of human essence, Kosík shifts his rhetorical usage of 'man' (that is, of 'the human being'). At moments like these, the human being ceases to serve as an answer to other questions and becomes a question itself. Kosík asks 'Who is man?'[31] and he challenges us to find the answer in the complexity of social relations, accumulated over time, in which humans have come to exist. The autonomy of the human being, a subject essentially free and self-determining, can be sought in concrete human history. Perhaps the autonomous human being can come into being at certain moments and at other moments may cease to exist. And the idea of the autonomous human being can persist as a moral imperative, guiding critics who attempt to step conditionally outside their social conditions, insisting that the human being *can* be something more than it *is*.

Still – from where do we get our ideas about what the human being should or could be?

---

27   Ibid.
28   Kosík 1995d, p. 33.
29   Kosík 1995d, p. 35.
30   Ibid.
31   Kosík 1995d, p. 34.

5 Man Abstract

In 'Our Current Crisis', although Kosík writes suggestively of the human being's inherent capacity to transcend its social conditions, Kosík does not characterise in any detail the conditions that might enable or shape this transcendence. In discussing 'the crisis of the nation', as we saw, Kosík asserts the nation's need to transcend its local particularity by inserting its problems into the problems of humanity as a whole.[32] In this process, he writes, 'everything depends' on the priority we give to one or the other of these two opposing terms, particular and universal, nature and humanity: Do we *begin* by reflecting on the specific situation of our nation and *then* consider how this character determines our human existence? Or do we begin by reflecting on the meaning of human existence, and on *this* basis proceed to the specific questions of our nation? Is the nation the measure of humanity or is humanity the measure of the nation? Kosík insists here on the priority of the universal, of humanity. If we began from the position of the particular nation – in the Czech case, from the position of a small and threatened nation – then we would limit our understanding of humanity by the terms of our struggle for national existence, and we would hardly have the occasion to ask how to make our national existence humanly meaningful. Instead, we should begin with our human existence and proceed from the meaning of humanity to the meaning of the nation.[33]

Four years earlier, in a paper from 1964 entitled 'The Nation and Humanism', Kosík articulated roughly the same idea. There he turns to the 'old-fashioned' philosophy of history of Johann Gottfried Herder. At least 'one of Herder's thoughts', he writes, 'should not be disregarded: the relationship of the nation and humanity'. As Kosík puts it, Herder understood that 'every single nation represents humanity to one degree or another' and that 'every nation takes upon itself the responsibility for humankind, because it itself is the realisation of humanity to some degree'.[34] Herder, in effect, appears as the mouthpiece not only for the long line of Czech thinkers who emphasised the nation's contribution to general human history, but also for Kosík's own synthesis of national

---

32 Kosík 1995d, pp. 28–9.
33 Kosík 1995d, p. 28. He writes: 'The Czech Question is a historical struggle over the *point of departure*. All depends upon whether or not one *begins* with an analysis regarding the meaning of human existence and, on this basis, one reflects on the politics of a small nation in Central Europe, or whether one begins with the question of whether or not belonging to a small and threatened nation determines the nature of human existence.'
34 Kosík 1995k, p. 142.

emancipation and philosophical humanism: National questions are human questions. Humanity is a 'constituent part' of each nation. Nations are 'responsible' for realising the potential of humanity as a whole. Through nations, people 'reach the stage of humanity' and *'become* humane'.[35]

The trouble with Kosík's reading is that this is not exactly what Herder called for. That Herder should be misread is nothing surprising (after Marx and the authors of the world's great religious texts, there is perhaps no other thinker who has been more frequently and disastrously – albeit often indirectly – reinterpreted). What is telling are the specifics of Kosík's misreading. Herder did indeed insist on the interrelationship between nations (or peoples, *Völker*) and 'humanity' (*Humanität* or *Menschheit*). But in Herder's view individual peoples (nations) did *not* take upon themselves 'responsibility' for humankind – if by humankind we understand a higher end existing above and before specific peoples. Herder shared with his former mentor Kant a concern for treating people as ends rather than means. But he also polemicised with Kant, especially after Kant responded critically to the first edition of Herder's *Ideas for the Philosophy of History of Humanity* by writing his own, very different 'Idea for a Universal History with a Cosmopolitan Purpose'. Herder rejected the notion that the history of humanity could be united in a single, universal, cosmopolitan purpose – that peoples could be made to serve as means to some higher ('cosmopolitan') end. Instead, he described the history of humanity (*Menschheit*) as the collected history of multiple peoples, each creating and perfecting its own aspect of humanity (*Humanität*) in its own way. Herder's cosmopolitanism demanded that the particularity of each people be respected and protected from subsumption by the universal.

This appears to be the reverse of what Kosík calls for in this passage. Whereas Kosík says that people 'reach the stage of humanity', Herder said that humanity's stages are different in every people. Whereas Kosík says that people 'become humane', Herder said in effect that humanity becomes national and popular, defined by people and derived from their unique cultural histories. Kosík, more in the spirit of Kant than of Herder, writes as if humanity *preexisted* any given nation and as if nations gave meaning to themselves primarily by contributing to a general human project, whose basic contours are not fundamentally altered by any single nation. In this picture, the human ideal enables the nation to escape its particular, isolated ends, to find common cause with people of other nations; but national specificity is not shown to have a significant impact on humanity. As such, it appears as an abstract force, unmediated by

---

35   Ibid. Kosík's emphasis.

the concrete praxis of people in the world – dangerously close, it would seem, to Kosík's own conception of 'bad totality' as developed in *Dialectics of the Concrete*.[36]

Must the choice be so stark? A particularistic ideal of peoples that find their own, varied humanness, or a universal ideal that develops independently of people? Must we begin with only one term – nation or humanity, particular or universal – and proceed as if this term were already formed and formative of the other? Or is it possible that they mutually form one another? Does the universal serve as the measure of the particular, or the particular as the measure of the universal? Or might there be a third term that measures and roots them both?

6   Man Concrete

In Kosík's more political texts, humanity appears to ground and give meaning to the people and the nation, but Kosík does not specify what might ground and give meaning to humanity. In Kosík's more social-philosophical writings on dialectics and materialism, however, an alternative attitude can be discerned. Similarly abstract and universalistic concepts do appear, but they are shown to develop in confrontation with concrete social and historical reality.

In his 1958 article 'The History of Philosophy as Philosophy', Kosík writes that every philosophical system represents 'a moment in the developmental process of humanity'.[37] This is what lends it universal meaning in spite of the fact that it is always a product of a specific situation and epoch. Much in the same way that particular nations gain legitimacy by cultivating their relationship to the human whole, particular philosophies gain validity through participation in the universal history of human thought. But in this article Kosík does not invoke universal human history as a *conclusion* to his argument. The concept presents one *moment* in the argument that leads to further precision in subsequent moments. Kosík *first* raises the issue of universal intellectual history in order to call into question the notion of history understood as continual progress toward final, objective truth. In what could be read as a polemic with the Kantian idea of history with a 'cosmopolitan purpose', Kosík holds that a Marxist history of philosophy refuses to recognise progress as a process that unfolds *on its own*, as an abstraction independent of the concrete philosophies that suc-

---

36   Kosík 1976, pp. 30–1.
37   Kosík 1958b, p. 24.

ceed one another in history. Such an abstract notion of progress, self-contained and complete, would be a metaphysical concept, and Kosík (at this stage in his career) rejects metaphysics. Nevertheless, Kosík also regards it as inadequate to adopt the apparently opposite view that the history of philosophy is merely a 'succession of philosophical currents', each independent of the others and 'equally truthful and legitimate'. History *does* move forward, because each new system of thought includes and responds to the thought that came before it. The systems are interrelated, and the totality of their interrelations forms the general 'developmental process of humanity'. Humanity and its history, in other words, are necessary abstractions, but they are taken neither as given before investigation nor as the endpoint of investigation. Rather, they are questions to be worked through. To borrow a term from Kosík's 1958 article 'Classes and the Real Structure of Society', written that same year (a term which would later become central to *Dialectics of the Concrete*), such abstractions should be subsequently concretised and brought into mutual confrontation and connection, in order to reveal the form of the whole as a *'concrete totality'*.[38]

In *Dialectics of the Concrete*, too, Kosík would problematise the status of 'humanity'. Although Kosík writes of the 'essence' of the human being ('the unity of objectivity and subjectivity'[39]), the entire book is an attempt to specify and clarify the practical, social meaning of essences (or 'things themselves'). At times in *Dialectics of the Concrete*, Kosík seems to refer to the essence of humanity as if it were a fixed and acknowledged idea that can explain and justify other ideas: He identifies human critical praxis with 'the humanisation of man', without (at that moment) explaining the meaning of 'man' in any terms other than man's own humanness.[40] He discusses the widespread call to 'return to the sources' (*ad fontes*) as a call to 'find the 'real reality' of concrete man behind the reified reality of reigning culture', without clarifying whether he himself shares this view and whether he, therefore, accepts that man has a 'real reality', unaffected by the accretions of reified culture, to which humanity could eventually return.[41] Kosík concludes the book, however, with a more guarded and contextually specific (or, we could say, historical and materialist) consideration of the human being. He proposes that we understand the human being not purely in its own subjective terms, as if it were separate from the universe – the way the human being appears in 'philosophical anthropology', from which Kosík distin-

---

38 Kosík 2017, p. 196.
39 Kosík 1976, p. 70.
40 Kosík 1976, p. 8.
41 Ibid.

guishes his own approach[42] – but rather as a being that 'exist[s] in the totality of the world'[43] and is understandable as part of this *global* (not only 'human') totality.

The human being, in other words, understood in its totality, is both abstract and concrete. According to the view of praxis and cognition developed in *Dialectics of the Concrete*, the abstract notion of humanity provides a starting point for understanding human affairs and enables us to see unity and interrelation rather than random and isolated empirical facts. This notion, however, comes into confrontation with multiple historical and social mediations. It is concretised in each epoch and society, structured by differing social systems, variously reflecting those systems' structures of thought and action. But this moment of concretisation is not the final moment in understanding, because these various systems are interrelated. The multiplicity of humanities, in relation to one another, form humanity as a concrete totality, made up of and mediated by its variously conditioned humanities.

7   Man the Product, Man the Problem

At certain moments in his work, Kosík raises the question of just how universally valid the notion of 'humanity' can be. In *Dialectics of the Concrete*, for example, Kosík refers to Max Scheler's assertion that 'at no time in his history has man been so much of a problem to himself as he is now',[44] and he cites Heidegger's suggestion that philosophical anthropology should be understood as a '"*tendency*" of a time that has made man problematic'.[45] The conception of man put forth by philosophical anthropologists like Scheler, Kosík explains, has developed in 'epochs of homelessness, isolation, and problematisation'.[46] Especially disorienting social conditions have led people to question who they are as humans and what they might become, how they have treated and should treat other humans, what they can know about themselves and their world. Kosík takes this as an occasion to criticise the narrowness of philosophical anthropology's conception of the human being, which draws transhistorical conclusions from the historically contingent figure of a being who is alienated and dislocated at a specific moment in history. Kosík, however, does not ques-

---

42   Kosík 1976, p. 149.
43   Kosík 1976, pp. 152–3.
44   Scheler 1961, p. 6; cited in Kosík 1976, p. 148.
45   Heidegger 1962b, p. 216; cited in Kosík 1976, p. 149.
46   Kosík 1976, p. 149.

tion the validity of the concept of humanity as such; rather, he proposes a more general concept that can encompass the various manifestations of the human *within* and *in relation to* its shifting context. Each iteration of the human being in history is a product of its historical moment, but the figure that is repeatedly iterated would seem to transcend the sum of its historical moments.

Yet the early pages of 'Our Current Crisis' raise further questions about the origin and historical status of the human notion. Here, as is typical in humanistic reflections, 'the human being' appears both individual and universal. The notion can be variously specified in varying social conditions, but the notion itself brackets those specifications, framing its subject-object, the human being, as a universalisable individual. Humanity, as a universalised collection of human beings, bears a striking resemblance to another notion discussed in this part of Kosík's essay: the mass. People 'become masses' in a system that places them in the category of an 'anonymous majority'[47] without internal differentiation. Might it also be the case that people become 'humans' when they are abstracted from their concrete communities and placed together in a homogeneous mass? Might the abstract human being be a *product* of modern alienation, even while it represents a revolt against that alienation? The human being is typically presented as a figure that *once existed* in a pre-alienated past and has now been lost; is it possible that that the human being is, rather, historically achieved precisely in the moment that is felt as a loss? That it has come into being just as social relations have become more global and more uniform, beginning in ancient empires, where the notion of the human first appeared when claims of global domination were accompanied by dreams of global subjecthood, then reaching its higher development alongside the economic globalisation and cultural homogenisation of today?

Does humanism represent a *negative* protest against global alienation, redeeming its content but reproducing its external form, substituting the standardised 'mass' with the universalised 'human'? Or can humanism offer a counter-conception of the subject, fundamentally distinct from the alienation that it opposes? A *radical* humanism, perhaps, should be one that grasps humanity by its roots – a humanity *already* deracinated by globalisation, homogenisation, and alienation – and replants it in more fertile ground.

---

47 Kosík 1995d, p. 18.

8   The Human Being in Plural

In 'Democracy and the Myth of the Cave', as we saw, Kosík describes the democratic subject, 'the people', as 'the human being in plural'.[48] His point was that the people could be reconceptualised and redeemed if seen through the lens of the human being. But this assertion hardly clarified the issue, because the human being itself was so abstractly conceptualised. The notion of the human being can hardly specify the meaning of other problems if it remains unspecified itself. Like all abstract philosophical concepts, its meaning becomes clear and is filled with content – i.e. it ceases to be an empty phrase – only when it is translated into terms other than its own, and this happens as the abstract concept passes through forms of social mediation, becoming increasingly concretised – when it ceases to be an independently existing category, absolute and metaphysical, and begins to be a dialectical category, existing within a totality of social relations. Kosík wavered in his conception of the human being, never definitively abandoning the concept of an absolute, independent human essence, even while he repeatedly pointed toward the human being's relational, socially determined existence.

Much of the conceptual power of *Dialectics of the Concrete* stems from Kosík's ability to take widely used philosophical concepts, concepts typically defined in purely *philosophical* terms, and to translate them into terms that are *socially* meaningful. Kosík engages the discourse of metaphysics, epistemology and phenomenology, which are so frequently elaborated within closed conceptual systems whose terms are defined in relation to one another, whose meaning barely escapes tautology, and which in the worst cases degenerate into collections of high-sounding jargon that masks conceptual emptiness.[49] Kosík brings such terms into confrontation with one another and inserts them into living human praxis, pulling them out of their metaphysical isolation.[50] Yet Kosík hesitated in bringing this critical approach to bear on one category of his own system: the human being.

The human being, in Kosík's work, lacks another term into which its meaning could be translated. Other terms are defined in terms of the human being, while the human being is defined in terms of itself. Man is rooted exclusively

---

48   Kosík 1996, p. 122.
49   Adorno 1973.
50   I would argue that Heidegger's *Being and Time*, for example, in spite of its stated aims, only ceases to be a work of metaphysics when pulled out of its closed, self-referential system by interpreters like Kosík.

in man. But Kosík's notion of 'the human being in plural' suggests a way out; it points to another set of socially concretised terms. In Kosík's usage, the phrase was meant to ask how the problem of the people is reframed by the notion of the human being. But what if we reverse the terms and ask how the notion of the human being is reframed by the notion of the people? What if, instead of asking how the people becomes singular, refracting the abstract human, we ask how the human being becomes plural, concretising itself in the praxis of the people?

The notion of the people, of course, can be just as abstract and almost as general as the notion of the human being. Unlike the human being, however, the people and its political project, democracy, were the object of extended, concrete investigation in Kosík's work. While Kosík seems (at least at times) to have been devoted to the eternal and transcendently critical character of the human ideal, his commitment to democracy was historically situated, framed in terms of democracy's specific contents and adversaries. While his devotion to the human being seems to have been unconditional and absolute, his commitment to democracy was partisan and always framed in concrete terms – when democracy became a question, he took the people's side. In his book *Czech Radical Democracy*, Kosík was thus willing to say something of the people that he did not quite bring himself to say of the human being: '"the people" is a concretely historical category, whose content changes depending on the conditions of social development'.[51] This meant, first of all, that one could investigate the historical development of 'the people' and 'democracy' as *ideas* – and this was a central feature of *Czech Radical Democracy*, which interpreted the philosophical systems of Czech radical democrats within the historical context of nineteenth-century politics. But the concretely historical character of 'the people' also meant that 'the people' could serve as a *social* category for investigating the shifting composition of 'the people' over time.

With his social conception of 'the people', Kosík distinguished his notion of 'democracy' from the liberal notion. The democratic subject, for him, was not an abstract human-citizen bearing formal-legal rights. Rather, more in line with the nineteenth-century usage (shared by the democrats themselves and by liberals who generally *opposed* pure 'democracy'), Kosík understood the democratic subject as a socially structured entity wielding and demanding power. The people could therefore be defined in terms of the social structure in which people participate as 'the immediate producers of material goods, that is, of the overwhelming majority of the population, which lives by its labor, clothes soci-

---

51   Kosík 1958a, p. 18.

ety, builds cities and villages, creates the material basis and the spiritual culture of humanity'.[52] The specific class composition of this group would change over time, being predominantly peasant at one moment, predominantly working-class at another.[53] A 'democrat', then, is someone who, in a given social situation, defends this social group and works toward its emancipation. And since the people 'creates the material basis and the spiritual culture of humanity', the emancipation of the people would mean the liberation of the creative potential of humankind.

'The people' is the name for the group that, in a given historical moment, creates the conditions for the possibility of liberated humanity. The root of man may be man, but if we apply Kosík's dialectical approach to his own notion of man and specify the meaning of each of these 'men', we can see that the root of man-as-abstract-humanity is man-as-the-concrete-people. The radical, who would grasp the root of humanity with the aim of realising humanity's potential, must do so as a democrat. Then, on this basis, the radical can return to the abstraction of the human being, having passed through the mediating structure of the people. *Then* it would be possible to say that the people should be humanised, that is, made into a free, self-determining subject, because this process of humanisation would take on social meaning as a process of democratisation – that is, as a process by which social structures are changed, enabling 'the overwhelming majority of the population' to determine the material basis and spiritual culture of humanity.

In 'the people', the human being becomes plural without immediately becoming universal. If understood as a category that must be socially specified, 'the people' can frame the human being as a question of pluralisation – a question of how a creative subject in a given time and place is or might be collectively organised. 'The people' leaves open the question of whether there may be a single people or multiple peoples. But in the face of mass society, which has left people feeling rootless, and in contrast with 'the human being', which presents people as a universalised individual, the people presents the possibility of a differentiated yet interwoven system of roots. There appears to be a tension between radical democracy and humanism that Kosík did not see. Radical democracy, insofar as it posits specific social structures, offers a counterweight to any humanism that merely negates mass society and defines the integral human being as the opposite of alienated man (and is therefore determined by the form of alienated man). But the human being that grasps its

---

52 Ibid.
53 Ibid.

own democratic roots might establish a different, differentiated, socialised and pluralised humanism.

9 The Roots of Humanity – the People

The people creates the historically conditioned manifestations of humanity, but during most historical moments the people does not effectively control this process of creation. As Kosík argued in 'Democracy and the Myth of the Cave', the people in its present, undemocratic form cannot be expected to refound humanity. So Kosík fell back on the idea of humanity as a standard by which to judge the people. He preserved it as an idea that transcends given social conditions, making it possible to imagine those conditions more generally transcended. Yet even this transcendent idea must have socially grounded roots. It is an idea that can only grow in a specific time and place, even if it is projected beyond.

Kosík did not fully resolve this tension in his work. But his dialectical understanding of history and practice points toward a possible resolution. He provides a framework within which an abstract ideal – the human being – can be confronted with its own historical conditions and contingency; then, passing through concrete mediations, the human being can be redeemed as an abstract standard whose claim to absoluteness is relative – valid only under certain social conditions, yet still, under those specific conditions, valid. Specific historical conditions, including the globalisation and standardisation of social relations, may have generated an idea of the human being as a figure standing outside its specific historical conditions. But this figure may nonetheless offer a critical perspective on those historical conditions, pointing beyond those conditions in ways that only these conditions have made imaginable. If this figure is not taken to be the *original* or *final* moment in a critical process, but a figure that passes through the mediation of socially grounded *peoples* – and Kosík made this conceptual move sometimes, but not consistently – the human being can be understood in its critical, dialectical totality.

The standpoint of humanity may well be a product of ideology.[54] Like any ideological product, it fails to serve the cause of human emancipation when it is taken as absolute, unchanging, unassailable, when it serves as the beginning and end of reflection rather than developing together with other terms. Kosík's conception of the human being is ambivalent, but his philosophy provides a

---

54 Althusser 1986.

means for moving beyond the metaphysical humanism – absolute and ahistorical – that he sometimes himself invokes. His radicalism – his passion for uprooting – points away from the metaphysics of man and toward a genealogy of the human being, in which the human being is grasped by its democratic roots.

CHAPTER 10

The Dialectic of Concrete Totality in the Age of Globalisation: Karel Kosík's *Dialectics of the Concrete* Fifty Years Later

Anselm K. Min

The purpose of this essay is to draw out the implications of the dialectic of concrete totality for the age of globalisation in which we find ourselves. The dialectic of concrete totality is *the* central idea of Karel Kosík's *Dialectics of the Concrete*, and it has always been central to the tradition of Hegel and Marx.[1] The distinguishing mark of the Hegelian-Marxian tradition is the interpretation of reality and history as a dialectic of concrete totality, and it is Kosík's particular merit to spell out this dialectic for the European world of the 1960s and 1970s. I am further convinced that this dialectic is especially compelling and relevant today, as globalisation cries out for a dialectical interpretation of its central movement in all its oppressive and liberating potential. I will, first, briefly review Kosík's idea of the dialectic of concrete totality; second, I will indicate the strengths and weaknesses of his idea; and third, I will develop the core of the idea of concrete totality for an analysis of our globalising world.

1 *Dialectics of the Concrete* Then

Let me begin with a brief review highlighting the basic insights of each of the four chapters of *Dialectics of the Concrete*.[2] In the *first* chapter Kosík gives us an insightful description of the capitalist world as a world of total reification, alienation and mystification, where things are isolated from the totality of the processes and relations that produce them; things gain independence and self-sufficiency in their isolation and givenness, and they exercise the power of the given on human beings, the ultimate producers, and their relations with one another. It is this appearance of things in their atomistic self-sufficiency that

---

1 For a scholarly history of the concept of totality in the Marxist tradition, see Jay 1984.
2 For my comprehensive review of this book from many years ago, see Min 1981, pp. 247–54.

constitutes the 'pseudoconcrete' that dominates the everyday consciousness of the capitalist world. To unmask and demystify the pseudoconcrete is to dereify them by restoring all the relations and movements that produce things, analysing them as products of a particular form of society in its contradictions, and recognising them ultimately as products of the praxis of human beings in their social relations, however fetishised such praxis may be.

The task of demystification and dereification, therefore, requires nothing less than the renewal of dialectical thinking or what Hegel called *begreifendes Denken*, which sees all reality as a movement, a movement of differentiation and contradiction, a movement of parts among themselves and between the parts and the whole, and therefore as a totality that differentiates itself into parts, suffers the internal contradictions among them, seeks to sublate the contradictions into a new whole, and constitutes itself as concrete because it is self-differentiating, self-contradicting and self-sublating. Behind this movement of concrete totality, even behind the dialectic of base and superstructure, however, there is the reality of human praxis, the ultimate producer of concrete totality, whose reality is reified in the many forms of false concreteness and false totality. For Kosík this dialectic is both the structure of reality as such and our heuristic way of grasping or comprehending [*begreifen*] the world as it truly is in its essence.

It is the failure to attend to all these essential moments of the dialectic that produces false totalities in their triple form as 'empty', 'abstract', and 'bad'. The totality is 'empty' without the determinate differentiation of the individual moments, the province of analytic reason, 'abstract' without the genesis and movements of internal relations and mutual mediations, and 'bad' when it is hypostasised into autonomous structures and tendencies at the expense of the complete elimination of the real human subjects of praxis. In light of the dialectic of concrete totality, Kosík provides a penetrating critique of empiricism, positivism, existentialism, and structuralism for absolutising atomistic facts, reifying the appearances of givenness, taking as normal the phenomenal world as given to reified consciousness, and reifying the structures themselves, and for equating reality with these appearances of what is really false concreteness and false totality.

In the *second* chapter, dealing with the relation between economics and philosophy, Kosík faults Heidegger for taking the particular reified, alienated, superficial world of capitalism with its preoccupation with manipulating and procuring, with its anonymity and everydayness, as the normal existential of human life for all time, when such a world is no more than the alienated expression of reified human praxis. In this regard Kosík dismisses Heidegger's call to existential authenticity as 'aristocratic Romantic Stoicism', quite the contrary of a revolutionary transformation of society, which is what we need. Capitalism reduces man to economic man, an abstraction from subjectivity that can be manipulated as an object, which makes economics as a science possible. Economy, however, is not a particular 'factor' or sphere among others that can be isolated and discussed in purely positivistic terms. It is a 'structure' as the totality of the social relations we enter in the sphere of production and therefore as the basis of all social relations, whether political or cultural. And responsible for this very structure is the subjectivity of human praxis in its social existence. The economic structure should not be reified by being separated from the involvement of human praxis. The capitalist structure is only a particular historical form of the objectification of human praxis and of human praxis in its alienation at that.

In dealing with the relation between philosophy and economy on the basis of the dialectical nature of *Capital*, the *third* chapter makes three very important points. First, it is false to interpret the transition from the young Marx to the Marx of *Capital* as a transition from philosophy to economy, because the real genius of *Capital* is precisely the union of philosophy and economy. Kosík dismisses the idea that the transition implies any kind of abolition of philosophy either idealistically, by reducing it to class consciousness, or materialistically, by transforming it into a dialectical theory of society. In the process of the praxis whereby humans form reality, they also develop an openness to being or reality in its totality and infinity, where there loom all the philosophical, ontological questions that transcend human subjectivity in its social and class form. Humans are not only relative and conditioned by the historical but also transcendent by being able to ask questions about the totality of history and nature as such. This is the transcendent function of philosophy that cannot be abolished either idealistically or materialistically. Philosophy is more than a projection of a particular time and society, and human beings cannot be locked up in their social subjectivity.

Second, by unmasking capitalism as a system of total reification and showing the movements and internal relations of the commodity, social relations, the contradiction between base and superstructure and the formation of the revolutionary subject, Marx also reveals the connection between philosophy and economy. To understand economy requires philosophy in the form of a dialectical ontology of social existence; economy is a modality of social existence and economic categories are historically particular forms of social existence that can only be transcended by human praxis. As a modality of social existence, economy produces not only material goods but also human beings in their social relations; only, capitalist economy subverts the relation among human beings into a relation among things and produces reified consciousness, which is only one historical form of consciousness. The nature of economy can only be properly understood on the basis of a dialectical ontology of social being.

Third, only a philosophical ontology of concrete totality is capable of truly comprehending the full meaning of labour. Specialised approaches to labour – psychology, sociology, economics, theology, anthropology, and physiology of labour – reify particular aspects of labour and ignore the essence of labour, which lies in the humanisation of nature and naturalisation of humanity in the sphere of external necessity, and in the process actualising the unification of human existence in its constitutive duality: internal and external, subjective and objective, ideal and real, universal and particular, freedom and necessity, teleology and causality, humanity and animality, history and nature. As such, labour is not one aspect of human existence among others but the event that defines human existence in its human specificity and internally permeates the totality of human existence, the very locus and active centre of the genesis of the human. It is in the process of labour that human beings transform nature and actualise human meanings, and thereby also discover the temporality of human existence. This is human activity in the sphere of external necessity, but it is precisely a condition of human existence and human freedom.

Economy, therefore, is not some simply given, ready-made reality. It is a socio-human reality in the process of formation on the basis of human practical activity. Economy is not one sphere among others concerned with the production of things, but a central sphere of human existence, which forms and produces the very humanity of the human being as a reasonable, social creature. Labour in the philosophical sense refers to this objective and practical activity that forms our sociohuman reality. Labour in the economic sense refers to the creation of a specific historical form of wealth under a determinate structure of social relations in the sphere of production, and it presupposes labour in the philosophical sense. It is only a particular form of labour, not labour in general.

In the *fourth* and last chapter Kosík brings together all the preceding analyses and critiques into a comprehensive ontology of the human being as an anthropocosmic being, centred on the three moments of praxis: labour in the sphere of external necessity, the struggle for freedom, and the search in art and philosophy for the ultimate meaning of being in its totality and depth. We should distinguish praxis from the practice of manipulation and procuring, which is only a particular historical form of praxis as reified in a capitalist society, as well as from practical activity as opposed to theory, which is to reduce it to action without reflection. For Kosík, praxis is first and foremost the activity of self-objectification in which human beings actively and creatively form, discover, and define their sociohuman reality in their human specificity rather than taking their existence passively as something simply given. It is an answer to the question: what is a human being, what is his or her sociohuman reality, and how is this reality formed? Praxis defines the sphere of the human being as such and reveals him or her as an ontoformative being. It is in the process of objectifying themselves and forming their sociohuman reality that human beings also comprehend and interpret that reality, both human and non-human, as a totality, discovering their own mortality, their temporality, and their finitude. In this ontoformative process human beings actively produce themselves by actualising the unity of humanity and the world, matter and spirit, subject and object. In this sense, then, praxis is not one aspect of human existence among others, something accidental and external to human existence: it is the specific human mode of being that permeates human essence in all its manifestations and determines it in its totality.

As such, there are three related moments of praxis. Praxis contains the moment of labour whereby human beings form themselves by transforming nature and procuring the material conditions of human freedom. It also contains the moment of the struggle for recognition, i.e. the process of actualising freedom, in the process of which human beings also experience such existential moods as anxiety, nausea, fear, joy, laughter, and hope. Kosík insists that without this struggle for freedom and the existential moods that accompany it labour ceases to be a moment of praxis, which in turn sinks to the level of technique and manipulation. This unity of labour and the struggle for freedom is the true lesson of the master/slave dialectic in Hegel's *Phenomenology of Spirit*, a lesson often missed. Praxis as objectification of humanity is both the mastery of nature and the realisation of human freedom. There is also a third moment, not often included in the traditional Marxist account of praxis, the moment of the disclosure of reality in its ultimacy and totality, the moment of art and philosophy. The *ontoformative* process of praxis is also an *onto-logical* process: the process of forming our sociohuman reality also opens us toward reality in general and leads us to ask ontological questions about the universe. Praxis does not lock up human subjects in their sociality and historicity; rather, it opens their horizon towards being in general beyond themselves. Praxis reveals human beings as anthropocosmic beings.

Taken as a unity of these three moments, then, praxis constitutes the active centre of human existence as the real historical mediation of spirit and matter, culture and nature, humanity and the universe, theory and action, even existence and existents, epistemology and ontology. The spiritual and intellectual reproduction of reality, for Kosík, is possible only in the process of forming our sociohuman reality; knowledge of the world is itself an aspect of our practical human relationship with the world. It is this openness to being in general, developed in the process of praxis, which makes it possible for us to comprehend the world as a totality, to transcend our finitude and to strive for infinity, through language and poetry, through art and philosophy. I am afraid that this comprehensive conception of praxis as a unity of labour, politics, and philosophy, quite distinctive of Kosík, is lost in many accounts that limit praxis to labour and politics.

2   *Dialectics of the Concrete* Today

Now a few words of critical appreciation of Kosík's work from today's perspective, half a century later.

Let me begin with my appreciation of Kosík's ontology or ontoformative conception of human existence. One can say that instead of reducing the human being to an atomistic economic object, Kosík restores the human being as an active social subject; instead of reducing the human being to a social subject as determined by a particular society, Kosík restores the human being as a transcendent subject irreducible to his or her social subjectivity as an anthropocosmic being that seeks to comprehend the totality in its ultimate depth. Instead of treating the spheres of the production of things, the realisation of freedom and contemplation of truth as three distinct but unrelated spheres of economics, politics and philosophy, or *poiesis*, *praxis* and *theoria* as Aristotle did, Kosík brings these spheres together as three internally related moments of human existence whose unity and totality lies in praxis as an ontoformative activity. In doing so, Kosík has disclosed the creative potential of dialectical thinking that used to be understood only as a dialectical theory of society and history and opened it up to the sphere of philosophy. One can argue that Kosík has the merit of renewing the Hegelian dialectic in its full scope but without its idealism, under the impact of Heidegger's search for the ultimate meaning of being but without his existentialist individualism. In the process, Kosík has also significantly broadened and deepened our understanding of human existence and praxis beyond the standard Marxist views.

Secondly, Kosík's dialectical insights into the mystifying and alienating logic of capitalism have lost none of their force today. His demystification of the many forms of false concreteness and false totality produced by capitalism, his critique of various theories from empiricism to structuralism and existentialism that assume and legitimate false concreteness and false totality, and his humanistic retrieval of the praxical subjectivity of the human being reducible to neither the subjectivity of consciousness nor the objectivity of social existence: all these, it seems to me, are to his great credit, and we can only admire his great originality in the application and renewal of dialectical thinking or *begreifendes Denken*. These insights and projects remain even more compelling today because our world has been globalising according to the imperative of capitalism – now called *Empire* by Michael Hardt and Antonio Negri[3] – and in the process it has only been intensifying false concreteness and false totality. Non-dialectical and even anti-dialectical positivism has been strengthening its grip on the neoliberal ideologues of today, and the humanity of the human being in his or her praxis, the ultimate producer of concrete totality, has been subjected to even more systematically demystifying and alienating processes of degradation in many parts of the world in all three constitutive aspects of praxis, namely the economic field of labour, the political field of freedom and the philosophical field of the search for truth and meaning, to the point that we even speak of the 'death of the subject': capitalism now produces our subjectivity itself in what, after Foucault, Hardt and Negri call 'bioproduction', perhaps the ultimate in our self-alienation.[4]

Rereading Kosík's *Dialectics of Concrete Totality* fifty years later, in a rather different world, also raises many issues with regard to what Kosík did *not* do. There are two things in particular that strike me at this distance in time as rather odd. With regard to the concept of concrete totality, Kosík was strong on the formal aspect of that concept; he was interested in separating the true concept of concrete totality from many of its capitalist counterfeits as envisioned by empiricism, positivism, functionalism, and mathematical formalism. No wonder that his work was translated and published in English as Volume 52 of the *Boston Studies in the Philosophy of Science*. He was not interested in providing a concrete critical analysis of his time from the perspective of concrete totality and presenting its actual material content, and I wonder why. Was it because he felt the contemporary contextual references of his theory were clear enough to all in his country and in his generation? Perhaps so.

Likewise, in his presentation of the threefold aspect of praxis as ontoformative activity, he seems more interested in delineating the formal characteristics of praxis as labour, as the struggle for freedom, and as the search for the meaning of being than in presenting the historically appropriate content of praxis, especially of political praxis. While he went farther than the usual Marxist account of human being in opening up human being to being as such

---

3 Hardt and Negri 2000.
4 Hardt and Negri 2000, pp. 22–41.

in its totality and depth, and while he discerned something of the infinite in the human being beyond history, he was less interested in offering a determinate content of praxis for organising a political existence that will actually produce the historical conditions of authentic human existence in its threefold praxis than he was in exploring the formal structure of praxis as the totalising centre of human existence. The compelling question from the Marxist point of view of *any* time, it would seem, is how to *actualise* the historical conditions of authentic human existence and how to determine the historically appropriate mode of praxis necessary to bring about those historical conditions, something for which we do not find any answer in Kosík's book, perhaps because of the external political constraint so clearly evident in the situation of the East European Communism of his day.

3 The Dialectic of Concrete Totality in the Age of Globalisation: Towards a Trinitarian Dialectic of Totality, Infinity, and Solidarity

In trying to retrieve the dialectic of concrete totality for the age of globalisation, therefore, I would like to focus on two issues. The first is the concept (*Begriff*) of globalisation from the dialectical perspective. What are the concrete characteristics of globalisation when interpreted as a dialectic of concrete totality? What is the central movement that is driving globalisation? What are its various moments, and what are the possibilities of human liberation and oppression that it offers? This is an issue of theoretical analysis. The second issue is the nature of the political praxis appropriate to actualising the liberating possibilities inherent in globalisation or at least resisting its oppressive possibilities. What are the main challenges facing those of us with emancipatory interests? I would like to engage in some current debates on these two issues: on the first, some recent interpretations of globalisation; and on the second, some of the discussions of global or cosmopolitan solidarity by Jürgen Habermas, Ulrich Beck, and Antonio Negri, and of Emmanuel Levinas's opposition to totality in the name of infinity.

I would like to argue a) that it is essential to interpret globalisation as a movement of concrete totality, in order to be able to discern its central movement and its human challenges, and b) that the central challenge of globalisation in its manifold aspects is the challenge to provide normative resources for global human solidarity across the many empirical, often painfully divisive boundaries of identity. I would also argue that providing normative motivation for global solidarity is precisely the most difficult challenge to secular humanist thought, including Marxism, with its libertarian individualist bias, which makes a dialogue between secular political thought on the one hand and religion, especially Christianity, on the other, a compelling task for our time.

In this regard Levinas makes a critical contribution to the issue through his phenomenology of the face of the Other through which the infinite shines forth, but while infinity provides a protection against bad totalities, I also believe that Levinas's identification of all totality with bad totality is based on an illusion: we cannot protect the infinite dignity of the Other without the institution of a humane totality, i.e. the sum of concrete historical conditions necessary for doing concrete justice to the infinity of the Other, who still have to live *in* history. The same critique also applies to much postmodern thought with its exclusive emphasis on difference and rejection of totality. The real issue, for me, is not difference as such, but how to live *together* with one another with all those differences, that is, how to sublate differences into the solidarity of the different so that invidious differences are negated, positive differences are preserved, yet also transcended in the reconciliation and solidarity of the different or what I call 'the solidarity of Others', and how to create a social structure, a system, a totality that embodies this solidarity. My ultimate argument here is that the way out of all totalitarianism, whether capitalist or collectivist, is the Trinitarian dialectic of totality, infinity, and solidarity. Without infinity totality becomes oppressive, but without totality infinity becomes empty, while it is precisely the politics of solidarity that protects both infinity and totality in their normative humanity by providing concrete historical conditions worthy of that infinity.[5]

4   Conceiving [*begreifen*] Globalisation as Concrete Totality

First, with regard to interpreting the phenomenon of globalisation. A wise man of the nineteenth century described the capitalist revolution as follows:

> Constant revolutionising of production, uninterrupted disturbance of all social conditions, everlasting uncertainty and agitation distinguish the bourgeois epoch from all earlier ones. All fixed, fast-frozen relations, with their train of ancient and venerable prejudices and opinions, are swept away, all new-formed ones become antiquated before they can ossify. All that is solid melts into air, all that is holy is profaned, and man is at last compelled to face with sober senses, his real conditions of life, and his

---

5   I provide a critique of Levinas's deconstruction of totality and a defence of totality as a dialectical concept in Min 2004; also Jay 1984, pp. 510–37 ('The Challenge of Post-Structuralism').

relations with his kind. The need of a constantly expanding market for its products chases the bourgeoisie over the whole surface of the globe. It must nestle everywhere, settle everywhere, establish connections everywhere. The bourgeoisie has through its exploitation of the world-market given a cosmopolitan character to production and consumption in every country. [...] All old-established national industries have been destroyed or are daily being destroyed. They are dislodged by new industries, [...] industries whose products are consumed, not only at home, but in every quarter of the globe. In place of the old wants, satisfied by the productions of the country, we find new wants, requiring for their satisfaction the products of distant lands and climes. In place of the old local and national seclusion and self-sufficiency, we have intercourse in every direction, universal interdependence of nations. [...] The bourgeoisie, by the rapid improvement of all instruments of production, by the immensely facilitated means of communication, draws all, even the most barbarian, nations into civilisation. The cheap prices of its commodities are the heavy artillery with which it batters down all Chinese walls, [...] It compels all nations, on pain of extinction, to adopt the bourgeois mode of production; [...] In one word, it creates a world after its own image.[6]

For all the differences between the nineteenth and the twenty-first centuries, these lines from the *Manifesto* sound as fresh, as relevant and as compelling today as in mid-nineteenth century. One can even argue that they are truer and more compelling today than at the time of their composition. A masterpiece of dialectical thinking, the *Manifesto* explores the central unifying role of the mode of production and consumption in its impact on the structure of an entire society and indeed of the globe as a whole, its politics, its culture, its self-consciousness.

Today, there is no lack of social scientific analyses and commentaries on the phenomenon of globalisation. Whether they enthusiastically support the theory of globalisation, remain sceptical about it, or realistically but critically accept it (David Held calls them 'hyperglobalizers', 'sceptics', and 'transformationalists' respectively), there is a certain pattern in their approaches.[7] To summarise the vast proliferating literature on globalisation for the sake of discussion, I can say that most are, in one word, simply undialectical, with three distinctive characteristics.

---

6 Tucker 1978, pp. 476–7.
7 Held, McGrew, Goldblatt and Perraton 1999, pp. 2–10. (For a brief description of these three different views.)

First, they are one-dimensional analyses limited to the purely economic, or political, or cultural aspect, without trying to see their internal relations and contradictions, discussing economic transformations largely in economic terms such as volumes of trade, financial transfers, new financial global institutions, etc., without also discussing their impact on politics and culture, or discussing politics only in terms of the erosion of national sovereignty without also discussing the relation of politics to the ongoing economic transformations, or discussing culture only in terms of the tension between tradition and modernity, between Westernisation and preservation of local culture, between identity and hybridity, but without also discussing the relation of culture to the economic and political changes going on all around them. Second, they fail to provide insight into the central driving force of the phenomenon in its totality. They often claim that globalisation is not reducible to any one dimension and that we have to consider the many different dimensions in their own right, as though all these dimensions are simply unrelated to one another, as though they are simply autonomous from one another, and as though they are all equally important. This is a result of the first failure to internally relate these different 'dimensions' or, in dialectical terms, 'moments' of the phenomenon of globalisation. They think of globalisation as simply a sum of these different dimensions or parts with no internal relationship and with no centralising, unifying, or totalising centre of the whole movement. Third, they deal with reifications such as sovereignty, financial institutions, international laws, economic statistics, demographics, quantified data of all sorts, covering up in the process the active role of the human subjects involved in these reifications, as well as their impact on the humanity of those human subjects; and they are silent about oppression and the possibilities of liberation.

These three characteristics, I am afraid, are true of most current approaches to globalisation, including those that are critical of globalisation led by capitalism. What Kosík said about 'empty', 'abstract', and 'bad' totality in the first chapter of his book remains true today. In short, contemporary capitalism, one can say, is still awaiting an analysis as insightful into the dialectic of history, as sensitive to its social contradictions, as relevant to the central, totalising movement, as awake to its impact on human dignity, as realistic and hopeful with regard to its liberating potential, in short, as dialectical as its nineteenth-century original and exemplar.

Without going into any of the complex discussions on the definition, theories, and evaluations of globalisation,[8] I will briefly describe the essential struc-

---

8 For a most critical, systematic, and comprehensive discussion of globalisation I recommend

ture and dialectic of globalisation and the seven challenges it poses which I consider humanly most compelling. Globalisation is the totality of the complex processes centrally led by market capitalism that bring the peoples, nations, cultures, and religions of the world together into a common space, sometimes called, as one CNN Sunday programme puts it, the Global Public Square. It makes the globe as such, not a region or nation, the context of our acting and the horizon of our thinking. It makes the peoples of the world interdependent, involves them in a dialectic of the struggle for domination and liberation, for imperialism and resistance, and sensitises them to the reality of difference, differences in power, in culture, in religion, while also pressuring them to find a way of living *together* despite and beyond such differences.

This global dialectic of interdependence among unequal nations, cultures, and religions is now posing seven major challenges, economic, ecological, political, military, cultural, religious, and migratory. Economically, globalisation globalises inequality and injustice, creating class divisions not only within nations but also between nations, globalising financial disasters, which used to remain local decades ago. The corollary of economic globalisation is the globalisation of ecological disasters due to the increasing exploitation of natural resources in the unlimited competition for production, consumption, and growth. Globalisation also globalises political inequality among nations and the danger of imperialism inherent in that inequality, involving nations in the global struggle for power, domination, and resistance.[9] Militarism is a corollary of imperialism, promoting instability, alienation, distrust, and hostility among nations.[10] Globalisation also brings together different religions and cultures into a common space and imposes the question of how we can live together in peace and justice despite all our differences. The globalisation of culture

---

Held, McGrew, Goldblatt and Perraton 1999, and Held and McGrew 2007. There are *three* basic perspectives on globalisation. Among the defenders of the first, *optimistic* perspective I include: Friedman 2005; Wolf 2004; Legrain 2004; Bhagwati 2004; http://www.polyarchy.org/essays/english/globalism.html. Among the defenders of the second, *more critical but realistic* view I include: Stiglitz 2003; Stiglitz 2006; Held et al. 1999, Hardt and Negri 2000, Tomlinson 1999. Among the defenders of the third, *oppositional perspective* I include: Bauman 1998; Martin and Schumann 1997; Mander and Goldsmith 1996; Kunstler 2005; Berberoglu 2005; Schirato and Webb 2003; Steger 2003; Barnet and Cavanagh 1994; Bigelow and Peterson 2002.

[9] For an excellent study of nineteenth-century British imperialism, whose insights into imperialism as such I consider still quite valid, see Hobson 2005 (originally published in 1902 by Allen and Unwin), pp. 113–52. On US imperialism, see Johnson 2004; Eland 2004; Bacevich 2002; Dorrien, 2004, available online at http://www.crosscurrents.org/Dorrieno204.htm.

[10] See http://www.globalissues.org/article/75/world-military-spending.

through the internet not only destroys monopolies, hierarchies, and elitisms in the realm of ideas and values, but also tends to erode our sense of identity by pluralising, destroy our sense of dignity by commercialising, impair our sense of objectivity by ideologising, and dissolve our sense of commitment by relativising, posing a threat to our religious and moral sensibilities as well as to our integrity as human beings.[11] Finally, globalisation also produces the migrant worker, the most visible and most suffering embodiment of the economic, political, and cultural contradictions of the age of globalisation, in much the same way that the working class, according to Marx, was the most visible product of the contradictions of a capitalist society.[12]

These seven challenges, I think, are the seven 'faces' or manifestations of a fundamental crisis posed by globalisation. The many crises of globalisation I have enumerated also disclose a crisis of human existence in its totality, revealing the truth about human existence and unmasking all the illusions we often harbour about ourselves, in much the same way that Marx said capitalism did in the nineteenth century: 'All that is solid melts into air, all that is holy is profaned, and man is at last compelled to face with sober senses, his real conditions of life, and his relations with his kind' (quoted above). The many crises of globalisation are manifestations of the one central crisis, the crisis of human solidarity and human dignity.

The recent financial crisis, originating in the crisis of the housing industry in the United States but crossing all the continents and oceans, has demonstrated, in the most painful way, how interdependent humanity has become for all its differences in nationality, culture, and religion and for all its claims to self-sufficiency. Economic globalisation means thoroughgoing interdependence among all human groups. We are thoroughly dependent on one another despite all our differences. In good times we try to exploit this interdependence for our own advantage. After all, not all are equally dependent on others. I am more dependent on you than you are dependent on me. You, therefore, try to exploit me all you can, and I of course resist that exploitation. Interdependence conceals the dialectic of domination and resistance. It also reveals the crying need for transforming that dialectic into a mode of genuine solidarity, the solidarity of mutual recognition (Hegel). No group, no culture, no religion accepts humiliation by another; the yearning to breathe freely indeed belongs to all groups, and demands to be recognised and protected.

---

11   I elaborate on the globalisation of cultural nihilism in my essay, 'The Deconstruction and Reconstruction of Christian Identity in a World of Difference' in Min 2014, pp. 38–45.
12   See Min 2008, pp. 177–201.

That yearning also conceals an insistence on a dignity that resists and transcends the arbitrary desires of another for subjection and exploitation. I am more than an object of your desire. We are more than objects of your imperialist domination. We do not want to be reduced to objects of your essentialisation and categorisation. We are worth more than you think we are. Each is worth more than the other thinks it is. Each claims a dignity that is transcendent. It is this dignity that is hurt and destroyed by economic, political, and cultural domination or oppression. It is this dignity each claims, but it is also a dignity which each can protect and promote only when each enters into solidarity with the other, only when we collaborate in creating the concrete historical conditions of that dignity.

Globalisation brings all humanity face to face with the truth about human existence, the truth that we are mutually dependent for the very dignity we all claim, and presents a choice to all: are we willing to recognise our mutual dependence or solidarity as our common destiny and to collaborate to create the concrete conditions of that dignity that transcends all of us, or, are we going to persist in the illusion of isolation and self-sufficiency and to continue to compete with and exploit one another for mutual destruction?

Globalisation also discloses our differences in the way we think and worship. Globalisation concretisings our otherwise very abstract idea of humanity and human nature and introduces differences into our otherwise very homogeneous conception of humanity, but this is not all. It also compels us to not only accept such differences but also live *together* with one another *with* such differences, *despite* such differences, and *beyond* such differences, something I am afraid postmodernist thinkers do not sufficiently recognise in their preoccupation with difference. We also need to find a sense of common humanity, not as an abstract concept but as a concrete concept that both allows and transcends internal differentiation into a unity of solidarity, a solidarity that accepts differences but also sublates them in a recognition of common destiny higher than any nationalism, any ideology, any religion, a solidarity where differentiation does not mean division or separation but is sublated into the recognition of a transcendence, a dignity that belongs to all. Are we willing to welcome our common destiny as human beings and our solidarity with one another in that destiny?

At the heart of the seven crises of globalisation I mentioned, then, is the crisis of human dignity and human solidarity. It is essential to note the internal relationship between this dignity and this solidarity. The Christian tradition considers this dignity transcendent because it is related to the image of God the transcendent; Kant considers it the critical source of the categorical imperative that overrules all arbitrary desires; and Levinas calls it infinite because it cannot be subjected to but overrides all categorical thinking and desiring. Thanks to the Hegelian and Marxian tradition, however, we now see that this dignity will be an abstraction unless it is concretely protected and promoted by legal, economic, political, and cultural conditions of life, a system that is sufficiently differentiated and applies to all in a fair and just way, a concrete, humane *totality*, which, however, can only be provided by the social labour or collaboration of an entire society in the common recognition that we depend on one another for the protection of our infinite dignity. Indeed, our infinity is not grounded for its validity on the democratic consensus of a society, which may always change and often brings in a reign of terror, but it is dependent for its protection on the consensus and cooperation of a society. The protection of *infinity* is contingent on our willingness to convert our factual, ontological interdependence into an ethical sense of mutual *solidarity* as the normative motivation for cooperation across the various divisive borders of exclusivistic identity. Are we willing to practice solidarity concretely for the sake of the infinity of all? How do we inspire a sense of solidarity so as to energise the political praxis that will create a liberating and transforming totality for the sake of all? In the context of globalisation, how do we inspire the political praxis of solidarity at the global level of cosmopolitan solidarity? Just as each of the seven crises is in its own sphere a sign of the contradiction between the universality of social labour and the particularity of the appropriation of its products, between the universal human interest and the particular contingent interest, as the Hegelian and Marxian tradition insightfully described, so the need for political solidarity is the fundamental challenge at the heart of all the crises I have mentioned and remains the essential or central demand of our time.[13] This leads me to the second issue, the issue of praxis, the praxis of solidarity.

5 Secular Humanism, Religion, and the Praxis of Global Solidarity

How does one organise infinite subjectivities to collaborate on a humane system of concrete totality? This, of course, is the enduring source of the near despair of all political activists. How do you get people to sign up for your democratic, liberating projects? What kind of motivation can we provide, espe-

---

[13] For my elaboration of the nature, need, and dialectic of solidarity, the solidarity of Others, over against the postmodern emphasis on difference and the critique of totality by Levinas and Derrida, see Min 2004, pp. 1–88.

cially in a world of competition where each is expected to seek his or her own interest? Marxism has always provided one important source, the revolutionary idea that it is unjust for some to appropriate for themselves the products of social labour on the part of all. This is still a very important motivation, derived from the recognition of the *facticity* of our mutual interdependence. The question, however, remains: why *should* we accept it and convert it into an ethical obligation of solidarity even at the cost of great personal disadvantage? After all, not all benefit equally from the process of interdependent labour. Why not take advantage of it for my own benefit? What is the normative source for motivating people with a sense of solidarity strong enough to override purely egotistic calculations?

Antonio Negri, a neo-Marxist analyst of globalisation, has been theorising Empire as opposed to imperialism: Empire is a new global, postmodern form of sovereignty no longer centred on territorial nation states, as was traditional modern imperialism, but comprising a truly global network of power exercised in a mixed constitution of monarchy and aristocracy, in which distinctions between inner and outer are no longer clear, all contradictions being internal to the structure. Empire is the form of sovereignty most appropriate to the demands of the global market. Empire is the global form of capitalism.

In this Empire a new form of labour, immaterial labour, is emerging with hegemonic power over all other forms of labour. Immaterial labour does not produce things or material products as in industrial labour; it produces immaterial products such as knowledge, information, communications, linguistic and emotional relations. Immaterial labour is of two kinds. Intellectual labour produces ideas, symbols, codes, texts, and images, while affective labour produces or manipulates affects such as the sense of relaxation, well-being, satisfaction, excitement, passion, etc. Immaterial labour produces not just material goods but also relations and social life itself and is in this sense bio-political labour, obscuring the conventional distinctions between the economic, political, social, and cultural as well as between labour time and free time. Although only a minority of global labour, immaterial labour has been dominating other forms of labour and society itself. Immaterial labour does not exploit by expropriating the value produced by determinate individual or group labour but by expropriating the value produced by cooperative labour now becoming common through social networks, exploiting communication, social relations, and cooperating itself. *Immaterial labour produces subjectivity and society itself*. Production of abstractions leads to greater socialisation of labour. By producing what is common, immaterial labour also reduces the distinction between different classes of workers and creates the conditions for a common political project of labour, which Negri calls 'the multitude'.

What, then, are the possibilities of social change in the age of Empire? For Negri there are many situations where political battles are directed to ends that are local and national but with the potential of impacting the global structure of power in its totality. For example, a movement against the construction of a dam in India, which focuses on the dam's local and national implications regarding the right to land, the national debt, and the redistribution of wealth, can at the same time struggle with the World Bank that encourages and provides funds for this kind of work. There are many movements of this kind, which contribute to the democratisation of the global system; they are struggling not only against the undemocratic character of their national governments but also against the undemocratic character of the global Empire itself. These movements provide resources for the construction of a post-socialist programme. Negri, however, recognises that this is far from establishing institutions of global democracy and a real concept of global democracy to legitimise those institutions.[14]

Along the same lines, in a global version of the *Communist Manifesto* entitled the *Cosmopolitan Manifesto*, Ulrich Beck sums up the problem of the age of globalisation which he calls second modernity, not postmodernity, because it suffers from the unforeseen consequences of the triumph of the first, as follows:

> The central problem is that without a politically strong cosmopolitan consciousness, and without corresponding institutions of global civil society and public opinion, cosmopolitan democracy remains, for all the institutional fantasy, no more than a necessary utopia. *The decisive question is whether and how a consciousness of cosmopolitan solidarity can develop.*[15]

As steps to an answer, Beck advocates the formation of cosmopolitan or world parties and post-national politics on the basis of shared global risks, common human values and traditions found in every culture and religion, with globality at the heart of their imagination, action, and organisation, multi-nationally based, each group struggling against the egoism of its own nation. He locates the possible bearers of such cosmopolitan movements precisely where global risks become an everyday problem of cooperation, in the big cities, transnational organisations and movements, and schools and universities. Beck is here providing a necessary step, discerning the concrete possibility of cosmopolitan

---

14   Negri 2008, pp. 117–60.
15   Beck 2010, in Brown and Held 2010, p. 225, emphasis added.

democracy in the actual conditions of shared global risks. However, this still does not answer the compelling question about the normative or ideal justification of cosmopolitan solidarity so necessary to win the culture war in the global forum of public opinion. Why should one person, group or nation be concerned about the well-being of another person, group, or nation across the globe?[16]

Perhaps no one in recent decades has struggled with the problem of legitimation or the normative foundations of the democratic constitutional state as much as has Jürgen Habermas. For him, a democracy requires more than laws and politics; it can thrive only on a form of civic solidarity among citizens who respect each other as free and equal members regardless of their ideological differences. In a democracy, citizens are co-legislators and as such they are expected to be willing to participate in public debates, take responsibility for anonymous fellow citizens and make sacrifices for the common good. Such willingness should be more than just a practical *modus vivendi*, a pragmatic accommodation; it should also be a conviction and a virtue. These are so essential to a democracy, yet they cannot be legally prescribed and mechanically produced. This civic solidarity is not something that the liberal state can produce from its own resources through legal enforcement. Such political virtues need nourishment through pre-political sources and are matters of a long process of learning through socialisation and habituation.

Yet it is precisely this sense of civic solidarity and the essential political virtues that Habermas sees being seriously eroded and even destroyed in the politically uncontrolled dynamics of the global capitalist economy and global society in general. Today we are left with isolated, self-interested monads using their liberties only against one another and against the common good. A sense of social solidarity that enables citizens to coordinate their actions through commonly shared values and norms is increasingly displaced from more and more domains of social life because of the dominance of the market mentality. No wonder that citizens no longer have confidence in the capacity of their collective action to shape the common conditions of their lives. The increasing social disintegration, the privatisation of concerns, the atrophy of normative sensibilities and other depoliticising tendencies all go hand in hand. Today, says Habermas, there is reason to doubt whether Enlightenment traditions can still sufficiently motivate social movements for preserving the normative contents of modernity. How, for instance, can we keep alive respect for the inviolability

---

16   Beck 2010, in Brown and Held 2010, pp. 225–8.

of human dignity and public awareness of the relevance of normative questions in the face of mounting social disintegration?

For Habermas there are certain insights that secular societies have lost and that professional expertise alone cannot recover, and which only religions articulate. These insights have to do with transgressions and salvation, redemption of lives experienced as hopeless, sensibility about lives squandered, social pathologies, distorted social relations, failed existences. In these substantive matters philosophy can learn from religious insights, and there is nothing strange or improper about this. Historically, philosophy has always assimilated genuine Christian concepts, in particular such normatively charged networks of concepts as responsibility, autonomy, justification, history and remembrance, emancipation, fulfilment, rebirth and renunciation. The idea of the equal, unconditional dignity of every human being is a paradigmatic case of the philosophical translation of the theological doctrine of creation, in which human beings are understood to have been created in the image of God. These are secularising recoveries of religious meaning. This is also what 'postsecular society' means for Habermas.[17] This is why, in the dispute between secularism and religion, Habermas is willing to defend Hegel's thesis that the major world religions belong to the history of reason itself. Postmetaphysical thinking misunderstands itself if it fails to include the religious traditions alongside metaphysics in its own genealogy. On these premises, it would be irrational to reject those 'strong' traditions as 'archaic' residua instead of elucidating their internal connection with modern forms of thought. Even today, religious traditions perform the function of articulating an awareness of what is lacking or absent. They keep alive a sensitivity to failure and suffering. They rescue from oblivion the dimensions of our social and personal relations, in which advances in cultural and social rationalisation have caused devastation. Who is to say that they do not contain encoded semantic potentialities that could provide inspiration if only their message were translated into rational discourse and their profane truth contents were set free?[18]

The secularisation of the state is not the same as the secularisation of society, and religious citizens are as much entitled to participate in the 'public use of reason' (Kant), in the formation of public opinion and will, as are secular citizens. The only condition is that they translate their views into generally accessible language, and secular citizens in turn must recognise the limits of purely secular reasoning and be willing to learn from religious insights. They

---

17   Habermas 2008, pp. 105–11.
18   Habermas 2008, p. 6.

must be aware of the religious origin of so much contemporary secular thought such as that of equal respect for every human being, and they should be willing to continue to learn from Christian sources. In this regard secular and religious citizens are mutually complementary. Their interaction may contribute to the recovery of the semantic potentials from religious traditions for the wider political culture. For Habermas, the democratic process is a learning process, and this learning process from religious sources is all the more compelling today when we have to develop a universalist meaning of human rights for the emerging multicultural world society.[19]

My point in discussing Negri, Beck and Habermas is not to agree or disagree with any particular point each is raising but to call attention to three things. First, in order to overcome the many contradictions and crises of globalisation and in order to create liberating totalities, we need a praxis of solidarity that transcends all the traditional, especially national, boundaries of identity and becomes truly cosmopolitan. Second, this very praxis requires appropriate motivation for activating and sustaining it against all the temptations to despair in the long, seemingly endless struggle against the oppressive powers and principalities of the world. Three, religions have provided these motivations for civic and global solidarity,[20] and political progressives including Marxists should not hesitate to learn from and work together with religious citizens and activists. The struggle against oppressive systems of identity and the struggle to create liberating totalities need effective collaboration among as many like-minded citizens as possible. This seems to be the demand of praxis in the globalising world. It is time for Marxists to drop their traditional opposition to religion and add 'religion' to 'art' and 'philosophy' in their equivalent of the Hegelian sphere of the absolute Spirit. Kosík mentions only art and philosophy in the third, ontological moment of praxis; he should have included religion where, after all, human beings concretely express their radical openness to being. Religion still functions, I regret to admit, as the opium of the people in many instances, but religion at its best also provides reflection on the ultimate meaning of life in its totality and depth, and it can provide motivation for solidarity across all the boundaries of identity, even with all creation, with all things that are. Perhaps there is something in the recent turn to religion among many secular atheist philosophers such as Žižek, Badiou, Agamben, Nancy, and, as we have seen, Habermas.

---

19   Habermas 2011, pp. 15–28.
20   I did not go into the concrete content that religion can provide in order to motivate people to engage in the praxis of solidarity. This is in fact the very content of liberation and political theologies of recent decades. I elaborate on this in Min 1989, pp. 91–230.

To conclude, then, we can say that human existence means interdependence among Others and requires for its actualisation the Trinitarian dialectic of infinity, totality, and solidarity. Infinity refers to our dignity as creatures whose very being is relational to the Infinite. Totality refers to the economic, political, and cultural conditions that make possible the incarnation of that infinity in concrete history. Solidarity refers to our ontological interdependence transformed into a vital sense of collaboration with one another in the creation of a liberating totality. It is clear that these three are dialectically united. Without a liberating or positive totality, infinity remains merely ideal and abstract and often exhausts itself in unrelieved negation. Without it, solidarity too becomes mere talk of 'community' and lapses into empty ideology. On the other hand, without infinity, which alone provides a critique of oppression and the moral stimulation for liberating praxis, totality becomes oppressive and totalitarian, while solidarity lapses into mere collectivism. Without the concrete praxis of solidarity, however, infinity becomes egoism absolutised, and totality becomes a war of all against all. If totality is the 'actualising' principle of human existence, infinity is its 'idealising' and solidarity its 'socialising' principle. The great challenge of human existence is to constructively maintain the tension and dialectic between infinity, totality, and solidarity, between transcendence, history, and sociality, and create, through a politics of solidarity, totalities that liberate us for our mutual infinity. Whether we can transform the globalising process into a liberating totality depends on whether we can motivate and establish a politics of solidarity on a global level.

PART 4

Intellectual Encounters

CHAPTER 11

Kosík's Notion of 'Positivism'

Tomáš Hříbek

1   Introduction

Karel Kosík's *Dialectics of the Concrete* is one of the key works of Humanist Marxism, and as such it has attracted plenty of scholarly attention in the last half century. Yet most commentators have concentrated on such topics as existentialist themes in Kosík's philosophy, his peculiar appropriation of certain concepts borrowed from Heidegger, and his reading of Marx's economic theory as a brand of philosophical anthropology. There is, however, at least one topic in the book which has so far been neglected, in my opinion. I am referring to the Czech philosopher's critique of what he called 'positivism'. I believe the topic should no longer be underestimated, since it has the potential to shed more light on Kosík's attitude toward a type of philosophy that has in the meantime grown into the dominant current of contemporary thought, i.e. so-called analytic philosophy. In so far as the early Kosík is an important representative of the dialectical school of thought, one might even consider his remarks to be informative regarding the relationship between dialectical and analytic thought in general. But there is a lot of interpretative work to do, because the precise content of what Kosík meant by 'positivism' is unclear. This lack of clarity is due to the enormous complexity of his viewpoint. He aimed at multiple targets simultaneously, and his critique drew on a wide variety of sources. In this chapter, I wish to distinguish some of these targets and to identify some of the sources. It will transpire that a better understanding of what Karel Kosík meant, in the early 1960s, by 'positivism', helps illuminate what he meant by such key terms as 'metaphysics' and 'the dialectic'. In addition, this analysis will help situate Kosík's work within twentieth-century Marxism.

I shall proceed as follows in this chapter. In the second section, I shall analyse Kosík's critical remarks on positivism in *Dialectics of the Concrete*. It ensues that by 'positivism', Kosík meant things such as a fragmentary conception of social reality, methodological individualism and a naturalistic reduction of the humanist dimension of the social sciences. I shall argue that these notions, rather than being results of a relatively recent doctrine called 'positivism', happen to reflect deeper problems within modern philosophy, and that Kosík's alternative theory of the 'concrete totality' remains too vague and inchoate to provide any solutions to those problems. In section three, I shall look for the origins of Kosík's ideas about positivism in the Marxist tradition. It transpires that Kosík's critique of positivism is largely derived from Lukács, although Kosík preserved some elements of Engels's naturalisation of the dialectic that was rejected by Lukács. Finally, in section four, we shall see that Kosík was also able to appreciate certain aspects of positivism as correct. In particular, he praised the logical positivists' elimination of metaphysics. Unfortunately, Kosík did not go beyond a few cursory remarks on these authors' ideas. Accordingly, I shall demonstrate that had Kosík studied the work of one of the logical positivists that he cited, namely Otto Neurath, more closely, he might have discovered that the latter's view was both 'positivist' and, in a way, 'dialectical' (or rather holistic). Indeed, he could have recognised in Neurath a fellow Marxist. Unfortunately, in his largely dismissive attitude towards the 'positivist' thinkers, Kosík continued the tradition initiated by one of his predecessors within the current of the twentieth-century Marxism, Max Horkheimer, who savaged Neurath's project already back in the late 1930s. Kosík is to be congratulated for giving any credit to Neurath at all. Yet only recent scholarship has revealed that Neurath was guilty of hardly any of the accusations levelled at him by the Marxists of the dialectical school. Moreover, he stands at the beginning of a tradition which has proved superior to the dialectical school by correcting, among other matters, its anti-science bias.

2 Kosík against Positivism

The few remarks Kosík makes on the subject of positivism can be found in Chapter 1 of his book, entitled 'Dialectics of the Concrete Totality'. Here, he uses positivism as a foil for introducing what he takes to be the authentically Marxist conception of reality, i.e. the 'concrete totality'. Like much of the rest of the book, it is so dense that I should better quote it in full before I attempt an analysis:

> Thus in the course of appropriating the world spiritually-practically, which is the basis for all other modes of appropriation – the theoretical, artistic, etc. – reality is perceived as an *undifferentiated whole of existents and of meanings*, and it is implicitly grasped in a unity of statements of fact and those of value. It takes abstraction and thematisation, a *project*, to select out of this full and inexhaustible world of reality certain areas, aspects and spheres, which naive naturalism and positivism would then consider to be the *only* true ones and the only reality, while suppressing

the 'rest' as sheer subjectivity. The physicalist image presented by positivism impoverishes the human world, and its absolute exclusiveness deforms reality, because it reduces the real world to but *one* dimension and aspect, to the dimension of extensity and of quantitative relations. In addition, it cleaves the human world, when it declares the world of physicalism, the world of idealised real values, of extensity, quantity, mensuration and geometric shapes to be the only reality, while calling man's everyday world a fiction.[1]

We can gather three things from this passage. Firstly, positivism, as Kosík understands it, drives a wedge between 'existents' and 'meanings', facts and values, and the objective and the subjective. Apparently, according to Kosík, these items are in fact interconnected, and dialectical thought has the advantage over positivist thought in that it can recognise this interconnectedness. Secondly, positivism allegedly reduces reality to a single dimension, that of extension and quantity. Yet reality is much richer, presumably including qualitative aspects as well. This, again, is revealed from the dialectical perspective. Thirdly, positivism postulates the world as described by the physical sciences as the only reality. Thus it completely disregards the contribution of the human sciences and the arts. By now we should not be too surprised by the suggestion that only dialectics can make room for the arts and humanities.

I wonder, however, whether the dialectical approach provides any genuine solutions to the problems of positivism. As for the separation of 'meanings' from 'existents', values from facts, the subjective from the objective, Kosík is not very forthcoming, to put it mildly, as to how their unification should be achieved. In the very last section of the final chapter of the book 'Praxis and Totality', he revisits this topic, claiming that positivism is one of two extreme viewpoints, the other being idealism: 'While idealism insulated meanings from material reality and transformed them into an independent reality, materialist positivism on the other hand deprived reality of meanings'.[2] This suggests that the 'dialectical' solution to the problem of connecting 'meaning' with 'material reality' should be some sort of a middle-ground position. By specifying 'meanings' as 'human meanings', I take it that Kosík's dialectical, middle-ground position amounts to a conception of the world as involving human values and interests, rather than either hypostasising these values and interests as an independent reality (as in idealism), or construing them as mere subjective feelings

---

1   Kosík 1976, p. 11. Emphasis in the original.
2   Kosík 1976, p. 148.

and preferences (as in positivism). However, we do not learn much as to how Kosík's dialectical position is to be prevented from collapsing into one of these two extreme positions.

The other two charges against positivism that are distinguished in the previously quoted passage are both concerned with a reductionist picture of reality. Positivism is said to be a tendency to eliminate all the qualitative aspects of reality, and then to proclaim such a reduced reality as all that exists. Kosík thus ascribes to positivists the notion that they are materialists, or – as Kosík prefers to put it – physicalists. Now, one might think that Kosík, who after all identifies himself as a materialist, would share the problem of accounting for the qualitative aspects of reality with the positivists. However, positivist physicalism is supposedly not identical to materialism:

> Positivist physicalism has substituted a certain *image* of reality for *reality* itself and has promoted a certain mode of appropriating the world as the only true one. Thereby it denied, first, the inexhaustibility of the objective world and its irreducibility to knowledge, which is one of the fundamental theses of materialism, and, second, it impoverished the human world by reducing the wealth of human subjectivity, formed *historically* through the objective praxis of mankind, to one single mode of appropriating reality.[3]

I take it that, for Kosík, physicalism regards all reality as accessible to the natural sciences, in particular physics; or, rather, physicalism disregards anything that resists the methodology of physics as illusory, whereas a genuine, Marxist materialism presumably admits that there are aspects of reality that can be accessed by either social or human sciences that are not themselves reducible to physics. However, as with the previous point about the desirability of reconnecting meaning and reality, which is assumed rather than argued for, Kosík simply assumes that the human sciences are irreducible to the natural sciences.

In another relevant passage in Chapter 1, Kosík compares the dialectical concept of reality as a concrete totality with the positivist notion of totality as an agglomeration of all the facts:

> There is a principal difference between the opinion that considers reality to be a concrete totality, i.e. a structural, evolving, self-forming whole, and the position that human cognition can, or cannot, achieve a 'totality' of

---

3 Kosík 1976, p. 11. Emphasis in the original.

aspects and facts, i.e. of *all* properties, things, relations and processes of reality. The second position takes totality as a sum of all facts. [...] Totality indeed does not signify *all facts*. Totality signifies reality as a structured dialectical whole, within which and from which *any particular* fact (or any group or set of facts) can be rationally comprehended. The accumulation of all facts would not yet amount to the cognition of reality, and neither would all accumulated facts amount to a totality. Facts are the cognition of reality only provided they are comprehended as facts and as structural parts of a dialectical whole, i.e. not as immutable, further irreducible atoms which, agglomerated, compose reality.[4]

It appears that what Kosík means by 'totality' has both ontological and epistemological aspects. Ontologically, totality is a structured, dynamic and developing whole. Epistemologically, gaining knowledge amounts to comprehending and mentally capturing this whole. Unlike in positivism, the whole is not a mere agglomeration of all the facts. Facts do not even make sense in isolation unless they are understood as parts of a concrete totality. If facts are understood as atomic facts, separated from their mutual interrelationships within the whole, knowledge necessarily fails in its task. Kosík makes these remarks in order to counter Popper's dismissal of dialectics as a doomed project of trying to capture the concrete in reality, when all knowledge is of necessity abstract.[5] Of special note in his response to Popper's charge is Kosík's claim that the concept of concrete totality implies a definite 'heuristic guide and epistemological principle' for the study of disciplines as diverse as 'physics or literary criticism, biology or political economy, theoretical problems of mathematics or practical issues of organising human life and social conditions'.[6] Yet if all these fields are, in Kosík's view, methodologically and epistemologically unified, the 'positivist physicalist' might well ask what prevents the more complex fields such as biology and political economy (if we put literary criticism aside) from being reduced to a single basis, say physics. So, as before, we are confronted with the issue of reduction. I should like to stress that I am far from saying that such a reduction is achievable. In fact, many philosophers of science in the past few decades have argued in detail that a reduction of the so-called special sciences to basic physics is not possible even in principle. These arguments might support Kosík's position, but we do not find anything like them in his book; instead,

---

4   Kosík 1976, pp. 18–19. Emphasis in the original.
5   Kosík 1976, p. 18.
6   Kosík 1976, p. 19.

his assumption of a methodological unity invites reduction, even though he officially rejects it.

I have criticised the lack of worked-out alternatives to positivist dichotomies in Kosík's book. However, despite this criticism, I believe that he put his finger on an issue that runs much deeper than positivism. Indeed, it is arguable that the dichotomies identified by Kosík haunt modern philosophical thought in general, including Marxism. This fact at least partly explains why Kosík has such a hard time overcoming these dichotomies in any convincing way. Three decades after the publication of *Dialectics of the Concrete*, the contemporary British philosopher John McDowell identified the elimination of meaning, value and quality from reality as the greatest blunder of contemporary philosophy. In his groundbreaking work, *Mind and World* (1994), McDowell suggests that an elimination of meaning from reality is a result of the triumph of modern science. There are indications that Kosík would concur with such a view, having adopted a similar idea from Husserl. And it is even more interesting that McDowell, whose work falls within the school of analytic philosophy which Kosík would likely have identified as an offshoot of positivism, looks for a solution to the problem of meaningless and valueless reality in the same place as Kosík did in the early 1960s: the young Marx's concept of the world as essentially inhabited by human beings.[7] Now, I do not have a space here to go into a detailed exploration of McDowell's solution of the deepest problems of modern philosophy. But it should not come as a big surprise that McDowell's work has met with strong resistance. A number of his critics have felt that his solution presupposes a return to a pre-modern, pre-scientific concept of reality. Yet it may very well be that such a regression is not conceivable, and therefore we might be stuck with the modern scientific view of the world. And so McDowell's attempts to mine the young Marx's poetic images of the 'second nature' might be no more satisfactory than Kosík's efforts thirty years earlier.

3   Between Lukács and Engels

In the previous section, I have tried to suggest that Kosík's critique of what he calls 'positivism' still has a relevance for contemporary philosophy, long after the demise of Humanist Marxism, in the context of which *Dialectic of the Concrete* was composed. Now I should like to conduct a mostly historical research,

---

[7] McDowell sums up Marx's notion of the world, which he sees as a connection between Hegel and Gadamer, as follows: 'the world is where a human being lives, where she is at home' (McDowell 1994, p. 118). I believe Kosík would endorse this.

tracing Kosík's concepts within the Marxist tradition. I shall argue that it combines certain elements of the broadly Hegelian brand of Marxism mostly pioneered by György Lukács with some vestiges of dialectical materialism, which in Kosík's time was the official East European version of Marxism, largely derived from the late work of Friedrich Engels. In particular Kosík wished, with help from Lukács, to tap into the philosophical core of Marxism, which he believed had been obscured by the officially mandated doctrine of dialectical materialism. Due primarily to Engels, Marxism had been misconstrued as a kind of positivism. Even more interestingly, this Marxist positivism was, according to Kosík and other Humanist Marxists, largely responsible for the pitfalls of the communist regimes in the USSR and Eastern Europe. Consequently, these philosophers set out to reverse this unfortunate development by exposing the error of Marxist positivism.

Starting with Lukács, the readers of his classic work, *History and Class Consciousness* (1923), would have noticed that Kosík's concept of 'concrete totality' is a direct descendant of 'totality', introduced four decades earlier by the Hungarian philosopher.[8] 'It is not the primacy of economic motives' that is specific to the Marxist style of thought, according to Lukács; rather, it is 'the point of view of totality'. And what this point of view amounts to is 'the all-pervasive supremacy of the whole over the parts'.[9] By contrast, bourgeois thought registers only the isolated parts; examples include '[t]he capitalist separation of the producer from the total process of production, the division of the process of labour into parts at the cost of the individual humanity of the worker, the atomisation of society into individuals who simply go on producing without rhyme or reason'.[10] These and other examples throughout Lukács's

---

8   The direct link between Lukács's 'totality' and Kosík's 'concrete totality' was pointed out already by the latter's older colleague on the Czech philosophical scene, Jan Patočka. See Patočka's 1970 Heidegger from the Other Shore (repr. in Patočka 2006b, pp. 214–29). To this day, Patočka's paper remains one of a very few insightful analyses of Kosík's philosophy. And yet, as a phenomenologist, it is true that he appreciates Kosík's project only to the extent that he sees it as moving away from Marxism to existential phenomenology. His advice to Kosík is to drop materialism completely and embrace Heidegger. I think Patočka fails to see a genuine novelty in Kosík's handling of some of the concepts borrowed from existentialism and Heidegger and regards it mistakenly as a mere misinterpretation; but I shall leave this point aside here. However, I believe that Patočka also underestimates the originality of Kosík's articulation of concrete totality via his critique of positivism. Kosík does not merely repeat Lukács after four decades, but reflects the philosophical development of the intervening years, as I shall explain in the following paragraphs.

9   Lukács 1971, p. 27.

10 Ibid.

book make it clear that he has in mind a specific view of social, rather than natural, reality. And it is equally clear that he considers totality to be not just a methodological, or epistemological concept, as might be suggested by the phrase 'the point of view'. Totality is also, and even more importantly, the supreme ontological category: the social reality *is* an interconnected whole. And the crucial Marxist insight, according to Lukács, is that this whole is not something static and timeless, but rather dynamic and developing. This development is propelled by contradictions among the various parts of the social reality. One of the key goals that Lukács set himself in his book was to demonstrate that these contradictions are embedded in the social reality, so they are neither transposed to the realm of thought, nor ultimately eliminated by a superior social theory. The former option, namely the relegation of contradictions to relations among ideas, is the dialectical idealism of Hegel; the latter view, which conceives of contradictions as errors to be eliminated, is a bourgeois social science. Lukács uses these two approaches as a foil against which to articulate his own theory, which is *both* dialectical – in that it regards contradictions as ineliminable – *and* materialist – in that it embeds them in the social reality.

The critical points that we saw distinguished by Kosík in Chapter I of *Dialectics of the Concrete* can also be traced back to *History and Class Consciousness*. The divorce between existence and meaning, or rather fact and value, is rejected by Lukács by way of his criticism of Kantian moral philosophy and its impact on the Marxist Revisionists (in particular within the Austrian Social Democracy). As for the omission of the qualitative aspect of reality, it results from a misbegotten application of the method of the natural sciences to social phenomena. I take it that it is acceptable, according to Lukács, to isolate natural phenomena in a lab, 'reducing [them] to their purely quantitative essence'.[11] However, if applied to the study of, say, economic production, it results in 'an abstract, rational analysis, without regard to the human potentialities and abilities of the immediate producers'.[12] Lukács also prefigures a critique of reductive physicalism, in the form of a rejection of the contradictory nature of social reality, which I have already mentioned earlier: since contradictions have no place in a successful physical science, they should not be postulated by a social theory either. There is no doubt that these insights are brought up to a new level, as well as up to date, by Kosík, who had the advantage over Lukács of having learned from later critics of positivism such as Husserl.

11   Lukács 1971, p. 6.
12   Ibid.

For our purposes *History and Class Consciousness* is best seen as a work unified by a deep opposition to positivism, within as well as outside of Marxism. On the most general level, Lukács understands positivism as a sort of anti-philosophical impulse. In the last few decades of the nineteenth century, there prevailed an opinion that social thought should be modeled on the natural sciences, in that it should seek general sociological laws by means of testing hypotheses based on observation of facts. From a positivist point of view, philosophy was something redundant. Not only 'bourgeois' sociology, but Marxism of the Second International as well, came to be understood in this positivistic fashion. Marxists during this period judged their doctrine as superior to the bourgeois social sciences insofar as the former was better than the latter in terms of explanation and prediction. Once some Marxists, such as Bernstein, concluded that certain facts contradicted Marx's 'predictions', the doctrine reached a crisis. For Lukács this whole judgement was a fundamental mistake, since it missed the standpoint of totality. In an earlier essay, he wrote: 'To understand reality in the Marxist sense is to be master and not the slave of the imminent facts'.[13] In other words, only a subject involved in an active struggle can overcome the fragmentary vision of a passive observer of facts. Clearly enough, Lukács assumes a particular conception of science: as an inherently contemplative endeavor, incapable of grasping totality, and he blames Engels primarily for engendering this positivist interpretation of Marxism. Lukács writes:

> Engels' deepest misunderstanding consists in his belief that the behavior of industry and scientific experiment constitutes praxis in the dialectical, philosophical sense. In fact, scientific experiment is contemplation at its purest. The experimenter creates an artificial, abstract milieu in order to be able to *observe* undisturbed the untrammeled workings of the laws under examination, eliminating all irrational factors both of the subject and the object.[14]

It was Engels's erroneous understanding of dialectical thought as a description of a reality given in observation – instead of a theoretical consciousness of the subject involved in transforming that reality – that led him, according to Lukács, to extend the dialectic from history and society to nature.

---

13   Lukács 1972, p. 26.
14   Lukács 1971, p. 132. Emphasis in the original.

> It is of the first importance to realise that the [dialectical] method is limited here to the realms of history and society. The misunderstandings that arise from Engels' account of dialectics can in the main be put down to the fact that Engels – following Hegel's mistaken lead – extended the method to apply also to nature. However, the crucial determinants of dialectics – the interaction of subject and object, the unity of theory and practice, the historical changes in the reality underlying the categories as the root cause of changes in thought, etc. – are absent from our knowledge of nature.[15]

Lukács is thus responsible not only for the popular view of a theoretical split between Marx and Engels, but also for a deep anti-science attitude, shared by many Western Marxists throughout the last century. As for the former view, it is debatable as to what extent it is correct. Karl Marx often spoke of overcoming philosophy. Kosík's famous predecessor in the history of Czech philosophy, Thomas G. Masaryk, was probably the very first scholar to interpret Marx as an early convert to positivism, partly on the basis of an apocryphal story of a meeting between the young German journalist and the founder of positivism, Auguste Comte, in Paris in the early 1840s.[16] However, Masaryk suggested this long before Marx's early philosophical writings became available. Since their publication it has become clear that a certain anti-philosophical attitude on the part of Marx is due to a Hegelian view of history, rather than to any positivist notion that science should substitute speculation. Things are not so simple, however. The historian Jonathan Sperber has recently argued that Marx's attitude towards science changed after the 1850s, as can be seen in his fascination with Darwinism.[17] In other words, he moved away from the Hegelian *Wissenschaft* toward English science. So when by the 1870s Marxism grew into a mass political movement and a need arose for a popular text summarising the main tenets of the doctrine, it was quite natural that Engels, to whom it fell to carry out the task that his ailing friend Marx no longer could, wrote a book very much influenced by positivism. This is *Anti-Dühring* (1878), notorious for the introduction of the 'dialectical laws' that Lukács dismissed some four decades later. One of these laws is that of a development through contradiction and a mutual connection between opposites. Engels seems to suggest that contradictions, rather than being found only in language or thought, are embedded in external reality itself. For example, he declares:

---

15 Lukács 1971, p. 24.
16 Masaryk 1936, p. 52.
17 See Sperber 2013, chap. 10.

Motion itself is a contradiction: even simple mechanical change of place can only come about through a body at one and the same moment of time being both in one place and in another place, being in one and the same place and also not in it. And the continuous origination and simultaneous solution of this contradiction is precisely what motion is.[18]

I can see why Lukács regards such 'dialectical laws' as positivistic. Dialectics, instead of a method of achieving concrete totality, becomes a contemplation of certain very general regularities in a passively observed nature. Dialectics thus ceases to be philosophical and becomes reduced to one of the sciences of nature. It seems to me, however, that a different perspective is possible. This is because Engels suggests a rather elevated view of philosophy or, more precisely, dialectical logic. It achieves a sort of cosmic significance as a study of the ultimate nature of reality, inaccessible to ordinary sciences such as physics, chemistry or biology. In a way, dialectical logic becomes a super-science, a venerable successor to classical metaphysics. One can imagine that it was passages like the one just quoted that later functioned as a source for the patronising attitude on the part of Soviet-style dialectical materialists towards scientists. One of the things Humanist Marxists rejected was this sort of attitude. It is important to note, however, that while the Soviet dialectical materialists patronised science, many Humanist Marxists, following Lukács, mistrusted science, thus both versions of Marxism had a troubled relationship with science.

Given that Kosík is, as we have seen, so indebted to Lukács, who dismissed the dialectic of nature, it is curious to find in Kosík's book statements reminiscent of Engelsian dialectical materialism. For example: 'Only such a concept of matter that in matter itself discovers negativity, that is, the potentiality to produce new qualities and higher stages of development, can materialistically explain the new as a property of the material world'.[19] And similarly: 'Polemics against dialectical materialism relentlessly impute to modern materialism the mechanical and metaphysical concept of matter of eighteenth-century theories. Why should *only* the spirit, and not matter, have the property of negativity?'[20] One cannot help interpreting these statements as incarnations of Engels's view that contradictions are aspects of the world out there.[21]

---

18   Engels 1975, p. 111.
19   Kosík 1976, p. 14.
20   Kosík 1976, p. 33.
21   Patočka believes that Kosík is confused on this point: 'The issue is, whether the matter of natural science and the matter, which Kosík postulates for his dialectical view of nature, is really the same matter. Of the matter of natural science we must learn from natural sci-

I think the cosmic interpretation of dialectics, suggested in Engels and later codified in Soviet dialectical materialism, justifies the self-understanding on the part of Soviet philosophers as opponents of positivism. If we view positivism as driven, as argued by Lukács, by a certain anti-philosophical attitude, we must view dialectical materialism – i.e. the official Soviet doctrine that ossified into a rigid dogma by the 1940s and following World War II was spread around the entire Soviet bloc – as an anti-positivistic, cosmic philosophy, a kind of successor to older metaphysics. This was the philosophy that Kosík imbibed during his studies at the Moscow and Leningrad universities in the late 1940s and early 1950s, and the dissemination of it by teaching and paraphrasing was supposed to be his day job afterwards. To be sure, instead of becoming another state-appointed priest of the official ideological dogma, Kosík soon began to think independently. By the late 1950s he was a Humanist Marxist freeing himself from the official dialectical materialism.[22]

While I can see how – in view of their advocacy of a pretty heavy metaphysics of the material world governed by a set of rational principles – it made sense for the Soviet-style dialectical materialists to see themselves as anti-positivists, there is also a good reason for the opposing Humanist Marxists to view diamat as a type of positivism. Their reason for classifying dialectical materialism as positivism was somewhat different from Lukács's. Recall that what Lukács opposed in Engels – who was the ultimate source of the later Soviet dialectical materialism – was the dialectics of nature. The Humanist Marxist, like Kosík, did not extricate himself completely from dialectics of nature; what he missed in the official diamat was rather the humane dimension. This is something he could not find in *History and Class Consciousness*, either – Lukács speaks only of entire classes, not individual human beings. The exclusive emphasis on class is understandable in Lukács's book, which was published shortly after the October Revolution with the intention of making sense of and justifying this historic event. Yet the absence of the theory of subjectivity in Lukács became more perspicuous with the passage of years, which speaks volumes about the Hungarian philosopher's troubling attitude towards the Stalinist regime. At any rate, the needed theory of subjectivity could not have been found in his work, and that is why Lukács does not really belong within the group of Humanist Marxists.

Hence a critique of 'positivism' in application to a theoretical reflection of life under a Stalinist regime constituted a major advance by Humanist Marxists, such as Kosík, over Lukács's version of Marxism. The experience of Stalinism,

---

ence, not from philosophy; however, the matter of natural science *in concreto* neither sees nor presupposes negativity anywhere'. Patočka 2006a, p. 325.

22 See Tomáš Hermann's chapter of this book.

with its dismissal of the individual point of view, made these philosophers realising the glaring absence of a theory of individual subjectivity in the official doctrine. They came to view diamat as 'positivistic' in the sense of a collection of allegedly objective knowledge supplied by special sciences, with 'dialectical laws' thrown into the mix. But there was no conceptual apparatus to articulate how these facts and laws affected the individual human being – and, in particular, how individual human beings produced social reality. Various Humanist Marxists sought for this missing apparatus in the young Marx, or in theories outside of Marxism, such as existentialism or psychoanalysis.

Kosík's contribution in this area is, in my opinion, superior to efforts of various other authors, in that it does not have the character of an inorganic importation of some foreign ideas into Marxism. Thus, he reverses the category of 'concrete totality' into that of 'the pseudoconcrete', which turns out to be a close cousin of Lukács's experience of reality as fragmented – except that in Kosík's version, it does not describe merely the experience under a capitalist system, but also the world of Stalinism. According to Kosík, the world of 'the pseudoconrete' includes:

> the world of external phenomena which are played out on the surface of real essential processes;
> the world of procuring and manipulation, i.e. of man's fetishised praxis (which is not identical to the revolutionary-critical praxis of mankind);
> the world of routine ideas which are external phenomena projected into man's consciousness, a product of fetishised praxis; they are ideological forms of the movement of this praxis;
> the world of fixed objects which give the impression of being natural conditions and are not immediately recognizable as the result of man's social activity.[23]

This world of fixed things and relations is also the object described and explored by social science under Stalinism, which is thus a socialist counterpart of bourgeois positivist science. The Stalinist social science is similarly complicit in masquerading the subjective constitution of this reality. An analysis of this constitution, which Kosík carried out in Chapter IV of *Dialectics*, falls outside of my topic, but it should be noted that only here Kosík completes his overcoming of positivism, because he reveals a 'thing in itself' behind the appearances recorded by the positivist science – namely, 'man and his place in the universe'.[24]

---

23   Kosík 1976, p. 2.
24   Kosík 1976, p. 152.

4 Neurath on Holistic Empiricism

In this last section, I shall show that Kosík is not exclusively dismissive of positivism. He appreciates one particular contribution; and, had he studied it more closely, Kosík could have found a certain version of positivism even more congenial. Let me start by what Kosík could have uncovered even in Engels, who sometimes writes in a strictly positivist mode. That is, in contrast to his cosmic philosophy, which piles dialectical super-laws on top of humble scientific ones, Engels also hints – in a manner recalling Mach – that we should dispense with philosophy altogether and replace it with a set of natural sciences. Thus, in another work of his old age, *Dialectics of Nature* (1886), he claims:

> Matter as such is a pure creation of thought and an abstraction. We leave out of account the qualitative differences of things in lumping them together as corporeally existing things under the concept of matter. Hence matter as such, as distinct from definite existing kinds of matter, is not anything sensuously existing. When natural science directs its efforts to seeking out uniform matter as such, to reducing qualitative differences to merely quantitative differences in combining. Identical smallest particles, it is doing the same thing as demanding to see fruit as such instead of cherries, pears, apples, or the mammal as such instead of cats, dogs, sheep, etc., gas as such, metal, stone, chemical compound as such, motion as such.[25]

Engels seems to be saying that there is no entity called 'matter', an entity presumably in the category of substance theorised by traditional metaphysics. It is pointless to speak of any such substance as different from, and perhaps hidden behind, a complex of empirical facts; rather, matter is but an abstraction from these facts. It seems as if Engels himself, although he went down in history as the author of the canonical formulation of dialectical materialism, also made room for a 'grandiose purification of philosophy from remnants of the *theological* conception of reality, as a hierarchy of degrees of perfection [...] [and] the creditable destructive and demystifying role of modem positivism'.[26] When mentioning positivism in *Dialectics of the Concrete*, however, Kosík speaks largely of a version of the doctrine that could not have been known to Engels. He cites Rudolf Carnap and Otto Neurath, two leading figures

---

25   Engels 1975, p. 533.
26   Kosík 1976, p. 20. Emphasis in the original.

of the so-called Vienna Circle that included scientists and mathematicians, as well as philosophers. The Circle was active from the late 1920s and throughout the '30s, with active participants not only in Vienna, but also in other cities such as Prague and Berlin. Though the Central European network very soon dispersed due to the rise of Nazism and World War II, the contributions of the members of the Circle to theorising language, logic and science shaped the later developments within the analytic school of philosophy, which is today enjoying dominant status on the world stage. Contemporary analytic philosophy thus partly originates in Viennese pre-war positivism, although the example of John McDowell, mentioned in the second section, should make it clear that the use of the label 'positivist' with respect to such contemporary figures would hardly be intelligible. In the remainder of this section, I wish to suggest that the same label is at least problematic, if not downright misleading, even with respect to the work of some of the inter-war philosophers cited by Kosík. Though his interest in the Vienna Circle remained quite marginal, the fact that *Dialectics of the Concrete* includes *any* appreciation of recent positivism whatsoever makes it quite exceptional within the tradition of the dialectical Marxist thought of the last century. We shall see that other, better known representatives of this tradition were usually nothing but dismissive.

Here is remarkable praise expressed by Kosík for the Viennese philosophers: 'Positivism of the Viennese school played a positive role in destroying the pseudoconcrete, when it opposed surviving metaphysical conceptions by stating that matter is not something behind phenomena or the transcendence of phenomena, but that it is rather material objects and processes'.[27] As we saw earlier, Kosík could have found and praised similar remarks scattered around Engels's later texts. Instead, Kosík here references a particular book by one of the aforementioned Viennese authors, the sociologist and economist Otto Neurath. The book, *Empirical Sociology* (1931), is a fascinating attempt to conceive of Marxism as a scientific, indeed physicalistic, sociology. It is to be regretted that Kosík did not say more about Neurath's volume, since it is nearly contemporaneous with Lukács's *History and Class Consciousness*, while providing a sharply divergent interpretation of Marxism. I shall come back to this difference later; first, let me explain what Kosík apparently appreciates in Neurath's approach. Kosík refers to pages 59–61 of the first German-language edition, in which we are told, among other things:

27   Kosík 1976, p. 33.

> Sociology deals with human behavior, i.e. with spatio-temporal events. Sociology is for Physicalism part of the physical structure, like every actual science. Formulated like this, it is clear that all statements about things called 'mental' as opposed to 'material' can only mean that certain spatiotemporal things which are found together with a given person are in contrast to other spatio-temporal things. All statements concerning different kinds of causality of non-living, living, and social events, are without meaning. In this way, physicalism succeeds materialism.[28]

In other words, Neurath suggests that we dispense with metaphysically loaded terms such as 'matter' or 'mind', and speak simply of objects and processes in space-time. He claims that as 'theory of the mind' disappears, only 'theory of the matter' remains, which means that only physics remains.[29] Accordingly, physicalism prevails. However, as Neurath explains in an important article, published in the same year as his book, 'Sociology in Physicalism' (1931), the thesis of physicalism does not require that we attempt to go as far as the microstructural level in every case. This is both useless and impossible. There are similar limits to what physicalist sociology can predict: not every individual event can be predicted, nor is it necessary.[30]

Neurath further denies that his physicalist sociology breaks society into isolated facts. In an important passage from *Empirical Sociology*, he makes it quite explicit that his physicalism is holistic:

> The materialist conception of history begins with the total process of life. If one continues to use the traditional delimited terms such as 'religion', 'art', 'science', 'law' and so on, these formations appear as 'interwoven' into the total social process. This interweaving might perhaps be described in this way: one might of course predict the course of modes of production and social changes, but it would be hopeless to write an autonomous 'history' of religion, art, mathematics and so on; such histories could be written only within the framework of a historical account of the total process.[31]

It is remarkable that Neurath believes that he pretty much translates here into a metaphysically harmless idiom the text of Marx and Engels's *Deutsche Ideo-*

---

28   Neurath 1973, p. 359.
29   Ibid.
30   Neurath 1931/32, pp. 293, 303.
31   Neurath 1973, p. 352.

logie (1846). We should note that he concurs with Marx and Engels that social science ought to start with totalities, which we might identify as 'religion', 'art', 'science', etc. He goes beyond the classics by suggesting that these common-sense totalities might eventually prove less appropriate for explanatory and predictive purposes. Accordingly, we should expect to keep on revising our view of these wholes as we go on:

> But much indicates that these formations are in any case not suitable elements for setting out the functional relations in society. It is most probable that in the elaboration of sociology on a materialist basis and of a more perfect behaviorism the account of social processes will no longer use the traditional delimited terms. It is conceivable that one will distinguish a sphere of nutrition, of dwellings, of play and so on. What we emphasize today as 'art history' might well cut across quite different social compartments [...][32]

Neurath coins the technical term 'congestions' (*Ballungen*) to denote the imprecise terms of everyday usage that we shall begin with as we build the vocabulary of a unified physicalistic language. We should never expect exact precision, let alone any independent ground against which to adjudicate the appropriateness of our vocabulary. Thus, Neurath's conception is not only holistic, but also non-foundationalist.[33]

5 Conclusion

Without exploring Neurath's sociology in detail here, let me note several concluding points. First off, the charges that Kosík levels against 'physicalistic positivism' might prove difficult for any position that accepts the scientific description of the world. However, Neurath might have an easier time than some others answering them. He argues that we ought to start with everyday, imprecise language describing everyday spatio-temporal objections, with no presumption of entities hidden behind the observables. Secondly, his theory is non-foundationalist and holistic, so that we ought to give up unrealistic expectations of certainty and precision. This point should also make it clear that it is fairly inaccurate to label Neurath as a 'positivist'. Thirdly, it is quite amazing that

---

32 Ibid.
33 For an excellent and meticulous analysis of Neurath's non-foundationalism and holism, see Cartwright et al. 2008, esp. Part 3.

two rival holistic versions of Marxism arose at roughly the same time and place, with the two authors working independently of each other. Neurath offered his 'empirical sociology' as a streamlined Marxism in 1931, while Lukács articulated his Hegelian project only a few years earlier. Despite their shared holism, it is hard to think of two more diverse conceptions of Marxism. Neurath avers that Marxism is the most complete 'strictly scientific unmetaphysical physicalist sociology',[34] while for Lukács any construal of Marxism as sociology, i.e. a positive science, is anathema. This should be clear enough from our exposition of *History and Class Consciousness*, although additional evidence is provided by Lukács's negative review of Bukharin's textbook of Marxism, which was another attempt to turn Marxism into sociology.[35] However, Lukács might hold this opinion because he assumes without argument, as we saw, that science is essentially contemplative and atomistic.

In any case, while Lukács's Hegelian Marxism achieved enormous influence as a founding text of the whole tradition of the Western Marxism, and proved formative even in the case of certain East European Humanist Marxists such as Kosík, Neurath's peculiar Marxist sociology fell into obscurity, from which it is recovered only by a new generation of scholars. I am afraid this is largely due to malicious treatment of Neurath, and the rest of the Viennese 'positivists', at the hands of certain Western Marxists. It seems that it all started with a savage critique of the whole programme of the 'scientific philosophy' of the Vienna Circle, and the work of Otto Neurath in particular, in a paper by Max Horkheimer, of the Institute for Social Research at Frankfurt, called 'Der neueste Angriff auf die Metaphysik' (1937). Horkheimer initiated a tradition of using the term 'positivism' in a very expansive, unclear sense as a slur to be hurled at all people who had respect for science, evidence and logic. Neurath was crushed by this criticism because he thought of the Frankfurt School Critical Theorists as allies in a struggle against fascism and obscurantism. He wrote a reply which he asked Horkheimer to publish in his journal (*Zeitschrift für Sozialforschung*), but the latter declined.[36] The Marxist tradition of dismissing 'positivism' continued after World War II, not only in Europe, to which the exiled members of the Frankfurt School triumphantly returned, but even in the United States, where many 'positivists' from Vienna and elsewhere found a new home. The low point of this caricaturing was probably reached in Herbert Marcuse's popular book, *One-Dimensional Man* (1964).

---

34 Lukács 1973, p. 347.
35 Lukács 1972.
36 Neurath's manuscript was for decades presumed to have been lost. Recently it was rediscovered and published in Symons et al. 2011.

It should be evident that the Western Marxist tradition of misinterpretation and simplification of twentieth-century scientific philosophy left its mark even on the work of the Czech Humanist Marxist, Karel Kosík. A closer look at the positions of different philosophers might have revealed to him that the general label 'positivism' did not do justice to them. Yet unlike many of his Western colleagues, Kosík never stooped to slander, and he even singled out Neurath's critique of metaphysical materialism for praise. It is to be regretted that Kosík did not find use for Neurath's holism, whose totalities appear more manageable than Lukács's rather arcane totality.

CHAPTER 12

Kosík's Concept of 'Concrete Totality': A Structuralist Critique

Vít Bartoš

Karel Kosík's central work – *Dialectics of the Concrete* is one of only a few books of Czech philosophical production that transcends the narrow intellectual framework of the domestic milieu. Its international success is thanks to both the general cultural context of the revolutionary 1960s and the intrinsic quality of the book. *Dialectics of the Concrete* is a specific attempt at a comprehensive Marxist philosophy whose central theme is, as Karel Kosík himself puts it, the issue of the relationship between man and the world. This issue is developed naturally and treated in terms of basic Marxist categories, but these are interpreted and discussed in this book in an innovative manner.

My aim is to examine and criticise one of the central concepts of Kosík's book, namely the notion of a 'concrete totality'. The concept in itself concentrates upon basic questions of Marxist ontology, epistemology and methodology, and establishes a certain type of interconnection between them. This is directly related to the basic question we are currently asking. In the preparatory studies[1] for *Dialectics of the Concrete* Kosík had already explicitly argued that it is precisely the conceptual scheme of the so-called 'concrete totality' which provides a more efficient method than the terms of a structure, as would henceforth be employed by both structuralists and system theorists working in the field of cybernetics and biology. In the introductory part of *Dialectics of the Concrete*, entitled 'Dialectics of the Concrete Totality', which is merely an elaboration upon an earlier article from 1962, we encounter an identical claim concerning the privileged concept of concrete totality. But is this really the case? In what sense does the specific aspect of the concept of concrete totality overcome notions of a structure or a system?

It is therefore clear that through a confrontation of the concepts of concrete totality and the concepts of structure and system, we get to the fundamentals of Marxist ontology and methodology (epistemology). It should be noted that Kosík himself did not make any detailed comparison. However, it seems that

---

1 Kosík 1962, in Kosík 1962, pp. 24–35.

he explicitly formulated the basic onto-methodological problem for Marxist philosophy, which is worth exploring.

I believe that despite his deep insights and often brilliant formulations, Kosík failed to formulate precisely the onto-methodological foundations of Marxism, and yet his criticism, mainly directed towards structuralism, is vitiated by a number of inaccuracies and omissions resulting from an insufficiently precise analysis of structuralist positions (e.g. Piaget's genetic epistemology). In my view we can concede that Kosík's intuitions concerning the conceptual merit of the notion of 'concrete totality' are correct but not sufficiently justified, poorly reflecting the conceptual fullness of structuralism and systems theory.

Within this context I would like to mention what we may call an 'obstacle', which is worth keeping in mind. Kosík's ontology is implicitly an ontology of social reality, and as such is at least inherently connected with the theory of subjectivity developed by German idealism. This in turn means that the relationship between human 'praxis' and physical reality ('material objects and processes') is, from a modern naturalistic point of view, somewhat distorted. The reason why we feel that there is something counterintuitive in traditional Marxian subject-object theory could be formulated as follows: 'Within Western Marxism materialism was increasingly emptied of any relation to nature and was reduced to practical materialism (the transformative actions of humans in the production of social life), particularly in relation to the economic conditions underpinning human society'.[2]

Of course, what is in this case valid for Western Marxism is valid also for Eastern Marxism. Briefly stated: modern Marxism is still deprived of an adequate theory of physical nature (and 'matter'). The Marxian concept of nature and matter is narrow, and at first glance it does not allow for a convergence with systems theory (or structuralism). It is not only human beings within their historical practice that are agents actively transforming and generally processing ontological reality. Marxist ontology should accept that natural systems of all kinds are as active as human subjects, and that all around us there are self-sustaining systems striving and struggling for the preservation of their existence. Simply speaking, everything that is also complex is always an active and 'self-creating' system within a process. Therefore when I speak here about a 'structure' or a 'system', I am not reducing my claims to the traditional narrow 'subject-centric' principles of Kosík's – and broadly speaking Marxist – ontology. I am talking about systems (or structures) in the most general way.

---

2   Clark, Brett and Richard York 2005.

Therefore, in attempting to critically develop the concept of 'concrete totality' and its dialectic, we should try to respect the progress made especially in modern systems theory, and accept the new theoretical tools which proved to be universally usable in possibly all the sciences that deal with systems in the broadest sense of the word.

I shall start by reproducing Kosík's arguments against a 'false', i.e. nonconcrete concept of totality, and try to formulate more sharply the fundamental ontological basis of the problem of the concrete totality in terms of modern structuralist and systems or complexity theory approach.

1 On False Totality

False totality is essentially a lack of understanding of architecture, process, structure, emergence, disintegration and contextual interdependence among the parts and relative units (totalities) of reality. False totality is also primarily based on an undialectical mode of relation:

> There are at least two steps that lead from the dialectical to the undialectical. First, because that which is dialectical is a real unity in difference, the undialectical would have to disunite the moments of the unity. Second, because the real unity in difference requires the maintenance of each of the dual moments as different despite their thoroughgoing dependence and in fact sees such moments as dependent precisely because of their difference, the undialectical would have to eradicate such difference by collapsing one into the other and in this again eradicate their interdependence. In other words, the undialectical involves separation and reduction.[3]

In essence, there are two basic approaches in their naive forms intuitively expressing the basic concept of false totality.

There is naive atomism of disparate facts (elements) and naive holism of totally dependent parts of the whole. Atomism means general separation, as there is no unity of opposites. Holism means the disappearance of any concrete entity in a superior organic wholeness – there are no opposites at all. For both, there is no place for developmental conflict or contradiction.

---

3 Pomeroy 2004, p. 15.

These are extreme positions. There is, of course, a grey zone of compromises (mostly verbal) between them. To overcome this false conception of totality is to formulate a more sophisticated theory of totality, which would be much better construed than the previous original naive intuition, both atomistic and holistic. The question is whether it is possible and meaningful to improve our understanding of concrete totality only by the application of the concepts of 'concreteness' and 'dialectics' which, in their traditional vagueness, do not significantly overcome the vagueness of naive atomism and holism. What are Kosík's arguments against the basic idea of a false totality? Or more generally, how do we construct our theories of totality which – in historical perspective – always prove themselves to be inadequate. Kosík says: 'Spinozism and physicalism are the two most wide-spread varieties of the reductionist method which translates the wealth of reality into something basic and elementary. All the richness of the world is jettisoned into the abyss of an immutable substance'.[4]

These are primary intuitions about 'totality'.

Let us start with an atomistic doctrine which expresses the simple belief: reality is divisible into individual atomic elements, whose combination altogether constitutes the facts. The 'keynote statement' of this approach is the bible of logical atomism, i.e. Wittgenstein's *Tractatus Logico-Philosophicus*. Here on the very first page we find such formulations:

> The world is everything that is the case. The world is the totality of facts, not of things. The world divides into facts. Any one can either be the case or not be the case, and everything else remain the same.[5]

What makes this position indefensible from the point of view of Kosík's concept of totality? Kosík says: 'Totality indeed does not signify all facts. Totality signifies reality as a structured dialectical whole, within which and from which any particular fact (or any group or set of facts) can be rationally comprehended'.[6]

The biggest problem of the atomistic conception of totality is simply the absence of structure and thus the absence of certain asymmetrical relationships between the entities and processes that make up the world. The world, i.e. concrete totality or reality in Kosík's terminology, is not a collection of facts, as Wittgenstein says. If it were so, then there would be no sufficient reason for a particular object to be structurally more dependent on one set of things (facts)

---

4   Kosík 1976, p. 13.
5   Wittgenstein 1922, p. 25.
6   Kosík 1976, pp. 18–19.

rather than on a completely different set of things (facts). Such an approach would paradoxically be reminiscent of astrological speculation about the interdependence of totally unrelated systems of nature (human viscera, minerals, stars etc.). The facts of logical atomism lack the real ontic anchoring (in concreteness or specificity) that we can see everywhere in our world, and that allows us to formulate certain laws and proportional relationships defining the functioning of reality.

Another unacceptable consequence of logical atomism is the belief that, as Wittgenstein says above: 'Any one can either be the case or not be the case and everything else remain the same'. From this it follows that facts are mutually independent, thus arbitrarily variable and also arbitrarily causally connected. However, this does not reflect our experience and scientific determinism. Logically then, the main concern is to locate the criteria and reasons why the existing systems (both natural and social) are built and structured just the way they are. But what are the true criteria of this anchoring or logic of correlation of facts? Before we move on to at least a partial attempt to formulate these criteria, let us look briefly at the second false conception of totality – naive holism.

Naive holism is built on hypostasis of the whole, in which parts or elements of the system are completely interconnected. Historically, this holism was tied together with pantheism, which in essence does not need the category of mediation because it has everything going on within a synchronous coordination mechanism without any contradictions, in a kind of 'pre-established harmony'. Kosík formulates this fact as follows: 'Hypostatising the whole and favoring it over its parts (over facts) is one path that leads to a false totality instead of to a concrete one. If the whole process represented a reality which would be indeed genuine and higher than facts, then reality could exist independently of facts, independently in particular of facts that would contradict it'.[7]

The same argument can be applied to naive holism as to naive atomism: the way of linking facts is either completely random and arbitrary, or mysterious (perhaps even both). Rather we should say that there are no individual facts, but only one unstructured all-embracing fact. If such a totality has to undergo a process of development, it is not clear as to how it will happen and why this should be happening.

There is a simple conclusion ensuing from the above: the totality concept of traditional ontologies based on both naive atomism and holism is so abstract that their explanatory and explicative value is close to zero. The problem of Marxist ontology (in Kosík's interpretation) rests upon the fact that it can see

---

7   Kosík 1976, p. 27.

correctly the shortcomings of previous ontologies of totality; however, the only terminological innovation[8] which is expressed by the term 'dialectic of the concrete totality' brings no positive information or idea. Therefore, is there any development of this theme which would lead to positive results and formulations? I will try to suggest that systemic and structuralist thinking has more to offer than Marxist (Kosík's) thought.

But before doing so, I would like to point out that there is a congenial, or better said complementary, concept to Kosík's notion of 'concrete totality'. The term 'fallacy of misplaced concreteness' was invented by Alfred North Whitehead and originally meant a critique of modern physics and metaphysics (since the seventeenth century), with their common assumption that there are separated parts of physical reality – in Whitehead's term 'simple locations' – which can be conceived as ultimate elements of reality with their own ontological and epistemological autonomy. The fallacy from Whitehead's point of view rests upon our fallacious understanding of what it means to be 'concrete'. To be 'concrete' does not mean to have definite spatio-temporal co-ordinations as we usually comprehend them, because to have definite spatio-temporal co-ordinations means to be positioned within an abstract and conventional frame of reference, i.e. Cartesian co-ordinates. This is in fact merely scientific abstraction. To be concrete means to be continuing an actual occasion[9] which is contextually located in an intertwined series of other different actual occasions with their own durations. This is, of course, a direct criticism of logical atomism.

Within this context it could be very inspiring to think about a possible intersection of implicit Marxist ontology with explicit Whiteheadian metaphysics. The reason is quite obvious:

> As an initial expression, therefore, we see three similarities between Marx and Whitehead's projects. First, there is a similarity of method [...] Second, [...] there is a denial of the possibility of uncritical universality and a specificity acceptance of the historical or epoch of the project. Third, [...] there is a similarity of critique of those positions that commit the fallacy of misplaced concreteness either by beginning with the

---

8   Here I mean that innovative verbal expressions are of value only when there is at the same time a new cognitive model of reality expressed by those new terms (through new metaphors, analogies etc.).

9   'Actual occasion' is engaged in Whitehead's metaphysics as a fundamental given fact (positum). We can imagine it very imprecisely like small and discrete electro-magnetic fields, which in their mutual interactions constitute physical reality.

abstract and uncritically determining the concrete by it, or by universalising or trans-historicising the concrete determinations such that they are torn out of their processive form of being-becoming or, in Marx's terms, out of their production within specific material-historical conditions.[10]

To be clear, my personal opinion is that the principles of Whiteheadian metaphysics could really serve as a basis for a Marxian philosophy of nature. And as far as I know, Whitehead is the only 'scientific' philosopher who emphasised the 'concreteness' of reality as an irreducible fact, from which it cannot be abstracted even in scientific theories. From Whitehead's perspective our reality is rather a blending process of abstract universals and entangled actual occasions, which – as Whitehead himself admits – is originally an idea of late Plato's. The misleading concept of false totality from this Whiteheadian point of view is then based on a reduction of fully-fledged reality into abstract universals, the cognitive tendency of which is unfortunately deeply embedded in the structure of human language.

2   Structure in Process versus the Dialectic of Totality

Marxists have traditionally opposed structuralism and the systems approach in its abstract conception of human subjectivity and practice. For Marxist criticism, structuralism is just another example of fetishisation and reification, because structuralism does not see the immanent activity of historical subjects within the social system, which historically transforms their own social and natural reality. Structuralism seems to be unable to appreciate the contradiction and productivity of a dialectical process that shapes itself through its own forces and thus independently of virtually immobile autonomous structures, as usually understood by traditional structuralism. Structuralism is supposed to be a doctrine which conceives the totality of reality as a union of autonomous areas or dimensions which have a priori clear and sharp demarcations of their mutual relationships. The consequence is that it is obviously impossible to change the ultimate destiny of the social or natural system. Contradictions are then merely a by-product and do not play a fundamental role in 'constructing' reality. Kosík states: 'The dialectical relationship of contradictions and totality of contradictions within totality and the totality of contradictions, of the concreteness of a totality formed by contradictions and the lawful character of

---

10   Pomeroy 2004, p. 13.

contradictions within totality, all this is one of that the distinctions set apart the Marxist and the Structuralist conceptions of totality'.[11]

It is difficult to argue briefly with this criticism, which is certainly not entirely unjustified. Let us choose the type of structuralism, but one that is inherently probably the closest to dialectical materialism, namely the genetic structuralism of Jean Piaget. The reason why Piaget is so close to the Marxist method is probably clear. Genetic structuralism simply understands cognitive structure as a result of a certain historical process (ontogenesis) and accepts qualitative processuality as the fundamental character of reality. Piaget's structuralism is not really the structuralism of almost eternal and unchanging mathematical structures, as in the tradition of Bourbaki or even Claude Lévi-Strauss.

It is precisely Piaget's concept of structure here that complements in many ways what we intuitively lack in both the Marxist theory of the dialectic totality and in the traditional 'static' structuralist approach. Piaget defines the structure of three attributes: totality, transformation and self-regulation.[12] On the other hand, Marxists tend to understand as fundamental principles of the dialectic the following trio of concepts: totality, change and contradiction.[13] The difference between the dialectic and the structure seems to be evident. The structuralist term 'self-regulation' is in opposition to the Marxist term 'contradiction'. However, as we will see further, there is in fact no conflict. A problem formulated this way is in itself a typical example of undialectical thinking, and we should be very cautious not to be caught in some kind of ideological partisanship: 'A dialectical view begins from the opposite end: change is universal and much is happening to change everything. Therefore, equilibrium and stasis are special situations that have to be explained'.[14]

Well, changes without equilibria cannot establish any internal relations or structures, and what is even worse, there could be no history embedded in the development of a given (natural or cultural) system. The equilibrium of a given system is some kind of pattern (attractor) which comes into being through the 'dialectical' conflict between historically older ontic domains. When there is no equilibrium there is no history and no 'logic' of history – there would be only an irreducibly complex lawless chain of changes. Equilibrium is not a 'special situation'. It is a constitutive and fundamental moment in the process of

---

[11] Kosík 1962, p. 8 (translation by the author).
[12] Piaget 1971, pp. 6–16.
[13] There is a clear article about the possibility of dialectics in biology and understanding of 'contradiction' in Marxist philosophy. See Sullivan 2015.
[14] Levins 2008, p. 40.

constructing new structures of reality. This moment makes up the necessary condition for dialectical transformation.

Finally, an important concept that newly emerged in structuralism (but mainly in systems theory) is certainly the concept of self-regulation. In contrast with traditional Marxism (including Kosík), Piaget emphasised the real fact that systems tend to maintain their existence within certain values. Those values originally arose from the organisation of the structurally simpler systems that historically preceded them (it is irrelevant as to whether we consider the evolution of spatial systems, biological evolution, natural or intellectual ontogeny – it is the general rule). The homeostasis or equilibria that systems achieve through using negative feedback is somewhat neglected in Marxism, while these play a central role in Piaget's theory. Marxists by contrast emphasising the negativity and lack of such fundamental processes governing the forms of totality. A dispute is also established – is the reality (totality) rather built on the principle of equilibrium (equilibria), or (on the contrary) upon the principle of contradiction and dialectical negation. Piaget prefers the process of integration (totalisation) and unification, which does not mean that reality is not contradictory. However, the Piagetian concept of contradiction is different in comparison with the Marxist point. It is worth conducting a deeper analysis of the Piagetian concept of contradiction (negation):

> [...] given a completed structure, one negates one of its seemingly essential or at least necessary attributes. [...] Euclidean geometry has by 'negation' (of the parallel postulate) engendered the non-Euclidean geometries; two-valued logic with its principle of excluded middle has [...] become supplemented by multivalued logic, and so on. [...] Given a certain structure, one tries, by systematic negation of one after another attribute to construct its complementary structures, in order later to subsume the original together with its complements in a more complex total structure.[15]

As we can see, Piaget interprets contradiction – not only in mathematics and not only within the bounds of cognitive processes; he is convinced that this is generally how new systems are constructed – as a way of building up a bigger and more general structure. The new structure, which is made up of the previous structure and its partial negations, is a new encapsulated totality with newly organised internal relations. This process could hypothetically

---

15 Piaget 1977, pp. 775–9.

be repeated ad infinitum. The principle of negation of the negation could be understood in this manner. It is interesting that within this context it is not usually considered that the process of negation of the negation necessitates something that I would call the 'endless horizon' for totalisation. The term 'endless horizon' conceals a simple rationale that says that there always has to be space for additional (external or internal) actions which create negative alterations to previously historically given natural or cultural systems. If this were not the case then there would be no dialectic at all (no negation of the negation). There is therefore a profound question as to whether the dialectical process could ever be enacted if there had not been at least a potentially endless reservoir of events acting beyond the given system. However, be that as it may, it is now clear that a dialectical process is some kind of genesis and 'genesis is never anything but the transition from one structure to another [...]'[16] There is no sharp distinction between the dialectical process of totalisation and the process of transition or transformation within the structure.

Directly related to the above, there is one important question which, as it seems to me, Piaget formulated very properly. What is the contradiction? Do Marxists distinguish sufficiently between real (i.e. logical) contradiction or inconsistency and, let us say, physical conflict (vector conflict), or as we mentioned above the process of encapsulation of opposites (negation of the negation in Hegelian terms)? Piaget states: 'But the point here is precisely what dialectics calls contradiction is not a logical or formal contradiction, otherwise it could never be, transcended but only corrected and eliminated [...]'.[17]

This again simply means that Marxist and Hegelian negation, to be constructive and if it is to explain the emergence of new things, should not be equated with logical contradictions, which are completely unconstructive. It may seem to be an obvious finding, but it is not. Let us then consider the fact that some Marxist theorists have tried to create so-called dialectical logic, which violates the traditional non-contradiction principle in logic.[18]

I propose that the concept of totality and dialectics of totality of Marxist philosophy should be systematically confronted with Piaget's genetic structuralism, which, with its emphasis on self-regulation and 'constructive' contradictions, could help to develop the concept of the dialectic and totality in greater (more specific) depth.

---

16   Ibid.
17   Piaget 1980, p. 304.
18   In the Czech context see: Jindřich Zelený and his *Dialektická ontologie* [Dialectical Ontology], 1997.

3   Robustness and Concreteness

When we have analysed Kosík's term 'false totality' we only come to the negative conclusion that the atomistic and holistic idea of wholeness is untenable. However, the statement of 'the concrete totality' is only a verbal revision, even though it expresses a correct intuition of how to overcome the naive abstractness of atomism and holism. I dare say that we should not be satisfied only with vague intuitions and verbal expressions. For this reason, I suggest that we employ new more fine-grained concepts and intuitions borrowed from systems theories in order to specify better our idea of the concrete totality. The question is therefore what do we really mean when we stress that atomism and holism miss the target because of their unstructured and abstract conception of totality? What do they lack or omit? I believe that a necessary (but probably not sufficient) condition of constituting a concrete totality is for whatever system to have a space-time differentiation between relatively autonomous domains (modules) of reality as they have evolved over time (history).

Let me present a few simple examples and questions in order to grasp our problem more deeply. As we all know, there are many system domains which compose our reality – from quarks and atoms, molecules, cells, organisms, populations, human societies etc. to planets, stars, galaxies and whatever else may exist. But there has to be a certain reason or architecture which explains why those domains are arranged in the particular way we perceive them and as we describe them in scientific terms. The space-time relations between all of these domains from my point of view make up the concrete arrangement of our world – the concrete totality, if you wish. And that totality has at least one very interesting property we are all familiar with: I call this property the 'asymmetry of binding', or 'asymmetry of linkage'. The intuition expressed by those terms is simple and could be exemplified even within a Marxist conceptual framework: why is there any problem whatsoever with the relation between the social or economic basis and superstructure in Marxist methodology? What is the fundamental level of social or natural reality, and what is only the emergent level? What determines what and how? (Now we can shift the identical structure of the problem to another level of reality, i.e. why do quarks determine the structure of an atom but not vice versa, or why does DNA determine the structure of proteins but not vice versa). Let's consider this for a moment. Do you think that the problem could ever have emerged if we had adopted the naive atomist or holistic point of view? It is unlikely, because both neglected the above-mentioned asymmetry, and this is why they fail to explain the real and concrete architecture of our reality.

Finally, we can employ our new system category, which is usually called 'robustness', or 'resilience', in order to understand the nature of 'concreteness' better. Robustness is roughly a property of a system that says what it is possible to change in the system without the given system ceasing to function. More concretely, robustness should be viewed from at least three perspectives:

I. [...] that robustness is a measure of feature persistence for systems, or for features of systems, that are difficult to quantify ...
II. [...] that represents changes in system composition, system topology, or in the fundamental assumptions regarding the environment in which the system operates.
III. [...] that is especially appropriate for systems whose behavior results from the interplay of dynamics with a definite organisational architecture.[19]

But probably the best formulation is this one:

Usually we don't care about the robustness of a rock. In many of these cases, robustness may be interpreted as an index of the relative strengths and weaknesses – what might also be called the 'fitness' – of the set of 'strategic options' that either have been designed top-down or have emerged bottom-up for the system. The options available to the system serve in other words as a 'strategy' for how to respond to perturbations.[20]

It implies a simple conclusion: Robustness is a matter of internal symmetries and their possible transformations on many scales of the given system (totality). It is also a matter of the plasticity of those internal symmetries of the system (either physical, biological, or man-made). The more transformation with the given system can be achieved without the system being violated, the more robust the system and the more fundamental the level of reality we observe. Robustness of a system is criterion distinguishing what is fundamental and what is emergent.

From our point of view, the concrete analysis of entity (process, system, event etc.) firstly rests on a bottom-up and top-down categorisation of the basic domains which make up our reality – and categorisation is, of course, a matter of empirical inquiry based on historically given scientific knowledge and its limits.

---

19   Jen 2002.
20   Ibid.

Secondly, we must determine the so-called 'relative powers' of domains in their interactions ('what determines what' question). Those causal and structurally restrictive powers could be measured precisely through the above-mentioned numerical richness of possibilities (possible transformations of the system within adaptive space) for strategic options in the particular investigated domain.

If we have general categorisation of physical[21] domains and their relative powers within their interactions, then we also have the concrete architecture of our world.

4   Conclusions

My aim has been to criticise and elaborate on Kosík's notions of 'concrete totality' and 'dialectical totality', which have been understood to mean the same thing. I am in basic agreement with Kosík when he emphasises the need for concrete analysis of the concrete fact. The concrete fact is always a matter of multi-level, contradictory processes shaping the totality of relevant relations creating that concrete given fact. We also endorse Kosík's condemnation of so-called 'bad totalities' – holistic and atomistic concepts of totality – as insufficient abstractions.

In general, I believe, similarly to Whitehead or Kosík, that abstraction itself is an ambivalent intellectual instrument. Abstraction often means oversimplification, creating meaningless generalisations. Abstract schemes, in order to achieve logical coherence, tend to cover over real contradictions. On the other hand, we have to engage in abstraction because of the limited 'computational' powers of our minds, and abstraction is basically a simplification that permits effective understanding. The notions, concepts and languages we employ are by their nature abstractions, and that fundamentally limits what they can uncover in reality. It is therefore extremely difficult to express concrete reality in abstract terms. But we believe that new meaning expressing 'concreteness' can be constructed through the mutual intersection of abstract schemes. I have therefore examined the constructive character of the terms 'concrete totality' and 'dialectical totality', especially in comparison with the structuralist ideas of 'structure' and 'system'. I have tried to reconcile their mutual contradictions, above all the dispute about the ontological priority of permanent change or

---

21   I mean 'physical' in the broadest sense – even human institutions, historical duration, artefacts, mental states etc. are in some sense physical events.

contradiction over relative structural stasis. I determined that these concepts are in fact dialectically complementary. Finally, I have tried to express more intuitively the concept of 'concrete totality' through the categories of a systems approach, like the robustness or resilience of the system. Put simply, I see the 'concreteness of the fact' and 'concrete totality' as results of mingled and intertwined, differently robust domains of reality.

Concrete totality then could be understood as some kind of matrix that is built out of interacting domains of different space-time scales and different causal and structural powers.

Or in other words: when we think about concreteness and totality, we should be thinking about a hierarchy of differently robust and intersecting systems in their interactions. I hope this might be a plausible way to understand the nature of the concrete totality.

CHAPTER 13

The World of the Pseudoconcrete, Ideology and the Theory of the Subject (Kosík and Althusser)

Petr Kužel

The main focus of this paper is to compare certain aspects of Karel Kosík's concept of the 'world of the pseudoconcrete' with Louis Althusser's concept of ideology. Although Kosík belonged to the tradition of humanist Marxism, while Althusser called for Marxism to be understood as theoretical anti-humanism, we will point out significant similarities between Althusser's concept of ideology and Kosík's concept of the world of the pseudoconcrete. We will also discuss how each of these conceptions is linked with a specific theory of the subject, and we will focus on the problems surrounding the conceptualisation of a subversive subject that is capable of undermining and radically transforming given social conditions.

We begin with the conviction that the question of the subversive subject is narrowly linked with the question of ideology. The problem of conceptualising this type of subject is a central concern for both Althusser and Kosík. Their conceptualisation of subversion is, however, entirely different. In Althusser's conception of ideology, the subversive subject does not have the character of a subject overcoming ideology as such. The subversive subject can merely overcome a *dominant* ideology (an ideology that ensures the reproduction of given relations of production), but the subject remains ideological as a subject – it remains an effect of ideological state apparatuses. For Althusser, the subject (even a revolutionary subject) is ideological by definition. Revolutionary subjects and revolutionary ideologies are reproduced (as 'by-products' of ideological state apparatuses) in 'ritual practices', which are governed by ideological apparatuses.[1] Even revolutionary ideology is therefore materialised in these apparatuses and in the actions of subjects determined by them. If the

---

1 Ideological state apparatuses produce, above all, the dominant ideology, which helps to reproduce existing capitalist relations of production. As a by-product, however, they may also produce subversive ideology. See Althusser 2014, p. 187. Althusser's essay 'Ideology and Ideological State Apparatuses' is an extract from the much more extensive work *Sur la reproduction* (published in English as *On the Reproduction of Capitalism*). The discussion of 'secondary ideology' as a 'by-product' of ideological apparatuses was omitted from 'Ideology and Ideological State Apparatuses' when published as a separate article.

subject (even a revolutionary subject) is always an effect of ideological interpellations, then subversion is always in a certain sense incorporated in advance into the function of the given system of apparatuses. More precisely, the process of creating a subversive subject (a subject that undermines the dominant ideology materialised in ideological state apparatuses) is *at the same time* a process of transforming these apparatuses. It is a process of struggling for the transformation of these apparatuses in order to change their 'final product' from a dominant ideology (which enables the reproduction of a given order) to a subversive ideology (which enables the reproduction of social relations in which capitalist logic no longer prevails).

With this approach, Althusser tries to avoid the dualism between people with their actions and ideas on the one hand and the conditions and function of the social structure on the other. He tries to overcome the antinomy between the internal and the external (and between the ideal and the material). According to Althusser, the separation of the internal and the external into distinct instances leads to a certain form of dualism between *ideal* consciousness and *material* action, where the *ideal* is something that we could call transcendent, or separated from the real material world and inexplicable by means of it. This dualistic approach is not logically sustainable, as many have observed since the earliest critiques of Cartesian philosophy. On this point, Althusser productively develops the Spinozist approach of psycho-physical parallelism, which resolves the antinomy between the ideal and the material. What is traditionally represented as *ideal* is in reality, for Althusser, also a certain form of materiality. For this reason, he conceives of ideology too as material. There is no separation between ideology and the actions of a subject. The subject's ideology, its set of *internal* convictions, is in fact its *material* and *external* action.

As we will see, this approach was not foreign to Kosík, yet there are important differences between Kosík's and Althusser's conceptions of the subject. Whereas in Althusser's concept of ideology a subject cannot transcend and overcome ideology as such, Kosík's conception of the destruction of the world of the pseudoconcrete involves a conception of a subversive, potentially revolutionary subject that *transcends* given conditions.

As we have indicated, the problem of the subject is linked with a problem of ideology and, in Kosík's conception, with the so-called 'world of the pseudoconcrete'. Let us start with the second concept. What is Kosík's definition of 'the world of the pseudoconcrete'? According to Kosík, 'dialectical thinking' should distinguish between the phenomenal forms of a thing and the *concept* of the thing.[2] In Kosík's philosophy these phenomenal forms are related to

---

2 Kosík 1976, p. 1.

the practical-utilitarian treatment of things, which is a primary and *immediate* approach of man to reality. These phenomenal forms of reality are immediately reproduced in the mind of agents of historically determined praxis as complexes of ideas or as categories of *'routine thinking'*[3] (this concept, chosen by the English translators of Kosík's *Dialectics of the Concrete*, corresponds to the concept of 'common sense' or to the French concept of *'connaissance commune'*, which was theorised by Gaston Bachelard and subsequently became one of the starting points for Althusser's theory of ideology). The categories of *routine thinking* are not *concepts*; they are, as Kosík claims, 'considered only out of a 'barbarian habit' to be concepts'. Kosík adds that 'these phenomenal forms are diverse and often contradict the *law* of the phenomenon, the *structure* of the thing, i.e. [...] the corresponding concept'.[4]

This epistemological approach is evidently derived from Marx, but we can see here also a similarity with the epistemology of Gaston Bachelard, whose philosophy strongly influenced Althusser's conception of ideology (especially in his 'theoreticist period', but this influence persisted in subsequent periods of Althusser's work and is present also in his essay 'Ideology and Ideological State Apparatuses').

Like Kosík, Bachelard argued that scientific knowledge contradicts the 'true nature' of 'common sense'. One of the best known of Bachelard's concepts, the concept of the *epistemological break*, which was borrowed and productively used by Althusser, is, put very simply, a break from this 'true nature' of common sense. This break enables theorists to enter into the field of science, which Althusser conceives as the field in which the imaginary naturalness of the phenomenal surface of living reality loses its semblance of autonomy and its unquestionability.[5]

---

3 Ibid.
4 Ibid.
5 The epistemological break is, very roughly speaking, a break from concepts that are taken for granted in everyday life. These are concepts that contaminate the theoretical field; they are conceived as *given* (and not *produced*), and they cannot prove their theoretical genesis within the theoretical system. The process of epistemologically breaking with them is a process of separating ourselves from these ideological concepts (a process of moving away from the field of ideology) and entering into the field of theoretical concepts. What comes first in this process is a new theoretical praxis. We can only retrospectively recognise and theoretically reflect upon concepts from which we have already separated ourselves. Ideological concepts with which we have not yet epistemologically broken (concepts which still 'contaminate' the field of science) cannot be seen within a given theoretical structure as ideological. The very theoretical structure (contaminated as it is by ideological concepts) systematically conceals these ideological concepts and renders their ideological nature invisible. In order to make this ideological contamination visible, it is necessary to transform the theoretical field through

For Althusser, as for Kosík, ideological categories are related only to common sense, to living reality, and they can be *recognised* as ideological (but not abolished) only by theoretical praxis, which produces and expresses *concepts* of things rather than their imaginary reflection. For both Althusser and Kosík, to intellectually reproduce the structure of the thing, i.e. to comprehend it, means to express its *concept*. The question is what 'concept' means for them. According to Kosík 'the concept of the thing means comprehending the thing, and comprehending the thing means knowledge of the thing's structure'.[6]

This theoretical recognition sets the task of attaining a concept of things which is not immediately or purely empirically approachable. This is also why Kosík wrote that 'because things do not show man immediately what they are, [...] mankind arrives at the cognition of things and of their structure via a detour'.[7] Althusser's famous critique of empiricism[8] and his emphasis on the need to recognise the inner structure of 'objects of knowledge' and their immanent causality, points in the same direction. In his view, theoretical recognition is an effect of theoretical praxis, which is associated with the construction of the concept and of the object of knowledge, and can neither be reduced to empirical data nor simply abstracted from empirical data. This recognition does not cancel the phenomenal, imaginary forms (because these forms are, as Marx stressed, 'socially valid, and therefore objective'[9]), but it enables us to explicate these forms as well as the contents of what historically determined subjects thought about the actions in which they 'freely' participate.[10]

As we have indicated, Althusser's distinction between what he called Generalities I (ideological concepts or concepts adopted from everyday life,[11] con-

---

new theoretical praxis and to demonstrate how the invisibility was theoretically produced. Every science is thus in a certain sense a science of ideology.

6 Kosík 1976, p. 4.
7 Kosík 1976, p. 9.
8 According to Althusser, empiricism includes all epistemologies that 'oppose a given subject to a given object and call knowledge the abstraction by the subject of the essence of the object'. Althusser 2005, p. 249.
9 Marx 1982, p. 169.
10 As Marx said, the 'scientific discovery that the products of labour, in so far as they are values, are merely the material expressions of the human labour expended to produce them, marks an epoch in the history of mankind's development, but by no means banishes the semblance of objectivity possessed by the social characteristics of labour'. Marx 1982, p. 167. Similarly to how Copernicus's scientific discovery of heliocentrism enables us to better understand the motion of cosmic bodies but does not dissipate the *semblance* that the sun is turning around the Earth, scientific discovery does not dismiss inadequate semblance, but it is capable of explaining it. Marx uses this example in: Marx 1982, p. 2117.
11 This was a problem of political economy which 'has generally been content to take, just as

cepts that are not able to prove their *theoretical genesis*) and what he called Generalities III (theoretical concepts) is also present – when we look closer – in Kosík's conceptualisation of concepts on the one hand and the pseudoconcrete on the other. Moreover, Kosík asserted that 'man has to exert an effort to emerge from his "state of nature" [...] to recognize reality for what it is'.[12] Recognition is characterised as 'overcoming that which is natural'.[13] This is the basis of his definition of the pseudoconcrete. For Kosík, therefore, the 'collection of phenomena that crowd the everyday environment and the routine atmosphere of human life and which penetrate the consciousness of acting individuals with regularity, immediacy and self-evidence that lend them a semblance of autonomy and naturalness, constitutes the world of the *pseudoconcrete*'.[14] This world of the pseudoconcrete includes, among other things, the world of routine ideas that are external phenomena projected into man's consciousness, and which are a product of *fetishised praxis*; they are 'ideological forms of the movement of this praxis'.[15] 'Routine ideas' are identified by Kosík as ideology: 'Routine thinking is the ideological form of everyday human activity'.[16] This definition is very close to Althusser's conception of ideology as a material activity of the subject.

We can see that in spite of the fact that Althusser and Kosík represent opposing currents of Marxist tradition, they came, independently and around the same time, to conceptions of ideology that were in many aspects analogous (Kosík's *Dialectics of the Concrete* was published in 1963, the same year as Althusser's paper 'Marxism and Humanism', in which Althusser discussed the problem of ideology). Both of them identified 'routine ideas', as well as the ordinary, everyday social praxis governed by these ideas, as ideology, which penetrates the mind of the *subject*. Both also spoke, albeit in different ways, about a certain dual character of ideology, about its illusive and allusive function[17] (or about what Althusser called a duality between ideological *recognition* and *misrecognition*).

---

      they were, the terms of commercial and industrial life, and to operate with them, entirely failing to see that by so doing, it confined itself within the narrow circle of ideas expressed by those terms'. Engels's Preface to the English Edition of *Capital I*. See Marx 1982, p. 111.

12   Kosík 1976, p. 9.
13   Ibid.
14   Kosík 1976, p.2.
15   Ibid.
16   Kosík 1966, p. 14. In the English translation this sentence is missing. See Kosík 1976, p. 5.
17   'The world of the pseudoconcrete is the chiaroscuro of truth and deceit. It thrives in ambiguity. The phenomenon conceals the essence even as it reveals it'. See Kosík 1976, p. 2. 'However, while admitting that they do not correspond to reality, i.e. that they constitute an illusion, we admit that they do make allusion to reality, and that they need only be

Nevertheless, although there are certain similarities between Kosík's conception of the world of the pseudoconcrete and Althusser's conception of ideology, they differ significantly in their concepts of the possibility of destroying this world of the pseudoconcerete, or ideology.

Whereas for Kosík the destruction of the pseudoconcrete 'results in the liberation of the "subject"',[18] for Althusser 'man is an ideological animal by nature'.[19] The very claim that ideology could be entirely removed from society is, according to Althusser, itself ideological.[20] Although ideologies change, ideology as such is – in its general form – eternal and is inextricably linked to the category of the subject. For Kosík, by contrast, this form of the subject, a subject whose mind is governed by routine thinking and whose action represents fetishised praxis, is identified as a *mystified subject* or *false subject*.[21]

Within this context Althusser proclaims two important theses: 1) 'There is no practice except by and in an ideology; 2) There is no ideology except by the subject and for subjects'.[22] There is no social activity without ideology.[23] Social action presupposes the category of the subject, which is fundamentally identified with ideology.[24] The subject, for Althusser, is always an ideological

---

"interpreted" to discover the reality of the world behind their imaginary representation of that world (ideology = illusion/allusion)'. Althusser 2008, p. 36; Althusser 1976, p. 102.

18   Kosík 1976, p. 8.
19   Althusser 2008, p. 45; Althusser 1994, p. 70.
20   Ideology as such is for Althusser 'an organic part of every social totality. It is as if human societies could not survive without these specific formations, these systems of representations (at various levels), their ideologies. Human societies secrete ideology as the very element and atmosphere indispensable to their historical respiration and life. Only an ideological world outlook could have imagined societies without ideology and accepted the utopian idea of a world in which ideology (not just one of its historical forms) would disappear without trace, to be replaced by science'. Althusser 2005, p. 232.
21   See Kosík 1976, p. 56.
22   Althusser 2008, p. 44.
23   'In reality, the social practices and the ideas men form of them are intimately linked. It can be said that there is no practice without ideology, and that every practice – including scientific practice – realizes itself through an ideology. In all the social practices (whether they pertain to the domain of economic production, of science, of art or law, of ethics or of politics), the people who act are subjected to corresponding ideologies, independently of their will and usually in total ignorance of the fact'. Althusser 2011, p. 256.
24   'Ideology is the system of the ideas and representations which dominate the mind of a man or a social group'. Althusser 2008, p. 32. 'Ideology represents the imaginary relationship of individuals to their real conditions of existence'. Althusser 2008, p. 36. 'Ideology has material existence'. Althusser 2008, p. 40.

subject; ideology in this conception always 'hails or interpellates individuals as subjects'.[25] And 'all ideology hails or interpellates concrete individuals as concrete subjects, by the functioning of the category of the subject'.[26]

Consequently, there is no subject in the field of science. Entering into the field of science, by epistemologically breaking off from ideological concepts, involves the destruction of the category of the subject – it is a destruction of our subjection.[27] The problem is that our self-perception, self-awareness, and identity (however imaginary) are based on precisely this subjection. By this subjection we recognise ourselves as subjects. This is also why it is so difficult to enter into the field of science and achieve this epistemological break. We are obliged to cut ourselves off from our deepest convictions, based on unreflected everyday praxis, convictions on which we base our intuitive comprehension of the world and our role within it.[28]

According to Althusser, as we have indicated, the subject is entirely an effect of ideological apparatuses; his imaginary autonomy is a consequence of the efficacy of ideological state apparatuses. This thesis is linked of course with Althusser's concept of the materiality of ideology. 'An ideology [whether dominant or revolutionary – note P.K.] always exists in an apparatus, and its practice, or practices. This existence is material'.[29] According to Judith Butler, Althusser's distinctive contribution was, after all, to 'undermine the ontological dualism presupposed by the conventional Marxist distinction between a material base and an ideal or ideological superstructure'.[30]

The subject, according to Althusser, is *completely* subjected to ideology, and consequently there is no part of the subject that escapes this subjection, this submission to the rules of the ideology. Significant consequences follow from this fact. Since there can be nothing that transcends the system of ideology, it would be idealist to presume the existence of ideas not materialised and

---

25 Althusser 2008, p. 49.
26 Althusser 2008, p. 47.
27 Of course we can never divest ourselves entirely of our ideological subjection (this would result in total autism), but as I understand Althusser, the breaking off from ideological concepts and entering the field of science is at the same time a process of certain desubjectivation.
28 This enables us to understand the end of Marx's Preface to *A Contribution to the Critique of Political Economy*: '[A]t the entrance to science, as at the entrance to hell, the demand must be posted: *Qui si convien lasciare ogni sospetto / Ogni vilta convien che qui sia morta.* [From Dante, *Divina Commedia*: Here all mistrust must be abandoned; And here must perish every craven thought.]'
29 Althusser 2008, p. 40.
30 See for example Butler 1997, p. 121.

produced by the structure of ideological state apparatuses, and the existence of such ideas would be inexplicable. This would bring us to an idealistic conception of ideology. Furthermore, this idealistic approach would lead to the liberalist ideology of 'independent' man, thus masking the existence of class struggle and supporting the dominant ideology.[31] Althusser's line of reasoning is understandable, but it presents us with an important problem: how can one theoretically grasp the possibility (if this possibility exists at all) of the emergence of a subject that truly subverts a given system and that goes beyond the logic of the system? Within Althusser's framework, this type of subject cannot be constructed.

In contemporary Marxist and post-Marxist philosophy, this problem in Althusser's conception of subject has been recognised. The approaches of philosophers like, for example, Alain Badiou and Slavoj Žižek can be understood (from this point of view) as efforts to overcome this theoretical problem. Kosík's conception of the destruction of the world of the pseudoconcrete, however, also involves an effort to conceptualise a subversive subject and at the same time to anchor this subject (as well as praxis and labour *as general categories*) ontologically. From this perspective his conception can contribute to contemporary discussions.

1 The Destruction of Ideology

On the problem of the destruction of ideology, Kosík could agree with Althusser that phenomenal forms *as such* (those forms that have an ideological character) could not be abolished simply by their adequate recognition. This recognition is not sufficient for their abolition, because they exist *objectively*, not merely subjectively. What could (and would have to) be abolished is the 'apparent autonomy of the world of immediate everyday contacts'.[32] According to Kosík,

> thinking, which abolishes the pseudoconcrete in order to reach the concrete, is also a process that exposes a real world under the world of appearances, the law of the phenomenon behind the appearance of the phenomenon, the real internal movement behind visible movement, the essence behind the phenomenon. What lends these phenomena a

---

31 See Althusser 1973a.
32 See Kosík 1976, p. 6.

pseudoconcrete character is not their existence as such but the apparent autonomy of their existence.[33]

In destroying the pseudoconcrete, dialectical thinking does not deny the existence or the objective character of these phenomena'[34] (this assertion of the objective character of such phenomena is analogous to Althusser's concept of the material existence of ideology); dialectical thinking rather 'abolishes their fictitious independence [the independence of ideological phenomena] by demonstrating their mediatedness, and counters their claim to autonomy with proving their derivative character'.[35] (Althusser would of course deny that this critical method is 'dialectical'. His rejection of dialectics naturally leads to very important consequences, but we must set aside those issues in this paper.)

The destruction of the pseudoconcrete is thus for Kosík linked with a 'dialectical-critical method of thinking'. But Kosík adds to his previous sentence about the 'dialectical-critical method of thinking', saying that 'to interpret the world critically, the interpretation itself must be grounded in revolutionary praxis'. This revolutionary praxis is, for Kosík but of course not for Althusser, identical with 'the humanisation of man'.[36]

The process of destroying the pseudoconcrete thus contains not only an *epistemological* aspect, a process of recognition, but also a *practical* process. The destruction of the pseudoconcrete is linked to the ontological process of forming 'the *concrete*'.[37] It is insufficient simply to recognise the fetishised character of the everyday, and it is insufficient simply to reject it in the name of so-called 'authenticity'. This approach is criticised by Kosík when he speaks about the limits of the Heideggerian approach, according to which the transition to authenticity is 'a rejection of the everyday'. According to Kosík, by contrast, 'if the everyday is the *phenomenal* "layer" of reality, then the *reified* everyday is overcome not in a leap from the everyday to authenticity but in practically abolishing both the fetishism of the everyday and that of History, that is, in practically destroying reified reality both in its phenomenal appearance and its real essence'.[38] This process, according to Kosík, refers to an 'authentic historical subject', to a 'concrete man'.

---

33 We can add here that according to Kosík it is just this 'apparent' autonomy that gives the subject its mystified form: the 'fetishized subject'.
34 Kosík 1976, p. 6.
35 Ibid.
36 Kosík 1976, p. 8.
37 Ibid.
38 Kosík 1976, p. 45.

This is a crucial point that distinguishes Kosík's thought from Althusser's, since for Althusser there is no subject of history. History is, for Althusser, a 'process without subject',[39] and the concept of 'man' is, for Althusser, an ideological concept. Kosík, on the other hand, argues that when 'social reality is conceived of as a sum or a totality of autonomous structures influencing one another',[40] as thinkers like Althusser propose, this conception becomes 'a captive of fetishist intuiting and results in a bad totality',[41] in which 'the subject vanishes, or more precisely, the place of the real subject, i.e. of man as an objective-practical subject, is taken by a subject that has been mythologised, reified and fetishized: by an autonomous movement of structures'.[42]

2   The Mystified Subject

Of the various forms of mystified subject mentioned by Kosík, two are especially worthy of discussion. The first involves the category of 'procuring'. Procuring is for Kosík 'praxis in its *phenomenally alienated form* [...] it expresses the praxis of everyday manipulation, with man employed in a system of ready-made "things", i.e. implements. In this system of implements, man himself becomes an object of manipulation. The praxis of manipulation (procuring) transforms people into manipulators and into objects of manipulation. Procuring is manipulation (of things and people). Its motions repeat daily, they have long ago become a habit and are performed mechanically'.[43] This means that procuring reproduces nothing authentic; it is the mechanical reproduction of ready-made things. Man is merely an object of manipulation, which has transformed him into a cog in the machine. He is a mystified subject, not a true subject. (We can say that this mystified subject is analogous to Althusser's subject, which is produced and reproduced by ideological state apparatuses and which is in reality an object of manipulation.) It is a subject linked with the everyday. In the everyday, 'activity and way of life are transformed into an instinctive, subconscious, unconscious and unreflected mechanism of acting and living'.[44] Kosík in this context also analogously emphasises that the everyday has no his-

---

39   Althusser 1982, pp. 49–71; Althusser 1973b, pp. 91–8.
40   Kosík 1976, p. 30.
41   Ibid. Kosík borrows the term 'bad totality' from Czech theoretician Kurt Konrad.
42   Kosík 1976, p. 31.
43   Kosík 1976, p. 39.
44   Kosík 1976, p. 43.

tory; it is itself 'devoid of history and outside of history'.[45] (Compare Althusser's claim that 'ideology has no history'.[46])

Kosík also depicts a second type of mystified or 'derivative' subject.[47] Whereas 'man as care is the pure subjectivity',[48] there are also subjects that objectify themselves. 'In order to understand who he is, the subject becomes objectual. The subject abstracts from his subjectivity and becomes an object and an element of the system'.[49] It should be emphasised that this reduction is not just a change of theoretical standpoint but rather reflects, according to Kosík, the *real* metamorphosis of man that is performed by capitalism.[50]

> *Not theory, but reality itself reduces man to an abstraction. Economics is a system and set of laws governing relations in which man is constantly being transformed into the 'economic man'.*[51]

Classical economics represent a reflection of this reduction of man to *homo oeconomicus*. Due to this real reduction of man,

> [m]an becomes a reality only by becoming an element of the system. Outside the system he is unreal. He is real only to the extent to which he is reduced to a function of the system and to which the requirements of the system define him as homo oeconomicus. He is real only to the extent to which he cultivates those abilities, talents and inclination that the system requires for its own operation. Other talents and capacities which are not indispensable for the system are superfluous and unreal. They are unreal in the true and original sense of the world. They cannot be actualised and realised, they cannot become the *real* activity of man, or transform into a

---

45   Kosík 1976, pp. 44–5.
46   Ideology has no history in two senses. 1) Ideology has no autonomy; it is only a reflection of processes that are external to it. Its history is outside of it. This is why Althusser proclaims that 'ideology has no history, which emphatically does not mean that there is no history in it (on the contrary, for it is merely the pale, empty and inverted reflection of real history) but that it has no history *of its own*' (Althusser 2008, p. 34). 2) Ideology *in general* (ideology as such, not its particular historical forms) is 'omni-historical', in the sense that its 'structure and functioning are immutable, present in the same form throughout what we can call history'. Althusser 2008, pp. 34–5.
47   Kosík 1976, p. 46.
48   Kosík 1976, p. 50.
49   Ibid.
50   Ibid.
51   Kosík 1976, p. 52 (Kosík's emphasis).

real world for man to live in. They amount to an unreal world of privacy, irrelevance, of the romantic.[52]

As a result, a mystified subject governs over the real subject. In the capitalist system it is the commodity that plays the role of this 'mystified and mystifying subject'.[53] Things and persons become interchangeable. 'Things are personified and persons are reified. Things are invested with will and consciousness [...] and people turn into agents and executors of the movement of things'.[54] The response to this should be that a true subject (i.e. man) comes to replace the mystified subject by means of an emancipatory act, thus becoming real, no longer a simple function of the requirements of the system, becoming someone who determines his proper life and action. Under capitalism, truly human activities, i.e. activities that develop humans' universal potentiality, are considered in certain sense 'unreal' if they do not valorise capital and do not reproduce the dominant social relations. This means that this potential cannot be fully realised under capitalism. For Kosík emancipation means the transformation of this 'unreal' true subject into a real true subject. This process of the humanisation of man is at the same time a process of what might be called the 'de-reification' of man. Man, in other words, ceases to be a mere vehicle of the logic of capital and becomes the proper subject of his own actions. Kosík thus disagrees with the frequently expressed conviction that the law determining the social movement of things, that is, the law of capital, is the *real* subject of the movement of the capitalist system. This law, he says, represents only a 'real semblance',[55] not a fundamental reality.[56]

In this context, Kosík observes that Marx's *Capital* is not only a *critique* or *critical* theory of capital but is also an analysis of the replacement of persons by things.[57] Furthermore, besides 'describing objective formations of capital's social movement and the *forms of consciousness* of its agents that correspond to these formations, andbesides tracing the objective laws of the system's *func-*

---

52 Kosík 1976, pp. 54–5.
53 Kosík 1976, p. 110.
54 Kosík 1976, p. 116.
55 Ibid.
56 According to Althusser, history is, on the contrary, a 'process without subject'. Moishe Postone on this question claims that Althusser's thesis is transhistorical and is thus in opposition to Marx's methodological principle that categories (if they are not pure abstractions) are always historically specific. The concept of history as a process without subject is thus for Postone correct only for the capitalist period, but incorrect as a transhistorical conception of history. See Postone 2003, p. 77.
57 Kosík 1976, p. 116.

tioning [...] [*Capital*] also investigates the genesis and the process of forming the *subject* who will carry out a *revolutionary destruction of the system*'.[58]

This emancipation is accomplished, according to Kosík, by '*revolutionary* practical action based on [the] cognition' of what the human being really 'is in itself'.[59] This means that a true subject will recognise that it is in fact a true subject, and it will act in accordance with this recognition.

3   The Non-reductionist Conception of the Subject

Kosík devotes most of *Dialectics of the Concrete* to various types of mystified subjects that are reducible to and determined by external forces. As we indicated in the previous section, however, we can also find in Kosík's work another type of subject, one that is irreducible to anything else. This conception of the subject is based on a non-reductionist theory of reality and on a non-reductionist ontology of man. It draws on the idea that man is 'always more than a system, and *as man* he cannot be reduced to one. The existence of the concrete man spans the distance between his irreducibility to a system and the possibility to transcend it, and his actual location and practical functioning in a particular system (of historical circumstances and relations)'.[60]

This means that man, in Kosík's conception, is not fully determined by the logic of the system but rather escapes this logic. Man is a form of subject characterised by a *cleavage* between his subordination to a system and his irreducibility to that system.[61]

Kosík, in line with the tradition of humanist Marxism, refuses to see man as an absolute and total effect of the system, and he refuses to see man's thought and actions as pure products of ideological praxis and of ideological state apparatuses. According to Kosík, exterior determination can never be 'complete' or absolute. The ontological structure of reality is understood (for ontological and logical reasons that I must leave aside in this paper) as a space of randomness and possibility, which are not reducible in advance to causes. The fact that something escapes exterior determination also makes possible the creation of the 'ontologically new' and onto-formative character of the reality,[62] which is crucial for Kosík's philosophy.[63] (If everything were determined

---

58   Kosík 1976, p. 112.
59   Kosík 1976, p. 111.
60   Kosík 1976, p. 56.
61   Kosík 1976, p. 44.
62   Kosík 1976, p. 102.
63   This is interconnected with Kosík's effort to conceptualise a non-mechanical form of

by exterior mechanical causality – in other words if mechanical causality were the only existing type of causality – reality would be a mechanical machine in which nothing is *newly* created and the old merely manifests itself over time.[64]) For Kosík it is of central importance that the ontologically new *can* be created, that the human being is fundamentally 'onto-formative'.[65] Man is characterised by Kosík as an 'onto-formative being'[66] and praxis is characterised as a process of creating the ontological new. Labour, by contrast, refers to external economic necessity, while praxis permeates the essence of man's being in all its manifestations. 'Praxis permeates the *whole* of man and determines him in his totality. Praxis is not an *external* determination'.[67] But there is also another dimension of praxis. Praxis also includes 'an *existential moment*: it manifests itself both in man's objective activity by which he transforms nature and chisels human meanings into natural material, and in the *process of forming* the human subject in which existential moments such as anxiety, nausea, fear, joy, laughter, hope, etc. stand out not as positive 'experiencing', but as a part of the struggle for recognition, i.e. of the process of realising human freedom. Without the existential moment, labor would cease to be component of praxis'.[68]

4 Badiou's Conception of the Subject

This 'demystified subject' as conceived by Kosík is of course foreign to Althusser's conception of subjection. Nevertheless, it bears certain similarities to

---

causality. This is, by the way, another similarity with Althusser's philosophy. Consider Althusser's concept of structural causality (which is not, of course, a multiplication of mechanistic causality, but something completely different).

[64] This is also why Kosík argues against reductionism. Reductionism makes impossible the creation of the ontologically new and denies in fact the onto-formative character of all (not only the human) being. '[R]eductionism cannot rationally explain *new* phenomena, or qualitative development. It will reduce anything new to conditions and prerequisites; the new is 'nothing but' the old'. Kosík 1976, p. 14.

[65] The category of the 'onto-formative', as well as the category of the 'ontologically new', have been described and systematically analysed in relation to various ontological models by the Czech philosopher Egon Bondy (given name Zbyněk Fišer). Erich Fromm called Egon Bondy 'one of the most outstanding, though little-known, Czech philosophers', and added that 'unfortunately, his work has been published only in the Czech language and hence has been inaccessible to most Western readers. (I know it from a private English translation.)' See Fromm 1997, p. 22. We would like to note here that since that time Bondy's most important work has been made available to English readers: See Bondy 2001.

[66] Kosík 1976, p. 137.

[67] Ibid.

[68] Kosík 1976, p. 138.

the theory of the subject put forth by Alain Badiou. Badiou's theory is naturally very sophisticated, and we do not want to discuss it here in detail. But since Badiou's theory represents a currently influential attempt to work through some of the problems posed by Althusser's theory of the subject, it is worth very roughly sketching out certain features of this theory and comparing them with Kosík's theory.

Badiou's conception of the subject, however, raises an important problem. As Nick Hewlett has stressed, 'the role of the subjects of a political event is, paradoxically, a highly passive one until the event has taken place, at which point the role of the subjects becomes crucial. [...] For Badiou true politics is about sudden and serious change in the form of an event, and not about ongoing power struggles which sometimes erupt into emancipatory events'.[69] Hewlett adds that in Badiou's theoretical framework 'subjects play no part in causing events'.[70] Thus, although Badiou has revived the concept of the active subject, this subject remains limited in its capacity for action.

For Althusser, as we have said, the subject is basically an ideological subject incapable of interrupting the logic of the system, because it is an effect of ideological interpellations and ideological state apparatuses. Badiou's theory of the subject, for its part, has difficulty explaining how we can *prepare* an event if the event is defined as *unpredictable* and if the subject is defined by an act of fidelity to the event (after the event has already passed), and is rather a consequence of the event than its cause. What is missing is a concept of praxis or of 'revolutionary praxis', which was central to Kosík's conception of the subject.

5   Kosík's Conception of the Subject

Unlike Althusser's and Badiou's conceptions of the subject, Kosík's conception is closely linked to an ontology of man and to the concepts of praxis and labour.[71] Kosík characterises labour in terms of a variety of dichotomies, such as animality versus humanity, causality versus teleology, subject versus object. Labour itself stands out as an active centre in which the dialectical unity of these pairs is *realised*.[72] Labour is for Kosík 'involved in the realm of *necessity*',[73]

---

69   Hewlett 2010, pp. 81–2.
70   Hewlett 2010, p. 54.
71   'The problem of labour as a *philosophical* question and as a *philosophy of labour* is based on an ontology of man'. Kosík 1976, p. 119.
72   Kosík 1976, p. 123.
73   Kosík 1976, p. 124.

but at the same time it transcends this necessity and creates conditions for the realisation of freedom. Economics is the realm of necessity (of the objective doing of labour) in which the historical prerequisites of human freedom are *formed*.[74] Since Kosík approached 'the investigation of economics from an analysis of labor', economics appeared to him 'to be primarily not a *ready-made* economic structure of reality, [...] but rather a socio-human reality *in the process of formation*, a reality based on man's *objective-practical* doing'.[75]

The forming of the new, that is, the *ontologically new*, which is not reducible to given conditions or prerequisites, is directly linked to the onto-formative character of human praxis.[76] Reality in its concreteness is comprehensible only from the standpoint of practice. It is described as a process of forming and re-forming reality. Reality *is* this process, the process of *qualitative* development.

Incidentally, on this point we can see a similarity between Kosík and Badiou, for whom the ontologically new represents a supernumerary point of given conditions, of a 'situation'. But whereas for Badiou this supernumerary point represents an inexplicable and unpredictable *event*, for Kosík the possibility of transcending given conditions is drawn from a conception of emancipatory praxis.

Kosík tries to avoid the dualism of subject and object, internal and external,[77] and 'conditions and people'.[78] These pairs are mutually mediated. 'People enter conditions independently of their consciousness and of their will but 'once there', they transform these conditions. Conditions do not exist without people, nor people without conditions. This is the basis for the development of a *dialectic* between *conditions* that are *given* for every generation, epoch, class, and action that unfolds on the basis of ready-made and given prerequisites'.[79]

For Kosík, 'social reality' is infinitely more variegated and concrete than conditions and circumstances (which correspond roughly to Badiou's concept of *situation*[80]), precisely *'because it includes human objective praxis* which forms

---

74 Kosík 1976, p. 126.
75 Ibid.
76 Kosík 1976, p. 137.
77 Kosík 1976, p. 47.
78 Kosík 1976, p. 74. We can observe a similarly 'antidualistic' approach in Althusser's undermining of internal and external and of materiality and ideality.
79 Kosík 1976, pp. 146–7.
80 A situation is defined by Badiou as a 'presented multiplicity' [*multiplicité présentée*] (Badiou 2006, p. 181. See also Badiou 1988, p. 24). Badiou defines the event as the supernumerary [*surnuméraire*] point of the situation. 'If there is an event, *its belonging to the situation of its site is undecidable from the point of view of the situation itself*'. Ibid.

these conditions and circumstances'.[81] The concept of *objective-practical* doing is key to conceptualising the possibility of the emergence of a subversive subject.

Praxis inserts into reality meaning and values, which cannot be deduced from given conditions. Kosík refers to the following example: 'For the peasant serf, "conditions" [are] the immediate natural situation of life; indirectly, through his action, resistance or in a peasant uprising, he gives them the signification of [...] *more* than a part of conditions'.[82] This 'more than' can be compared to Badiou's term 'supernumerary'. For Kosík, the essence of this 'more than' is located, as we have said, in the nature of emancipatory praxis.[83]

Throughout his philosophy, Kosík stresses the importance of the category of the subject, and this category's importance is especially salient in his evaluation of Marx's *Capital*. In a passage from *Dialectics of the Concrete* criticising Plekhanov's understanding of *Capital*, Kosík writes that

> Plekhanov parts ways with Marx in the *cardinal point* at which Marxist materialism has succeeded in transcending both the *weaknesses* of all previous kinds of materialism and the strong points of *idealism*: that is, in its grasp of the subject. *Objective praxis, Marx's most important discovery, consequently entirely drops out of the materialist conception of history*. Plekhanovist analyses [...] lack the constitutive elements of objective human praxis. [They lack] 'human sensory activity' which cannot be reduced to 'psyché' or to the 'spirit of the times'.[84]

If Kosík is right, it should be asked whether contemporary conceptions of the subject and philosophies of emancipatory politics might not do well to return to this 'cardinal point', to 'Marx's most important discovery', and to analyse the possibility of the subversive subject on the basis of the categories of concrete praxis, labour and mediation, which are practically missing from contemporary post-Marxism.

On the other hand, it should also be emphasised that the concept of praxis did not only disappear from post-Marxist discourse in general; over time it also decreased in importance in Kosík's own thought. This was symptomatic and no accident. An explanation should be sought in the extra-theoretical conditions that prevailed after 1968. We can keep in mind that for Kosík the destruction

---

81   Kosík 1976, p. 74.
82   Kosík 1976, p. 147.
83   See Kosík 1976, p. 147.
84   Kosík 1976, pp. 76–7.

of the pseudoconcrete could be realised in three ways: 1) *estrangement*, that is, by maintaining a certain distance from the 'alienated everyday' and 'forcing it', that is, doing away with its familiarity; one manner of this 'forcing' is present in art;[85] 2) *existential modification*; and 3) *revolutionary transformation*.[86] It is clear that for Kosík the third way is the most important and fundamental.[87]

Nevertheless, it also seems that in the 1960s Kosík overestimated the possibilities for realising 'revolutionary praxis'. After 1968 it became obvious that there was very little chance of praxis overturning the given social relations, and the concept of praxis disappeared from the centre of Kosík's intellectual attention. (This fact fundamentally conditioned the qualitative shifts in Kosík's later philosophical development – but that is not our theme here.[88]) Something similar was experienced by Marxist theorists in the West. We stand before a problem. If Kosík was right when he claimed that *'If we want to explain the world critically, the explication itself must be grounded in the field of revolutionary praxis'*,[89] then we face the question of how to 'explain the world critically' in a period when it is not possible (for objective reasons) to enter the 'field of revolutionary praxis'.

This reveals certain limits to Kosík's applicability to our times. Even still, Kosík's effort to investigate the world of the pseudoconcrete and the possibilit-

---

85 Art plays an important role in this process. The role of the artist (if we may take an expression from the Czech poet Karel Kryl) is to let others see in reality what they do not see or what they *do not want to see* (Kryl 1990). This presupposes that art can shape or transform (or 'force') reality by specifically artistic activity, in which reality and our role in society are seen suddenly very differently than in everyday (alienated) life. This disproportion between reality and the artistic shaping of reality is the very condition of art as such. Kosík discusses, in particular, the example of modern art: 'One of the main principles of modern art, poetry and drama, of painting and film-making is, we feel, the "forcing" of the everyday, the destruction of the pseudoconcrete'. Kosík 1976, p. 49. Kosík adds that simply 'presenting the truth about human reality is rightly felt to be something other than this reality itself, and it is therefore insufficient'. Kosík 1976, p. 49. We can see in this a key to understanding why contemporary art such as conceptualism, which programmatically dismisses the distance between the everyday and itself, is not satisfactory, and why most people simply ignore it.
86 Kosík 1976, p. 48.
87 'The existential modification is not a revolutionary transformation of the world but *the-drama of an individual in the world*. [...] *This* form of existential modification is, however, not [...] the most adequate way for an individual's authentic realisation to take place. It, too, is only an historical choice with a quite precise social and class content'. Kosík 1976, p. 49.
88 On this point, see Jan Černý's contribution in this volume, pp. 281–303.
89 Kosík 1966, p. 16. I have altered the existing English translation, which is somewhat inaccurate. See Kosík 1976, p. 7. Kosík's emphasis.

ies of its overcoming, his analysis of phenomenal forms of reality and their genesis, his analysis of how a 'necessary real semblance' is created in this process, his analysis of the real process of replacing people by things, his investigation into the mechanism by which a true subject is made invisible, paralysed and transformed into a simple agent of the capitalist mechanism – all this remains stimulating today in spite of changing social conditions.

Kosík's effort to conceptualise the possibility of a subversive subject capable of radical emancipatory politics – on the basis of an analysis of everyday fetishised reality, in which people are reduced to agents and 'holders' of functions of the social mechanism – is still worthy of attention, as we have tried to demonstrate.

Even if a concept of 'revolutionary praxis', in the sense assigned to it by Kosík, seems to be inapplicable in the foreseeable future, Kosík's thought presents contemporary philosophy with the challenge of conceptualising a subject of radical emancipation at a time when no revolutionary practice is on the agenda.

CHAPTER 14

Karel Kosík and Martin Heidegger: From Marxism to Traditionalism

Jan Černý

The widespread acceptance of Karel Kosík's *Dialectics of the Concrete*[1] was due to the fact that Kosík's book presented Marx's philosophical heritage, which had been rendered petrified and sterile under the control of the ideological apparatus of 'bureaucratic socialism' (as Kosík himself later called the regime at the time), as vivid and capable of dialogue with other currents of philosophical thought. *Dialectics of the Concrete* managed to incorporate phenomenological, existentialist or hermeneutical elements within the framework of a Marxist philosophy of praxis. However *concrete* these elements were, they were submitted to the course of historical-materialistic *dialectics*, i.e. to the course of a Marxist methodology. Implementing elements from non-Marxist philosophies was Kosík's way of broadening the political-economic horizons of the thinking of the mature Marx and of making explicit Kosík's ontological concern – yet the resulting ontology of human praxis was clearly a Marxist, or more precisely a Neo-Marxist one.

I will argue in this essay that while the thinking of Martin Heidegger was just one (albeit important) non-Marxist element present within the pattern of *Dialectics of the Concrete*, the later development of Kosík's thought, especially the later phase of his work presented in the texts from the 1990s, made the Czech philosopher a Heideggerian thinker and, in a certain sense, a traditionalist whose 'critical thinking' simply incorporated *some* Marxist elements. I will also examine more closely the discrepancies to be found in such an attempt to synthesise traditionalist thought with the emancipatory aim of a politically progressive line of thought, and especially the tension between Kosík's democratism and traditionalist hierarchical ontology.

---

1 Miroslav Pauza writes that according to the witnesses of the publication of *Dialectics of the Concrete*, the book was almost a 'revelation' to its Czech readers. See Pauza 2011, p. 96. *Dialectics of the Concrete* was also translated into several languages and earned Kosík an international reputation.

1 Heidegger within *Dialectics of the Concrete*: A Critical Dialogue

The dialogue with Martin Heidegger within *Dialectics of the Concrete* is a critical dialogue – it handles Heideggerian concepts from the critical standpoint of historical dialectics. The dialogue takes place, first of all, in the chapter entitled 'Metaphysics of Everyday Life', which opens with an analysis of 'care' understood as '[t]he primary and elementary mode in which economics exists for man'.[2] Initially the Heideggerian origin of the term remains hidden,[3] but it comes to Heidegger explicitly soon after. Kosík incorporates the term into the dialectics of the individual and the social: care is the way in which the individual is entangled in the social world and thus to the element of the anonymous as the objective aspect of the social order (because the subject does not view the network of social relations objectively in her everyday care). This interpretation of care is not alien to its rendering in *Being and Time*: For Heidegger also, care (*Sorge*) is the basic pattern of our being embedded within the world, the expression of our basic ontological characteristics as being-in-the-world.[4] For Heidegger, however, the worldliness of our existence is specified not primarily or exclusively as a social relation: it concerns others as well as things. Care is the manner in which we understand ourselves and the world we live in. This understanding of the whole of our being unfolds itself, first and foremost, as an inauthentic one, as falling prey (*Verfallen*) to the anonymity of a general public point of view (*das Man*). Yet there is also another option: to understand myself not from the public point of view, but from my own adoption of the authentic possibility to be myself as a finite being.

In contrast with this double self-understanding of the caring self, Kosík lays down only the first, inauthentic one. The author of *Dialectics of the Concrete* does not locate the opposition of authentic/inauthentic mode of being and understanding in care, but transforms it into the opposition of praxis (or labour)[5]/procuring; procuring is a sub-type of care and designates handling with natural and – more often – cultural objects and relations in labour for

---

2   Kosík 1976, p. 37.
3   As noted by Miroslav Pauza (in the above-mentioned article), Kosík often hides the primary source of his philosophical inspiration behind the authors who held an ideologically more neutral position in the perspective of the dominating 'orthodox' philosophical discourse; it is Johann Gottfried Herder who is cited as the source of the term 'care'. See Kosík 1976, p. 37.
4   See Heidegger 1996, pp. 178–83.
5   Kosík protests against the merging of praxis and labour found in Marxist literature (cf. Kosík 1976, p. 119, n. 42), yet labour represents just one part of praxis in his definition of praxis at the same time – this gives Kosík an opportunity to speak of both the opposition of labour/procuring and praxis/procuring (on p. 39 and p. 41).

Kosík.[6] Praxis, understood by the Czech philosopher as labour plus the existential moment of 'the struggle for recognition, i.e. of the process of realising human freedom',[7] is an authentic way of understanding our being and the whole of reality, for in praxis humans create *and* understand reality as socio-human reality.[8] Care as procuring, on the other hand, is for Kosík 'the phenomenal aspect of abstract labor'.[9] The dialectical opposition of phenomenon and essence is the basic structure of the ontology of *Dialectics of the Concrete*, and it is clear that care (as procuring) falls by the wayside of the phenomenal world of 'the pseudoconcrete' for the Czech thinker.

This stance towards care is rooted in the Marxist methodology of *Dialectics of the Concrete*, in its historical-material dialectics. Kosík offers criticism of Heidegger's notion of care by historicising it. The existential ontology provided in *Being and Time* is trans-historical – it describes the transcendental features of human existence (and understands the historicity of existence as one of them). *Dialectics of the Concrete* tries to locate the analysis of *Being and Time* in the specific phase of the development of capitalist production in the twentieth century.[10] Procuring as a 'phenomenally alienated form' of praxis is, for Kosík, the expression of the fetishisation of human relations, which has reached its apex within a technically highly developed society.[11] The human handles technical inventions in procuring her life, giving everything meaning only within this availability of manipulation.[12]

The criticism of the 'philosophy of care' (as Kosík names it) of the German philosopher culminates in the rejection of Heidegger's understanding of care as the source of the (authentic) temporality of human existence.[13] Because care,

---

6   Kosík 1976, p. 38. The conceptual couple care/procuring also has its origin in *Being and Time*: Heidegger understands by procuring (*Besorgen* – Stambaugh's translation of *Being and Time* renders the term 'taking care') the specific case of care (*Sorge*) – procuring is the actual handling of inner-worldly being. See Heidegger 1996, p. 180.
7   Kosík 1976, p. 138.
8   See the chapter 'Praxis' in Kosík 1976, pp. 133–40.
9   Kosík 1976, p. 38.
10 Kosík mentions this explicitly in a footnote, where he accuses Heidegger of a romantic hiding of the reality of twentieth-century capitalism behind his patriarchal examples of the smith and ironwork. See Kosík 1976, p. 40, n. 2.
11 See Kosík 1976, pp. 38–42.
12 This critique of the technological understanding of both things and people reminds one, in fact, of Heidegger's later criticism of technology as our only mode of understanding being. See Heidegger 1977, pp. 3–35. Kosík denies, however, that he was familiar with Heidegger's later criticism of technology at the time of working on *Dialectics of the Concrete*. See Kosík 1993e, p. 14.
13 See Heidegger 1996, p. 281.

for Kosík, bears in itself only an alienated mode of self-understanding of the human, it brings us to an inauthentic understanding of the timing of our existence: in care we find ourselves always in the future and never really in the actual present. According to Kosík, the being of the human opens up in care as a 'fetishised future'.[14] Heidegger's category of 'anticipation' (of death, *Vorlaufen zum Tode*), which stands for the whole of our existence and represents the authentic mode of being for the German thinker,[15] is explicitly rejected – for Kosík, 'to anticipate' is to live in nothingness and inauthenticity; to live in the future does not mean overcoming alienation; on the contrary, it can be an 'alienated escape from alienation'.

Later, Kosík advances his own competing version of the source of the (authentic) temporality of human existence. In developing his philosophy of labour as an ontology of human being understood as working being, Kosík utilises the Hegelian opposition of animal and human craving (Hegel's *Begierde* and *Trieb*) within the dialectical process of differentiating the human from the animal.[16] Kosík finds the origin of human temporality in the harnessing of craving in labour: '[...] only a being which transcends the nihilism of its animal craving in labor will, in the act of harnessing its craving, uncover a *future* as a dimension of its being'.[17] The human understands the present as a function of the future, and utilises the past in the act of harnessing. It is only through labour as objective doing (producing a product), Kosík argues against Heidegger, that we are aware of our temporality and death.[18] Joining the uncovering of the temporality of our existence with labour – harnessing craving is the moment of labour – is also Kosík's polemic with the manner in which Heidegger distinguishes authentic from inauthentic temporality. Besides harnessing craving, which might be considered the origin of authentic temporality, concerning the whole of a human's being, Kosík writes about the objectivity of labour as the source of the three-dimensionality of time: The labour process gives rise to the temporal sequence, to progression in time, and at the same time to the duration of a product of labour as the condensation or abolition of the succession of time.[19] While for Heidegger this would be a perfect example of inauthentic temporality born out of procuring a particular thing

---

14 See Kosík 1976, p. 42.
15 See Heidegger 1996, pp. 240–6.
16 See Kosík 1976, p. 121.
17 Ibid.
18 See Kosík 1976, p. 123.
19 See Kosík 1976, p. 122. Kosík has in mind Marx's analysis of labour as a cycle of being in motion and producing a product without motion in the first book of *Capital*. See Marx 1967, p. 189.

in the world,[20] Kosík consciously joins the temporality of harnessing craving with the temporality of the process of objectification in labour. By contrast, as I have argued above, for Kosík inauthentic temporality represents the procuring of one's existence within the alienated apparatus of modern technology, where labour is not experienced and understood as creating socio-human reality.

Kosík's theory of the origin of temporality is a good example of his critical dialogue with Heidegger in *Dialectics of the Concrete*. Joining the ontology of the human with her temporality, the ontological concern itself, distinguishing authentic temporality from inauthentic – all of these thoughts are of Heideggerian inspiration. Yet at the same time Kosík expends much energy in contrasting his Marxist, materialistic position with the 'idealistic' – as he finds it – position of Heidegger: he refuses to consider care to be the source of the authentic temporality of human existence and replaces it with labour. By doing this, he inverts Heidegger's opposition of authentic/inauthentic mode of being – care cannot be at the origin of authentic temporality (it is on the contrary the source of inauthentic existence within the technological understanding of being), and objectification is not a form of flight from authenticity, because it fundamentally belongs to labour, which is the real source of authentic temporality.[21]

Kosík sums up his critical position towards Heidegger's existential ontology of *Being and Time* by saying that the 'philosophy of care' is 'mystifying-demystifying'.[22] It is demystifying because it rightly describes prevalent everyday life as inauthentic – in procuring one's existence in familiarity with things, the human in fact remains far removed from herself, falsely united with the surrounding world.[23] Yet it is also mystifying, for it does not see the everyday as a historical-social construct and therefore does not possess the methodological tools for explaining the alienation that arises in the everyday. The objectification of humanity arises with the fact that the human produces reality as socio-human reality, that the objectivity of reality is objectified human praxis. Now, it can ensue only from the very praxis of a single human and of mankind that the anonymity of the objective aspect of reality will be permeated by authen-

---

20 See Heidegger 1996, pp. 310–11.
21 Jan Patočka, himself a pupil of Heidegger, finds Kosík's attempt to explain the original structure of time out of labour reductive and unsatisfying. Patočka rejects Kosík's attempt to build ontology on labour, and argues that a mere instrumental activity (labour) cannot relate itself to the whole of the world. See Patočka 2004a, p. 209; see also Zouhar 2009, pp. 69–73. Patočka's critique had a major influence on the next development of Kosík's thinking and contributed to his shift towards a more positive acceptance of the Heideggerian heritage. See the essay of Ivan Landa in this volume, pp. 75–106.
22 See Kosík 1976, p. 46.
23 See Heidegger 1996, pp. 118–22.

tic humanity in the destruction of the pseudoconcrete.[24] Three ways of this destruction are described: the estrangement of the pseudo-concrete in modern art; the existential modification of individual life; the revolutionary transformation of the social world. The second way, specified as living an individual life *sub specie mortis*, is once more inspired by Heidegger's existential ontology. Yet Kosík also notes, in contrast with Heidegger's transcendental attitude, the historical-social and class condition of such an existential modification. And he adds that '[t]*his* form of the existential modification is, however, not the only way, or even the most frequent or the most adequate way for an individual's authentic realisation'.[25]

The wording 'mystifying-demystifying', used for the assessment of Heidegger's fundamental ontology, thus encapsulates Kosík's general attitude towards Heidegger in *Dialectics of the Concrete*. Kosík accepts the need to relate the human to the whole of that which is, and the need to uncover alienating structures of the everyday which obscure that relation. Yet he finds Heidegger's phenomenology of the everyday insufficiently critical. Moreover, the purified phenomena of Dasein's *authentic* life remain for Kosík within the realm of the pseudoconcrete: these do not reveal the essence of life as praxis. Although Heidegger's starting point for the analysis of human life is (everyday) action, Heidegger does not come to an understanding of praxis as *historical* activity bearing in itself *creation* and understanding of reality. Human activity is, for Heidegger, the manner in which a human understands reality and herself, but it is considered only as a step on the way towards uncovering the sense of being as such. The later development of Heidegger's thought after *Being and Time* further underscores the primacy of being over the human, who is now appropriated ('en-owned', '*er-eignet*') by being.[26] Yet for Kosík's Marxist humanism of *Dialectics of the Concrete*, it must be the human who stands at the centre of creating reality as socio-human reality.

2   Kosík and Heidegger in the 1960s: Heideggerian Marxism

As we know, Karel Kosík did not publish any major work after *Dialectics of the Concrete*.[27] The only sources for examining the subsequent development

---

24   See Kosík 1976, pp. 47–9.
25   Kosík 1976, p. 49.
26   See Heidegger 1999, p. 19, p. 169, p. 173.
27   In fact, Kosík did publish – besides the collections of his essays, lectures and articles – a

of his thought are his lectures, essays, articles, conference contributions and unpublished manuscripts. The critical edition of all of these texts has not yet been completed;[28] the most important published texts can be found in another three Czech collections[29] and in several collections in other languages.[30] The remainder of my essay will examine the relation of Kosík to the thought of Heidegger in the texts gathered in these collections.

There are – in my opinion – two major currents of thought to be found in Kosík's work of the 1960s after the appearance of *Dialectics of the Concrete* in 1963. The first, represented by texts such as 'The Dialectics of Morality and the Morality of Dialectics',[31] or 'The Individual and History'[32] can be labelled as contributions to 'Humanist Marxism', the effort to prevent the reduction of the human to mere historical-social categories; the sacralisation of history, not allowing for the removal of the alienation of the individual, was considered by many Marxists of that era to be the main heritage of the Stalinist ideology. These texts of Kosík prolong the philosophical direction proposed in *Dialectics of the Concrete*, not only in this humanist respect, but also in respect of methodology: they comprise – however brief – materialistic dialectical analysis. And regarding the main interest of this paper – the reader does not find any major Heideggerian influence or dialogue with Heidegger therein.

Yet very soon after the publication of *Dialectics of the Concrete*, readers were presented with yet another type of Kosík's texts: texts in which criticism of the modern technological attitude to reality is one of the key issues, and the Stalinist deformation of socialism falls within the description of the broader crisis of modern civilisation. From a certain time, certainly from 1968 (the year of the publication of the essays 'Our Current Crisis' and 'Socialism and Crisis of Modern Man') onwards, the description of the crisis of modern civilisation works with the conceptuality of the later Heidegger. It is difficult to determine the exact time when Kosík became acquainted with the writings of the later Heidegger, Heidegger after his 'turn',[33] but it is clear that, at least from 1968 on,

---

'book', the 40-page long essay, *A Youth and Death* in 1995, perhaps his most Heideggerian text ever. See Kosík 1995m. I will examine this text later.

28   A critical edition of Kosík's collected writings is being prepared at the Institute of Philosophy of the Czech Academy of Sciences; the first volume to be published (volume four) covers essays from the period between 1955 and 1969. See Kosík 2019.
29   Kosík 1993; Kosík 1997; Kosík 2004.
30   For example: Kosík 1995; Kosík 2003b; Kosík 1969c.
31   In Kosík 1995h, pp. 63–76.
32   In Kosík 1995i, pp. 123–34.
33   'The turn' ('*die Kehre*') is a notion signifying the reorientation of Heidegger's thought after *Being and Time* in the 1930s. The interest in temporal structures of human existence was

they exercised a major influence on his thought.[34] The questions of technology, truth and art, the nihilism of the modern era, the need for salvation of the world gradually become the focal point also in the work of the Czech philosopher. Karel Kosík later declared in the 1990s that he considered Heidegger the thinker who analysed 'the reality of the 20th century' with the same analytical depth as Marx did in his analysis of the reality of the nineteenth century.[35]

Kosík's *Kehre*, if we may borrow the term, was, similarly as in the case of Heidegger, motivated by literary texts. It was not, however, the pre-technological world of 'mortals and gods' of Hölderlin that accompanied Kosík in moving the direction of his thought; it was, on the contrary, a description of the grotesque features of alienated human existence in the midst of the modern world found in the works of two authors born in Prague: Jaroslav Hašek and Franz Kafka. In 1963, the year of publication of *Dialectics of the Concrete*, Kosík published the essay 'Hašek and Kafka, or the World of the Grotesque',[36] where he portrays Hašek's 'good soldier Švejk' as a figure mirroring and at the same time transcending the absurd bureaucratic machinery of a modern war. According to Kosík, this machinery creates 'the Great Mechanism' which 'adjusts the man to its own needs, modifies him according to its own logic, and forces him to accept a certain behavior'.[37] The 'Great Mechanism' is the first appearance of and the first name given to, within the collections of Kosík's essays, the system of the modern rational and manipulative attitude to reality, which became the main target of Kosík's criticism for the rest of his career.

There is a positive solution to the problem offered in the essay: Švejk overcomes the 'rationalized and calculated system' of the Great Mechanism through his *autonomous* behaviour – he cannot be reduced to the demands of the system. This solution marks another important feature of Kosík's essays:

---

replaced by the examination of the history of being itself, as found within the history of Western metaphysics. The current age was then understood as nihilistic, as the emptying of the sense of being in a technological understanding of being. Heidegger's works after the turn were less systematic than *Being and Time* and the source of inspiration for them were both philosophical and literary texts – the features we find also with Kosík after *Dialectics of the Concrete*.

34 To my knowledge, the first mention of the later Heidegger's work by Kosík is to be found in his contribution to the collection of essays edited by Erich Fromm under the title *Socialist Humanism: An International Symposium* in 1965. See Kosík 1965b. The reference, however, is critical: Kosík accuses 'the later philosophy of Heidegger' of overburdening being insofar as it gains a certain independence in relation to the human, whose being is in question.

35 See Kosík 1993e, p. 14.

36 In Kosík 1995b, pp. 77–86. The literary work of Hašek and Kafka was a frequent subject of Kosík's interpretation throughout the 1960s and the 1990s.

37 Kosík 1995b, p. 83.

democratism and democratic humanism.[38] Švejk is an emblematic figure of the 'common human' facing the dehumanised systems of a modern anonymous power; and there is a deep faith in the ability of the 'common people' to act authentically and to overcome the alienating structures of a reified reality in Kosík's writings.

If we take into consideration Kosík's statement that he was not familiar with the writings of the later Heidegger in 1963, we can view his later development as a Heideggerian conceptualisation of his own critical enterprise. Two important essays from the time of the Prague Spring in 1968, 'Our Current Crisis',[39] and 'Socialism and Crisis of Modern Man',[40] offer a synthesis of Marxist thinking with the type of criticism towards modern civilisation which we find in later Heidegger; the synthesis thus represents a specific type of Heideggerian Marxism. Both essays place the Stalinist deformation of socialism within the broader crisis of modern civilisation; Kosík speaks of '[...] a system of generalized manipulation in both of its currently reigning forms: both as bureaucratic Stalinism and as democratic capitalism'.[41] The crisis of modern civilisation is described in a clearly Heideggerian fashion: it is based upon the description of the affinity of modern science and technology and of the hermeneutical and ontological consequences of their epistemological hegemony in modern civilisation; Kosík finds that 'the essence of technology' is 'the technical rationality that organizes reality into a system that can be grasped, perfected, and objectified', or that 'The basis of modern science and technology is the technical understanding that converts reality (being) into a secure, verified, and manipulated object'.[42] Yet similarly, as in many places of *Dialectics of the Concrete*, Kosík conceals the Heideggerian origin of his thoughts, and ascribes this criticism of technological reasoning to other thinkers – Hegel, Condorcet, Kant and Marx in this case – directly following the passage of his text using manifestly Heideggerian thoughts and Heideggerian vocabulary.[43]

---

38   The 'democratic' line of Kosík's writings returns to his first book *Czech Radical Democracy* (Kosík 1958), examining the political and philosophical thought of Czech radical and revolutionary democrats of the nineteenth century on the background of the European radical democratic movement.
39   Kosík 1995d, pp. 17–51.
40   Kosík 1995f, pp. 53–62. The lecture *Socialism and Crisis of Modern Man*, in fact, takes most of its motifs and formulations from the essay *Our Current Crisis*, but adds the important motive of dialectics.
41   Kosík 1995f, p. 55.
42   Kosík 1995d, p. 38. For Heidegger's criticism of technological reason see Heidegger 1977.
43   See Kosík 1995d, p. 38 and p. 58.

The synthesis of Marxism with later Heideggerian thought then runs as follows: Heideggerian conceptuality serves as a critical tool for the description of the modern crisis of both socialist and capitalist society; Marxian historical dialectics (in theory and in political praxis) provides an escape from the prison of technological reason. In 'Socialism and the Crisis of Modern Man', Kosík identifies the system of generalised manipulation, promoted by technical science, with a false consciousness unable to distinguish between truth and untruth, good and evil. Now, it is the task of dialectical reasoning to eliminate the false identification of technical rationality with rationality in general.[44] Kosík underscores at the same time that dialectics is not just a method of thinking, but a kind of wisdom linked to the ontological questions of being, truth and time. And he finds a specific political realisation of such dialectics at work in the Prague Spring: democratic socialism, realised in the popular movement of 1968 (the alliance of all classes with the possibility of inner opposition, renewed political democracy, workers' councils or councils of producers), is a liberating alternative to the system of universal manipulation and it brings an 'absolutely different conceptualisation of man, nature, truth and history'.[45] Dialectics is the means of recognising and eliminating everything which is not humanist from socialism. We find a similar account of the aim of democratic socialism in the chapter 'The Crisis of Socialism' in 'Our Current Crisis', yet without the emphasis on dialectics.

I conclude from the above that Kosík's Heideggerian Marxism in the late 1960s views democratic socialism as an answer to the later Heidegger's call for such a reorientation of our thinking and our cultural paradigm, which would liberate us from the technological understanding of being. Of course, democratic socialism does not represent the specific form of the reorientation that Heidegger had in mind; the German philosopher was in favour of the renewal of a traditional (i.e. rather receptive) relation to the surrounding world, and of thinking and imagination adequate to such a receptive relation to the world; the *concrete* form, proposed by Kosík, is the answer of a Marxist thinker, keeping human activity, (*dialectical*) *historical* praxis, as the only way of liberating the human from self-alienation.

Yet this is not the end of the story of Kosík's relation to Heidegger's thinking. The last two chapters of the essay 'Our Current Crisis' ('The Crisis of Modernity', 'The Crisis of Principles') were added – and most probably also written or rewritten – much later when the essay was included in the collection *The Cen-*

---

44 Kosík 1995c, pp. 56–8. Kosík equals this procedure with 'the destruction of the pseudoconcrete', familiar from *Dialectics of the Concrete*.
45 Kosík 1995f, p. 59.

tury of Grete Samsa in 1993. They do not contain, even implicitly, the idea of democratic socialism. And on the contrary, they contain many more ideas of the later Heidegger than the first six chapters published in 1968, such as the loss of a natural 'measure' for the non-technological relation to reality, the idea of a modern nihilism as shown in the process of transforming everything into 'values' and thus losing the autonomous being of things, the idea of the subjection of the human to the truth understood as the openness of being, the loss of the essential in one's life, etc. These two chapters mark a new phase of Kosík's relation to Heidegger, in which Marxian historical dialectics withdraw and give way to the primacy of Heideggerian thinking in Kosík's writings.

3   1990–97: Metaphysical Democracy

Kosík's position, emerging at the end of the 1960s, viewing both bureaucratic socialism and democratic capitalism as mere subtypes of one system of a universal manipulative attitude to reality, was the background of his early (in comparison with other critical thinkers) rejection of the new regime established in Czechoslovakia after 1989, the regime of democratic capitalism. Yet it seems that with the end of socialism as the attempt to build a historical alternative to capitalism, Kosík resigned from elaborating the Marxist answer to the crisis of modern civilisation.[46] With the diminishing of their Marxist basis, Kosík's writings in 1990s became, first of all, a specific type of Heideggerian analysis of the crisis of modern civilisation, without offering a real solution to the problem. The main difference with Heidegger's thought, however, was represented by Kosík's democratism: the philosophical-political position of the Czech thinker remained democratic throughout his whole career, whereas Heidegger's non-egalitarianism was not really compatible with democratic principles.[47]

In the essays published in the first half of the 1990s – 'The Third Munich?' (1992), 'Truth of Exile – Exile of Truth' (1992), 'Democracy and the Myth of the Cave' (1993), 'The Prague Spring, the "End of History" and the Show Maker' (1993), 'Infernal Circles' (1994) and others – Kosík's critique of modern civilisation reaches its fully-developed form. It describes – under the titles 'system',

---

46   Kosík said in his interview in the *Concordia* journal that Marx's assigning of the mission of liberating humankind to the proletariat had been proved wrong. See Kosík 1993e, p. 19. Kosík adds, at the same time, that Heidegger's assigning of this mission to the German nation had not been proven right either. See Kosík 1993e, p. 20.

47   For Heidegger's non-egalitarianism see Guignon 1993, p. 36.

'modernist system', 'mechanism', 'system of needs' and the like – the globally dominant cultural paradigm as a manipulative attitude to reality, ordering everything, including the human that orders, into the complex of global availability. In this manner it repeats Heidegger's critique of the technological understanding of being,[48] but with a certain moralist overtone: Kosík's description of the 'system of needs' incorporates a more explicit criticism of modern consumerism and stresses the endlessly *growing* reach of the system. Yet similarly to Heidegger, Kosík praises the non-technological or rather pre-technological way of understanding the world surrounding us. The Czech philosopher thus introduces two competing ways of life and cultural practices: One, predominant in the modern world, is brought about by the symbiosis of economy, technology and science and closes us into a 'cave' where everything is at our disposal, everything except for the real: the world, reality, being. This cave expands itself aimlessly and makes this expansion the only sense of everything that is. The metaphor of a cave suggests the meaning of being closed, isolated from the openness of the world and has Platonic, but also Aristotelian origins. Kosík speaks of two different types of cave – the Platonic one[49] is austere, military-like, while the Aristotelian one is, contrariwise, abundant in richness and comfort,[50] but they both represent oblivion from the real world. According to Kosík, the change of regime in Czechoslovakia after 1989 meant, for that society, a mere shift from one type of cave to another, from the cave of control to that of consumption, yet people are not free in either of them; on the contrary, they are subjected to the needs of the system and therefore ultimately to the 'pseudo-subject' of the system.

What we really need is to leave the cave and to live our life within the sphere of 'the Open' – Kosík is citing Rilke's *das Offene*,[51] but he has in mind the meaning of the term which was given to it by Heidegger in his criticism of

---

48 According to Heidegger, the power of modern technology covers the original relation of the human towards being and replaces it with the 'ordering' or 'challenging' of all beings – including the human herself – for their technical exploitability. Technology thus displaces everything mysterious and poetic and leads us to forget the dimension where truth as the 'unconcealment' of things is rooted. See Heidegger 1977, pp. 16–28.

49 Kosík has in mind the famous parable of the cave in *Politeia*. See Platon, *Politeia* VII, pp. 514–16.

50 Aristotle uses the metaphor of the cave in his dialogue *Peri filosofias* [On Philosophy], of which only fragments have survived; see Jaeger 1923, pp. 167–8. The use of the metaphor of the cave is ubiquitous in Kosík's texts from the 1990s; explicit rendering of both *types* of cave is to be found in the essay 'The Commanding Instance', in Kosík 1997c, pp. 225–6.

51 See Kosík 1993d, p. 169 (English translation see Kosík 1993g). This seems to be the only case where the term is assigned to Rilke; in all other cases Kosík uses it without ascribing it to anyone.

Rilke's understanding of the term: the Open is the 'truth' (*aletheia*) of being, being which hides itself while giving things to appear.[52] The Open is also often equated with 'the world' by Kosík, and world is understood as an ontological structure; the structure is that of Heidegger's *Geviert* (fourfold)[53] – it is measured out by a community of divinities, mortals and sky and earth.[54] Fourfold is often reduced to twofold structure by Kosík, to the contrast of the earth and that which is above the human, or simply to the contrast of two distinct spheres of meaning, of 'the essential' or 'the sublime' on one side, and 'the trivial' or 'the secondary' on the other.

Kosík does not cease to be a political thinker even in the most Heideggerian phase of his thinking. The Czech philosopher therefore stresses the communal aspect of living within the fourfold (or twofold) of the world – the ideal of open life outside the cave represents the founding of the *polis*, a living community of people who have freed themselves from the hidden authoritarian pseudo-subject of the system operating within the cave. Founding a 'political state' is one of the ways 'in which truth occurs', says Heidegger in the famous passage from *The Origin of the Work of Art*;[55] yet Kosík makes this *the* way of a human life lived truthfully, in openness for being. The greatest tension in his late thinking, moreover, arises with this option. Kosík's deep faith in democracy leads him to the rejection of 'a god' who only could save us, according to the well-known Heideggerian dictum; it is perhaps only democracy that could save us, says the Czech thinker.[56] Yet it is not so simple a matter to put the Heideggerian god aside, for he – or more exactly the god-like measure of that which is the counterpart of the earth, the sky – is the integral part of the 'the Open' where Kosík's *polis* should be founded. To meet the demands of later Heideggerian ontology, Kosík suggests replacing 'social democracy' (because the social reduces the human to a system of needs) with 'metaphysical democracy', which urges the human 'to found the world where people could dwell poetically'.[57] Yet

---

52 See Heidegger 1992, p. 208, p. 218. For Heidegger's criticism of Rilke's understanding of the term 'the Open' see ibid, pp. 227–40.

53 In his lecture cycle 'Insight Into That Which Is' from 1949, Heidegger describes, for the first time, being as the field of the interaction of the four terms: the 'earth', the 'sky', 'mortals' and 'divinities'; see Heidegger 2012, pp. 3–74.

54 Once again Kosík conceals the Heideggerian inspiration of his thought by ascribing the origin of the concept directly to the Greek thinking (where it was, in fact, rediscovered, through Hölderlin, by Heidegger). See Kosík 1993b, p. 21; Kosík 1993c, p. 145.

55 Heidegger 1971, p. 62.

56 See Kosík 1993a, p. 183. The English translation of the essay is to be found in the journal *Thesis Eleven*, Kosík 1996.

57 Kosík 1993a, p. 185.

for both Heidegger and Kosík, dwelling poetically means not losing the measure which contrasts (and unites at the same time) the earth with the sky,[58] the sublime with the trivial.[59] To live poetically means maintaining a receptive relation towards the way things appear to the human, and 'measuring' that way is bound together with looking up 'toward the divinities', with the human relation to the 'unknown' god, i.e. with a certain hierarchy found within the fourfold.[60] Nietzsche's statement 'God is dead' indicates, for Kosík, the loss of this hierarchy and with it the loss of the dimension of the sublime and the essential from the life of modern society.[61]

Yet such ontology is not so easily compatible with the sovereignty of the human, which is one of the preconditions of democracy. 'Metaphysical democracy' flirts with the pre-Enlightenment conception of the human position within the world; and its nature is still more problematic if it becomes a conceptual tool of a socialist thinker. A good example of a problem in which Kosík finds himself, in his enthusiasm for metaphysical democracy, is an interview with the Italian author Antonio Cassuti from May 1993:

> *Question*: You are interested in the future of socialism and democracy; it seems that the European left, and mainly the socialist movement, is currently in crisis. The end of so called real socialism has brought democratic socialism to a crisis as well. Is this so?
>
> *Answer*: The socialist movement is and *must* be in crisis, because it moves *within* the ruling paradigm which is historically exhausted, sterile and mindless, and it lacks not only the courage, but also the imagination for its transcending and breakthrough.
>
> The crisis of the modern age, or more precisely its agony, lies in the fact, that there is no liberating alternative to the ruling paradigm implemented in Europe, Japan and North America. This alternative is not *something*

---

[58] See Heidegger's lecture '[...] Poetically Man Dwells [...]', in Heidegger 1971, pp. 213–29, especially pp. 219–23.

[59] In the essay 'The City and the Architectonics of the World', Kosík complains about the loss of the poetic from modern cities ('[...] where there the poetic has been removed, suppressed, expelled, the community, the *Polis* disintegrates', p. 70) and writes that the poetic comprehends 'the beautiful, the sublime, the familiar', but pays the greatest attention to the sublime afterwards; its effect on the human is described as follows: 'In meeting the sublime the human feels fear and horror in the beginning, but both lead him *upwards*: the sublime appears as a power which liberates and uplifts the human'. Kosík 1997e, p. 66.

[60] See Heidegger 1971, p. 220 and p. 222.

[61] See Kosík 1993d, p. 169.

else, but just the *measure*, the *dimension* which would break through the limitedness of the cave, whether a barracks-like or luxurious one, so that we can set out to the Open, to the founding of the world. Return to the ancient *polis* or to the medieval Christian community, both of which had that dimension, is not possible; life in them would be unbearable for the modern human. The liberating alternative can be born out of the creative thinking imagination, from *seeking* the dimension that the modern age lacks.

If the political left does not become aware of this fact, it will compete, but also cooperate with the political right in our current farce, which is sterile, awkward, ridiculous, but it can change into a bloody farce, into endless catastrophe.

Thinking must remain faithful to itself. Its highest mission is: to think. So it must not fantasize and try to conceive a new paradigm; it will suffice if it analyses the symbiosis which rules the present: science, technology, economy. I once wrote that there are *liberating* possibilities hidden within this trinity, and thinking is called to ask again: what is economy (what is a house, what is it to run a household), what is science (what does it mean for a human to know about the essential and to be able to distinguish it from the secondary) and what is technology (what is the *art* to be in the world and not within the cave that does not know about the world or denies it)?[62]

As we can see, Kosík in his answer proposes what is in fact a Heideggerian critique of modern civilisation as a programme for the political left. The critique and the programme are centred on Heidegger's later ontology and represent a remarkable shift in Kosík's thinking. The ontology of human praxis in *Dialectics of the Concrete* postulated the destruction of the pseudoconcrete through the revolutionary-critical praxis of humankind, through dialectical thinking and through 'the ontogenetic process' of an individual creating the world of truth.[63] Now it is not human praxis (and dialectical thinking as a spiritual-practical activity) which is to liberate the human from the alienated existence within the system of general availability of everything – it is imaginative thinking; and it is not the human who stands at the centre of the ontological plan, it is being itself and the truth of its unfolding-concealing within the fourfold.

---

62 Kosík 1997k, pp. 28–9. Kosík's emphasis.
63 See Kosík 1976, p. 8.

4 Economy, Science, Technology

Let us examine more closely the manner in which Kosík seeks the missing dimension of the modern age by exploring the hidden meaning of economics, science and technology, as he suggested in the cited interview. Incorporating the economy into the trinity of powers creating the plan of the modern cave can be considered a Marxist element of the later Kosík's ontology (the emphasis on the political way of life within the sphere of the Open could be considered the same).[64] Yet the philosophical treatment itself of economy is once again Heideggerian: it is drawn from Heidegger's organic concept of language as a structure of sense corresponding to the structure of the sense of being; philosophical etymologisation then ascribes to words themselves a deeper, ontological meaning. And also, the conviction that the biggest danger contains within itself the possibility of salvation and that we must search for it in the essence of the threatening power (economy in this case), is drawn from Heidegger.[65] As we have read in the interview, the task of thinking what economy is, for Kosík, conceals within itself the appeal to consider what the *oikos* is: a house; so the question leads us to architecture, or more precisely, to architectonics representing a saving power. In his lectures 'The Victory of Method over Architectonics'[66] and 'The City and the Architectonics of the World',[67] Kosík juxtaposes modern architecture with its ancient and medieval counterparts: according to him, the latter was based on an *architectonical* plan of *reality*. Ancient architecture did not lose contact with the manner in which the world (in an ontological sense) unfolds itself in the opposition of the essential and the insignificant, of the

---

64 In the interview with the journal *Concordia*, Kosík connects his trinity with Marx, who in *Outlines of the Critique of Political Economy* anticipated that the ruling power of society will be not just the old capitalist economy, but something broader. In the same interview, Kosík also speaks about the deficit of praxis in Heidegger's philosophy – although Heidegger works with the notion of praxis, it is mere 'Zeug' for him. Yet we find a different picture 'in antiquity and in Marx', according to Kosík, where praxis does not mean the mere handling of instruments, but the founding of the *polis*, a community. See Kosík 1993e, p. 17 and p. 16.

65 According to Heidegger, technology, although representing the highest danger for the human, could also become a guideline for the needed turn and for salvation from modern nihilism: Technology is also a certain (calculative, manipulative) understanding of being; if we take into consideration the historicity of that understanding, we can open ourselves up to a new understanding of being, in which we will become its witnesses and the voices of its truth once again. See Heidegger 1977.

66 Kosík 1997i, pp. 52–61.

67 Kosík 1997e, pp. 62–81.

sublime and the trivial: the foundation of the *polis* is an 'event' which reveals this distinction. This is why ancient architecture works with a meaningful disposition of space, whereas modern architecture repeats the same sterile buildings that ensure the domination of the human over the space but are unable to create meaning within the City. The main concern in our modern cities has become transportation, aimless movement from place to place that makes us the part of the never-ending operation of the System.

Kant's notion of the sublime (*das Erhabene*) is the state of mind in which we relate ourselves to the infinite, which cannot be present itself. The sublime is, for Kosík, a founding power which enables us to inhabit the world, unites the finite and infinite, elevates us above the everyday and banal, but which at the same time gives meaning also to the trivial and bestows to it a certain poetry.[68] Architectonics reveals the hierarchical order of the essential and the secondary and makes the *polis* an event, a place of the unfolding of history – because history is this action in which the sublime and the beautiful are decided upon. The belonging of the human to a specific place then makes her responsible for this event and history.[69]

In speaking about the difference between the essential and the secondary, about the *polis*, history and responsibility, we are already answering together with Kosík the second question, the question of science, right 'architectonical' knowing. The right kind of knowing, according to Kosík, is precisely this knowledge of the difference between the sublime, which gives meaning to our life, and the trivial, which must be subordinated to the first. Right knowing is spiritual, it is 'the sense of the sublime', it presupposes that one is faithful to the truth of the sublime.[70] Kosík thus founds his existential hermeneutics on the correspondence of our knowledge to a certain hierarchy within the plan of being. The architectonic context of the explanation makes it manifest that this hermeneutics forms the basis for the authentic *social* and *political* life. Yet with every hierarchy there comes also the possibility of its turnabout – and Kosík sees such a turnabout at work in Western society today. Forgetting the ontological hierarchy and leveling everything to the system of general

---

68   See Kosík 1997e, p. 78.
69   This thesis resembles Heidegger's emphasis on rootedness (existence which is faithful to being) – and yet more so, when it is connected with the notions of earth and homeland: in Czech 'homeland' translates as '*vlast*', which comes from the verb '*vlastnit*', 'to own', and can be easily interpreted in the Heideggerian sense of the *Ereignis*, the event in which the mutual belonging of being and the human is revealed. In his lecture 'The Homeland of Mácha', Kosík describes the mutual belonging of homeland and the human; see Kosík 1997j, pp. 82–93.
70   See Kosík 1997e, p. 68.

availability leads to the perverted power-and-social hierarchy within the 'cave', comprising the anonymous powers of the System. In the essay 'The Commanding Instance'[71] Kosík enumerates particular levels of the perverted hierarchy: The highest place is occupied by the anonymous 'hidden planetary dictator'; beneath him stand the competing regional superpowers, then come corporations and consortia; the fourth place from the top is reserved for the administration, composed of generals, ideologists and managers; the fifth place hosts the most numerous group – the mass of consumers – and at the bottom end are two levels constituted by social roles – the first is the voter and the last, the lowest member of the hierarchy, is the human: yet not the human defined by her relation to the ontological capacity of 'the world', but an abstract human being, reduced to its social role.[72] This picture of a perverted hierarchy can obviously be understood as a criticism of the ruling global capitalist system; in the essay 'The Lumpenbourgeoisie and Higher Spiritual Truth', Kosík speaks directly about 'super-capital' and identifies it with the highest position of the anonymous dictator.[73] Yet the manner in which the human is defined within the 'right' hierarchy of the disposition of being and the whole reasoning and tone of the essays do not enable one to label Kosík's position and methodology as Marxist. The criticism of capitalism is to a far greater degree a moralist and traditionalist one.

The third question, the question of technology, is translated by Kosík into the question 'what is the *art* of being in the world and not within the cave that does not know about the world?' in the cited interview. Art is the prominent way of uniting the sky with the earth, the sublime with the trivial;[74] the poet is the emblematic figure of the one who is able to discern the fourfold of the world. Kosík finds his Hölderlin in the Czech romantic poet Karel Hynek Mácha: In the lecture 'The Homeland of Mácha', he explains Mácha's notion of 'homeland' as the range between being tied to the earth and the beyond-reach of the stars; and only rootedness in the earth, connected with the desire of the beyond-reach which cannot be made present, ensures the right measure of one's existence.[75] Similarly to Heidegger, Kosík wants philosophical thinking to follow this revealing disposition of art, and he links both art and philosophy with individual sacrifice as another manner of one's subjection to the truth

---

71 See Kosík 1997c, pp. 195–237.
72 See Kosík 1997c, pp. 233–4.
73 See Kosík 1997d, pp. 238–55, on 'super-capital' see pp. 251–2.
74 See Kosík 1997d, pp. 252–3.
75 See Kosík 1997j, p. 84 and p. 87.

of being.⁷⁶ Sacrifice is the main topic of his small book *A Youth and Death* from 1995:⁷⁷ One of Kosík's most Heideggerian texts preaches sacrifice as the act that gives birth to the ethical self that overcomes the innate egoism of the human and that founds community. Community is conceived in the sense of the fourfold as an order of things unfolding in the relation between the earth and the heavens; and the human is understood as 'homo religiosus' – which, according to the Czech thinker, means uniting the earth with the sky. Sacrifice is a foundation stone of such an order, and generally everything that founds community also becomes a sacrifice: works of art and philosophical works too are seen as kinds of 'altar sacrifices' brought to the festivity of a liberating relation to being.

5 Conclusion

It should be clearer now as to why I have labelled the later development of Kosík's thought as a move towards 'traditionalism' in the title of this essay. Kosík's later ontology connects the good future of humanity with a refocusing of our cultural practices to those that are connected with the appearance of the essential and the sublime as foundation stones of a hierarchical structure of the way being unfolds itself through us. Once it is being and not human praxis that governs the unfolding of history and destiny of humanity, the meaningful comes from above, from the authority transcending the social players; its source is sought in the spiritualised knowledge that makes it possible to portray the good future as the idealised past.⁷⁸ Kosík on the one hand does not deny

---

76 See part of the famous passage from Heidegger's treatise *The Origin of the Work of Art*: 'Still another way in which truth grounds itself is the essential sacrifice'. Heidegger 1971, p. 62.

77 Kosík 1995m. Also in Kosík 1997b, pp. 151–94. The very first version of the text is from 1969 – the title refers to the death of a young Czech student, Jan Palach, who immolated himself on Prague's main square as a public appeal to the people so that they do not fall into lethargy and remain vigilant in the effort to retain the liberating social movement of the Prague Spring also after the Soviet occupation of Czechoslovakia in August 1968.

78 The classical place of this traditionalistic shift of the past to the future is Heidegger's *Rectoral Address*, delivered in May 1933: 'The beginning still is. It does not lie behind us, as something that was long ago, but stands before us. As what is greatest, the beginning has passed in advance beyond all that is to come and thus also beyond us. The beginning has invaded our future. There it awaits us, as a distant command bidding us catch up with its greatness'. Heidegger 1985, p. 473; Kosík's political concern replaces Heideggerian 'beginning' (the German philosopher had in mind the Greek beginning of Western knowledge) with the 'founding' of the *polis*, but the ubiquitous lament over current civilisation and the feeling of the perversion of a good (old) order are similar to Heidegger's.

the Enlightenment and the effort to liberate the human from powers external to her; but at the same time he concedes that the modern emancipatory project has become perverted into the hegemony of the technological System that has spoiled morality and culture.[79] His rejection of modern 'nihilistic' culture and sometimes of the whole modern era is explicit in the texts from the 1990s. The 'missing dimension' of the modern era should be provided by the new 'imagination', but any attempt to specify it is vague or sounds traditionalist: Kosík speaks of 'the new culture', which will yet be born out of 'the big traditions';[80] he suggests counterbalancing the idea of a historical progress perverted into mere technological progress by cultivating our sensitivity for musing – but reminds us that the muses were the daughters of the highest god Zeus and Mnemosyne, the goddess of *memory*.[81]

In his lecture 'Faust the Architect' Kosík designates modernity as a Mephistophelian project: the evil is inherent in the promise of the never-ending growth of happiness and comfort ensured by the scientific and technological System.[82] Heidegger did not want to be – philosophically – a conscious traditionalist and neither did Kosík; yet the strong moral element of Kosík's criticism of the modern era makes his cultural and philosophical-political position still more traditionalist than the ontology of the fourfold would require. The emphasis on transcendent moral law, high culture, the belonging of the human to a particular place (on earth, or in *polis*) as against the modernist destruction thereof, make Kosík's later criticism of the modern era and modern culture traditionalist.[83]

The philosophical position of the later Kosík is self-contradictory, however. As we have seen, the Czech thinker is strongly influenced by the thought of Martin Heidegger, and at the same time represents a more politically and democratically oriented way of thinking. It is difficult to connect in a satisfying manner these two intellectual paradigms. Democracy is based on equality – and of course, Kosík does not call into question the political equality of people: that would contradict his democratism. Yet he is at the same time very fervent

---

79   Kosík 1997f, pp. 135–50.
80   Kosík 1997g, p. 126.
81   See Kosík 1997d, pp. 142–6.
82   Kosík 1997a, pp. 102–5.
83   I understand the term *traditionalism* broadly as an effort to preserve (or restore) traditional customs and values against any innovation which would destroy their sense. Kosík's later philosophical position is marked – in my understanding and against Kosík's own self-understanding – by the effort to reestablish the pre-modern cultural paradigm based on a hierarchy of meaning: the meaningful comes from the authority transcending social players and is built on the opposition of the sublime and the trivial.

in establishing the hierarchical order of meaning as a sphere where the life of people in his *polis* should be rooted. In the late 1960s, Heideggerian conceptuality served merely as a critical tool for the description of the modern crisis of both socialist and capitalist society; the answer to this crisis was sought in Marxian historical dialectics in theory and in political praxis – in democratic socialism. In the 1990s, Heideggerian conceptuality *also* provides the answer. The task of the citizens gathered within Kosík's *polis* is to be subjected to the truth of being, to be there *for* being in its meaningful disposition. And should the citizens proceed incorrectly, the perversion of culture and devastation of all meaning is always at hand. Humans seem to be subjected constantly to some subject other than themselves now – not only in the case of a perverted life within the technological System, but also if they leave its cave and found the *polis*.[84]

6   Postscript

However, there is a postscript to this conclusion concerning the later Kosík's thought. Between 1997 and 2000, Karel Kosík published a series of essays in the Czech newspaper *Právo*, in which he reacted to current events of both Czech and world politics. They were collected, and published after the author's death in the book titled *The Last Essays*.[85] The reader finds in them a certain intellectual shift, which has strengthened Kosík's line of democratic thought as against the traditionalist one. The point of departure remains the same; it is a critique of modernity based on the later Heidegger's ontology, followed by the ideal of the community of the *polis*, whose citizens should exercise the virtues of the kind of life that overcomes the alienating structures of the worldwide technological System. Yet the democracy we find depicted within this *polis* is no longer 'metaphysical' – we might refer to it rather as a plebeian democracy (a feature corresponding with the historically plebeian character of Czech society): it is

---

84   The ideal of Kosík's *polis* is, in fact, close to the (anti)political concept designated by Jacques Rancière as 'archipolitics'. Archipolitics is an originally Platonic project of replacing democratic politics with the ideal of a community permeated and united by its *arche*, by the law internalised by the members of the community as something natural; this naturalisation of the political-ethical order makes the law of the community sensually perceptible according to Rancière – in Kosík's case, this naturalisation and sensualisation of the *arche* of the community, i.e. of the way the truth of being unfolds itself, is made real in 'architectonics' and in the works of art. See Rancière 1999, pp. 65–70.
85   Kosík 2004.

based on the equality of those subjected to the rule of the System, which is *represented* by specific political or economic players. Likewise, the technological scientific reason that remains at the origin of the modern calculative attitude to reality is referred to as a 'nobility view' or 'nobility greed' now, and the omnipresent technological hand of the System belongs to those who have specific power, be it political, economic or military.[86]

The citizens of the *polis* are called upon to fulfil the ideal of the non-alienated life, which still has the Heideggerian form of the right 'measure', contrasting and uniting the earth and the sky, but fulfilling the ideal is now rather a rebellion against the stakeholders of the System. Kosík sees the prominent example of such rebellion in people gathered on Serbian bridges as living shields against the bombing by NATO forces in 1999. Humans on the bridges show, through their bravery, who they really are and plan out reality in terms of the essential and the secondary, not in terms of technologically handling it (this attitude is ascribed to the pilots of the bombing aircrafts): the Serbian bridges became the places where the truth is revealed.[87]

Stronger emphasis on democratic life brings a new emphasis on *plurality*, which overshadows the inherent ontological *hierarchy* of Kosík's *polis*. 'The people constitutes a plurality of human beings',[88] writes the Czech philosopher, and adds that there is also a plurality within each human: four players, 'private person, producer and consumer, voter, metaphysical being' meet inside of everyone in dialogue and dispute.[89] The trinity of reason – technological, poetical and moral – should save us from the one-sidedness of a mere technological reason; and the three should be in the relation of a mutual dialogue: one cannot dominate the other two.[90] Plurality is, in fact, an inherent feature of a Heideggerian ontology: from a number of 'existentials' in *Being and Time* to four agents of the 'fourfold' that meet in a particular 'thing',[91] we find plurality in the manner in which the sense of being is revealed or in the manner being itself makes things appear. Kosík utilises this feature, and in the very last phase of his writings he 'democratises' his social ontology by stressing the need of *dialogue* between the ontological agents or/and the particular social players of his *polis*. So the *polis* is still the place where the sublime and the banal, the sacred and the profane are distinguished, but these measures are born out of a dialogue of

---

86   See Kosík 2004c, pp. 141–5.
87   See Kosík 2004b, pp. 108–10 and pp. 113–14.
88   Kosík 1996, p. 122.
89   See Kosík 2004d, pp. 69–70.
90   See Kosík 2004c, p. 158.
91   See the lecture 'The Thing', in Heidegger 1971, pp. 163–86, pp. 171–4.

specific social players; it is not so much the instance transcending all members of the community that prescribes the right structuring of the world.

Kosík's *moral* critique of the current capitalist incorporation of the technological System remains strong even now. Yet the differentiation of the good and the evil is implicitly and sometimes also explicitly linked to the opposition between the powerless and those in power. In this way, in his last essays, Kosík wants the non-privileged to become the bearers of the salvation of the world, which means leaving the System of never-ending growth of the satisfaction of our needs. Salvation still has no specific historic form; the strong moral criticism of the historical progress which has taken on the form of mere technological progress makes it clear that such salvation would require a complete reorientation of the modernist project. Yet it is not reorientation in a pre-modern direction this time, for the meaning of human life and the meaning of being are sought *in* humans themselves and *for* humans themselves, although the truth of being is given in a certain hierarchical ontological structure. The ontological priority of human praxis is gradually re-established in Kosík's last essays, but we do not know, unfortunately, how far and where exactly it would have led the Czech philosopher had death not terminated his lifelong encounter and confrontation with the thought of Karl Marx and Martin Heidegger.

PART 5

Influence and Reception

CHAPTER 15

A Route of Critical Thought: Between Italian and Czech Intellectuals

Gabriella Fusi

> [...] La voce di Kosík è tra le più coraggiose e responsabili, anche perché non esprime il ribollire di un momento, ma riecheggia una lunga strada trascorsa senza compromessi intellettuali attraverso la selva del marxismo 'apologetico' e 'idealistico' [...]¹
> F.R.

∴

In the post-Stalinist years, theoreticians and philosophers of a generation partly educated in Moscow and Leningrad, an experience which was supposed to support and spread Marxism, started to refuse the reduction of Marxism to apologetics and propaganda for 'the socialist realisation', claiming Marxism's critical function with regard to existence from every point of view, socialism included. One of those philosophers was Karel Kosík, who said in 1993 to Antonio Cassuti: 'During a large assembly of Prague "philosophers" in 1958, I was urged to walk "with the spirit of the times" and to retract the sentence: "The rule of ideology is over, the age of the critical thought is beginning"'.² Kosík refused, and the need to establish the critical function of philosophy with regard to existence urged him to develop his most structured work: *Dialectics of the Concrete*.

Enzo Paci published, under the title *Diario Fenomenologico* [Phenomenological Diary],³ parts of the diary he kept between 14 March 1956 and 30 June 1961.

---

1   Kosík's voice is one of the most courageous and responsible, because it lacks the excitement of the moment. It is the echo of a long route covered, with no intellectual compromises, through the thick tangle of 'apologetic' and 'idealistic' Marxism, F.R. 1964, p. 3. (English translation – Gabriella Fusi; the identity of F.R. has not been determined.)
2   Kosík 1993f, p. 211.
3   Paci 1961.

In the passages he selected for the publication, he showed a great enthusiasm for Sartre, above all when he related in glowing terms the French philosopher's visit to Milan in April 1961. But even the year before, on 23 September 1960, he had written that the debate at Royaumont on dialectics had convinced him of two things: the need to re-examine Marx and the importance of Sartre.

In the diary there was no direct mention of Karel Kosík's speech on that occasion, but the following publication by *aut aut* of Kosík's essay 'Dialectique du Concret'[4] seemed to confirm the idea that the Prague philosopher's positions had particularly impressed Paci. The published speech was one of the four essays read at Royaumont, the first to make up *Dialectics of the Concrete*, Kosík's most structured work based on the need to re-establish the critical function of philosophy as regards existence.

And precisely the pursuit of critical thought was a sort of leitmotiv that in the 1960s bound together some of the Italian Communist Party intellectuals, Sartre, Paci, Kosík and Petrović.

Those were fundamental years for all those who felt an urgent need to start a debate between different positions, going beyond the conflict of the systems, being aware of the transformations that were taking place in socialist and capitalist countries, both afflicted by a crisis of their own fundamental values. They were important years for the discussion inside Marxism, for those who wanted to replace apologetics with criticism of loyalty to Moscow and with fidelity to Marx understood 'as a return to consequent reasoning and the application of materialistic dialectics to all the phenomena of the contemporary society, Marxism and socialism included'.[5]

Out of the need to start a debate beyond the East-West division, in 1964 in Zagreb Gajo Petrović, Rudi Supek and other Yugoslav philosophers and sociologists founded the review *Praxis*, which had a Serbo-Croatian and an international version, and the following year they established the so-called Korčula School. These two activities gathered intellectuals from the whole world on a programme of non-dogmatic, creative Marxism and revolutionary and humanistic socialism as the only solution to the problems of contemporary society, according to the editorial of the first number.[6] Every year the school on Korčula had the aim of calling philosophers, sociologists and psychologists to the Croatian island of Korčula to discuss various topics: from 'Meaning and Perspectives of Socialism' to 'Creation and Reification', 'Utopia is Reality' and 'Equality and Freedom'. In ten years of activity (from 1965 to 1974),

---

4 Kosík 1961.
5 Kosík 1964a, p. 113.
6 Petrović 1965, p. 3.

before being forbidden by the government authorities, *Praxis* and the school on Korčula involved Karel Kosík, Enzo Paci, Agnes Heller, Ernst Bloch, Erich Fromm, Herbert Marcuse and Zygmunt Bauman.

Kosík himself recalled in 2002 in a letter to Asja Petrović, the Yugoslav philosopher Gajo's wife, how the Korčula period, when scholars from all over the world used to meet, had been difficult but also full of hope: '[...] we thought that philosophy could make a big contribution to liberation'.[7]

In order to gain a better understanding of the relationships between Czech and Italian philosophers, I have to go back and examine the figure of Enzo Paci not only as a philosopher but also as a guide for his students. He studied with Antonio Banfi together with personalities who would become significant points of reference for Milanese cultural life in the 1970s (Remo Cantoni, Giulio Preti, Raffaele de Grada, Vittorio Sereni, Luciano Anceschi, Rossana Rossanda).

Emilio Renzi, one of his students, described Paci as a man whose culture was not restricted within the bounds of a specific area, but was broad, curious and 'interdisciplinary'. Another, Alfredo Marini, remarked that he was able to find unexpected connections between seemingly very different things: a talent for establishing wide-ranging connections and cultural relationships developed under the guidance of Banfi, who shared his idea of cultural life as something harmonious, organic, multifaceted and free. And free, intent and curious he was when I met him in 1968, and also able to communicate his curiosity and problematic nature to his listeners.

Conferences, meetings and seminars stimulated further in-depth studies. Undoubtedly Prague represented such an interesting meeting place because it was the city where Husserl had held his conferences, starting the reflection which would lead to *The Crisis of European Sciences and Transcendental Phenomenology*. On the other hand, Prague was the city of Franz Kafka, whose works were arousing the interest of Italian and French scholars. We know that Paci made Kosík's acquaintance at Royaumont, but he had probably already heard of Jan Patočka, even if the Czech philosopher had been dismissed from the university in 1948. Patočka was known for having organised a series of lectures by Husserl in Prague in 1935. Besides, as a secretary of the 'Prague Philosophical Circle' (Cercle philosophique de Prague) he had collected and rescued the unpublished works of the German philosopher from the Nazi threat. In fact, he had helped Leo van Breda to put them in a safe place in

---

7 A letter Kosík wrote on 15 December 2002 to Asja Petrović on the occasion of her husband's death. I was given a photocopy.

the Archives of Leuven, where Merleau-Ponty, Tran Duc Thao and Enzo Paci among others had the opportunity to study them.

Interest in phenomenology, but also in the socialist experiment, drove Paci's pupil and university assistant Guido Davide Neri to the difficult choice, at that time, to apply for a scholarship in Prague, beyond the Iron Curtain. During the year of his scholarship, Guido Neri made contact with Patočka and Kosík. The result of this relationship was the organisation of Paci's conference in Prague. The invitation came from the Academy of Sciences, where both Patočka and Kosík worked. The conference, organised by Neri and attended by Lorenzo Pacini, at that time a lecturer at the Italian Embassy, and by Renato Rozzi, a psychologist and Neri's friend, was held on 24 October 1962, and was translated from French into Czech by Jan Patočka. The paper *Il significato dell'uomo in Marx e Husserl* [The Meaning of Man in Marx and Husserl] was later published by *aut aut*.[8]

Undoubtedly Paci attributed a lot of importance to the conference in Prague and mentioned it several times in his university lectures, as I can personally testify. He mentioned it in the preface to Husserl's *Crisis of European Sciences and Transcendental Phenomenology*[9] (where he advanced the idea, if not of a Marxist phenomenology, then of a phenomenological Marxism) and in *Praxis* in a paper with the title 'Intersoggettività del potere' [Intersubjectivity of Power].[10]

A few years later, he wrote about it also in the more popular review *Tempo*, to which he contributed in the 1970s, in an article ('Husserl e Marx a Praga') on the main themes of the conference, those he thought were at the root of the ongoing debate between phenomenology and Marxism.[11]

At the Prague conference, Paci saw a close parallel between discussions of the objectification of man, the naturalisation of social relationships, the reduction of the real to an abstract worker and to a pure commodity, and on the other hand scientific objectivism, the reduction of living subjectivity to a 'psychic object' and the quantification of nature. Both social and scientific alienation were therefore two aspects of the same historical phenomenon.

From the letters in G. Neri's archives, we can deduce that Neri did not know Kosík personally at the beginning, and that their relationship would transform, over the years, from a formal one into friendship.[12]

---

8   Paci 1963.
9   Husserl 1968.
10 Paci 1970a.
11 Paci 1973.
12 Neri's archives were provided by his son, Gabriele, to the Department of Philosophy at the State University in Milan.

Kosík made several trips to Italy from 1963 to 1968 and met Paci and his younger pupils. A conference was held at Milan's 'Università degli Studi' in 1963 on 'La Ragione e la Storia', later published in *aut aut*.[13] The essay is a modified version of a part of the chapter 'Storia e libertà' – in *Dialectics of the Concrete*.

The 'Gramsci Institute' also used to invite the Czech philosopher to its conferences such as the one held in Rome in 1964 on 'Morale e Società' (Kosík's paper, 'La dialettica della morale e la morale della dialettica' [The Dialectics of Morality and the Morality of Dialectics], was published in *Critica marxista*[14]), and the one held in Cagliari in 1967 on 'Gramsci e la Cultura Contemporanea' (Kosík's paper, 'Gramsci et la philosophie de la praxis', was published in the journal *Praxis* in the autumn of 1967).[15]

Clear evidence of Kosík's knowledge of Gramsci's works and of his reflections on his thought would appear in the articles written during the Prague Spring, collected and published in Italy under the title *La nostra crisi attuale* [Our Current Crisis],[16] and since there was no hint of the Italian philosopher in *Dialectics of the Concrete*, we can infer that his acquaintance was closely connected with his meetings and exchanges with Italian intellectuals, made easier by the contribution of Lubomír Sochor, who could speak their language.[17]

At the same time there were close contacts between the reviews *Literární noviny* [Literary News] and *Plamen* [The Flame], of whose editorial boards Karel Kosík was a member, and the review *Il Filo rosso* [The Red Thread], where Guido Neri held the same position.

The Italian magazine, a monthly publication of political and cultural comments published by Feltrinelli in Milan, opened up the main themes concerning real socialism in its first issue, publishing the contribution by Renato Rozzi entitled 'Problemi della psicologia in un paese socialista' [Problems of Psycho-

---

13   Kosík 1964b.
14   Kosík 1964a. Now in Kosík 2013. In English Kosík 1995h.
15   Kosík 1967f. Republished as Kosík 2013a.
16   Kosík 1969c.
17   Editorial note: Lubomír Sochor prepared and translated two volumes of selections from Antonio Gramsci's *Prison Notebooks* – see Gramsci 1966; 1970. Nevertheless, Kosík's first reference to Gramsci appeared in a 1956 article published in *Literární noviny* – see Kosík 2019c. It referred to a text later published in Sochor's volume, which suggests that Sochor may have drawn Kosík's attention to the text, and that Sochor's role in propagating Gramsci among Czech Marxist intellectuals was crucial. Later, Kosík also reviewed the first, short volume of selections from Gramsci's *Prison Notebooks* to appear in Czech (Gramsci 1959) – see Kosík 2019b. It is thus likely that Kosík was somewhat familiar with Gramsci before developing his Italian contacts as described by Fusi. Gramsci's *Letters from Prison* (*Lettere dal carcere*, Milano: Giulio Einaudi, 1947) were also published in Czechoslovakia in 1949 – see Gramsci 1949.

logy in a Socialist Country],[18] which was the result of exchanges of experiences and visits to facilities in Prague. In the following issues, up to number 10 (the last was published in January–March 1965), articles by the economist Radoslav Selucký, by Kosík and by Gianlorenzo Pacini on the opposition of Czechoslovakian writers and by Guido Neri on Karel Kosík and the interpretation of praxis made their appearance, keeping constant attention on Socialist countries, from Yugoslavia to Poland and Hungary. The attention paid to Lukács with the translation of *Lenin* (later published by Einaudi in 1970 as *Lenin: unità e coerenza del suo pensiero*[19]), was particularly relevant from a philosophical point of view.

At the same time, in *Literární noviny* Františka Faktorová wrote a reportage on her experience at the Olivetti factory in Ivrea, a factory she had got to know through Roberto Rozzi. Karel Kosík was going to write a comment on *Il Filo rosso* and Rozzi's above-mentioned contribution 'Problemi della psicologia in un paese socialista'.

It is no accident that the first translation and edition of Kosík's *Dialectics of the Concrete* was published in Italy and in Milan by Bompiani, nor was it an accident that Kosík's works made their appearance in Italian journals as long ago as the early 1960s following his attendance at conferences in Italy.

So we come to 1968. Arrigo Lampugnani Nigri, Enzo Paci's assistant and publisher, among other things, of Jan Patočka's *Il senso dell'oggi in Cecoslovacchia* [The Meaning of Today in Czechoslovakia],[20] remembers being in Prague that year with his professor on the occasion of a number of conferences. Kosík's philosophical and political commitment actually reached its peak during his active participation and leading role in the Prague Spring. He was a protagonist whose criticism was not restricted to the ideology and practice of Stalinism, but also opposed any kind of new ideology, including the productivist and competitive one, which was supposed to produce a definite improvement towards a new and liberated society thanks to a simple quantitative growth of the technical and scientific factor.[21] Referring to Jan Hus, who chose between conscience and reason on the one hand and nihilism on the other, Kosík said that 'when the conflict between truth and nothing is radical', the choice cannot be anything other than radical.[22] And the Prague philosopher's position was radical throughout the upheaval of the Prague Spring, which Rossana Rossanda

---

18   Rozzi 1963.
19   Lukács 1976.
20   Patočka 2006c.
21   See Neri 1968; 1975.
22   Kosík 1968c, p. 142.

called 'the last train for socialism', an opportunity socialism could not miss,[23] for Kosík 'a rare historical moment when truth is unveiled'.[24] Critical thought had seen a chance, not only to confront the real, but above all to leave a mark on the historical and social reality, achieving a union of theory and praxis, of thought and action. Considering the global crisis, it was the right time to re-establish and to try to give socialism and politics new bases.

Soon afterwards, the tanks would appear. Kosík was isolated, at least publicly, from the international context he had interacted with until then, and he was reduced to silence. He wrote in 1969: the time of mirth is over. But for how long? Maybe forever? When he retrospectively contemplated the event of the Prague Spring, and considered how fast a system that seemed immovable had been overturned, he remarked: '[...] twenty years, a short time for a historical point of view but ages for an individual life'.[25] Kosík, among others, was not only prevented from publishing, but in 1973 all his works were removed from libraries. It was the *damnatio memoriae*.

Before going to Prague in the summer of 1970 I met Paci, who asked me to give Patočka the book published by Lampugnani Nigri, since we were not allowed to send it by normal channels. He gave me two addresses to turn to: the first was Dr Oliver Tenzer's, an intellectual who was less watched than others. I had to ask him whether contacting would be dangerous. Actually it was. Only two years later, in 1972, did I succeed in meeting the phenomenological philosopher, and in the same year I was able to make an acquaintance with Kosík. After that I took several trips to Prague, where I had many meetings. I took few notes anyway, because the sense (or certainty, according to my interlocutors) of being watched was strong.[26]

In 1973, after spending a month in Bratislava on a scholarship, I met Kosík several times. He introduced me to the philosopher Robert Kalivoda and to Pavel Machonin, a sociologist I had been interested in and whose research on Czechoslovak society had made up a chapter of my degree thesis. On the occasion of our conversations I had the opportunity to study Kosík's thought in

---

23   Rossanda 2003, p. 12.
24   Kosík 1968b, p. 22.
25   Kosík 1995m.
26   Those meetings enabled me to write my degree thesis in Philosophy: *Le posizioni filosofiche di Kosík e di Richta e le loro implicazioni politiche* [Kosík's and Richta's philosophical positions and their political implications] Enzo Paci supervisor, academic year 1971–72. In those years some more theses about *Dialectics of the Concrete* were written as reported by the *Bollettino dell'Associazione Italiana Slavisti* (Italian Slavist Association Journal), 1981, when Jitka Křesálková, a Czech language assistant at Milan State and Catholic Universities, was its secretary.

depth. These visits would turn out to be very useful, since a friend of mine, Giovanni Bossi, and I were particularly interested in confronting the different ideas of the philosophers of Prague and Budapest. For this purpose we had agreed that Giovanni would meet the exponents of the 'Budapest School'.

At that time we were both contributors to *aut aut*, and our notes, conversations, debates were used as the basis for a short essay which was published in Enzo Paci's journal in 1974 under the title 'Note sulla sinistra non ortodossa in Ungheria e Cecoslovacchia' [Notes on the Unorthodox Left in Hungary and Czechoslovakia].[27] Those were the years during which Kosík was working on a new essay that the German publisher Suhrkamp had already anticipated in 1972 in its catalogue, under the title *Kritik der technischen Vernunft* [Critique of Technical Reason]. This is why a 'dumb cover' with no drawings or words appears still today in online catalogues with the author's name and the title, but with the note *not available*.

The pages confiscated by the state police in 1972 and 1975 concerned this very project, where he tried to gather the essentials of the two systems – capitalist and socialist, seemingly antithetical – into a single common economic structure determined by the symbiosis between economics, science and technology, an economic structure that was developing in two different ways. In Kosík's opinion, 'the main element of both societies, capitalist and socialist – that is economics + science + technology – was developing in two ways, but it was always the same merging that took place and left its mark on both. Therefore the economic structure was basically the same. Actually in neo-capitalism, the personal interest could come into conflict with the interest of the state and through this antagonism it assumed a central role'.[28] The conflict between 'bureaucratic socialism' and 'liberal socialism' that had distinguished Kosík's position in his essays and in his contribution to the '68 Spring was now over.

However, it was not only the experience of sequestration that thwarted the work he had planned: reality, as he would tell me some years later, was becoming less and less transparent and the Prague philosopher had to put aside the idea of a philosophical paper that could tackle the system as a whole, as he had done in the *Dialectics of the Concrete*. His work condensed the need for critical thought that could analyse present and past events so as to understand the human condition in fragments of reflection. He always focused his attention on the triad (economics, science, technology), an unavoidable choice, since the

---

27   Bossi and Fusi 1974. The contribution was inspired by the conversations Giovanni Bossi and Gabriella Fusi had with some exponents of the Lukács school in Budapest and with Karel Kosík in Prague in the summer of 1973.

28   Bossi and Fusi 1974, p. 65.

liberating possibilities were hidden there. The liberation which critical thought had always aimed at consisted in regaining possession of culture and politics, keeping in mind the preservation of man as a being who establishes a relationship with truth. This thought rose now against the ideology that 'calculates and misrepresents',[29] so as not to reduce reason to personal and private interest and to simple utilitarian reason.

This was what made the relationship with Italian philosophers and intellectuals particularly close: 'We meditated, dreamed and wondered critically whether from Italy and Bohemia an impulse could come to remind everybody how joy, freedom and beauty are essential requirements for real life, and elements which could give birth to a dignified lifestyle of modern times'.[30]

29   Kosík 1993f, p. 215.
30   Kosík 1993f, p. 224.

CHAPTER 16

Karel Kosík in Mexico: Adolfo Sánchez Vázquez and *Dialectics of the Concrete*

Diana Fuentes

This paper intends to present the impact that Karel Kosík has had on Spanish-language philosophy owing to the interest and work of Adolfo Sánchez Vázquez. Karel Kosík participated in the Thirteenth International Congress of Philosophy in Mexico City in 1963. He delivered a speech entitled 'Was ist der Mensch?' which focused on the main ideas of his recently published book *Dialectics of the Concrete*. The lecture was attended by the Spanish-Mexican Marxist philosopher Adolfo Sánchez Vázquez, author of the 1967 landmark book *The Philosophy of Praxis*, who refers to Kosík's work as one of the most appealing, evocative and richest in Marxist literature. Such was Sánchez Vázquez's interest in the *Dialectics* that he actively promoted it to be translated into Spanish and published in Mexico. In 1967, the Mexican publishing house Grijalbo released the Spanish edition (which was translated from the Italian and German versions by Adolfo Sánchez Vázquez himself), and Karel Kosík began to be enthusiastically and widely read in Latin America.[1]

1   The Publication of *Dialectics of the Concrete* in Spanish

Dialectics of the Concrete has been known and read in the Spanish-speaking world since 1967 thanks to the translation and publishing arrangements made by Adolfo Sánchez Vázquez. The book was translated from the Italian version published by the Bompiani publishing house in 1965. As there has been no new edition or reprinting of the text since that year, it is still this edition that circulates on the Internet, and that new generations, who have no access to the printed book, obtain in a digital version. It can therefore be claimed that the early introduction of Karel Kosík into the Spanish-speaking critical thought of those decades is due to the great intellectual affinity that Adolfo Sánchez Vázquez professed for him.

---

[1]   Kosík 1967b.

There are many elements that can be pondered with regard to the relevance of the printing in Spanish of *Dialectics of the Concrete* so soon after its first appearance in Czech in 1963, but among them, the support from the Grijalbo publishing house enables us to perceive the influence the book would have in the Spanish-speaking world in the following decades. This publisher was responsible for many years for the publication and translation into Spanish of both classic texts and current discussions of Critical and Marxist thought. We need only consider the classic collection *Colección 70* from Grijalbo, which has been an indispensable scholarly reference over the decades, to appreciate the influence, prestige and impact that a book under this label had. The publishing house was founded by Juan Grijalbo, who like Adolfo Sánchez Vázquez had lived in exile in Mexico after the defeat of the Republic in the Spanish Civil War, before returning to Spain in 1965. Under his guidance, Grijalbo contributed to distribute important works that expanded the scope of Marxist discussions far beyond what was available through the books of the Progreso publishing house in Moscow. For example, Grijalbo printed *History and Class Consciousness* by György Lukács as well as Rosa Luxemburg's *The Accumulation of Capital*.[2]

In addition to Grijalbo, other Mexican publishing houses in those years, like Fondo de Cultura Económica, Siglo XXI Editores and Ediciones ERA, made enormous efforts to update the discussions in the field of political theory, social science and Critical Thought, making Mexico one of the most outstanding centres of book dissemination for the rest of Latin America. This is why insisting on the importance of the 1967 Spanish edition by Grijalbo enables us to understand the influence of its publication and, consequently, why *Dialectics of the Concrete* and Karel Kosík were known so early and so widely in the Spanish-speaking world. Since then, Karel Kosík has been regarded in Mexico as part of that powerful generation of critical Marxists where we can find Jindřich Zelený, István Mészarós, the Yugoslavian group Praxis, and, of course, Adolfo Sánchez Vázquez.

Nevertheless, it is clear that Marxist thought has not been a commercial priority for publishing houses since the 1990s, and for almost twenty years many of those books could only be found in second-hand bookstores. Nowadays many only circulate on the Internet, since some of them are actually unobtainable in their printed form. Even now that we are experiencing a kind of revival of Marxism, it is noteworthy how necessary it is to have new editions, commented on with new outlooks. Fortunately, in the case of Karel Kosík, the work of Adolfo Sánchez Vázquez and the emphasis he gave to him in his books has placed

---

2 Lukács 1969; Luxemburg 1967.

Dialectics of the Concrete as a fundamental and prevalent source of Critical Marxism for several generations; a Critical Marxism that was able to overturn the doctrinarian and simplistic thought that came from official Marxism by returning to the ontological foundations of the philosophy of praxis.

Before commenting on the theoretical affinities between both writers, it is worth explaining who Adolfo Sánchez Vázquez was and why his work is so widely renowned among those who promoted an innovative, critical and open Marxism, especially in Latin America; and also among those who tirelessly upheld the validity of the critique of political economy and the Marxist approach to understanding the world throughout the adverse turmoil that the fall of actually existing socialism brought about and the resulting elevation of capitalism as purportedly the only way forward for humanity.

2 Adolfo Sánchez Vázquez and the Path to *The Philosophy of Praxis*

Adolfo Sánchez Vázquez, poet and socialist philosopher, was born in Algeciras, Spain on 17 September 1919, and died at the age of 95 on 8 July 2011, in Mexico City. He was one of the many exiles who, as a consequence of the rise of fascism during the Spanish Civil War, were received in Mexico after 1939, when no other nation dared to assume responsibility for the survival of those persecuted by fascism. He spent the rest of his life in Mexico, where he built a brilliant intellectual career that places him as one of the most important exponents in the region of what is called 'non-orthodox Marxism'. His work was shaped in the complex scenario of an urgent critique of revolutionary thought and of the practices of 'actually existing socialism'; critiques that eventually led him to confront the dogmatism of Soviet Marxism and the theoreticist Marxism of Louis Althusser, who had a great impact in Latin America.

Bolívar Echeverría, another important Latin-American Marxist and also a naturalised Mexican, said that Adolfo Sánchez Vázquez deserved to be acclaimed for the commendable boldness, audacity and courage with which he practiced Marxism. That was especially true during those years in which promoting Marxist discourse provoked scorn and derision from those who attempted to close off and cancel out Marxist approaches, as well as from those who had faltered and let themselves be absorbed by what Echeverría called, 'The only totalitarian and repressive discourse there is – the all-embracing discourse that carries out a tireless aegis of capitalist modernity'.

Sánchez Vázquez's work falls within the efforts to redefine Marxism. This led him to undertake a critical analysis of Marx's early works, which, he claimed, had not yet received an adequate interpretation. Along these lines, he fashioned a discourse on the centrality of the category of *praxis* in Marxism, and on the Marxist approach to the distinctive characteristics of human activity, social life, historicity, and the fundamentals of emancipatory practice. The origin of his philosophy of praxis is a text from 1961 – *Aesthetic Ideas in Marx's Economic and Philosophic Manuscripts of 1844*.[3] The following year, the translation of Marx's *Economic and Philosophic Manuscripts*[4] into Spanish by Wenceslao Roces enabled Sánchez Vázquez to present a course on the texts and elaborate upon his conceptions. These elaborations were included in his subsequent book, *The Aesthetic Ideas of Marx* (1965).[5] In 1967 he published the landmark book *The Philosophy of Praxis*,[6] which was republished in 1980 with some modifications to update the text and reprinted in 2003 with new attachments. In 1982, he published another work of great interest for renewing an understanding of Karl Marx, *Philosophy and Economics in Young Marx: The Manuscrips of 1844*,[7] which was reedited in 2003 under the name *The Young Marx: The Manuscripts of 1844*.[8] But these are just the major texts; Adolfo Sánchez Vázquez also produced a vast amount of other philosophical essays in which he discussed and reflected on the meaning of ethics, politics and art.

It is now possible to state that Sánchez Vázquez's undertaking was not an attempt to create a new exegesis – yet another contribution to the vast disquisitions of Marxologists; on the contrary, his explicit objective was to uncover the concepts that underpin and make possible the assertion of a Marxist philosophy for revolutionary practice. This objective is embodied in his work *The Philosophy of Praxis* as a result of his analysis of the *Theses on Feuerbach* and the *Economic and Philosophic Manuscripts of 1844*, where Marx's essential concept of *praxis* can be found. Sánchez Vázquez's *The Philosophy of Praxis* builds on the tradition that bonds him to the reflections of Labriola, Lenin, Gramsci, Korsch and Lukács, who had already devoted important work to philosophy as part of Marxism. Therefore it is not surprising that he himself explained that the first source which enabled him to conceive the human being as a creating and practical being was the work of Marx, specifically his early works. However, he adds that it was under the influence of the Marxists of the 1920s and of those writers who criticised the official discourse of the Soviet Diamat that he managed to

---

3   Sánchez Vázquez 1961.
4   Marx 1968.
5   Sánchez Vázquez 1965.
6   Sánchez Vázquez 1967b.
7   Sánchez Vázquez 1982.
8   Sánchez Vázquez 2003.

engender his own understanding of the work of Marx and, specifically, a methodical and profound reflection on the fundamentals of Marxist philosophy.

Thus, Adolfo Sánchez Vázquez effectuated and promoted a reading of the critique of political economy from the perspective of a human project, which allowed him to characterise the philosophy of praxis as the unity of a project of emancipation, a critique of the existent, and the necessary knowledge of reality; since it is reality that we are to transform.[9] These elements entail a philosophical reflection that is centred on the thesis that the human being produces itself through its transformation of the world. This is why it is a philosophy, but not just any philosophy; it is a philosophy that places praxis at the centre of its reflection. Accordingly, the philosophy of praxis entails an ideological decision, that is to say, it entails the adoption of a class stance towards reality, which includes values and ideas, as well as specific conceptions of the human being and of its relations to its environment and to other human beings.

3 Affinities between Karel Kosík and Adolfo Sánchez Vázquez

The theoretical parallelism and almost simultaneity of *The Philosophy of Praxis* (1967) by Adolfo Sánchez Vázquez and the *Dialectics of the Concrete* (1963) by Karel Kosík should be appraised as part of a history of critical thought of the twentieth century, taking into account the emergence and manifestation of an epoch in which a revitalisation of the meaning Marxist critique was taking place. There was a strong necessity to deepen the ontological-methodological fundamentals of Marxist historical praxis by raising historical questions on the contradictions of actually existing socialism and of developed capitalism. From this perspective, their problematisations and commitments with an understanding of the present time as from a concrete-historical praxis must be incorporated into the spiritual atmosphere and the socio-historical reality to which they responded – as Kosík himself would insist with regard to reading and interpreting Marx's *Capital*. By this I wish to emphasise that a true appraisal of Karel Kosík and Adolfo Sánchez Vázquez's commitment to recover the richness and meaning of the materialistic theory of knowledge, as from the category of praxis, can only be fulfilled vis-à-vis the signs of exhaustion of those discourses, which turned out to be insufficient to deal with the severity of the crisis of

---

9 Sánchez Vázquez 1967a, p. 11.

civilisation that we are facing, especially after the surge of structuralism and post-structuralism and the propagated mistrust of all attempts to claim any sense or specificity of human activity.

It is therefore easy to understand that, on listening to and meeting Kosík, Sánchez Vázquez saw in him an eminent Marxist thinker in whom the depth and originality of his thought and the brilliance of his exposition were proficiently combined. The meeting took place during the Thirteenth International Congress of Philosophy in Mexico City in 1963, at which Karel Kosík delivered a paper in German entitled 'Wer ist der Mensh?' based on the main ideas of the recently published *Dialektika konkrétního* (*Dialectics of the Concrete*). Despite thinking that Kosík looked rather youthful and not very intellectual, and not being able to read the book in Czech, Sánchez Vázquez was deeply impressed by this congress delegate, by his lecture, and by the lively and firm manner in which he answered all his questions and critical observations, half in Russian and half in French. It was based on this indirect knowledge of the content of the book and the exchange of ideas it initiated that Sanchéz Vázquez recommended its publication in Spanish to the Grijalbo publishing house. Two years later, when he was finally able to read the whole work in its Italian version, he realised that he had not overestimated it at all. He was, in his own words, faced with one of the most appealing, evocative and richest works he had known in Marxist literature.

Locating Karel Kosík's thought in the preface to the Spanish edition of *Dialectics of the Concrete*, Sánchez Vázquez emphasises his participation in the revitalising and anti-dogmatic movement within Marxism that had been taking place since 1956 with mixed strength and results. It was a movement which, he explained, consisted of two undertakings: a) a return to the true Marx, free from the limitations, simplifications and myths that had for years been imposed by a dogmatic conception of Marxism, and b) an analysis of new realities, produced in our times and which Marx could therefore not possibly have known, but which should not be ignored by a creating and living Marxism.

Based on this framework, Sánchez Vázquez analyses Karel Kosík's philosophical relevance and transcendence into four themes. Firstly, Kosík recovered for Marxist discussions the reflections on 'the world of pseudo-concrete', i.e. the world of unilateral and fetishised praxis, for which humans and things are manipulating objects, and which is connected to a particular vision of things – false consciousness, naïve realism and ideology. Secondly, he restored the category of praxis to its central position, which enabled him to claim that knowledge is not contemplation – understanding *contemplation* as the immediate reproduction or reflection of things – given that the human being can only know in so far as it creates a social-human reality. Thirdly, the category of *concrete totality* made it possible for him to clearly explain the relations between social structure and praxis, and especially to show that the concrete human being cannot be reduced to the system. Finally, the distinction between *economic structure* and *economic factor* – the latter being alien to Marxism – which he identified with what he called the determining and prevalent role of economics, was key to his materialistic conception of history.

The core of the theoretical concurrences between both philosophers is thus based in their approach to what is human and to history, by examining the human being within the totality of the world. That is to say that far from those reductions that insist that the idea of *work* in Marx's writings displays a deterministic economicism, Karel Kosík and Adolfo Sánchez Vázquez share the idea that the objectivity of materialistic philosophy has *work* at its centre as a form of human praxis, without which there would not even be any knowledge of the world. This is the foundation and origin of the critique of political economy. In this way both authors are loyal to the meaning of the Second Thesis on Feuerbach, 'The question whether objective truth can be attributed to human thinking is not a question of theory but is a practical question. Man must prove the truth, i.e., the reality and power, the this-worldliness of his thinking, in practice'.

This is why Sánchez Vázquez stated that Kosík demonstrates that economic categories are incomprehensible if they are not seen as an expression of a subjective activity of human beings and of their social relations, which entails a specific understanding of the being of the human being. It might seem at a cursory glance that this would mean a relapse into a new anthropologism. However, what Kosík proposes is an ontology of man (or an examination of 'the problem of the human being within the totality of the world'), and not an anthropology or philosophy of man (or an ethical-existential complement to Marxism). Also Sánchez Vázquez, from his own philosophy of praxis, insisted that the human being is self-produced through its transformation of the world. This is why the philosophy of praxis is a philosophy, but not just any philosophy, but rather the philosophy that takes praxis as its centre of reflection, understanding *praxis* as an emancipatory practice.[10]

---

10   Sánchez Vázquez 1967a, p. 12.

4   Alienation and the World of Pseudo-concrete

Another aspect from which it is possible to open a dialogue between Sánchez Vázquez and Karel Kosík has to do with the way they approach what Lukács – in his famous essay on 'Reification and Consciousness of the Proletariat' in *History and Class Consciousness* – considered to be the specific phenomenon of our time, the phenomenon of alienation.

In the understanding and analysis of Sánchez Vázquez, the problem of social alienation, as characteristic of social relationships and of the relationship of the subject toward itself and toward others, becomes a key aspect of the critique of capitalism. Moreover, in his perspective and interpretation of Marx's work, the question is the reason for alienation; namely the way alienation can be interpreted in the course of history, which involves perceiving the historical process as a totality. In other words, it is only from the general historical process that you can understand the origin of alienated labour. Hence his coincidence with Kosík with respect to the centrality of the category of totality; because, it is only by seeing history as 'human development' that the characterisation and critique of the alienation of social life under capitalism makes sense.

On this point, Sánchez Vázquez clearly points out that the problem of the alienation of the human being in the process of history is not related to the loss and recovery of an abstract essence – in a teleological perspective. Far from it, he conceives the phenomenon of alienation as a historical form in the long evolution of the human being; an evolution that takes place in a material manner through the acts of both singular and collective individuals, i.e. through their concrete practices. Hence it is also in the realm of practice that the human being can overcome the contradiction between its essence and its actual existence, a contradiction that is clearly embodied in alienated labour. Therefore he believes that Marx's critique, through the category of alienation, exposes the contradiction between essence and existence as merely an illusory paradox of history; because in the process of this contradiction's evolution the possibility of its own abolition is also implied, denying on the one hand that it is a universal and permanent state of human affairs, and highlighting on the other that the important thing is the recognition of the role of the human practice in the construction of historical realities. Overcoming alienation means humanising the world.

This form of alienation, in the understanding of Sánchez Vázquez, entails what in Kosík's view shapes the fetishised praxis that acts upon the world and its processes, perceiving them as natural, independent and external phenomena – the world of pseudo-concrete. This is a world thriving in ambiguity, 'a chiaroscuro of truth and deceit' that reveals but at the same time conceals reality, where the contradiction between essence and existence renders phenomena inadequate to reveal their true nature, because the phenomenal aspect of things is considered to be their essence. It is a world where the widespread *quid pro quo* hinders the dividing and reproducing of 'the one', i.e. the knowledge of the structure of things, the comprehension of things.

Against that world, the critical thinking that Kosík posits – the dialectic of the concrete that grasps totality as a process – shows that the objectivity of phenomena does not lie in their simple perception, but in showing that they are not independent but derived and mediated. This is what enabled him to understand that human knowledge is never plain contemplation or passive reception; given that the human being only knows in so far as it creates.

The vindication of the active subject is the key element of the intellectual link between Kosík and Sánchez Vázquez, both central figures in the thinking of unorthodox Marxism in the Spanish-speaking world. What for Kosík is configured as the world of pseudo-concrete, for Sánchez Vázquez is related to the concepts of alienation and praxis. Ultimately, for both of them, it is a question of how it is that capitalist society subsumes social life under its dynamics, but, at the same time and in a contradictory way, it produces the conditions of possibility of its criticism and its overcoming. The elective affinity between both philosophers is something more than a historical and thematic coincidence since it presupposes the permanent need that has been given within Marxism to reformulate its basic anthropological and philosophical principles, hence the interest to recover for contemporary thought the legacy of these two figures.

Still, however, it is a pending task to establish more clearly the moments of dialogue between both authors, not only with a historiographic purpose but, above all, to recover the intention that articulates them, that is, the criticism of the naturalisation of the mode of configuration of the real in capitalism, as well as confronting the discourse that claims it as the most finished stage of human development. In other words, to show not only the delirious irrationality that accompanies capitalism but the rationality hidden in it; the normativity that articulates it, making manifest the contradictory sense that is constitutive to it. For this, the discourse of both authors is configured as a way of confronting and putting oneself face to face with reality, in order to turn the content of the apparent from an act of self-affirmation of the subject. These are two voices for which criticism works as a rejection of the theory working under the assumption of a reality in which individuals must accept as pre-established the basic destinations of their existence.

CHAPTER 17

Karel Kosík and US Marxist Humanism

Peter Hudis

1   Introduction: Marxism and Philosophy

Perhaps the most important contribution of Karel Kosík's *Dialectics of the Concrete*, not just for his time but also for our own, is its insistence on the *indispensability* of philosophy. Philosophy remains a vital form of human praxis so long as the revelation of the essence of things is not identical with their phenomenal appearance. Since philosophy is a distinct form of questioning that 'shatters the certainties of ordinary consciousness and everyday fetishised reality',[1] it 'continues to be a special form of consciousness indispensable for grasping the truth of the world'.[2]

Although it can be debated as to whether philosophy is vital for *all* stages of human development, for Kosík there is no question that it is indispensable so long as we live in *capitalism*. That is because capitalism is such a *mystifying* system. And it is mystifying because it is based on value production. As Marx showed in *Capital* and elsewhere, commodities can be universally exchanged only if they possess a common *quality*. This common quality is provided by a peculiar and historically specific kind of labour – abstract, homogenous labour. Strictly speaking, 'labour' is not the source of all value; its source is instead a specific *kind* of labour – labour that has been rendered abstract through the instrumentality of socially necessary labour time.[3] Abstract labour, according to Marx's *Capital*, is the *substance* of value; it serves as the condition for the possibility of universal commodity exchange. However, as Marx stated, 'Value does not have its description branded on its forehead; it rather transforms every product of labor into a social hieroglyphic'.[4] Since value can only show itself in a relation between one material product and another, it *appears* that what

---

1   Kosík 1976, p. 134.
2   Kosík 1976, p. 103.
3   See Dunayevskaya 2000 [1958], p. 105: 'Socially-necessary labor time is the handmaiden of the machine which accomplishes the fantastic transformation of all concrete labors into one abstract mass. Constant technological revolutions change how much labor time is socially necessary. [...] All must subordinate themselves to the newly set socially necessary time to be expended on commodities. Competition in the market will see that it is done'.
4   Marx 1976a, p. 167.

connects products, and increasingly people, is a quasi-natural property of the *things* themselves instead of a historically specific kind of labour. It follows from this that the mysterious nature of the commodity-form cannot be dispelled through a merely empirical analysis of existing conditions, since its fetishised reality is 'adequate' to the 'peculiar social character of the labor which produces' it.[5] Capitalism *has* to appear natural and immutable, and hence mystifying, precisely because it is a system of value production. *No system in human history so radically divorces the essence of things from their phenomenal appearance.*[6]

How ironic then that it is precisely in developed capitalist societies, in which truth shows itself *least* immediately to the knowing subject, that we face the most persistent effort to deny the indispensability of philosophy – a move that defines not only capitalism's apologists but also some of its most fervent critics. Marxism after Marx, much of which proclaimed that philosophy 'as such' comes to an end with Marx's critique of capitalism, is the most vivid expression of this tendency.

Although the notion of the end of philosophy 'as such' is often associated with Engels and the post-Marx Marxists of the Second International, it has its roots in Ludwig Feuerbach's critique of Hegel. In arguing that philosophy is an extension of religious illusion, in his *Essence of Christianity*, Feuerbach held that sense-certainty is the criterion of truth. In doing so he rejected Hegel's claim that sense-certainty is abstract[7] and that genuine positivity results from the negation of such abstractions through the 'negation of the negation'. Feuerbach instead championed a positivist turn in which philosophy becomes dissolved into the sciences of human subjectivity, such as psychology and anthropology.[8] Marx, however, began to part ways with Feuerbach in the concluding section of the *Economic and Philosophic Manuscripts of 1844*, the 'Critique of the Hegelian Dialectic'. As Herbert Marcuse noted, 'This is the point

---

5   Marx 1976a, p. 165. For both Marx and Hegel, the truth of a given phenomena is determined by whether or not it is adequate (or corresponds to) its concept. Since commodity fetishism is not an illusion but expresses capitalist social relations 'as what they are' (p. 168) it is adequate to the concept of capital. Commodity fetishism is capitalism's *truth*.
6   See Marx 1981, p. 956: 'All science would be superfluous if the form of appearance of things directly coincided with their essence'. Value appears, and *must* appear as a material relation between things, even though its essence is a specific form of *human* relations.
7   See Hegel 2018, p. 60: 'This *certainty* in fact yields the most abstract and the very poorest *truth*. It expresses what it knows as this: It *is*; and its truth only contains the *being* of the term'.
8   The full implications of this turn toward the 'concrete' did not becomes fully evident until Feuerbach's later work, which explicitly abandoned philosophy in favour of social criticism. In the 1840s, Feuerbach still tended to view his work as part of 'the philosophy of the future'.

in which Marx's critique of Feuerbach begins. Marx upholds Hegel as against Feuerbach. Hegel had denied that sense-certainty is the final criterion of truth, on the ground that, first, the truth is a universal that cannot be won in an experience that conveys particulars, and, second, that truth finds its fulfillment in a historical process carried forward by the collective practice of men'.[9]

Regardless of the provenance of the claim that philosophy 'as such' comes to an end with the emergence of Marxism, the critical question for today is: Where has this left us by the twenty-first century? Whether articulated by such crude tendencies as traditional Marxism or sophisticated ones such as structuralism and postmodernism, we have been led to a dead end – to a failure to envision the *transcendence* of capitalist value production. Even such well-meaning approaches as market socialism, which *tries* to pose an alternative to capitalism, seem unable to think outside the framework of social relations defined by exchange value, capital, and profit.

This situation makes especially relevant Kosík's critique of the position that the advent of Marxian critique heralds the 'abolition' of philosophy. He elaborated upon this in the same period that a similar argument about the indispensability of philosophy was developed by the Marxist-Humanist theorist Raya Dunayevskaya in that most *unphilosophical* land, the United States. She held, 'As against the familiarly-held view that Marx developed from providing a philosophic critique to an economic basis for his theory of revolution [...] dialectical philosophy was the basis of the totality of Marx's work, not only in philosophy but in practice, and in both politics and economics'.[10] The four volumes of Marx's *Capital*,[11] as well as his studies on the non-Western world at the end of his life, represented, she argued, not an *exit* from philosophy but rather its fullest *concretisation*. Philosophy maintains its objective importance so long as the social realities delineated in Marx's critique of the value form of mediation remain dominant.

Although Dunayevskaya commented on Kosík's work on various occasions, he was unacquainted with much of her philosophical work until after her death in 1987.[12] In *Philosophy and Revolution, from Hegel to Sartre and from Marx to*

---

9   Marcuse 1964b, p. 271.
10   Dunayevskaya 1991 [1981], p. xxxvii.
11   By the 'fourth' volume, I of course am referring to *Theories of Surplus Value*, which Marx had originally intended as an integral part of *Capital*. It only became conceived of as a separate, quasi-independent work after Kautsky's publication of it in 1905–10.
12   When I met with Kosík in 1992 he told me that he had first heard of Dunayevskaya in the 1950s, from reading a 1946 critique of the Soviet revision of the Marxian law of value published in *Revue internationale*, entitled 'Une nouvelle revision de la théorie économique marxiste'. This was a translation of 'A new Revision of Marxian Economics', originally pub-

Mao (1973)[13] Dunayevskaya explored the importance of *Dialectics of the Concrete*, singling out in particular the creative notion of the individual found in Kosík's concept that 'Each individual must absorb the culture and live his life without intermediary'.[14] In a speech to the Hegel Society of America delivered shortly afterward, she called the analysis of Marx's *Capital* in *Dialectics of the Concrete* 'one of the most rigorous studies' ever to come out of Central and Eastern Europe. She especially singled out Kosík's comment that the commodity-form represents 'this "absolute" of capitalist society'.[15]

Dunayevskaya wrote several letters to Kosík in 1968, following the translation into English of two chapters of *Dialectics of the Concrete* in *Telos*, but she was unable to sustain contact with him – largely because of the changed political situation following the Soviet invasion of that year. I met with Kosík in 1992 and had a lengthy discussion with him on Dunayevskaya's work. He was especially interested in her critique of György Lukács for presuming that 'externalisation' was the 'central philosophical' concept of both Hegel's *Phenomenology* and Marx's appropriation of it.[16]

Although these two thinkers developed their ideas largely independently of one another, an exploration of the points of philosophic affinity between their respective versions of Marxist Humanism may help illuminate how to break through the ideological illusion that dominates so much of contemporary discourse – namely that there is no alternative to capitalism.

2   Kosík on the Indispensability of Philosophy

There is a long history on the Left of the view that the 'realisation' of philosophy entails its dissolution into the 'positive sciences' of sociology, political economy and cultural theory. Kosík pinpoints the premise of this position as the claim that philosophy is 'nothing but' the reflection of class-based society, having no independent validity of its own.[17] The view that philosophy is merely

---

lished in *The American Economic Review* (September 1944). For the text of the essay, see Dunayevskaya 1992, pp. 83–8. A colleague of mine in Prague, Stephen Steiger, made contact with Kosík several years before our meeting and provided him with several copies of her books.

13   For the Slovak edition of this work, see Dunayevskaya 1995. This edition includes my epilogue, 'Teória štátneho kapitalizmu R. Dunayevskej'.
14   See Dunayevskaya 2003 [1973], p. 259.
15   Dunayevskaya 2002, p. 188.
16   For more on this issue see Hudis 1989, pp. 87–96.
17   One of the most sophisticated expressions of this position is found in the work of Alfred

a reflection of alienated realities, however, rests on a misplaced conflation of *philosophy* and *ideology*. Ideology is the uncritical acceptance of existing social forms that become imprinted upon the mind. Dialectical philosophy, whose core is *negativity*, is very different, since it posits a thoroughgoing critique of the present and anticipates a liberated *future*. However, when philosophy and ideology are conflated, it is easy to assume that the abolition of alienated realities will lead to the 'withering away' of their intellectual expression in philosophical discourse.

What makes Kosík's critique of those who proclaim the 'abolition' of philosophy most germane is that he shows that it characterises not only the vulgar Marxists of the Second International,[18] but also some of the most serious efforts to rethink Marxism in the twentieth century. This is seen in the philosophic denial of philosophy by a number of currents that contend that, 'In Marxism, philosophy has been abolished, that praxis is not a philosophical concept but a category of a dialectical theory of society'.[19] While sociologism may have some advantages compared with bourgeois philosophies that remain confined to the abstract *cogito*, it tends to share the assumption that 'philosophy is necessarily an alienated expression of an inverted world'. As a result, 'The historicity of conditions is substituted here again for the historicism of reality, and philosophy is vulgarly conceived as a manifestation of conditions rather than as the truth of reality'.[20]

Kosík's critique not only represents a response to the currents of his day (such as existentialism, structuralism and the Frankfurt School); it also anticipates the more recent standpoint of such tendencies as capital-logic theory (Backhaus, Postone, C.J. Arthur, and others), which holds that philosophy is 'nothing but' the expression of the alienated value form.[21] The critique of the

---

Sohn-Rethel, who argued that Western philosophy is inseparable from the notion of an 'autonomous intellect' that arises from the birth of commodification and a monetary economy in ancient Greece. For a critique of Sohn-Rethel's position, see Black 2014, pp. 1–41.

18 There are many instantiations of this tendency, from Frederick Engels and Georgy Plekhanov and from Rosa Luxemburg to the Anton Pannekoek. In 'The History of Philosophy as Philosophy', Kosík identified the central thrust of this tendency as follows: 'Franz Mehring espoused the opinion of his time, which reduced the history of philosophy to a mere reflection of class conflicts, and denied philosophy any cognitive value. The history of philosophy became the history of false consciousness, of historical putrefactions, reflections of the age, whose objective validity persisted for as long as the historical conditions which gave birth to them' (Kosík m.s., p. 1). I wish to thank Ivan Landa for providing me with a translation of this unpublished essay.

19 Kosík 1976, p. 135.

20 Kosík 1976, p. 102.

21 Some of the capital-logic theorists, such as Backhaus and Postone, proceed from Sohn-

value form is seen as rendering superfluous the positive exposition of a Marxian *philosophy*. But why should this evasion of philosophy be seen as a problem? It is a problem because capital-logic tends to 'wall' humanity into capital, insofar as an alternative to the value form is not clearly articulated when dialectical philosophy is left aside. As I argue in *Marx's Concept of the Alternative to Capitalism*, both objectivist and subjectivist Marxists have tended to shy away from directly tackling the most difficult question facing the radical movement: what specific social relations are needed for a revolutionary transformation to overcome value production?[22]

It is therefore worth recalling that Kosík offers a critique of those who champion the move *from* philosophy *to* a critical theory of society for 'walling man into his socialness'. This has rightly been taken as a strident critique of the bureaucratic-statist regimes of 'actually existing socialism', which confined all intellectual activity – including art and the imagination – to mere expressions of 'social reality'. However, it is often overlooked that the discussion of 'walling man into his socialness' in *Dialectics of the Concrete* actually appears in the context of a critique of what Kosík calls 'a different way of abolishing philosophy' than that found in orthodox Marxism – namely, in Herbert Marcuse's notion that with Marx's critique of capital, philosophy passes into a 'dialectical theory of society' or intellectually-informed social science.[23] Kosík says that while the first 'form of abolishing philosophy' in the history of Marxism is based on the false claim that Marx turned away from Hegel, the second and more recent form is based on the claim that Marx's *appropriation* of Hegel turns Marxism into radicalised 'social science or sociology'.[24] For Kosík, however, Marx's 'materialist inversion' of Hegel marks not the end of philosophy, but

---

    Rethel's claim that philosophy is an estranged expression of the value form that begins to emerge, even if partially, in ancient societies that experience the phenomenon of monetarised commodity exchange. This claim, however, tends to fall into a genetic fallacy by assuming that the content of a phenomenon is reducible to its origins. Kosík appears to largely dismiss the claim on the grounds that it conflates a certain kind of philosophy with philosophy 'as such'.

22   See Hudis 2013, pp. 9–36.

23   See Dunayevskaya 2012 for her extensive correspondence with Marcuse, which largely concerned the relevance of Hegel's Absolutes for the contemporary world. See also Marcuse 1958, pp. 7–12.

24   It should be noted, in Marcuse's defence, that it was only in his later work, beginning in the late 1950s, that he emphasised the alleged shift 'from' philosophy 'to' social theory. His earlier work, such as *Hegel's Ontology and the Theory of Historicity* and *Reason and Revolution*, were critically important contributions to dialectical philosophy. Dunayevskaya was especially indebted to *Reason and Revolution*, although its concluding chapters already point in this direction.

rather a transition from one philosophy into another. His critique of 'walling man into his socialness' therefore does not only take issue with established Marxism; it represents a challenge to *any* approach that views the 'realisation' of philosophy as entailing its dissolution. Kosík writes, 'Abolishing philosophy in dialectical social theory [...] turns into a closedness: socialness is a cave in which man is walled in [...] Man is *walled in* in his socialness. Praxis which in Marx's philosophy had made possible both objectivation and subjective cognition, and man's openness toward being, turns into social subjectivity and closedness: man is a prisoner of his socialness'.[25]

In the same period in which Kosík was developing these insights, Dunayevskaya, a Ukrainian-born Marxist who served as Leon Trotsky's Russian-language secretary in Mexico in 1937–38, was developing her own version of 'Marxist Humanism', which also focused on the indispensability of philosophy. After breaking from Trotskyism in the 1940s (when she developed the first economic analyses of Stalin's Russia as a state-capitalist society[26]), she issued the first English-language translation of parts of Marx's *Economic and Philosophical Manuscripts* of 1844, as well as Lenin's 'Abstract of Hegel's *Science of Logic*' of 1914–15. In *Marxism and Freedom* (1958), she argued that the startling phenomenon of counter-revolutionary state-capitalism emerging from *within* revolution signified that 'our life and times impart an urgency to the task of working out a new relationship of philosophy to reality'.[27] Hegel's impact on Marx's development was, she argued, not only pivotal in the *formation* of Marxism, but demonstrated most of all the need for a repeated *return* to Hegelian dialectics in order to meet the challenges of our era, in which the central question is no longer 'how to make the revolution' but rather 'can humanity be free in an era of unfinished and aborted revolutions'. As she wrote in an essay in Erich Fromm's *Socialist Humanism* in 1965, published two years after *Dialectics of the Concrete*, the task is not to 'abolish' philosophy but rather 'to abolish the

---

25 Kosík 1976, p. 106.
26 See 'An Analysis of the Russian Economy' [1942–43] and 'The Nature of the Russian Economy' [1946–47] in Dunayevskaya 1992, pp. 35–82. By the 1990s, it appears that Kosík had likewise come to the conclusion that 'Soviet-type' societies were state-capitalist. He said in an interview in 1992: 'The disintegration of the Soviet empire is a liberating step in the search for an alternative. Whatever the ideologists of neo-capitalism assert, it belongs to the irony of the twentieth century that this system fell apart not because it was Soviet and communist, but because it liquidated the soviets (the workers' councils) and replaced them with a police-bureaucratic dictatorship, because it suppressed communism as a liberating modern alternative and instead asserted itself as poorly functioning, inefficient, *state* capitalism' (translation by Ashley Davies, for Czech original, see Kosík 1997k).
27 Dunayevskaya 2000, p. 16.

conditions preventing the "realisation" of Marx's philosophy, i.e., the reunification of mental and manual abilities in the individual himself, the "all-rounded" individual who is the body and soul of Marx's humanism'.[28]

For both Kosík and Dunayevskaya, the development of a Marxism adequate for the realities of the second half of the twentieth century – Marxist Humanism – entailed a thoroughgoing commitment not only to the Hegelian roots of Marx's thought, but also to their *development* as a part of an enduring *philosophical* enterprise. But why were both Czech and US Marxist Humanism so committed to the permanence of the philosophic project? What is lost by not emphasising it? And what respective contributions did their emphasis on the indispensability of philosophy make for the development of Marxism?

3 Hegel's Absolutes and Marxism

What makes dialectical philosophy indispensable is that it can disclose what traditional rationalism and empiricism obscure – the essence of human praxis. Traditional rationalism, as has long been noted,[29] proceeds from the isolated, atomised individual and tries to comprehend the whole from its standpoint. But the whole is never *actually* comprehended. In Kosík's terms, *concrete totality* escapes it. This is because it considers 'reality' to be that which can be known quantitatively, in terms of discrete parts; what cannot be accounted for in mathematised terms is considered 'unreal' and outside the scope of analysis. Whole arenas of the life-world – immaterial entities, 'metaphysical' ideas, emotions – are ignored or reduced to mere 'reflections' of material reality. The universal is thereby subsumed under the particular, and 'the absolute' is detached from history. Needless to say, these defects open the door for anti-rationalism, which tries to account for what traditional rationalism leaves out. One such form is empiricism, which seeks to counter rationalism by returning to the concrete. Empiricism, however, suffers from some of the same defects as rationalism. Despite the common view that they are opposed to one another, they presuppose an individual subject that is incapable of grasping social life and lived experience as a totality. Yet another counter to rationalism is intuitionism. Irrationalism and intuitionism proceed from the standpoint of the whole, from the totality, but one that lacks any determinate content. It races to 'the absolute' like a shot out of a pistol. The particular is subsumed under the

---

28 Dunayevskaya 1965, p. 69.
29 The most outstanding critique of the pitfalls of modern rationalism is found in Husserl 1970.

universal, and 'the absolute' is once again detached from history. Traditional rationalism and intuitionism are opposite sides of the same coin; the former brings forth and necessitates the latter, just as the increasing rationalisation of social relations creates the basis for irrational mysticism in 'highly developed' capitalist societies.

While their limits are clear enough, it bears repeating that both traditional rationalism and irrationalism detach the whole, 'the absolute', from history – albeit in different ways. Dialectical reason, however, does not detach 'the absolute' from history, since it proceeds from neither the atomised individual nor an empty immediacy that lacks internal differentiation and specification. According to Kosík, 'The absolute and the universal are *formed in the course of history*. Ahistorical thinking knows the absolute only as non-historical, and thus as eternal, in the metaphysical sense.[30] Historicism culls the absolute and the universal out of history altogether. In distinction from both, dialectics considers history to be a unity of the absolute in the relative and of the relative in the absolute, *a process in which the human, the universal, and the absolute appear both in the form of a general prerequisite and as a specific result*'.[31]

Kosík's discussion of the immanence of 'the absolute' in history may not be the most widely discussed aspect of his contribution, but it is surely worth exploring. He insists, 'History is more than historicity, temporality, transience, and irreplicability which exclude the absolute and the transhistorical, as historicism would have it'.[32] He does not, of course, view history as the mere emanation or expression of some 'absolute' – as is the case with German idealists such as Schelling. 'The absolute' is not a person apart that operates behind our backs; such an inverted concept is alien to Marxism. Instead, 'the absolute and the universal *are formed in the course of history*'.[33] But what does Kosík actually mean by this? What does it mean to state, 'the absolute [...] is not divorced from the relative. It is rather "composed" of the relative or, more precisely, is formed in the relative'.[34] What 'absolute' is he referring to, and what role does it play in his thought?

The answer, I believe, is found in Kosík's analysis of the dialectic of capital in Chapter 3 of *Dialectics of the Concrete*. Marx's *Capital*, he says, is a kind of odyssey – but a very different one than an odyssey of consciousness (as in Hegel's

---

30   Kosík is referring to the Platonic and Neo-Platonic view of the absolute as an eternal Form residing outside of and beyond historical contingency.
31   Kosík 1976, pp. 82–3.
32   Kosík 1976, p. 82.
33   Ibid.
34   Kosík 1976, p. 83.

Phenomenology) or of subjective discovery (as in many works of literature).[35] It is instead an odyssey of capital, the objectual form assumed by human praxis under capitalism. However, Marx's aim in *Capital* is not to trace out capitalism's *development* as much as its tendency toward *dissolution*. *Capital* shows that what drives capitalist development at one and the same time fosters its tendency toward self-destruction.

Marx's *Capital* presents the odyssey of human praxis in its objectual, de-subjectified form, since in capitalism the object, dead labour, dominates the subject, living labour. Human relations *appear* to take on the form of things because that is what they *really are*. In delineating this objectual form, Marx's *Capital* is *adequate to its concept*. Capitalism, however, is inherently unstable and contradictory. *The dialectic of its development is the dialectic of its dissolution.* The critical analysis of the objectual, alienated expression of human praxis thereby discloses its absolute opposite: the essence of *non-alienated* human praxis – our capacity for freely creative, purposeful activity – which Marx refers to as the capacity for 'a totality of human manifestations' of life.[36]

The disclosure of the essence of human praxis – also referred to by Marx as 'human power as its own end'[37] and 'the absolute movement of becoming'[38] – shows that the absolute is immanent in history. This cannot be disclosed by intuitionism or traditional rationalism. It becomes known only through a detour, through a critical analysis of its alienated form of appearance. Yet this is an absolute that is *within* history; indeed, it is *formed* through the course of history. It is what Gramsci had in mind in writing, 'The philosophy of praxis is absolute "historicism", the absolute humanism of history. It is along this line that one must trace the thread of the new conception of the world'.[39]

Kosík's critique of those who 'cull the absolute and the universal out of history' may be somewhat abstract, which *may* explain why it has been passed over by many commentators of his work. But its importance can be illuminated by comparing it to the work of Dunayevskaya, who also argued for the immanence of the absolute in history.

As early as 1953 Dunayevskaya turned to a direct study of Hegel's Absolutes.[40] It was a subject that held her attention for many decades. Her fullest discussion

---

35   See Dunayevskaya 2002, p. 198 for a very similar view: 'Take [Maurice] Merleau-Ponty. He said that the greatest work since the *Phenomenology of Mind* was [Marx's] *Capital*. But *Capital* is not the application, so to speak, of the *Phenomenology*'.
36   See Marx 1975a, p. 306.
37   Marx 1981, p. 959.
38   Marx 1986, p. 306.
39   Gramsci 1971, p. 465.
40   See Dunayevskaya 2002, pp. 15–34.

of Hegel's Absolutes appeared in *Philosophy and Revolution* (1973). In contrast with interpretations that view Hegel's absolute as no different than Fichte or Schelling's empty Absolutes, she argues, 'Hegel himself did not displace reality when he entered the realm of "pure thought". Quite the contrary. The pull of objective history grounded Hegelian philosophy in the principle of freedom, so much so that the successive "manifestations of the World Spirit" are forever finding themselves inadequate to task of realising this principle and "perishing"'.[41] No one, of course, denies that Hegel's thought is deeply rooted in history. But the general consensus among Marxists, certainly from the time of Lukács's *The Young Hegel* onward, has been that Hegel's concept of the absolute lacks historical content. Did not Marx himself, after all, *criticise* Hegel's 'Absolute Knowledge' in 1844 for representing 'the annulling of objectivity'?[42] Did he not *praise* Feuerbach for 'opposing to the negation of the negation, which claims to be the absolute positive, the self-supporting positive, positively based on itself'?[43] Nevertheless, Dunayevskaya argues, 'The truth is that nowhere is the historic character of Hegel's philosophic categories more evident than in Absolute Knowledge'.[44]

Dunayevskaya does not deny that Hegel *dehumanises* the Idea by treating it as stages of consciousness and self-consciousness – instead of as live men and women.[45] She was surely aware that the *subject* of the *Phenomenology* is not humanity as such, but humanity in the shape of abstract consciousness. However, she also emphasises that Marx *departed* from Feuerbach when it came to the latter's wholesale rejection of 'the negation of the negation'. Even when Marx is most critical of Hegel he finds a *positive* dimension within the absolute, which he seeks to appropriate. His 1844 '*Critique of the Hegelian Dialectic*' singles out 'The outstanding achievement of Hegel's *Phenomenology* and of its final outcome, the dialectic of negativity as the moving and generating principle'.[46] He later adds, 'But because Hegel has conceived the negation of the negation, from the point of view of the positive relation inherent in it, as the true and only positive, and from the point of view of the negative relation

---

41 See Dunayevskaya 2003, p. 4.
42 Marx 1975a, p. 338.
43 Ibid.
44 Dunayevskaya 2003, p. 11.
45 This claim is itself a highly debated one in Hegel scholarship. For a different understanding of Hegel's *Phenomenology*, but one which also argues for a connection between Hegel's Absolutes and Marx's thought, see Rose 2009.
46 Marx 1975a, p. 329. I have emphasised 'and of its final outcome' to stress that Marx is speaking of the culmination of the *Phenomenology* in 'Absolute Knowledge'.

inherent in it as the only true act and spontaneous activity of all being, he has only found the *abstract, logical, speculative* history of man as a given subject [...]'.[47]

What could Marx mean by referring to the 'negation of the negation' as 'the true and only positive'? Surely, he does not think that positivity in the sense of material existence as such is a 'result' of a logical movement of the 'negation of the negation'. But surely that is not the only meaning of 'positivity'. Is the *existing* world the same as *true* positivity? Is sense-certainty best able to apprehend it? Feuerbach surely thought so. But as noted earlier, Marx departs from Feuerbach on this point. In his 'Critique of the Hegelian Dialectic' – the very document in which Marx praises aspects of Feuerbach's critique of Hegel – he refers to '*positive* humanism, beginning from itself'.[48] Indeed, he refers to this as 'the insight [of Hegel], expressed with the estrangement, concerning the appropriation of the objective essence through the supersession of this estrangement'.[49] Through his critical encounter with both Hegel and Feuerbach, Marx is reaching for a more adequate understanding of the 'positivity' that results from 'the negation of the negation'. That positive result is *communism*. Vulgar communism, Marx contends, stops at the first negation – the mere abolition of private property. He defines genuine communism, on the other hand – which for him is inseparable from 'humanism' – as 'the position as the negation of the negation'.[50]

Feuerbach, on the other hand, counterposes 'the negation of the negation', which is abstract, to positivity, which is concrete. Yet this 'positivity' is actually what Kosík referred to as the pseudo-concrete. It is the world of fetishised reality, which *appears* concrete. But it is not the actual, positively constituted concrete, since it represents the objectual form of human praxis in the era of alienation. To reach 'the true and only positive', 'positive humanism, beginning from itself', requires undergoing the 'negation of the negation'. Marx's focus on 'the negation of the negation', even when he is most searing in his criticism of Hegel, indicates that there is more to 'Absolute Knowledge' than appears at first sight.[51]

---

47 Ibid.
48 Marx 1975a, p. 342. The emphasis is in Marx's original.
49 Marx 1975a, p. 341.
50 Marx 1975a, p. 306.
51 It should be noted that virtually the entirety of Marx's discussion of Hegel's *Phenomenology* in his 1844 'Critique of the Hegelian Dialectic' consists of a discussion of the chapter on 'Absolute Knowledge'. For a translation of his excerpt-notes on 'Absolute Knowledge', which he wrote in conjunction with the 1844 Critique, see Hudis 2013, pp. 216–22. These excerpt notes have received almost no discussion in the critical literature on Marx.

In discussing these and related issues, Dunayevskaya notes that Hegel states in the chapter on 'Absolute Knowledge' in the *Phenomenology* that 'The process of carrying forward this form of knowledge of itself is the task which spirit accomplishes as actual History'.[52] Moreover, at the very end of the *Phenomenology*, Hegel tells us that Absolute Knowledge 'appearing in the form of contingency, is History', while its non-contingent expression is 'History (intellectually) comprehended'.[53] History seems to be integral to 'Absolute Knowledge' – at least in terms of how *Hegel* understands it.

But what *is* the absolute in Hegel? Is it a mere synthesis of prior knowledge, the resolution of contradiction, a closed ontology? Hegel writes, '[Absolute] Knowledge is aware not only of itself but also of the negative of itself, or its limit'.[54] Negativity pervades all of Hegel's categories, *including the absolute*. Dunayevskaya takes this to mean, 'In a word, Hegel is not standing stock still just because he has reached the absolute. Its negation will become the foundation for a new level of truth'.[55] In a word, the 'absolute' turns out to be *absolute negativity*. It is not a mere closure or the end of movement, but the comprehension of the movement of history itself.

Kosík does not enter into a detailed discussion of Hegel's Absolutes in *Dialectics of the Concrete*. But he does state, in terms strikingly similar to Dunayevskaya, that 'The unreason of reason, and thus the historical limitation of reason, is in its denial of negativity. The reasonableness of [dialectical] reason is in that it assumes and anticipates negativity as its own product, in that it grasps itself as a continuing historical negativity'.[56] Non-dialectical thought detaches negativity from reason, and is therefore incapable of grasping the actual movement of history. Hegelian reason has negativity at its inner core, and is therefore is able to grasp the 'active' side of history – albeit only abstractly, as Marx said in the first Thesis on Feuerbach.[57] For Dunayevskaya, much as Marx may have *wanted* to break from Hegel, he could never free himself from the 'spell' cast by his 'master', because the dialectic 'as a continuing historical negativity' *absolute negativity* – was integral to the dialectical reason that he employed as well.

But is Marx not averse to 'Absolutes'? Did he not also 'cull' the absolute from history? Dunayevskaya argues that this is not as self-evident as it may appear. Surely, Marx did not believe in fixed and eternal 'Absolutes'; every universal is,

---

52 Hegel 2018 [1807], p. 466.
53 Hegel 2018, p. 467.
54 Hegel 2018, p. 466.
55 Dunayevskaya 2003, p. 18.
56 Kosík 1976, p. 60.
57 Marx 1976b, p. 3.

for Marx, a moment of a *historical* reality and exists only in *relation* to it. But that hardly means that he dispensed with Absolutes or universals *tout court*, as seen in the section of Volume One of *Capital* that discusses 'the *absolute* general law of capitalist accumulation'. The 'absolute general law' sums up the ultimate logic of capital accumulation. 'The greater the social wealth' congealed in the objectified form of capital, the 'greater is the mass of a consolidated surplus population, whose misery is in inverse ratio to the amount of torture it has to undergo in the form of labor'. Increased accumulation of capital at one pole leads to increased 'pauperisation ... of sections of the working class' on the other. '*This is the absolute general law of capitalist accumulation*'.[58] This absolute, however, is not free of internal contradiction and differentiation. Instead, the 'absolute general law' encounters 'new passions and new forces' – especially of the army of the unemployed and underemployed – that *resist* capital's 'process of suction'. This internal antagonism leads, by the end of the book, to the 'negation of the negation' – the expropriation of the expropriators.[59] To be sure, in *Capital* the transcendence of capitalism is only intimated.[60] But a decade later, in his *Critique of the Gotha Program*, the conception of a post-capitalist society is spelled out in much greater detail.

Dunayevskaya concludes from this that for Marx, *as for Hegel*, the absolute contains 'the highest opposition within itself'.[61] Though the absolute general law posits the subsumption of the subject by the object, its absolute opposite is immanent in it, in the struggles of the subject to free itself of its dominance. *Negativity pervades Marx's categories no less than Hegel's*. The dialectic of negativity in *Capital* may not provide any 'blueprint' for the future, but it does *intimate* a transcendence of value production.

The question for *our* age, however, is whether it is enough to merely *intimate* the new society. Given the legacy of so many failed revolutions, must we not make much more explicit what represents a truly *viable* alternative to capitalism? For Dunayevskaya this question compels us to go further, to a *renewed* turn to Hegel, on the basis of his concept of *absolute* negativity.[62] In doing so,

---

58 See Marx 1976a, p. 798. The emphasis is Marx's.
59 See Marx 1976a, p. 929, where Marx distinguishes between 'the first negation' and 'the negation of the negation' in discussing the supersession of capitalism.
60 It should be noted, however, that Marx has a rather extensive discussion of a post-capitalist society at the conclusion of the section on commodity fetishism in Chapter 1 of *Capital* ('Let us finally imagine, for a change, an association of free men working with the means of production in common [...]'). See Marx 1976a, p. 171.
61 Hegel 1969, p. 824.
62 See Dunayevskaya 1991, pp. xxxvii–xxxviii: 'At the point when the theoretic-form reaches philosophy, the challenge demands that we synthesise not only the new relations of the-

she argues, we discover that 'So strong [...] is the objective pull of the dialectic of history – and Hegel considered philosophy to run "parallel" with it – that one could, not too misleadingly, "translate" the absolute as the new society'.[63]

Of course, any recourse to some abstract 'a' directing human affairs beyond our backs is out of the question, since such an inverted notion is an idealist delusion. The 'absolute' is either immanent in the praxis of the self-acting human subject, or is it not part of history at all. But is there any actual evidence of its immanence within reality? Dunayevskaya argued that it can be found in specific mass struggles that seek to go beyond the first negation – the mere abolition of private property and the market, a standpoint that Marx called 'vulgar communism' – by reaching for 'the negation of the negation', which is what Marx defined genuine communism or humanism to be. She discerned such a movement from practice that is itself a form of theory in pivotal freedom struggles at such historical turning points as the 1953 East German workers' uprising and the 1956 Hungarian Revolution, both of which sought to go beyond statist Communism and 'free market' capitalism. This revolutionary challenge represented a radical confrontation with existing society – which is why both were so quickly crushed. Nor was its significance only a matter of practical activity, since the Hungarian Revolution helped pry Marx's *1844 Manuscripts* from the archives and led to wide-ranging *theoretical* discussions of the humanism of Marx. Of these, and other pivotal social struggles, she argued, 'It was as if Hegel's Absolute Method as a simultaneous subjective-objective mediation had taken on flesh. Both in life and in cognition, "Subjectivity" – live men and women – tried shaping history via a totally new relationship of practice to theory. It was as if the "Absolute Universal", instead of being a beyond, an abstraction, was concrete and everywhere'.[64]

4   The Future Inherent in the Present

It is surely not easy today to discern the 'absolute universal' in everyday reality – especially since the movements that brought down the regimes of 'actually

---

ory to practice, and all the forces of revolution, but philosophy's "suffering, patience and labor of the negative", i.e. experiencing absolute negativity. *Then and only then* will we succeed in a revolution that will achieve a classless, non-racist, non-sexist, truly human, truly new society. That which Hegel judged to be the synthesis of the "Self-Thinking Idea" and the "Self-Bringing Forth of Liberty", Marxist-Humanism holds, is what Marx called the new society. The many paths to get there are not easy to work out'.

63   Dunayevskaya 2003, p. 36.
64   Dunayevskaya 2003, p. 42.

existing socialism' in 1989 (unlike those in 1956) did not reach to transform reality radically through a new relationship of practice to theory. The 'postmodern moment', as well as the retreat into various other forms of non-revolutionary theory (be it communicative ethics or the elevation of democratic discourse into the panacea for all social ills) reflects this historical limitation. However, it is one thing to acknowledge that a fundamental challenge to existing reality has not yet arisen in our generation, and quite another to presume that it is inconceivable that it can ever occur. Beneath the surface are many expressions of profound social dissatisfaction with existing society that the predominant variants of social theory are unwilling or incapable of addressing – as especially seen in how many recent spontaneous movements, from the anti-austerity protests in Europe to the Occupy Movement and emergence of a powerful anti-racist movement in the US, have stimulated important new discussions about the need to envision a fundamental break from capitalism. This is not to suggest, of course, that radical theoreticians need only await the spontaneous emergence of new instantiationsofefforts that seek to free humanity from capitalism. In light of the severe crisis and discrediting of both socialism and liberal democracy in recent years, the theoretical work of developing aviable conception of an *emancipatory* alternative to capitalism is sorely needed.

Actualising this brings us back to the indispensability of philosophy – or at the very least, of a philosophy that can point the way to a negation of capitalism that does not stop at a mere first negation that fails to target the social relations that are the condition for the possibility of private property, the market, and statist domination. In other words, is it possible to make a new beginning from the standpoint of absolute negativity? Dunayevskaya wrote in *Philosophy and Revolution*, 'The real question, therefore, is not the one concerning Hegel's specific ontological covering over human relations. The real question is this: Is it possible for another age to make a new beginning upon Hegel's Absolutes, especially absolute negativity, without breaking totally with Hegel? Marx did not think so'.[65] Marx did not think so because he lived in an era when it seemed that revolution was sufficient to bring forth a new society. We, however, are living in an era when it is obvious that revolutions do not by themselves lead to a new society – especially when left bereft of a perspective that can disclose a viable alternative to both existing capitalism and statist 'Communism'.

Did Kosík, who was witness to an era defined by these realities, think it was possible to make new beginning upon Hegel's Absolutes without breaking totally with Hegel? Toward the end of *Dialectics of the Concrete*, in the

---

65 Dunayevskaya 2003, p. 45.

section entitled 'History and Freedom', Kosík makes some cogent comments about 'the absolute'. He writes, 'When man considers himself a tool or a spokesman of providence, of the absolute spirit, History, etc., i.e. of an absolute force that infinitely transcends his own possibilities and reason, he falls into mystification'.[66] This critique of a 'providential' absolute resonates with Marx's critique of Hegel for inverting the subject/predicate relation. Hegel's mystification, Marx contends, resides in treating 'man' as the predicate of the Idea instead of as its subject and progenitor. Yet in contrast to virtually all Marxists, Kosík does not conclude that 'the absolute' is a mere mystification that has no historical basis or existence. As noted earlier, he argues, 'Ahistorical thinking knows the absolute only as non-historical, and thus as eternal, in the metaphysical sense. Historicism culls the absolute and the universal out of history altogether. In distinction from both, dialectics considers history to be a unity of the absolute in the relative and of the relative in the absolute, *a process in which the human, the universal, and the absolute appear both in the form of a general prerequisite and as a specific result*'.[67] This is a far more stridentembrace of 'the absolute' than found even in any text of Marx. Kosík follows Marx in critiquing the shortcomings of Hegel's conception of the absolute, but nevertheless affirms its immanence within history. Did he therefore conclude that it is 'possible to make new beginning upon Hegel's Absolutes without breaking totally with Hegel?' The evidence is unclear; his work concludes without any further discussion of Hegel's Absolutes, and as a whole it does not attempt to relate such concepts as 'the negation of the negation' to political or social concerns. This dimension of his work is left unfinished, at least judging by the text of *Dialectics of the Concrete*.

But that does not mean that our work in developing a concept of an emancipatory alternative to capitalism that is grounded in the dialectic of negativity need be left aside. As I argue in Marx's *Concept of the Alternative to Capitalism*, 'The realities of our time, in terms of its triumphs as well as its tragedies, call on us to develop a much more explicit and articulated alternative to capitalism than appeared necessary in Marx's time, and even to Marx himself. We do the most justice to a thinker like Marx, not by repeating what he said and did, but by rethinking the meaning of his legacy for the realities of our times'.[68] This rethinking cannot afford to bypass dialectical philosophy, for it is what makes it possible to discern the future that is embedded in the present. We surely cannot afford not to engage in the hard theoretical labour needed to articulate an

---

66   Kosík 1976, p. 146.
67   Kosík 1976, pp. 82–3.
68   Hudis 2013, p. 215.

alternative, since, as Kosík stated, 'Man [...] chooses his present from the perspective of the future, and thus forms his present on the basis of a project of the future'.[69] The extent to which the Marxist-Humanist legacy of Kosík and Dunayevskaya will live on largely depends on whether or not we rise to the task of orienting ourselves to this challenge.

69   Kosík 1976, p. 138.

Postscript: Looking Backwards

CHAPTER 18

Spirit of Resistance: Notes for an Intellectual Biography of Karel Kosík

Michael Löwy

1   Meeting Karel Kosík: A Publication of His Collected Essays (1994–2003)

In 1993 several articles by Karel Kosík were published in the French Journal *Le Messager européen*. Deeply impressed by these essays I wrote him a letter, which includes the following comment:

> I read with great joy your essays translated by the Journal *Le Messager européen*. For a long time I haven't seen writings with such breadth, such an elevated perspective, such lucidity in the analysis and critique of the modern world! [...] One can find more matter for serious reflection on the condition of modern humanity in your three short essays than in thousands of pages scribbled by the 'philosophers' who occupy the top ranks in the European and US cultural scene.
> Letter from 30 January 1994

An exchange of correspondence followed, and on 1 March 1994, Kosík invited me to take part in an international conference on Central European culture held in September 1994 in the town of Český Krumlov (South Bohemia), organised by the Bernard Bolzano Endowment Fund from Prague. I proposed to give a lecture on Kafka as an example of the intersection between Jewish, German and Czech cultures, which he agreed to.

In September 1994 I came with my wife Eleni Varikas to Prague, where we stayed for one or two weeks before the conference. On that occasion we had the chance to meet several times with Karel Kosík, who took us around the town and explained to us his (critical) assessment of the situation in the Czech Republic after the end of the bureaucratic dictatorship (but also the beginning of the capitalist restoration). A real friendship developed between us, which would last until his death. Karel Kosík showed a friendly interest in my presentation on Kafka at the Český Krumlov symposium, which emphasised the writer's connection to Prague Anarchist circles. The papers of the conference were published in Prague in a bilingual edition, Czech and German: *Ve světle tmy / Im Licht der Dunkelheit*.[1]

A few years later, in 2000, I proposed to Karel Kosík to publish a collection of his essays written after *Dialectics of the Concrete*, and we conducted a substantial correspondence on the issue. Our first letters were in French, but we soon moved, by mutual agreement, to German. It was a common initiative of myself and an Argentinian friend and admirer of Kosík, the historian Horacio Tarcus. With his help, we started collecting essays published in French, German, English, and of course Czech. We wanted to show that *Dialectics of the Concrete* was not his only writing, and that he had made a very substantial and important philosophical and political contribution in the following decades. We hesitated for a long time over the title, and finally decided, with his agreement, upon *The Crisis of Modern Times: Dialectics of Morality*.

In one of his letters, from 16 September 2001, Kosík made the following suggestion, both for how we should collect his writings and for the introduction we were writing:

> Ich habe eine wichtige allgemeine Bemerkung: ich bin überzeugt, dass für die französischen, spanischen Leser von Interesse und auch lehrreich sein könnte, die *Kontinuität* meines Denkens kennen zu lernen, d.h. sowohl die Kritik des Stalinismus, als auch meine Kritik des heutigen Kapitalismus, bzw. der Restauration des Kapitalismus, welche in meinem Texten nach 1989 enthalten ist. Könnten Sie diesen Umstand berücksichtigen?[2]

This is a very significant statement, which illuminates his entire intellectual and political itinerary, and of course, we took it into consideration. For sure, this does not mean that nothing changed in his philosophical views between the 1960s and his last writings – the Heideggerian *topoi* have greater weight after 1989 – but one cannot ignore his own perception of a decisive continuity.

We wanted to include in the collection an interview with Kosík, which would both shed light on his biography and discuss his writings. In fact, Kosík was extremely reluctant to speak about himself. We sent him a list of questions, but after a few months he answered with the following argument:

---

1 Becher et al. 1995.
2 I have an important remark: I am convinced that for French as well as for Spanish readers it could be interesting and illuminating to see the *continuity* of my thought; which means to see the critique of Stalinism together with the critique of contemporary capitalism, or, better put, of capitalist restoration, which is explored in my post-1989 texts. Could you take this into consideration? (English translation – J. Mervart).

> In der letzten Zeit habe ich mehrmals Ihre Fragen gelesen und habe auch mehrmals versucht, meine Antworten zu formulieren, doch das Ergebnis war ein totaler Misserfolg [...]. Meine Unfähigkeit präzise und sinnvolle Antworten zu geben ist für mich zu einem Alptraum geworden. Es tut mir sehr leid dass ich Ihnen zusätzliche Schwierigkeiten bereite, doch bitte ich sie dringend [...], schliessen Sie das Interview aus. Ich bin nicht im Stande es zu realisieren, für einen platen Text würde ich mich schämen.[3]
>
> Letter from 25 February 2002

The book was published first in Greek and soon after in French, thanks to Marc Perelman, both unfortunately a few months after Kosík's death.[4] Our plans for having the book translated into Spanish, Portuguese, Italian and English did not materialise.

My introduction of the book, with the help of Horacio Tarcus, was a brief summary of his political and intellectual evolution. On the following pages a substantially enlarged version of the original text is presented.

2   Karel Kosík's Intellectual Evolution

Karel Kosík was not only one of the most important philosophers of the second half of the twentieth century, but one of those who better embodied the spirit of resistance of critical thought. He is also one of the few that fought, in succession, all three great forces of oppression of modern history: Fascism during the 1940s, Stalinism after 1956, and the dictatorship of the Market after 1989. At a time when so many thinkers surrendered their autonomy in order to serve the powers that be, or turned their back on historical reality the better to enjoy academic linguistic games, Kosík appears as a man who stands up, refuses to surrender and does not hesitate to think against the current.

Karel Kosík was born in Prague in 1926 in a working-class family. As a young activist of the Czech Communist Party, he participated after September 1943 in the clandestine resistance against the Nazi occupation in a group called *Před-*

---

[3] Recently I have been reading your questions, and I have tried to formulate my answers many times. However, the result was a complete failure. The impossibility of giving you precise and thoughtful answers became a nightmare for me. I am deeply sorry for these additional inconveniences; but I would be very pleased if you could leave out the interview. I am not in a proper state to conduct it and I would feel ashamed of such a poor text. (English translation – Jan Mervart).

[4] Kosík 2003a; Kosík 2003b.

voj (The Vanguard). He was also editor of the illegal anti-fascist Journal *Boj mladých* (The Fight of Youth). Arrested by the Gestapo on 17 November 1944, and accused of 'high treason', Kosík was first imprisoned in Pankrác jail and later deported to the prison of Terezín, where remained from 20 January to 5 May 1945, i.e. until the end of the war. Submitted to forced labour, he succeeded in establishing a network of information with the outside thanks to the complicity of a female German railway worker. He would later comment, in a letter to Jean-Paul Sartre from 1975: 'I am the living memory of my comrades killed in Terezín'.[5]

After the liberation of Czechoslovakia, the young Kosík chose to study philosophy. His first teacher was Jan Patočka. In spite of their philosophical differences, Patočka had great esteem for his 'Marxist friend', whom he would later refer to as the most important representative of Czech philosophy in the present period. As was usual at those times in Eastern Europe, Kosík continued his philosophical *Bildung* in Moscow between 1947 and 1949. Back in Prague, in 1953 he published an anthology of insurgent voices from the 1848 revolution, and a few years later a book of his own on the same topic, *Czech Radical Democracy* (1958). In 1953 Kosík became a member of the Institute of Philosophy of the Czech Academy of Sciences. One of his first philosophical texts – an article on Hegel from a Marxist perspective – appeared in 1956. To what extent did he accept the Soviet-style 'Marxist-Leninist' philosophy (he seemed to believe in 'science as ideology')? Did he have doubts about the Stalinist trials in Prague (1949–53)? Can we consider his writings on the Czech democrats of the nineteenth century, as well as his friendship with Patočka and his interest in phenomenology, as manifestations of intellectual autonomy, a form of critical distance towards the official doctrines? I lack the information to answer these questions.[6] What appears very clearly, however, is that after 1956, the year of the Soviet Party's Twentieth Congress and Khrushchev's denunciation of Stalin's crimes – a watershed for many Marxists, both East and West – Kosík became increasingly committed to the struggle for a critical renewal of Marxism. His writings and conferences were received with growing interest among the critical intelligentsia, though obviously rejected by the Stalinist orthodoxy. Thus, at a public local party meeting in Prague in 1959, the representatives of the bureaucratic Party apparatus demanded, in vain, that he recant his iconoclastic statement published in the article 'Hegel and Our Epoch' in the Journal *Literární noviny*, from 1956: 'the domination of ideology is finished, now begins the

---

5 Kosík and Sartre 1975.
6 Other papers in this volume, such as those by Joseph Grim Feinberg, Tomáš Hermann and Jan Mervart, deal with this period and may provide some answers to these questions.

time of critical thinking'. His first contributions at international conferences soon attracted the attention and sympathy of those who were interested in the renewal of Marxist philosophy and culture. In September 1960, he took part in the International Philosophical Encounters of Royaumont (France), devoted to dialectics, with a paper on 'The Dialectics of Concrete Totality' – an initial version of the first chapter of his future book – that would be translated into Italian by the Journal *aut aut*.[7]

1963 saw the publication of the book that would immediately bring him a worldwide audience: *Dialektika konkrétního* (*Dialectics of the Concrete*), which was soon translated into Italian, German, Spanish, French and many other languages, and was compared to the main writings of Sartre, Lukács and Adorno. I shall not comment on this book, since it is the object of most of the papers in this volume.

In 1963 Kosík took part in the Thirteenth International Congress of Philosophy in Mexico City, where he presented a paper called 'Wer ist der Mensch?', which takes up some of the ideas of his book. The celebrated Spanish-Mexican Marxist philosopher Adolfo Sánchez Vázquez was deeply impressed with this unknown young scholar.[8] In 1964 Kosík travelled to Italy, where his ideas had already attracted attention both inside and outside the Communist Party. He took part in the international conference entitled Morals and Society in Rome, with a paper on 'The Dialectics of Morality and Morality of Dialectics', and gave a lecture entitled 'Reason and History' at the University of Milan.

During these years his essays began to be published in journals interested in the renewal of Leftist and/or Marxist thinking. Translations of his articles appeared in Italian Journals such as *aut aut*, *Carte segrete* or *Il Contemporáneo*, French ones such as *Recherches internationales à la lumière du marxisme* or *L'Homme et la société*, American publications such as *Telos*, and Argentinian such as *Nuevos aires*. The inclusion of his essay 'Man and Philosophy' in the collective volume *Socialist Humanism* (1965) edited by Erich Fromm – soon translated into several languages – also contributed to the dissemination of his ideas.[9] In this article, Kosík compares Machiavelli's system of government, based on the functional manipulation of human beings, to the similar one developed by technology in the modern industrial system. These articles are clearly based on the same philosophical premises as *Dialectics of the Concrete*, but they deal with theoretical or political issues less developed in his book.

---

7 See the paper by Gabriella Fusi in this volume, pp. 307–15.
8 For more on this see Diana Fuentes' contribution, pp. 316–24.
9 Kosík 1965b.

Until 1968 Kosík was engaged in intensive political-philosophical activity in Czechoslovakia, which culminated in the Prague Spring. As a fellow of the Institute of Philosophy of the Academy of Sciences, later Professor at the Faculty of Philosophy of Charles University in Prague, a member of the Central Committee of the Union of Czech Writers and director of its prestigious publication *Literární noviny*, he contributed significantly to the cultural-political changes that led to the watershed of 1968. One of the most important essays from this period is 'The Individual and History', which contains a sharp rejection of the determinist metaphysical conception of history: the future, argues Kosík, is a risk and a wager, always open and unpredictable, and it depends on human historical activity. Moreover, all victories of reason against irrationality are never definitive, because history is always incomplete.

On the occasion of the Summer 1967 Conference of the Writers' Union, Kosík gave a powerful speech in defence of the 'unity between reason and consciousness'. He mentioned as an example the great Czech 'heretic' revolutionary Jan Hus (fifteenth century), who refused to submit to the orders of the Church, preferring to die on the scaffold (1415) rather than renounce his convictions. Kosík's argument was obviously aimed at Stalinism, which required the sacrifice of reason and consciousness to the interests of the Party.[10] As one of the critical intellectuals who met at the headquarters of the Writers' Union, and later as co-director of the Journal *Plamen*, he appears as one of the main intellectual figures of the Prague Spring.

The writer Pavel Kohout gave us a very lively eyewitness account of Kosík's intervention at a meeting in March 1968 in the town of Tábor: 'Karel Kosík's participation raised the discussion to a new level. [...] It was the first time he had taken part in such a meeting, and he didn't have the experience or the manners of a professional speaker'. However, while he talked, 'the packed full room religiously held its breath'. In precise and sharp words, the philosopher denounced the political regime of Czechoslovakia as a 'police and bureaucratic system, based on the monopoly of power by an uncontrolled group of leaders'. His conclusion was unequivocal: 'The process of democratisation cannot stop until it achieves the legal and constitutional form of a democratic socialist system. Stopping half-way, with half-measures, will only reproduce the same old bureaucratic police system, modernised and repainted, where all the present problems will multiply and lead to tragic conflicts'. This is precisely what happened in the following decades ...[11]

---

10   English translation see Kosík 1995.
11   Kohout 1971, p. 247.

Following the Soviet invasion of August 1968, Kosík was elected to the Central Committee of the Czech Communist Party, during its Fourteenth (underground) Congress – the last Congress which clearly condemned the invasion. His essay 'Our present crisis' – published during the Prague Spring, four months before the invasion – had an international echo, being quickly translated into German, Italian and French. Kosík argued that the capitalist market and the so-called 'socialist' societies (based on political manipulation) were variants of the same system, modern industrial society, where the mechanism of production and consumption, the modern *perpetuum mobile* – described by Heidegger as *das Gestell* – determines human life. The human being, which created this mechanism, has become prisoner of its gears, and is reduced to a simple appendage of this modern pseudo-subject, this perverted omnipotent force.

As a part of the so-called 'normalisation' of Czechoslovakia in the autumn of 1969, the new authorities imposed by the Soviet tanks, under the leadership of Gustáv Husák, demanded that all members of the Central Committee accept the legitimacy of the invasion by the troops of the Warsaw Pact. Kosík, in a declaration which is not without some resemblance to that of Jan Hus, declared that he refused to comply. He was soon expelled from the CC, then from the Communist Party, and then from his position as professor at the university (and researcher at the Philosophical Institute), under the accusation of 'right wing deviationism'. From that moment on a period of 20 difficult years began for him, as a persecuted philosopher and a citizen without rights.

In 1972 Kosík was apprehended and submitted to a long and humiliating interrogation. In April 1975 the police invaded his home, searched the premises for six hours and confiscated some thousand pages of the manuscripts of two books in preparation, *On Practice* and *On Truth*, which were considered 'proof of the criminal activity of subversion against the Republic'. He decided to break his silence by sending a moving letter to Jean-Paul Sartre, denouncing police repression and the interdiction of any critical thought in Czechoslovakia. I have been treated as suspect, he writes, because I consider that every human being has the right to have his own opinion and to communicate it freely. In other words, because 'I consider it a fundamental human right that each human being can have a spinal column'. Sartre answered him with words of encouragement: 'This abomination, or better said, this stupidity [of the police regime in Czechoslovakia] cannot last for much time as long as there remain men like you, my dear friend, to denounce it'.[12]

---

12   Kosík and Sartre 1975.

Karel Kosík remained an outlaw in his country until the end of the bureaucratic regime. I lack more precise information on his (difficult) living conditions in those years, his philosophical and political thought, and his writings (none apparently). He did not join Charter 77, probably, as Josef Zumr suggested in a private interview, because he considered the document to be too liberal and not socialist enough. Following the 'Velvet Revolution' of 1989, Kosík recovered his previous position as Professor at Charles University.

However, after 20 years of opposing the bureaucratic regime, he would soon become an oppositionist to the new right-wing governments which came to power in Prague. The critical thinker who refused the dictatorship of the party equally rejected market absolutism. He also sharply criticised the partition of Czechoslovakia in 1992, which in an essay he referred to as a sort of 'Third Munich'. As he explains in an interview given to an Italian friend, 'they told me that I should at last be reasonable, march with the "spirit of the times" and put myself, like many others, at the service of the newly ascendant ideology'.[13] Since he refused to comply, the new powers that be, of neo-liberal orientation, would expel him from his position at the university in 1992, exactly as the authorities imposed by the Soviet tanks had done in 1969. It was only thanks to his friend Josef Zumr that he was able to obtain a fellowship at the Philosophical Institute of the Czech Academy of Sciences.

Marching against the current, Kosík remained faithful to the radical democratic and socialist ideals of the Prague Spring. In 1995 he published a collection of his essays from that crucial period: *The Crisis of Modernity: Essays and Observations from the 1968 Era*.[14] As he ironically commented in a French interview from 1993, 'the Prague Spring had a strange destiny: it was condemned and buried twice: by the winners of yesterday and by those of today', i.e. by the 'normalisers' imposed by the Soviet invasion in 1968, and, after 1989, by the new anti-communist rulers.[15]

During the next decade, until his untimely death in 2003, he continued to develop a radical criticism of the modern world, obstinately refusing to join the chorus of the new capitalist/liberal 'consensus'. His essays appeared in Czech Journals and were translated in several European publications such as *Le Messager européen*, *Claves de razón práctica*, *Lettre internationale*, *Il Manifesto*, *Leviatan*, *Telos* etc. In this writings, in a typical Left-Romantic way, traditional and pre-capitalist values are used in order to criticise capitalist civilisation from a

---

13 Karel Kosík, 'l'Homme mesure de toute chose', interview with A. Cassuti, in Kosík 2003b, p. 135.
14 Kosík 1995.
15 Interview with Alain Finkielkraut, in Kosík 2003b, p. 147.

democratic and egalitarian perspective.¹⁶ Kosík's approach is not so different from the one proposed by Adorno in *Minima Moralia*: 'Not least among the tasks now confronting thought is that of placing all the reactionary arguments against Western Civilisation in the service of progressive enlightenment'.¹⁷ A leftist re-interpretation of Heideggerian concepts and arguments is part of this configuration (as in other radical philosophers, such as Herbert Marcuse or Jean-Paul Sartre).

His relation to Marx is important in order to understand the dialectics of change and continuity in his intellectual evolution. Of course, this relation was not the same in the 1990s as in *Dialectics of the Concrete*. However, unlike other former leftists – not only in Czechoslovakia – he refused to treat Marx as a *toter Hund*. In 1993 he gave a very interesting interview to an Italian friend, Antonio Cassutti, published in the Journal *Micromega* under the title 'The human being, the measure of everything'. Observing that the author of *Das Kapital* was being treated, like Hegel a century before, as a 'dead dog', and that his name – as well as that of Rosa Luxemburg – was being erased from the streets by the new powers eager to show their allegiance to the 'market economy', he concluded: 'In a situation of this kind; I consider it an act of elementary decency – but perhaps it is necessary to recall what was meant by decency, modesty, *aidos* in Ancient Greece? Decency is the basic principle of democracy – to publicly take the defence of this great thinker that was Karl Marx'.¹⁸

Those among us who had the chance to know Karel Kosík personally were impressed by his modesty, his generosity, his sense of humour, and the acumen of his critical spirit in confronting the social and cultural realities of the Czech Republic and of the world. He was a discrete, sober person, who enjoyed friendly intellectual exchanges, but talked very little about himself, his history and his struggles.

Karel Kosík was at the same time a thinker deeply rooted in Czech history and culture – from the fifteenth-century Hussites to the radical democrats of the 1848 revolution, and the reform Communists of the Prague Spring – and a truly universal spirit, whose writings deal with the great issues of the present

---

16 For an extended discussion on anti-capitalist Romanticism, see Löwy and Sayre 2002. I sent a French version of the book to Kosík in January 1994, and he answered me in a letter from 1 March that he found it 'very interesting'. It was probably after reading it that he decided to invite me to the Český Krumlov symposium.

17 Adorno 2005, p. 192.

18 Interview with Cassuti, Kosík 2003b, p. 133. The ancient Greek concept of *aidos* meant, at the same time, honour, dignity, modesty, loyalty and solidarity. It would be interesting to compare Karel Kosík's celebration of decency with George Orwell's viewpoint that *common decency* is the key value of socialism.

times. He was an authentic man of the Enlightenment, but he distinguished clearly between the original *Aufklärung* of Kant and Mozart and the modern superficial rationalism 'which Husserl ironically called *Aufklärerei*'.[19] In his eyes, this first commitment was not contradictory to a keen interest in the Romantic anti-capitalist tradition, the tradition of cultural and ethical protest against industrial civilisation, in the name of past, pre-capitalist values. It is therefore not an accident that there are so many references in his writings to Rousseau, Hölderlin, Schelling and Novalis – who in 1799 compared modern society to a gigantic and monotonous mill that crushes everything under its grindstone. However, unlike the First German Romantics, his thinking is not conservative or past-oriented: 'a return to the ancient polis or the Medieval Christian community is not possible; to live inside their walls would be unbearable for the modern man. An emancipatory alternative can rise only from the creative and reflexive imagination'.[20] Like all Revolutionary Romantics – such as the young György Lukács – his perspective is not a *return* but a *detour* via the past towards a radically new utopia.

Beyond the changes that correspond to historical transformations and to the internal evolution of his ideas, one can perceive certain deep lines of continuity which run through his whole *oeuvre*, giving it a profound coherence, and a singular, even unique position in the intellectual landscape of the second half of the twentieth century:

1) A critique of modern civilisation, rooted in Marxism, Romanticism and Phenomenology, but truly original insofar as it deals with both its capitalist and its pseudo-socialist (bureaucratic) forms.

2) An ethical perspective, humanist and radical, which challenges the reified and fetishised forms of modern economy, society and politics.

3) A Principle of Resistance, against the totalitarian religions of the State, the Party and the Market, inspired by Jan Hus's 'No' to the Ecclesiastical powers of his time.

4) A passionate interest in the rich cultural forms of the past, from Ancient Greece to the Enlightenment, not as blueprints to be imitated, but as sources of inspiration for imagining an emancipated future.

---

19   Kosík, 'Aufklärung et Culture', in Kosík 2003b, p. 213.
20   Interview with Cassuti, in Kosík 2003b, p. 143.

References

Adorno, Theodor W. 2005, *Minima Moralia: Reflections on a Damaged Life*, translated by E.F.N. Jephcott, London: Verso.
Adorno, Theodor W. 1973, *The Jargon of Authenticity*, translated by Knut Tarnowski and Frederic Will, Evanston: Northwestern University Press.
Althusser, Louis 1973a, 'Réponse à John Lewis', in *Réponse à John Lewis*, Paris: Maspero.
Althusser, Louis 1973b, 'Remarque sur une catégorie: «Procès sans Sujet ni Fin(s)»', in *Réponse à John Lewis*, Paris: Maspero.
Althusser, Louis 1976, *Positions*, Paris: Éditions Sociales.
Althusser, Louis 1982, 'Sur le rapport de Marx à Hegel', in *Lénine et la philosophie. Marx et Lénine devant Hegel*, Paris: Maspero.
Althusser, Louis 1986, 'Marxism and Humanism', in *For Marx*, translated by Ben Brewster, London: Verso.
Althusser, Louis 1994, *Sur la philosophie*, Paris: Gallimard.
Althusser, Louis 2005, *For Marx*, translated by Ben Brewster, London: Verso.
Althusser, Louis 2008, 'Ideology and Ideological State Apparatuses', in *On Ideology*, London: Verso.
Althusser, Louis 2011, 'Transformation of Philosophy', in *Philosophy and the Spontaneous Philosophy of the Scientists*, London: Verso.
Althusser, Louis 2014, *On the Reproduction of Capitalism*, translated by G.M. Goshgarian, London: Verso.
Andělová, Kristina and Jan Mareš 2014, 'Hledání české radikální demokracie. Karel Kosík a filozofie (českých) dějin', *Dějiny – teorie – kritika*, 11, 2: 183–211.
Angus, Ian 2000, *(Dis)figurations: Discourse/Critique/Ethics*, London: Verso.
Angus, Ian 2005, 'Walking on Two Legs: On The Very Possibility of a Heideggerian Marxism'. A review essay of Andrew Feenberg, *Heidegger and Marcuse: The Catastrophe and Redemption of History*, in *Human Studies*, 28, 3: 335–52.
Angus, Ian 2009, 'Herbert Marcuse's *Heideggerian Marxism*', *Symposium: Canadian Journal of Continental Philosophy*, 13, 1: 113–36.
Arendt, Hannah 1958, *The Human Condition*, Chicago: University of Chicago Press.
Aristotle 1962, *Nicomachean Ethics*, translated by Martin Ostwald, Indianapolis: Bobbs-Merrill.
Arnason, Johann P. 1991, 'Praxis and Action: Mainstream Theories and Marxian Correctives', *Thesis Eleven*, 29: 63–81.
Badiou, Alain 1988, *L'être et l'évenement*, Paris: Éditions du Seuil.
Badiou, Alain 2007, *Being and Event*, translated by Oliver Felham, New York: Continuum.

Bakan, Mildred 1978, 'Review of Dialectics of the Concrete', *Telos*, 35: 242–53.

Bakan, Mildred 1983, 'Karel Kosík's Phenomenological Heritage', in *Phenomenology in a Pluralistic Context*, edited by William L. McBride and Calvin O. Schrag, Albany: State University of New York Press.

Ballard, Bruce W. 1990, 'Marxist Challanges to Heidegger on Alienation and Authenticity', *Man and World*, 23, 2: 121–41.

Barnet, Richard J. and John Cavanagh 1994, *Global Dreams: Imperial Corporations and the New World Order*, New York: Simon and Schuster.

Bartošek, Karel 2003a 'Naše nynější krize a revoluce', in *Češi nemocní dějinami. Eseje, studie, záznamy z let 1968–1993*, Litomyšl: Paseka, 52–64.

Bartošek, Karel 2003b, 'Mohli jsme se bránit? Mnichovský komlex v české politice a mentalitě', in *Češi nemocní dějinami. Eseje, studie, záznamy z let 1968–1993*, Litomyšl: Paseka, 65–86.

Bauman, Zygmunt 1998, *Globalisation: The Human Consequences*, New York: Columbia University Press.

Becher, Peter, et al. 1995, *Ve světle tmy / Im Licht der Dunkelheit*, Prague: Prago Media.

Beck, Ulrich 2010, 'The Cosmopolitan Manifesto', in *The Cosmopolitanism Reader*, edited by Garrett Wallace Brown and Devid Held, Malden, MA: Polity, 217–28.

Benjamin, Walter 1977, *The Origin of the German Tragic Drama*, translated by John Osbourne, with an introduction of George Steiner, London: LNB.

Berberoglu, Berch (ed.) 2005, *Globalisation and Change: The Transformation of Global Capitalism*, Lanham, MD: Lexington Books.

Bergson, Henri 2013, *Laughter: An Essay on the Meaning of the Comic*, London: Macmillan.

Bhagwati, Jagdish 2004, *In Defence of Globalisation*, New York: Oxford University Press.

Bigelow, Billand and Bob Peterson (eds.) 2002, *Rethinking Globalisation: Teaching for Justice in an Unjust World*, Milwaukee: Rethinking Schools Press.

Black, David 2014, *The Philosophic Roots of Anti-Capitalism: Essays on History, Culture, and Dialectical Thought*, Lanham, MD: Lexington Books.

Blažek, Vratislav 1963, 'Človek uprostred sveta, človek proti mýtu', *Kultúrny život*, 18, 45: 6 and 8.

Blattner, William D. 1999, *Heidegger's Temporal Idealism*, Cambridge: Cambridge University Press.

Blattner, William D. 2006, *Heidegger's Being and Time: A Reader's Guide*, New York: Continuum.

Bodnár, Ján 1963, 'Filozofia a problémy človeka', *Kultúrny život*, 18, 46: 3.

Boella, Laura 2013, 'Milena Jesenská (1896–1944)', in *Le imperdonabili*, Milano: Mimesis.

Bondy, Egon 2001, *The Consolation of Ontology: On the Substantial and Nonsubstantial Models*, Boston: Lexington Books.

Bondy, Egon 2013, *Filosofické dílo, sv. IV. Postpříběh, příležitostné eseje a rekapitulace*, Prague: DharmaGaia.

Bondy, Egon 2016, *Pracovní analýza*, edited by Petr Kužel, Prague: Filosofia.

Bonefeld, Werner 1997, 'Notes on Anti-Semitism', *Common Sense*, 21: 60–76.

Bonefeld, Werner 2010, 'Abstract Labour: Against its Nature and on its Time', *Capital & Class*, 34, 2: 257–76.

Bossi, Giovanni and Gabriella Fusi 1974, 'Note sulla sinistra non ortodossa in Ungheria e in Cecoslovacchia', *aut aut*, 140: 55–69.

Bren, Paulina 2010, *The Greengrocer and His TV: The Culture of Communism after the 1968 Prague Spring*, Ithaca: Cornell University Press.

Brett, Clark and Richard York 2005, 'Dialectical Nature', *Monthly Review*, 57, 1, available at: http://monthlyreview.org/2005/05/01/dialectical-nature/.

Brockhaus, Richard 1984, 'Review of Carol C. Gould's *Marx's Social Ontology*', *Philosophy and Social Criticism*, 10, 1: 91–5.

Buber-Neumann, Margarete 1989, *Milena: The Story of a Remarkable Friendship*, New York: Schocken Books.

Butler, Judith 1997, *The Psychic Life of Power*, Stanford: Stanford University Press.

Camus, Albert 1955, *The Myth of Sisyphus, and Other Essays*, translated by Justin O'Brien, New York: Knopf.

Carlyle, Thomas 1906, *The French Revolution: A History*, London: J.M. Dent.

Cartwright, Nancy, Jordi Cat, Lola Fleck and Thomas E. Uebel 2008, *Otto Neurath: Philosophy between Science and Politics*, Cambridge: Cambridge University Press.

Červinka, František 1964, 'Asociace citace a perspektivy', *Dějiny a současnost*, 6, 1: 11–15.

Cvekl, Jiří 1963, 'Filosofie tvořivá', *Kulturní tvorba*, 1, 49: 5.

Debray, Régis 2007, 'Socialism: A Life Cycle', *New Left Review*, 46: 5–28.

Desanti, Jean-Toussaint 1963, *Phénoménologie et Praxis*, Paris: Éditions Sociales.

Dorrien, Gary 2004, 'Imperial Designs: Theological Ethics and the Ideologies of International Politics', *Cross Currents*, 54, 2: 97–115.

Doskočil, Zdeněk 2006, *Duben 1969. Anatomie jednoho mocenského zvratu*, Brno: Doplněk.

Dreyfus, Hubert 1990, *Being-in-the-World: A Commentary on Heidegger's Being and Time. Division I*, Cambridge, MA: The MIT Press.

Dunayevskaya, Raya 1965, 'Marx's Humanism Today', in *Socialist Humanism*, edited by Erich Fromm, New York: Doubleday.

Dunayevskaya, Raya 1989, *Philosophy and Revolution*, New York: Columbia University Press.

Dunayevskaya, Raya 1991, *Rosa Luxemburg, Women's Liberation, and Marx's Philosophy of Revolution*, Champaign-Urbana: University of Illinois Press.

Dunayevskaya, Raya 1992, *The Marxist-Humanist Theory of State-Capitalism: Selected Writings by Raya Dunayevskaya*, edited and introduced by Peter Hudis, Chicago: News and Letters.

Dunayevskaya, Raya 1995, *Filozofia a Revolúcia*, translated by Jozef Lysý, Bratislava: IRIS.
Dunayevskaya, Raya 2000, *Marxism and Freedom, from 1776 Until Today*, Amherst, NY: Humanity Books.
Dunayevskaya, Raya 2002, *The Power of Negativity: Selected Writings on the Dialectic in Hegel and Marx by Raya Dunayevskaya*, edited by Peter Hudis and Kevin B. Anderson, Lanham, MD: Lexington Books.
Dunayevskaya, Raya 2003, *Philosophy and Revolution, from Hegel to Sartre and from Marx to Mao*, Lanham, MD: Lexington Books.
Dunayevskaya, Raya 2012, *The Dunayevskaya-Marcuse-Fromm Correspondence, 1954–1978: Dialogues on Hegel, Marx, and Critical Theory*, edited by Kevin B. Anderson and Russell Rockwell, Lanham, MD: Lexington Books.
Engels, Friedrich 1940, *Dialectics of Nature*, translated by Clemens Dutt, New York: International Publishers.
Engels, Friedrich 1941, *Ludwig Feuerbach and the Outcome of Classical German philosophy*, edited by C.P. Dutt, New York: International Publishers.
Engels, Friedrich 1975, *Anti-Dühring, Dialectics of Nature*, in *Collected Works*, Volume 25, New York: International Publishers.
Engels, Friedrich 2010, 'To Arnold Ruge, 26 July', in *Marx-Engels Collected Works*, Volume 2, New York: International Publishers, 545.
Falk, Barbara 2003, *The Dilemmas of Dissidence in Central-Eastern Europe: Citizen Intellectuals and Philosopher Kings*, Budapest: Central European University Press.
Freire, Paulo 1984, 'Education, Liberation, and the Church', *Religious Education*, 4: 524–45.
Freud, Sigmund 1960, *Jokes and Their Relation to the Unconscious*, edited by James Strachey, New York: Norton & Co.
Friedman, Thomas 2005, *The World is Flat: A Brief History of the Twenty-First Century*, New York: Farrar, Straus and Giroux.
Fritsche, Johannes, 1999, *Historical Destiny and National Socialism in Heidegger's Being and Time*, Berkeley: University of California Press.
Fromm, Erich 1997, *To Have or To Be*, New York: Continuum.
Gadamer, Hans-Georg 1977, 'Theory, Technology, Practice: The Task of the Science of Man', *Social Research*, 44, 3: 529–61.
Golan, Galia 1971, *The Czechoslovak Reform Movement: Communism in Crisis 1962–1968*, Cambridge: Cambridge University Press.
Golan, Galia 1973, *Reform Rule in Czechoslovakia: The Dubček Era 1968–1969*, Cambridge: Cambridge University Press.
Gould, Carol C. 1978, *Marx's Social Ontology: Individuality and Community in Marx's Theory of Social Reality*, Cambridge, MA: The MIT Press.
Gramsci, Antonio 1959, *Sešity z vězení*, edited and translated by Jaroslav Pokorný and Mario Cervi, Prague: Československý spisovatel.

Gramsci, Antonio 1966, *Historický materialismus a filosofie Benedetta Croceho*, edited and translated by Lubomír Sochor, Prague: Svoboda.
Gramsci, Antonio 1949, *Dopisy z vězení*, translated by Eliška Hošková-Ripellino, Prague: Svoboda.
Gramsci, Antonio 1970, *Poznámky o Machiavellim, politice a moderním státu*, edited and translated by Lubomír Sochor, Prague: Svoboda.
Gramsci, Antonio 1971, *Selections from the Prison Notebooks*, edited and translated by Quintin Hoare and Geoffrey Nowell Smith, New York: International Publishers.
Gubser, Mike 2014, *The Far Reaches: Phenomenology, Ethics, and Social Renewal in Central Europe*, Stanford: Stanford University Press.
Guignon, Charles 1993, 'Introduction', in *The Cambridge Companion to Heidegger*, edited by Charles Guignon, Cambridge: Cambridge University Press, 1–41.
Habermas, Jürgen 1968, *Knowledge and Human Interests*, translated by Jeremy J. Shapiro, Boston: Beacon Press.
Habermas, Jürgen 1973, *Theory and Practice*, translated by John Viertel, Boston: Beacon Press.
Habermas, Jürgen 1976, *Zur Rekonstruktion des Historischen Materialismus*, Frankfurt a. Main: Suhrkamp.
Habermas, Jürgen 2008, *Between Naturalism and Religion*, Malden, MA: Polity.
Habermas, Jürgen 2011, '"The Political": The Rational Meaning of a Questionable Inheritance of Political Theology', in *The Power of Religion in the Public Sphere*, edited by Eduardo Mendieta and Jonathan Vanantwerpen, New York: Columbia University Press, 15–28.
Hardt, Michael and Antonio Negri 2000, *Empire*, Cambridge, MA: Harvard University Press.
Hauser, Michael 2012, *Cesty z postmodernismu. Filosofická reflexe doby přechodu*, Prague: Filosofia.
Hayes, Kathleen (ed.) 2003, *The Journalism of Milena Jesenská: A Critical Voice in Interwar Central Europe*, New York: Berghahn Books.
Hegel, Georg Wilhelm Friedrich 1969, *Science of Logic*, translated by A.V. Miller, Atlantic Highlands, NJ: Humanities Books.
Hegel, Georg Wilhelm Friedrich 1973, *Phenomenology of Mind*, translated by J.B. Baillie, London: George Allen & Unwin.
Hegel, Georg Wilhelm Friedrich 2018, *The Phenomenology of Spirit*, translated by Terry Pinkard, Cambridge: Cambridge University Press.
Heidegger, Martin 1962a, *Being and Time*, translated by John Macquarrie and Edward Robinson, Oxford: Blackwell.
Heidegger, Martin 1962b, *Kant and the Problem of Metaphysics*, translated by James S. Churchill, Bloomington: Indiana University Press.

Heidegger, Martin 1971, *Poetry, Language, Thought*, translated by Albert Hofstadter, New York: Harper & Row.
Heidegger, Martin 1977, 'The Question Concerning Technology', in *The Question Concerning Technology and Other Essays*, translated by William Lovitt, New York: Harper & Row, 3–35.
Heidegger, Martin 1985, 'The Self-Assertion of the German University', translated by Karsten Harries, *Review of Metaphysics*, 38, March: 467–502.
Heidegger, Martin 1986, *Sein und Zeit*, Tübingen: Max Niemeyer Verlag.
Heidegger, Martin 1992, *Parmenides*, GA 54, Frankfurt am Main: Klostermann.
Heidegger, Martin 1996, *Being and Time*, translated by Joan Stambaugh, Albany: State University of New York Press.
Heidegger, Martin 1999, *Contributions to Philosophy (From Enowning)*, translated by Parvis Emad and Kenneth Maly, Bloomington: Indiana University Press.
Heidegger, Martin 2012, *Bremen and Freiburg Lectures: Insight Into That Which Is and Basic Principles of Thinking*, translated by Andrew J. Mitchell, Bloomington: Indiana University Press.
Hejdánek, Ladislav 1963, 'Filosofie člověka', *Plamen*, 5, 3: 118–20.
Hejdánek, Ladislav 2010, *Setkání a odstup*, Prague: OIKOYMENH.
Hejdánek, Ladislav 2010a, 'Ontologie a pojem praxe', in *Setkání a odstup*, Prague: OIKOYMENH, pp. 35–63.
Held, David, Anthony McGrew, David Goldblattand, Jonathan Perraton (eds.) 1999, *Global Transformations: Politics, Economics, and Culture*, Stanford: Stanford University Press.
Held, David and Anthony McGrew (eds.) 2007, *Globalisation / Anti-Globalisation: Beyond the Great Divide*, Cambridge: Polity Press.
Heller, Agnes 1999, *Der Affe auf dem Fahrrad*, Berlin: Verlag Philo.
Heller, Agnes 1977, 'On the New Adventures of the Dialectics', *Telos*, 31: 134–42.
Hermann, Tomáš 2012, 'Proměny sporu o svobodu české filosofie', in *Hledání české filosofie. Soubor studií*, edited by Erazim Kohák and Jakub Trnka, Prague: Filosofia, 49–73.
Hewlett, Nick 2010, *Badiou, Balibar, Rancière: Re-thinking Emancipation*, New York: Continuum.
Hobson, John A. 2005, *Imperialism: A Study*, New York: Cosimo.
Horkheimer, Max 1937, 'Der neueste Angriff auf die Metaphysik', *Zeitschrift für Sozialforschung* 6, 2: 4–53.
Hrubec, Marek and Axel Honneth 2004, 'O kritice a uznání', in *Filosofický časopis*, 52, 4: 621–9.
Hrubý, Karel 2018, *Cesty komunistickou diktaturou. Kritické studie a eseje*, Prague: Argo.
Hudis, Peter 1989, 'Toward Philosophic New Beginnings in Marxist-Humanism', *Quarterly Journal of Ideology*, 13, 4: 87–96.

Hudis, Peter 1995, 'Teória štátneho kapitalizmu R. Dunayevskej', in Raya Dunayevskaya, *Filozofia a revolúcia*, translated by Jozef Lysý, Bratislava: IRIS.

Hudis, Peter 2013, *Marx's Concept of the Alternative to Capitalism*, Chicago: Haymarket Books.

Husserl, Edmund 1968, *'La crisi delle scienze europee e la fenomenologia trascendentale'*, translated by Enrico Filippini, Milano: Il Saggiatore.

Husserl, Edmund 1970, *The Crisis of European Sciences and Transcendental Phenomenology*, translated by David Carr, Evanston: Northwestern University Press.

Jaeger, Werner 1923, *Aristoteles: Grundlegung einer Geschichte seiner Entwicklung*, Berlin: Weidman.

Jauss, Hans Robert 1970, 'Literary History as a Challenge to Literary Theory', *New Literary History*, 1: 7–37.

Jay, Martin 1984, *Marxism and Totality: The Adventures of a Concept from Lukács to Habermas*, Berkeley: University California Press.

Jen, Erica 2002, 'Stableor Robust? What's the Difference?', available at: https://www.santafe.edu/research/results/working-papers/stable-or-robust-whats-the-difference.

Jesenská, Milena 1983, 'Refugees from Hitler in Czechoslovakia, 1937–1939', *Cross Currents*, 2: 183–94.

Joós, Ernest 1983, *Lukács' Last Autocriticism*, Atlantic Highlands, NJ: Humanities Press.

Kalandra, Záviš 1994, 'Nadskutečno v surrealismu', in *Intelektuál a revoluce*, edited by Jiří Brabec, Prague: Český spisovatel, 16–24.

Kalivoda, Robert 1961, *Husitská ideologie*, Prague: Nakladatelství Československé akademie věd.

Kalivoda, Robert 1968a 'Demokratizace a kritické myšlení', *Literární listy*, 1: 10 and 11: 1 and 13: 6.

Kalivoda, Robert 1968b, 'O perspektivách socialistické demokracie', *Rudé právo*, 48, 122: 3.

Kalivoda, Robert 2018, 'Marx and Freud', translated by A. Davies, *Contradictions: A Journal for Critical Thought*, 2: 135–56.

Koch, Anton F. 2006, *Wahrheit, Zeit und Freiheit. Einführung in eine philosophische Theorie*, Panderborn: Mentis Verlag.

Koch, Anton F. 2006, *Versuch über Wahrheit und Zeit*, Paderborn: Mentis Verlag.

Kohout, Pavel 1971, *Journal d'un contre-revolutionnaire*, translated by Pierre Daix, Paris: Christian Burgeois.

Kołakowski, L 1978, *Main Currents of Marxism. Volume 3, The Breakdown*, translated by P.S. Falla, Oxford: Clarendon Press.

Konrád, György and Ivan Szelényi 1979, *The Intellectuals on the Road to Class Power*, Brighton: Harvester Press.

Kopeček, Michal (forthcoming), *Quest for the Revolution's Lost Meaning: The Origins of Marxist Revisionism in Central Europe 1953–1960*, Leiden: Brill.

Kosík, Karel 1948, 'Třídní boje v české revoluci 1848' [Class Struggles in the Czech Revolution of 1848], *Tvorba*, 17, 35–36: 693–4, 716–17.

Kosík, Karel 1951a, 'Sovětský svaz – bašta marxismu-leninismu' [The USSR – a Bastion of Marxism-Leninism], *Tvorba*, 20, 47: 1116–18.

Kosík, Karel 1951b, 'Stalin nás učí lásce k vlasti a nenávisti k jejím nepřátelům' [Stalin Teaches us to Love our Homeland and Hate its Enemies], *Tvorba*, 20, 51: 1211–12.

Kosík, Karel 1952a, with Růžena Grebeníčková, 'Některé poznámky o vztahu českého demokratického myšlení k revolučnímu Rusku v 19. století' [Some Notes on the Relationship of Czech Democratic Thought to Revolutionary Russia in the Nineteenth Century], *Sovětská věda – Filosofie*, 2, 1: 56–62.

Kosík, Karel 1952b, 'Příspěvek k dějinám české demokratické kultury 19. století' [Contribution to the History of Czech Democratic Culture of the Nineteenth Century], *Tvorba*, 21, 7: 159–61.

Kosík, Karel 1953a, with Růžena Grebeníčková, 'J.V. Frič a ruští revoluční demokraté' [J.V. Frič and Russian Revolutionary Democrats], *Praha – Moskva*, 3, 10: 73–86.

Kosík, Karel 1953b, 'Místo a význam radikálních demokratů v dějinách pokrokové české politiky a ideologie' [The Position and Importance of Radical Democrats in the History of Progressive Czech Politics and Ideology], in *Čeští radikální demokraté (Výbor z politických statí)* [Czech Radical Democrats: A Selection of Political Essays], edited by Karel Kosík, Prague: Státní nakladatelství politické literatury: 5–46.

Kosík, Karel 1953c, 'N.G. Černyševskij a české osvobozenecké hnutí' [N.G. Chernyshevsky and Czech Liberation Movement], *Literární noviny*, 2, 34: 3.

Kosík, Karel 1953d, 'Politické názory Emanuela Arnolda' [The Political Attitudes of Emanuel Arnold], *Filosofický časopis*, 1, 3–4: 184–202.

Kosík, Karel 1953e, 'Zdeněk Nejedlý a pokrokové české myšlení' [Zdeněk Nejedlý and Czech Progressive Thought], *Literární noviny*, 2, 5: 3.

Kosík, Karel 1954, 'O sociálních kořenech a filosofické podstatě masarykismu' [On the Social Roots and Philosophical Basis of Masarykism], *Filosofický časopis*, 2, 3: 196–215.

Kosík, Karel 1955, 'Evropská revoluční demokracie devatenáctého století a její význam' [European Revolutionary Democracy in the Nineteenth Century and its Significance], *Nová mysl*, 9, 10: 1188–1204.

Kosík, Karel 1956, 'Josef Václav Frič – český buržoasní revolucionář' [Josef Václav Frič – A Czech Bourgeois Revolutionary], in *J.V. Frič a demokratické proudy v české politice a kultuře. Sborník statí* [J.V. Frič and Democratic Currents in Czech Politics and Culture, an Edited Volume], edited by Václav Žáček and Karel Kosík, Prague: Nakladatelství Československé akademie věd: 7–42.

Kosík, Karel 1958a, *Česká radikální demokracie. Příspěvek k dějinám názorových sporů v české společnosti 19. Stoletî* [Czech Radical Democracy: Contribution to the History of Ideological Disputes in Nineteenth-Century Czech Society], Prague: Státní nakladatelství politické literatury.

Kosík, Karel 1958b, 'Dějiny filosofie jako filosofie' [The History of Philosophy as Philosophy], in *Filosofie v dějinách českého národa. Protokol celostátní konference o dějinách české filosofie v Liblicích ve dnech 14.–17. dubna 1958* [Philosophy in the History of Czech Nation. Conference Proceeding], edited by Jiřina Popelová-Otáhalová and Karel Kosík, Prague: Nakladatelství Československé akademie věd: 9–24.

Kosík, Karel 1961, 'Dialectique du concret' [Dialectics of the Concret], *aut aut*, 63: 203–13.

Kosík, Karel 1962, 'Filosofické problémy struktury a systému' [Philosophical Problems of Structure and System], in *Problémy marxistické jazykovědy*, Prague: Nakladatelství československé akademie věd: 24–35.

Kosík, Karel 1963a, 'Čeští radikální demokrati' [Czech Radical Democrats], in *Antologie z dějin československé filosofie I*, edited by Robert Kalivoda and Josef Zumr, Prague: Nakladatelství Československé akademie věd: 487–93.

Kosík, Karel 1963b, *Dialektika konkrétního. Studie o problematice člověka a světa* [Dialectics of the Concrete: A Study on Problems of Man and World], Prague: Nakladatelství Československé akademie věd.

Kosík, Karel 1964a, 'La dialettica della morale e la morale della dialettica' [The Dialectis of Morality and the Morality of Dialectis], *Critica marxista*, 3: 113–30.

Kosík, Karel 1964b [1963], 'La ragione e la storia' [Reason and History], *aut aut*, 83: 7–15.

Kosík, Karel 1965a, *Dialettica del concreto*, translated by Gianlorenzo Pacini, Milano: Bompiani.

Kosík, Karel 1965b, 'Man and Philosophy', in *Socialist Humanism: An International Symposium*, edited by Erich Fromm, Garden City, NY: Doubleday, 162–71.

Kosík, Karel 1966, *Dialektika konkrétního. Studie o problematice člověka* [Dialectics of the Concrete: A Study on Problems of Man and World], Prague: Nakladatelství Československé akademie věd.

Kosík, Karel 1967a, *A konkrét dialektikája*, translated by Bojtár Endre, Budapest: Gondolat.

Kosík, Karel 1967b, *Dialéctica de lo concreto*, translated by Adolfo Sánchez Vázquez, México: Grijalbo.

Kosík, Karel 1967c, *Dialektika konkretnega*, translated by Frane Jerman, Ljubljana: Cankarjeva založba.

Kosík, Karel 1967d, *Die Dialektik des Konkreten*, translated by Marianne Hoffman, Frankfurt am Main: Suhrkamp.

Kosík, Karel 1967e, *Dijaletika konkretnog*, translated by Krešimir Georgijević, Beograd: Prosveta.

Kosík, Karel 1967f, 'Gramsci et la philosophie de la praxis' [Gramsci and Praxis's Philosophy], *Praxis*, 3: 328–32.

Kosík, Karel 1968a [1963], 'Dialectic of the Concrete Totality', *Telos*, 2: 21–37.

Kosík, Karel 1968b, 'La crisi dell'uomo contemporaneo e il socialismo' [The Crisis of the Contemporary Man and the Socialism], *Rinascita*, 26: 22–4.

Kosík, Karel 1968c [1967], 'Ragione e coscienza' [Reason and Consciousness], in *La svolta di Praga*, edited and traslated by Gianlorenzo Pacini, Roma: Samonà e Savelli.

Kosík, Karel 1969a, *Dialéctica do concreto*, translated by Célia Neves and Aldérico Toríbio, Rio de Janeiro: Paz e Terra.

Kosík, Karel 1969b, *Gutaisei no benshōhō* [Dialectics of the Concrete], translated by Kohei Hanazaki, Tokyo: Seika Shobo.

Kosík, Karel 1969c [1968], *La nostra crisi attuale* [Our Current Crisis], translated by Lorenzo del Giudice and Alberto Scarpone, Roma: Editori Riuniti.

Kosík, Karel 1969d [1963], 'Reason and History', *Telos*, 3: 64–71.

Kosík, Karel 1969e [1963], 'The Concrete Totality', *Telos*, 4: 35–54.

Kosík, Karel 1970, *La dialectique du concret*, translated by Roger Dangeville, Paris: François Maspero.

Kosík, Karel 1976, *Dialectics of the Concrete*, translated by Karel Kovanda and James Schmidt, Dordrecht: D. Reidel.

Kosík, Karel 1977, *Dialéctica do concreto*, translated by Célia Neves and Aldérico Toríbio, Lisbon: Dina livro.

Kosík, Karel 1993, *Století Markéty Samsové* [The Century of Grete Samsa], Prague: Český spisovatel.

Kosík, Karel 1993a, 'Demokracie a mýtus o jeskyni' [Democracy and the Myth of the Cave], in *Století Markéty Samsové*, 177–86.

Kosík, Karel 1993b [1992], 'Století Markéty Samsové', in *Století Markéty Samsové*, 11–31.

Kosík, Karel 1993c [1969], 'Tetraktys', in *Století Markéty Samsové*, 145.

Kosík, Karel 1993d [1992], 'Třetí Mnichov' [The Third Munich], in *Století Markéty Samsové*, 156–71.

Kosík, Karel 1993e, 'Dass die Bürger es sind, die eine freie Welt gründen' [A Free World Depends on Its Citizens], in *Concordia: International Journal of Philosophy*, 24: 13–23.

Kosík, Karel 1993f, 'L'uomo, misura di ogni cosa' [Man, Measure of all Things] (conversation with Antonio Cassuti), *MicroMega*, 4: 211–24.

Kosík, Karel 1993g [1992], 'The Third Munich', *Telos*, 94: 145–54.

Kosík, Karel 1995, *The Crisis of Modernity: Essays and Observations from the 1968 Era*, edited by James H. Satterwhite, Boston: Rowman & Littlefield.

Kosík, Karel 1995a [1964], 'Culture Against Nihilism', in *The Crisis of Modernity: Essays and Observations from the 1968 Era*, 103.

Kosík, Karel 1995b [1963], 'Hašek and Kafka, or, the World of the Grotesque' [Hašek a Kafka neboli grotesknî svět], in *The Crisis of Modernity: Essays and Observations from the 1968 Era*, 77–86.

Kosík, Karel 1995c [1969], 'On Laughter' [O smíchu], in *The Crisis of Modernity, The Crisis of Modernity: Essays and Observations from the 1968 Era*, 183–98.

Kosík, Karel 1995d [1968], 'Our Current Crisis' [Naše nynější krize], *The Crisis of Modernity: Essays and Observations from the 1968 Era*, 17–51.

Kosík, Karel 1995e [1967], 'Reason and Conscience' [Rozum a svědomí], in *The Crisis of Modernity. Essays and Observations from the 1968 Era*, 13–15.

Kosík, Karel 1995f [1968], 'Socialism and Crisis of Modern Man' [Socialismus a krize moderního člověka], in *The Crisis of Modernity: Essays and Observations from the 1968 Era*, 53–62.

Kosík, Karel 1995g [1969], 'Švejk and Bugulma or the Birth of Great Humor' [Švejk a Bugulma neboli zrození velkého humoru], in *The Crisis of Modernity: Essays and Observations from the 1968 Era*, 87–99.

Kosík, Karel 1995h [1964], 'The Dialectics of Morality and the Morality of Dialectics' [Dialektika morálky a morálka dialektiky], in *The Crisis of Modernity: Essays and Observations from the 1968 Era*, 63–76.

Kosík, Karel 1995i [1966], 'The Individual and History' [Individuum a dějiny], in *The Crisis of Modernity: Essays and Observations from the 1968 Era*, 123–34.

Kosík, Karel 1995j [1967], 'The Irreplaceable Nature of Popular Culture' [Nezastupitelnost národní kultury], in *The Crisis of Modernity: Essays and Observations from the 1968 Era*, 101–2.

Kosík, Karel 1995k [1964], 'The Nation and Humanism' [Národ a humanizmus], *The Crisis of Modernity: Essays and Observations from the 1968 Era*, 137–42.

Kosík, Karel 1995l [1968], 'The Only Chance – An Alliance with the People' [Jediná záchrana – spojenectví s lidem], in *The Crisis of Modernity: Essays and Observations from the 1968 Era*, 211–15.

Kosík, Karel 1995m, *Jinoch a smrt* [A Youth and Death], Prague: Hynek.

Kosík, Karel 1995n [1994], 'La Primavera di Praga: la fine della storia e lo Schauspieler' [The Prague Spring: The End of History and the Schauspieler], *Dimensioni e problemi della ricerca storica*, 1: 115–29.

Kosík, Karel 1996 [1993], 'Democracy and the Myth of the Cave', translated by Johann P. Arnason, *Thesis Eleven*, 45: 116–23.

Kosík, Karel 1997, *Předpotopní úvahy* [Antediluvian Reflections], edited by Eva Červinková, Prague: Torst.

Kosík, Karel 1997a [1995], 'Faust – stavitel' [Faust the Architect], in *Předpotopní úvahy*, 94–105.

Kosík, Karel 1997b [1994], 'Jinoch a smrt' [A Youth and Death], in *Předpotopní úvahy*, 151–94.

Kosík, Karel 1997c [1994], 'Komandující instance' [The Commanding Instance], in *Předpotopní úvahy*, 195–237.

Kosík, Karel 1997d [1997], 'Lumpenburžoazie a vyšší duchovní pravda' [The Lumpenbourgeoisie and Higher Spiritual Truth], in *Předpotopní úvahy*, 238–55.

Kosík, Karel 1997e [1995], 'Město a architektonika světa' [The City and the Architectonics of the World], in *Předpotopní úvahy*, 62–81.

Kosík, Karel 1997f [1994], 'Osvícenství a kultura' [The Enlightenment and Culture], in *Předpotopní úvahy*, 135–50.

Kosík, Karel 1997g [1994], 'Pražské jaro, "konec dějin" a šaušpíler' [The Prague Spring: The End of History and the Schauspieler], in *Předpotopní úvahy*, 106–26.

Kosík, Karel 1997h [1991], 'Úsměv a ústa' [The Smile and the Mouth], in *Předpotopní úvahy*, 32–9.

Kosík, Karel 1997i [1993], 'Vítězství metody nad architekturou' [The Victory of Method over Architectonics], in *Předpotopní úvahy*, 52–61.

Kosík, Karel 1997j [1993], 'Vlast Máchova' [The Homeland of Mácha], in *Předpotopní úvahy*, 82–93.

Kosík, Karel 1997k [1993], 'Všechna moc vychází z imaginace' [All Power Arises from the Imagination], in *Předpotopní úvahy*, 17–31.

Kosík, Karel 1997l [1991], 'Výsměšnost' [Mocking], in *Předpotopní úvahy*, 40–51.

Kosík, Karel 2003a, *Η κρίση της νεωτερικότητας* [The Crisis of Modernity], Athens: Ψυχογιός (Psychogios).

Kosík, Karel 2003b, *La Crise des temps modernes. Dialectique de la morale* [The Crisis of Modernity: The Dialectics of Morality], edited by Michael Löwy, Paris: Éditions de la Passion.

Kosík, Karel 2004, *Poslední eseje* [Last Essays], edited by Irena Šnebergová and Josef Zumr, Prague: Filosofia.

Kosík, Karel 2004a [1998], 'Chodit pánům předsedům pro pivo' [Going to Fetch the Leaders Their Beer], in *Poslední eseje*, 17–34.

Kosík, Karel 2004b [1999], 'Mosty přes evropskou řeku' [Bridges over the European River], in *Poslední eseje*, 103–14.

Kosík, Karel 2004c [2000], 'Setkání s Třicetiletou válkou' [An Encounter with the Thirty Years' War], in *Poslední eseje*, 141–64.

Kosík, Karel 2004d [1998], 'Událost (Pražské jaro 1968)' [The Event (the Prague Spring of 1968)], *Poslední eseje*, 67–82.

Kosík, Karel 2013, *Un filosofo in tempi di farsa e di tragedia. Saggi di pensiero critico 1964–2000* [A Philosopher in Times of Farce and Tragedy: Essays in Critical Thought], edited by Gabriella Fusi and Francesco Tava, Milano: Mimesis.

Kosík, Karel 2013a [1967], 'Gramsci e la filosofia della prassi' [Gramsci and the Philosophy of Praxis], in *Un filosofo in tempi di farsa e di tragedia. Saggi di pensiero critico 1964–2000*, edited by Gabriella Fusi and Francesco Tava, Milano: Mimesis, 93–98.

Kosík, Karel 2017 [1958], 'Classes and the Real Structure of Society', translated by Ashley Davies, *Contradictions*, 1, 2: 187–204.

Kosík, Karel 2019, *Dialektika, kultura a politika. Eseje a články z let 1955–1969. Sebrané spisy Karla Kosíka, sv. 4* [Dialectics, Culture and Politics: Essays and Other Articles, 1955–1969. Collected Writings of Karel Kosík, vol. 4], edited by Jan Mervart, Prague: Filosofia.

Kosík, Karel 2019a [1956], 'Hegel a naše doba' [Hegel and Our Epoch], in *Dialektika, kultura a politika. Eseje a články z let 1955–1969*, 39–46.

Kosík, Karel 2019b [1959], 'Gramsci o kultuře' [Gramsci on Culture], in *Dialektika, kultura a politika. Eseje a články z let 1955–1969*, 105–6.

Kosík, Karel 2019c [1957], 'Slepá ulička neplodného myšlení' [Blind Alley of Sterile Thinking], in *Dialektika, kultura a politika. Eseje a články z let 1955–1969*, 61–7.

Kosík, Karel and Jean-Paul Sartre 1975, 'Exchange of Letters', translated by Andrew Feenberg, *Telos*, 25: 192–5.

Kryl, Karel 1990, *Interview on the program Slovíčka – literární pásmo*, Slovenská televízia, Štúdio Košice.

Křesťan, Jiří 1999, 'Nejedlého projev Slovo o české filosofii v historickém kontextu', in *Věda v Československu v letech 1945–1953. Sborník z konference*, edited by Blanka Zylinská and Petr Svobodný, Prague: Karolinum, 307–19.

Kundera, Milan 1984, 'The Tragedy of Central Europe', *New York Review of Books*, 26: 33–8.

Kunstler, James Howard 2005, *The Long Emergency: Surviving the End of the Oil Age, Climate Change and Other Converging Catastrophes of the Twenty-First Century*, New York: Atlantic Monthly Press.

Kusák, Alexej 1991, *Stalin. Horor XX. století*, Prague: Svépomoc.

Kusák, Alexej 1998, *Kultura a politika v Československu 1945–1956*, Prague: Torst.

Kusin, Vladimir V. 1971, *The Intellectual Origins of the Prague Spring: The Development of Reformist Ideas in Czechoslovakia 1956–1967*, Cambridge: Cambridge University Press.

Lachout, Václav and Vendula Běláčková (eds.) 2005, *Sborník příspěvků ke sdružení domácího odboje a partyzánů Předvoj. Historie-vzpomínky-dokumenty, 1943–1945*, Prague: Historická skupina Předvoj.

Landa, Ivan 2012, 'Kosíkova dialektika konkrétního', in *Hledání české filosofie*, edited by Erazim Kohák and Jakub Trnka, Prague: Filosofia.

Landa, Ivan 2017, 'György Lukács, otázka marxistické ortodoxie a český marxismus: Úvodní slovo k Lukácsově eseji "Co je ortodoxní marxismus?"', *Kontradikce. Časopis pro kritické myšlení*, 1, 1: 39–48.

Landa, Ivan 2018, 'Kosík, Heidegger a praktický materialismus', in *Imaginace a forma. Mezi estetickým formalismem a filosofií emancipace*, edited by Ivan Landa and Jan Mervart, Prague: Filosofia.

Lange, E.M. 1980, *Das Prinzip Arbeit. Drei metakritische Kapitel über Grundbegriffe, Struktur und Darstellung der Kritik der Politischen Ökonomie von Karl Marx*, Frankfurt am Main: Ulstein.

Legrain, Philippe 2004, *Open World: The Truth about Globalisation*, Chicago: Ivan R. Dee.

Leonov, M.A. 1950a, 'Lenin a Stalin o konkretnosti marxistické dialektické metody', in *O vědeckém světovém názoru. Soubor statí sovětských autorů*, edited by Jindřich Zelený, Brno: Rovnost, 82–104.

Leonov, M.A. 1950b, 'Soudruh Stalin o dialektice jako metodě revoluční činnosti', in *O vědeckém světovém názoru. Soubor statí sovětských autorů*, edited by Jindřich Zelený, Brno: Rovnost, 57–81.

Levins, Richard 2008, 'Dialectics and Systems Theory', in *Dialectics for the New Century*, edited by Bertell Ollman and Tony Smith, New York: Palgrave Macmillan.

Li, Baowen 2011, *Jutidebianzhengfayuxiandaijingpipan. Kexikezhexuesixiangyanjiu* [《具体的辩证法与现代性批判：科西克哲学思想研究》; *Dialectics of the Concrete* and the Critique of Modernity: A Study of Karel Kosík's Philosophy], Harbin: University of Heilongjiang Press.

Liehm, A.J. 1968, 'Diktát moci a trhu', *Literární listy*, 1, 3: 11.

Liehm, A.J. 1970, *Politics of Culture*, translated by Peter Kussi. New York: Groove Press.

Lobkowicz, Nicholas 1964, 'Review of *Dialectics of the Concrete*', *Studies in Soviet Thought*, 4, 3: 248–51.

Lobkowicz, Nicholas 1967, *Theory and Practice: History of a Concept from Aristotle to Marx*, Notre Dame: University of Notre Dame Press.

Löwy, Michael and Robet Sayre 2002, *Romanticism Against the Tide of Modernity*, Durham, NC: Duke University Press.

Lukács, György 1949, 'Heidegger Redivivus', *Sinn und Form*, 1, 3: 37–62.

Lukács, György 1969, *Historia y conciencia de clase*, translated by Manuel Sacristán, México: Grijalbo.

Lukács, György 1971, *History and Class Consciousness: Studies in Marxist Dialectics*, translated by Rodney Livingstone, Cambridge, MA: The MIT Press.

Lukács, György 1972, *Tactics and Politics. Political Writings, 1919–1929*, translated by Michael McColgan, London: NLB.

Lukács, György 1975, *The Young Hegel: Studies in the Relations between Dialectic and Economics*, translated by Rodney Livingstone, London: Merlin Press.

Lukács, György 1976, *Lenin: unità e coerenza del suo pensiero*, transladed by Guido D. Neri, Torino: Einaudi.

Lukács, György 1979, *History and Class Consciousness: Studies in Marxist Dialectics*, translated by Rodney Livingstone, Cambridge, MA: The MIT Press.

Lukács, György 1980a, *The Destruction of Reason*, translated by Peter Palmer, Atlantic Highlands, NJ: Humanity Press.

Lukács, György 1980b, *The Ontology of Social Being, 3. Labour*, translated by David Fernbach, London: Merlin.

Lukács, György 2000, *A Defense of History and Class Consciousness: Tailism and the Dialectic*, translated by Esther Leslie, London: Verso.

Lukács, György 2009, *Lenin: A Study in the Unity of His Thought*, translated by Nicholas Jacobs, London: New Left Books.

Luxemburg, Rosa 1967 [1913], *La acumulación del capital*, translated by Raimundo Fernández O., México: Grijalbo.

Mander, Jerry and Edward Goldsmith (eds.) 1996, *The Case against the Global Economy and for a Turn Toward the Local*, San Francisco: Sierra Book Club.

Mandler, Emanuel 1995, 'Intelektuálové na cestě k nepolitické politice', *Soudobé dějiny*, 2, 1: 65–92.

Marcuse, Herbert 1958, 'Preface', in *Marxism and Freedom, from 1776 Until Today*, edited by Raya Dunayevskaya, 7–12.

Marcuse, Herbert 1962, *Eros and Civilisation*, New York: Vintage.

Marcuse, Herbert 1964a, *One-Dimensional Man*, London: Routledge & Kegan Paul.

Marcuse, Herbert 1964b, *Reason and Revolution: Hegel and the Rise of Social Theory*, Boston: Beacon Press.

Marcuse, Herbert 2005, 'On the Philosophical Foundation of the Concept of Labour in Economics', in Herbert Marcuse, *Heideggerian Marxism*, edited by Richard Wolin and John Abromeit, Lincoln: University of Nebraska Press.

Margolis, Joseph 1992, 'Praxis and Meaning: Marx's Species Being and Aristotle's Political Animal', in *Marx and Aristotle: Nineteenth-century German Social Theory and Classical Antiquity*, edited by George E. McCarthy, Maryland: Rowman & Littlefield.

Márkus, György 1986, *Language and Production: A Critique of the Paradigms*, Dordrecht: D. Reidel.

Martin, Hans-Peter and Harald Schumann 1997, *The Global Trap: Globalisation and the Assault on Democracy and Prosperity*, New York: Zed Books.

Marx, Karl 1933, *Das Kapital: Kritik der politischen Ökonomie. Dritter Band.* Zürich: Ring Verlag.

Marx, Karl 1967, *Capital, Vol. 1*, translated by Samuel Moore and Edward Aveling, New York: International Publishers.

Marx, Karl 1968, *Manuscritos económico-filosóficos de 1844*, translated by Wenceslao Roces, México: Grijalbo.

Marx, Karl 1972, *Capital, Vol. 3*, edited by Friedrich Engels, London: Lawrence and Wishart.

Marx, Karl 1973, *Grundrisse, Foundations of the Critique of Political Economy (Rough Draft)*, translated by Martin Nicolaus, Harmondsworth: Penguin.

Marx, Karl 1974, *Economic and Philosophic Manuscripts of 1844*, Moscow: Progress Publishers.

Marx, Karl 1975a, 'Economic and Philosophic Manuscripts of 1844', in *Marx and Engels Collected Works, Vol. 3*, New York: International Publishers.

Marx, Karl 1975b, 'On the Jewish Question', *Marx and Engels Collected Works, Vol. 3*, Moscow: Progress Publishers, 146–74.

Marx, Karl 1976a, *Capital, Vol. 1*, translated by Ben Fowkes, New York: Penguin.

Marx, Karl 1976b, 'Theses on Feuerbach', in *Marx and Engels Collected Works, Vol. 5*, New York: International Publishers.

Marx, Karl 1977a, *Capital, Vol. 1*, translated by Ben Fowkes, New York: Vintage Books.

Marx, Karl 1977b, *Critique of Hegel's Philosophy of Right*, translated by A. Jolin and L. O'Malley, New York: Cambridge University Press.

Marx, Karl 1978a, 'Contribution to the Critique of Hegel's Philosophy of Right: Introduction', in *The Marx-Engels Reader*, edited by Robert C. Tucker, New York: W.W. Norton & Company, 53–65.

Marx, Karl 1978b, 'Theses on Feuerbach', in *The Marx-Engels Reader*, edited by Robert C. Tucker, New York: W.W. Norton & Company, 143–5.

Marx, Karl 1981, *Capital, Vol. 3*, translated by David Fernbach, New York: Penguin.

Marx, Karl 1982, *Capital, Vol. 1*, translated by Ben Fowkes, New York: Penguin.

Marx, Karl 1986, 'Grundrisse', in *Marx and Engels Collected Works, Vol. 28*, New York: International Publishers.

Marx, Karl 1992, *The Poverty of Philosophy*, New York: International Publishers.

Marx, Karl 2000, *Selected Writings*, edited by David McLellan, New York: Oxford University Press.

Marx, Karl 2000a, 'Theses on Feuerbach', in *Selected Writings*, edited by David McLellan, Oxford: Oxford University Press.

Marx, Karl and Friedrich Engels 1982, *Gesamtausgabe* (MEGA) II/3.6 *Zur Kritik der Politischen Ökonomie* (Manuskript 1861–1863), Teil 6, Berlin: Dietz.

Masaryk, Tomáš Garrigue 1895, *Naše nynější krise. Pád strany staročeské a počátkové směrů nových*, Prague: Čas.

Masaryk, Tomáš Garrigue 1936 [1896], *Otázka sociální. Základy marxismu filosofické a sociologické*. Prague: Čin.

McTaggart, John 1908, 'The Unreality of Time', *Mind*, 68, 7: 457–74.

Mellor, Hugh 1998, *The Real Time II*, London: Routledge.

Mencl, Vojtěch 2005, 'Šedesát let od vzniku Předvoje', in *Sborník příspěvků ke sdružení domácího odboje a partyzánů Předvoj. Historie-vzpomínky-dokumenty, 1943–1945*, edited by Václav Lachout and Vendula Běláčková, Prague: Historická skupina Předvoj, 12–32.

Mervart, Jan 2012, 'Kosík, Kalivoda, Sviták a Pražské jaro 1968', in *Hledání české filosofie*, edited by Erazim Kohák and Jakub Trnka, Prague: Filosofia, 195–209.

Mervart, Jan 2017, 'Czechoslovak Marxist Humanism and the Revolution', *Studies in East European Thought*, 69, 1: 111–26.

Mészáros, István 1998, 'Dialectical Transformations: Teleology, History and Social Consciousness', *Science and Society*, 62, 3: 417–33.

Mészáros, István 2011, 'The Dialectical of Structure and History: An Introduction', *Monthly Review*, 63, 1: 17–35.

McDowell, John 1994, *Mind and World*, Cambridge, MA: Harvard University Press.

Michňák, Karel 1968, *Metafyzika subjektivity a její pojetí člověka jako animal rationale*, Prague: Univerzita Karlova.

Michňák, Karel 1969, *Ke kritice antropologismu ve filosofii a teologii*, Prague: Svoboda.

Min, Anselm K. 1981, 'Karel Kosík, The Dialectics of the Concrete', *The New Scholasticism* 55, 2: 247–54.
Min, Anselm K. 1989, *Dialectic of Salvation: Issues in Theology of Liberation*, New York: State University of New York Press.
Min, Anselm K. 2004, *The Solidarity of Others in a Divided World: A Postmodern Theology after Postmodernism*, New York: T & T Clark.
Min, Anselm K. 2008, 'Migration and Christian Hope: Historical and Eschatological Reflections on Migration', in *Faith on the Move: Toward a Theology of Migration in Asia*, edited by Fabio Baggio and Agnes M. Brazal, Manila: Ateneo de Manila University Press, 177–202.
Min, Anselm K. 2014, 'The Deconstruction and Reconstruction of Christian Identity in a World of Difference', in *The Task of Theology: Leading Theologians on the Most Compelling Questions for Today*, edited by Anselm K. Min, Maryknoll, NY: Orbis, 29–55.
Mlynář, Zdeněk, 1965, 'Filosofie aktivity – aktivita filosofie', *Kulturní tvorba*, 3, 30: 4–5.
Nejedlý, Zdeněk 1950, 'Slovo o české filosofii', *Var*, 3, 1: 1–16.
Nejedlý, Zdeněk 1953, *Za kulturu lidovou a národní*, Spisy, 35, Prague: Státní nakladatelství politické literatury.
Negri, Antonio 2008, *Empire and Beyond*, Malden, MA: Polity.
Neri, Guido Davide 1966, *Prassi e conoscenza. Con una sezione dedicate ai critici marxisti della fenomenologia*, Milano: Feltrinelli.
Neri, Guido Davide 1966a, 'Karel Kosík e la "prassi" marxista', in *Prassi e conoscenza*, Milano: Feltrinelli.
Neri, Guido Davide 1966b, 'Nozioni marxiste di prassi', in *Prassi e conoscenza*. Milano: Feltrinelli.
Neri, Guido Davide 1968, 'L'esperienza cecoslovacca', *Quaderni piacentini*, 36: 11–46.
Neri, Guido Davide 1975, 'Variazioni ideologiche del socialismo realizzato: l'umanismo scientifico-tecnologico', *aut aut*, 145–6: 51–73.
Neri, Guido Davide 1980, 'Karel Kosík. Filosofia e política tra il 56 e il 68 cecoslovacco', in *Aporie della realizzazione. Filosofia e ideologia nel socialismo reale*, by Guido Davide Neri, Milano: Feltrinelli, 130–55.
Neurath, Otto 1931, *Empirische Soziologie. Der Wissenschaftliche Gehalt der Geschichte und Nationalőkonomie*, Berlin: Springer.
Neurath, Otto 1931/2, 'Sociology and Physicalism', *Erkenntnis*, 2: 282–317.
Neurath, Otto 1937, 'Unity of Science and Logical Empiricism: A Reply', in *Otto Neurath and the Unity of Science*, edited by John Symons and John Pombo and Olga Torres et al. 2011, Dordrecht: Springer, 15–28.
Neurath, Otto 1973, *Empiricism and Sociology*, edited by Marie Neurath and Robert Cohen, Dordrecht: Reidel.
Ollman, Bertell 2012, *Alienation: Marx's Conception of Man in Capitalist Society*, London: Cambridge University Press.

Paci, Enzo 1963, 'Il significato dell'uomo in Marx e Husserl', *aut aut*, 73: 10–21.
Paci, Enzo 1970a, 'Intersoggettività del potere', *Praxis*, 1–2: 87–92.
Paci, Enzo 1970b, *Il senso dell'oggi in Cecoslovacchia*, translated by Gianlorenzo Pacini, Milano: Lampugnani Nigri Editore.
Paci, Enzo 1973, 'Marx e Husserl a Praga', *Tempo*, 27: 53.
Paci, Enzo 1974, *Diario fenomenologico*, Milano: Bompiani.
Patočka, Jan 1970, 'Heidegger vom anderen Ufer', in *Durchblicke. M. Heidegger zum 80. Geburtstag*, edited by Klostermann Vittorio, Frankfurt am Main: Klostermann, 394–411.
Patočka, Jan 1989, 'The Dangers of Technicalisation in Science according to E. Husserl and the Essence of Technology as Danger according to M. Heidegger', in *Philosophy and Selected Writings*, translated by Erazim Kohák, Chicago: University of Chicago Press.
Patočka, Jan 2004, *Umění a čas I*, edited by Daniel Vojtěch and Ivan Chvatík, Prague: OIKOYMENH.
Patočka, Jan 2004a, 'Gehlenovy názory o úloze umění v antropogenezi', in *Umění a čas I*, 204–10.
Patočka, Jan 2004b, 'Ještě jedna Antigona a Antigoné ještě jednou', in *Umění a čas I*, 389–400.
Patočka, Jan 2006, *Češi I*, Prague: OIKOYMENH.
Patočka, Jan 2006a, 'Česká filosofie a její soudobá fáze', in *Češi I*, 306–27.
Patočka, Jan 2006b, 'Heidegger z druhého břehu', in *Češi I*, 214–29.
Patočka, Jan 2006c, 'O smysl dneška', in *Češi I*, 231–338.
Pauza, Miroslav 2011, 'Husserl a Heidegger v Dialektice konkrétního aneb jak by to asi vypadalo bez nich?', in *Myslitel Karel Kosík*, edited by Marek Hrubec et al., Prague: Filosofia, 79–96.
Pešek, Jiří 1966, *Dialektika dělby práce, sebestrukturace a perspektivnost člověka*, Prague: Univerzita Karlova.
Petrović, Gajo 1965, 'A quoi bon Praxis', *Praxis*, 1, 1: 3–7.
Piaget, Jean 1971, *Structuralism*, New York: Harper & Row.
Piaget, Jean 1977, 'Structuralism and Dialectic', in *The Essential Piaget: An Interpretive Reference and Guide*, New York: Basic Books.
Piaget, Jean 1980, *Experiments in Contradiction*, Chicago: University of Chicago Press.
Piccone, Paul 1971, 'Phenomenological Marxism', *Telos*, 9: 3–31.
Piccone, Paul 1977, 'Czech Marxism: Karel Kosík', *Critique: Journal of Socialist Theory*, 8, 1: 43–52.
Pomeroy, Anne Fairchild 2004, *Process, Dialectics and the Critique of Capitalism*, New York: State University of New York Press.
Postone, Moishe 2003, *Time, Labor, and Social Domination: A Reinterpretation of Marx's Critical Theory*, Cambridge: Cambridge University Press.

Postone, Moishe 2006, 'History and Helplessness: Mass Mobilisation and Contemporary Forms of Anticapitalism', *Public Culture*, 18, 1: 93–110.

Průcha, Milan 1965, *La rencontre du cogito et du marxisme*, Nancy: Université de Nancy.

Průcha, Milan 1966, *Kult člověka*, Prague: Svoboda.

Rancière, Jacques 1999, *Disagreement: Politics and Philosophy*, translated by Julie Rose, Minneapolis: University of Minnesota Press.

Ricoeur, Paul 1965, 'Work and the Word', in *History and Truth*, translated by Charles A. Kelbley, Evanston: Northwestern University Press.

Richta, Radovan 1969, *Civilisation at the Crossroads: Social and Human Implications of the Scientific and Technological Revolution*, translated by Marian Šlingová, Prague: International Arts and Sciences Press.

Rödl, Sebastian 2011, *Selbstbewusstsein*, Frankfurt am Main: Suhrkamp Verlag.

Rossanda, Rossana 2003, 'Karel Kosík, la primavera di un filosofo', *Il Manifesto*, 1 March: 12.

Rose, Gillian 2009, *Hegel Contra Sociology*, London: Verso.

Rozzi, Renato 1963, 'Problemi della psicologia in un paese socialista', *Il Filo rosso*, 1: 64–72.

Sánchez Vázquez, Adolfo 1961, 'Ideas estéticas en los *Manuscritos económico-filosóficos* de Marx', *Revista de filosofía* DIÁNOIA, 7, 7: 236–58.

Sánchez Vázquez, Adolfo 1965, *Las ideas estéticas de Marx. Ensayos de estética marxista*, México: ERA.

Sánchez Vázquez, Adolfo 1967a, 'Prólogo', in Karel Kosík, *Dialéctica de lo concreto*, México: Grijalbo, 5–13.

Sánchez Vázquez, Adolfo 1967b, *Filosofía de la praxis*, México: Grijalbo.

Sánchez Vázquez, Adolfo 1977, *The Philosophy of Praxis*, translated by Mike Gonzales, London: Merlin Press.

Sánchez Vázquez, Adolfo 1982, *Filosofía y economía en el joven Marx: Los manuscritos de 1844*, Barcelona and México: Grijalbo.

Sánchez Vázquez, Adolfo 2003, *El joven Marx. Los manuscritos de 1844*, México: UNAM.

Šámal, Petr 2005, 'Česká otázka ve světle stalinismu. Karel Kosík a koncept levicového radikalismu', *Soudobé dějiny*, 12, 1: 45–61.

Satterwhite, James H. 1992, *Varieties of Marxist Humanism: Philosophical Revision in Postwar Eastern Europe*, Pittsburgh: University of Pittsburgh Press.

Scheler, Max 1961 [1928], *Man's Place in Nature*, translated by Hans Meyerhoff, Boston: Beacon Press.

Schelling, Friedrich 1978 [1800], *System of Transcendental Idealism*, translated by Peter L. Heath, Charlottesville, VA: University Press of Virginia.

Schirato, Tony and Jen Webb 2003, *Understanding Globalisation*, London: Sage.

Schmidt, James 1977, 'Praxis and Temporality: Karel Kosík's Political Theory', *Telos*, 33: 71–84.

Sperber, Jonathan 2013, *Karl Marx: A Nineteenth-Century Life*, New York: W.W. Norton.
Srovnal, Jindřich 1965, 'Filosofie aktivity – aktivita filosofie', *Kulturní tvorba*, 3, 30: 5.
Šrubař, Ilja 2007, *Phänomenologische und Soziologische Theorie. Aufsätze zur pragmatischen Lebenswelttheorie*, Wiesbaden: vs Verlag für Sozialwissenschaften.
Steger, Martin 2003, *Globalisation: A Very Short Introduction*, New York: Oxford University Press.
Stiglitz, Joseph E. 2003, *Globalisation and Its Discontents*, New York: W.W. Norton.
Stiglitz, Joseph E. 2006, *Making Globalisation Work*, New York: W.W. Norton.
Sullivan, Terry 2015, 'Dialectical Biology: A Response to Camilla Royle', *International Socialism*, 145, available at: http://isj.org.uk/dialectical-biology-a-response-to-camilla-royle/.
Sviták, Ivan 1965, 'Dialektika konkrétního', unpublished manuscript (15pp).
Symons, John, Olga Pombo and Juan Manuel Torres (eds.) 2011, *Otto Neurath and the Unity of Science*, Dordrecht: Springer.
Tava, Francesco 2020 (forthcoming), 'Tragic Realism: On Karel Kosík's Insight into Kafka', in *Literary Theory between East and West: Transcultural and Transdisciplinary Movements from Russian Formalism to Cultural Studies*, edited by Michal Mrugalski et al., Berlin: De Gruyter.
Taylor, Charles 1975, *Hegel*, Cambridge: Cambridge University Press.
Tomlinson, John 1999, *Globalisation and Culture*, Chicago: University of Chicago Press.
Tucker, Robert C. (ed.) 1978, *The Marx-Engels Reader*, New York: W.W. Norton.
Vico, Giambattista 1948, *The New Science*, translated by Thomas G. Bergin, Ithaca: Cornell University Press.
Vranicki, Predrag 1974, *Geschichte des Marxismus, Bd. 2*. Frankfurt am Main: Suhrkamp.
Wagnerová, Alena 2006, 'Ještě o Karlu Kosíkovi', *Listy*, 36, 4.
Wagnerová, Alena and Vladimír Janovic (eds.) 1968, *Neohlížej se, zkameníš*, Prague: Naše vojsko.
Wittgenstein, Ludwig 1922, *Tractatus Logico-Philosophicus*, London: Kegan Paul.
Wolf, Martin 2004, *Why Globalisation Works*, New Haven: Yale University Press.
Zimmerman, Michael E. 1984, 'Karel Kosík's Heideggerian Marxism', *The Philosophical Forum*, 15: 209–33.
Zouhar, Jan 2009, 'Jan Patočka a Kosíkova Dialektika konkrétního', *Studia philosophica*, 56, 1–2: 69–73.
Zumr, Josef 1963, 'Marxismus jako filosofie člověka', *Literární noviny*, 12, 30: 5.
Zumr, Josef 2011, 'Kosíkovo pojetí dějin českého myšlení 19. století', in *Myslitel Karel Kosík*, edited by Marek Hrubec et al, Prague: Filosofia, 21–31.

Index

Adorno, Theodor W.   146, 200, 349, 352
Agamben, Giorgio   224
Althusser, Louis   13, 14, 151, 192n25, 262–277, 318
Anceschi, Luciano   309
Andělová, Kristina   45n17
Anaxagoras   140
Angus, Ian   11, 109n3
Arendt, Hannah   62, 113
Aristotle   113–114n14, 140, 210, 292
Arnason, Johann Pal   9, 57n1, 191n17
Arnold, Emanuel   44, 47
Arthur, C.J.   329
Auersperg, Pavel   28
Azeri, Siyaves   11, 14

Baczko, Bronisław   4
Backhaus, Hans Georg   329
Badiou, Alain   224, 269, 275–278
Bachelard, Gaston   264
Bakan, Mildred   5n24, 111, 121–124, 127n51
Ballard, Bruce W.   102n87
Banfi, Antonio   309
Bartoš, Vít   13
Bartošek, Karel   21, 31n38, 36
Batishchev, Genrikh S.   76n5
Bauer, Bruno   149
Bauman, Zygmunt   309
Bayerová, Marie   47n21
Beck, Ulrich   212, 221, 224
Beneš, Edvard   22
Benjamin, Walter   73n63
Bergson, Henri   68–69
Bernstein, Eduard   237
Blattner, William   77n79, 96, 98n71
Bloch, Ernst   309
Boella, Laura   72
Bolzano, Bernard   47, 345
Bondy, Egon   36, 275n65
Bonefeld, Werner   146
Bossi, Giovanni   314
Breda, Leo von   309
Brockhaus, Richard   89n40
Bukharin, Nikolai   246
Butler, Judith   268

Camus, Albert   71–72
Cantoni, Remo   309
Carlyle, Thomas   69
Carnap, Rudolf   242
Cassuti, Antonio   294, 307, 353
Cibulka, Josef   75
Comte, Auguste   238
Condorcet, Nicolas de   289

Černý, Jan   14, 189n11, 279n88
Černý, Jiří   75
Čupr, František   48

Debray, Régis   22, 38
Derrida, Jacques   219n13
Desanti, Jean-Toussaint   78
Diderot, Denis   123
Dreyfus, Hubert L.   96n60
Dubček, Alexander   20, 31, 34
Dubský, Ivan   75
Dunayevskaya, Raya   6, 15, 325n3, 327, 328, 330n23 and 24, 331–332, 334–335, 337–340, 342
Dussel, Enrique   3

Engels, Friedrich   8, 25, 57n3, 103, 111, 115n19, 123–124, 125, 126, 151–155, 157, 235, 237–239, 242, 244–245, 266, 326
Echeverría, Bolívar   318

Feinberg, Joseph Grim   12, 348n6
Feuerbach, Ludwig   57n3, 79–80, 153, 171, 326, 327, 335–337
Fichte, Johann Gottlieb   153, 162
Fischer, Ernst   25
Foucault, Michel   192n25, 211
Freire, Paolo   3
Freud, Sigmund   69
Frič, Josef Václav   44
Fritsche, Johannes   149
Fromm, Erich   25, 275, 288n34, 331
Fuentes, Diana   2n6, 3n8, 15, 349n8
Fusi, Gabriella   2n4, 14, 307n1, 311n17, 314n27, 349n7

Gadamer, Hans Georg   113, 234n7
Garaudy, Roger   25
Goldmann, Lucien   4, 46, 75
Gould, Carol C.   77n79, 88n40, 90n45
Grada, Raffaele de   309
Gramsci, Antonio   25, 46, 61, 192, 311, 319, 334
Grijalbo, Juan   317
Gubser, Michael   78n10

Habermas, Jürgen   3, 22, 29, 38, 79n10, 113, 153, 212, 222–224
Hájek, Miloš   23
Hardt, Michael   211
Hašek, Jaroslav   30, 67, 288
Hauser, Michael   51n8, 59n8
Havlíček Borovský, Karel   48
Hegel, Georg Wilhelm Friedrich   1n1, 3n11, 12, 25, 29, 54, 60, 78n10, 83–84, 86, 87–88, 103, 109, 122–123, 129, 134, 138, 140, 142, 143, 152–155, 157, 159, 160, 162, 169, 170, 179, 183, 205, 206, 209, 210, 217, 234n7, 236, 238, 289, 326–328, 330, 331, 334–341, 348, 353
Heidegger, Martin   11–13, 14, 54, 75–78, 88, 95–100, 101–103, 106, 108, 109, 111, 112, 116, 119, 121, 122n42, 131, 143–146, 153, 157–158, 160, 161, 165, 167, 170, 175, 176, 185, 190, 198, 200, 206, 210, 229, 235n8, 281–297, 299–303, 351, 353
Hejdánek, Ladislav   7, 28n28
Held, David   214, 216n8
Heller, Agnes   5, 10n34, 309
Hemingway, Ernest   30
Herbart, Johann Friedrich   48n23
Herder, Johann Gottfried   194, 195, 282
Hermann, Tomáš   10, 24n15, 49n25, 240n22, 348n6
Hewlett, Nick   276
Hiršl, Karel   44
Hobbes, Thomas   155
Holát, Vratislav   44
Holbach, P.H.D. von   25
Honneth, Axel   3, 4
Hölderlin, Friedrich   292n54, 298, 354
Horkheimer, Max   48, 230, 246
Hrubec, Marek   4n13
Hrubý, Karel   40n4
Hříbek, Tomáš   13

Huang, Xiaohan   12
Hudis, Peter   15
Hus, Jan   30, 312, 313, 350–351, 354
Husák, Gustáv   34, 35, 37, 351
Husserl, Edmund   14, 75, 76, 78n10, 101n84, 103n88, 109n3, 153, 234, 236, 309, 310, 332, 354

Ilyenkov, Evald   26n21, 76n5, 152, 160

Janovic, Vladimír   23n9
Jauss, Hans Robert   3, 4
Jay, Martin   205n1, 213n5
Jesenská, Milena   72–73
Joós, Ernest   115n19

Kafka, Franz   30, 67, 70, 288, 309, 345
Kalandra, Záviš   82
Kalivoda, Robert   7, 8n32, 25, 28, 29, 32, 36n53, 54n39, 84n26, 313
Kant, Immanuel   12, 132, 153, 155, 159, 162, 170, 195, 196, 223, 289, 297, 354
Kautsky, Karl   327n11
Khrushchev, Nikita   19, 348
Koch, Anton F.   89n42, 98n71
Kohout, Pavel   350
Kołakowski, Leszek   3–5, 152, 153
Konrád, György   21n6
Konrad, Kurt   271
Korsch, Karl   25, 153, 319
Kosík, Karel   1–15, 19–38, 39–54, 57–74, 75–78, 81–91, 94–106, 107–128, 129–135, 137–139, 142–143, 148, 151–153, 155–162, 165–167, 168, 170–171, 174–183, 185–186, 187–203, 205–212, 215, 224, 229–236, 239–243, 246–247, 248–256, 258, 260, 262–267, 269–280, 281–303, 307–314, 316, 317, 320–324, 325, 327–336, 340–342, 345–353
Koucký, Vladimír   28
Kryl, Karel   279n85
Křesálková, Jitka   313n26
Kundera, Milan   27, 38n57
Kuroń, Jacek   20n3
Kusák, Alexej   42, 45n17
Kusin, Vladimir V.   19n1, 67n38
Kužel, Petr   14

Labriola, Antonio 319
Lachout, Václav 23n9
Landa, Ivan 11, 285n21, 329n18
Lange, Ernst M. 86n31
Lenin, V.I. 42, 50, 107, 151, 319, 331
Leonov, M.A. 50n29
Levinas, Emmanuel 212, 213, 219n13
Lévi-Strauss, Claude 255
Li, Baowen 165n1
Liehm, A.J. 20n2, 22, 31n37, 32, 34n47
Lobkowicz, Nikolaus 3, 127n51
Löwy, Michael 4, 9, 15
Lukács, György 3n11, 4, 25, 26n21, 29, 46, 51, 52, 75, 76n6, 109n3, 115, 152–155, 160, 162, 168, 169, 172–174, 175, 185, 230, 235–241, 243, 246–247, 312, 317, 319, 323, 328, 335, 349, 354
Luxemburg, Rosa 329n18

McTaggart, John E. 88–89
Mach, Ernst 242
Mácha, Karel Hynek 297–298
Machiavelli, Niccolo 192, 349
Machonin, Pavel 313
Machovec, Milan 25
Mandler, Emanuel 49n49
Marcuse, Herbert 13, 111–120, 125, 128, 134, 153, 246, 309, 326, 330, 353
Mareš, Jan 45n17
Margolis, Joseph 184n40
Marini, Alfredo 309
Márkus, György 5, 76n5, 85–86n30
Marx, Karl 12, 25, 26n21, 29, 42, 49, 52, 57n3, 58, 59n7, 62, 66, 75, 77, 79, 80–82, 85–86, 88n40, 90n45, 91–94, 97, 103, 105, 108–113, 116, 119–120, 124, 129–139, 149, 151–162, 169–173, 175, 177, 178, 183–185, 187–188, 195, 205, 207, 217, 229, 234, 237, 238, 241, 244, 245, 265, 268, 273, 278, 284n19, 288–290, 296, 303, 308, 318–320, 322–323, 325–328, 330–341, 353
Masaryk, Tomáš G. 22–24, 31n38, 42, 45, 192, 238
McDowell, John 84n25, 234, 243
Mehring, Franz 329n18
Mellor, Hugh 89n44
Mencl, Vojtěch 23n11
Merleau-Ponty, Maurice 310, 334n35

Mervart, Jan 8n33, 10, 53n37, 54n39, 348n6
Mészáros, István 178, 179
Michňák, Karel 75
Min, Anselm K. 9, 12
Mlynář, Zdeněk 28, 29, 36, 37
Modzelewski, Karol 20–21n3
Montagne, Michel de 25
Mozart, Wolfgang Amadeus 354

Nancy, Jean-Luc 224
Negri, Antonio 211, 212, 220, 224
Nejedlý, Zdeněk 24, 25, 43, 49
Neri, Gabriele 310
Neri, Guido Davide 2, 3, 15, 64, 76n5, 310, 311, 312
Neurath, Otto 230, 242–246
Nietzsche, Friedrich 294
Nigri, Arrigo Lampugnani 312, 313
Novalis 354
Novotný, Antonín 20, 30, 32

Ollman, Bertell 9, 168n9, 173n18
Orwell, George 353n18

Paci, Enzo 2, 15, 153, 307–310, 312–314
Pacini, Gianlorenzo 310, 312
Palach, Jan 73–74, 299
Palacký, František 4n13
Pannekoek, Anton 329n18
Parmenides 167
Patočka, Jan 1, 6, 7, 52, 73–74, 76n6, 77, 83–84, 87n33, 100–104, 235n8, 239n21, 285n21, 309, 310, 313, 348
Pauza, Miroslav 28n1, 282n3
Perelman, Marc 4, 347
Perraton, Jonathan 214n7, 216n8
Pešek, Jiří 75
Petrović, Gajo 5, 76n5, 153, 308
Petrović, Asja 309
Piaget, Jean 249, 255, 256, 257
Piccone, Paul 5, 109n3
Plato 70, 152, 160
Plekhanov, G.V. 278
Popper, Karl R. 233
Postone, Moishe 137n32, 150, 329
Preti, Giulio 309
Prilutskiy, Pavel 5n18
Průcha, Milan 75, 103n88

Rancière, Jacques 301
Renzi, Emilio 309
Richta, Radovan 21n4, 23
Richter, Václav 101
Ricoeur, Paul 122n41, 124
Rilke, Rainer Maria 292–293
Roces, Wenceslao 319
Rockmore, Tom 12
Rödl, Sebastian 81, 103n90
Rossanda, Rossana 309, 312
Rousseau, Jean-Jacques 354
Rovatti, Pier Aldo 2
Rozzi, Renato 310, 311, 312

Sabina, Karel 44, 47
Sánchez Vázquez, Adolfo 2, 3, 15, 76n5, 316–324, 349
Sartre, Jean-Paul 4, 308, 348, 349, 351, 353
Satterwhite, James H. 6, 30n35, 165
Selucký, Radoslav 312
Sereni, Vittorio 309
Schaff, Adam 3
Scheler, Max 198
Schelling, F.W.J. 66, 354
Schmidt, James 60n11
Skácel, Jan 27
Smetana, Augustin 47, 54
Smith, Adam 177
Sochor, Lubomír 311
Sohn-Rethel, Alfred 328–329n17
Sperber, Jonathan 238
Srovnal, Jindřich 30
Stalin, J.V. 23, 24, 42, 50
Steiger, Štěpán 328n12

Strobachová, Ingrid 50
Supek, Rudi 308
Sviták, Ivan 24, 25, 29
Szewczyk, Jan 76n5

Šrubař, Ilja 75n4
Štorch, Karel Boleslav 47

Tarcus, Horacio 346, 347
Tava, Francesco 11, 12, 105n95
Taylor, Charles 86
Tenzer, Oliver 313
Thao, Tran Duc 310
Trotsky, Leon 331

Varikas, Eleni 345
Vico, Giambattista 155
Vranicki, Predrag 5

Wagnerová, Alena 40n5
Weil, Simone 105
Whitehead, Alfred North 253, 254, 260
Wittgenstein, Ludwig 251, 252

Xiaoping, Deng 183

Zelený, Jindřich 257
Zimmermann, Michael E. 5n24, 102n87, 165n1
Zhang, Xinruo 12
Zumr, Josef 7, 9, 52n36, 352

Žižek, Slavoj 224, 269

www.ingramcontent.com/pod-product-compliance
Lightning Source LLC
Chambersburg PA
CBHW071228070526
44583CB00017B/2088